PARKER HITT

American Warriors

Throughout the nation's history, numerous men and women of all ranks and branches of the US military have served their country with honor and distinction. During times of war and peace, there are individuals whose exemplary achievements embody the highest standards of the US armed forces. The aim of the American Warriors series is to examine the unique historical contributions of these individuals, whose legacies serve as enduring examples for soldiers and citizens alike. The series will promote a deeper and more comprehensive understanding of the US armed forces.

Series editor: Joseph Craig

An AUSA Book

PARKER HITT

THE FATHER OF AMERICAN MILITARY CRYPTOLOGY

Betsy Rohaly Smoot

UNIVERSITY PRESS OF KENTUCKY

Editorial and Sales Offices: The University Press of Kentucky
663 South Limestone Street, Lexington, Kentucky 40508-4008
www.kentuckypress.com

Portions of chapters 3, 5, and 7 previously appeared as "An Accidental
Cryptologist: The Brief Career of Genevieve Young Hitt" in *Cryptologia* 35,
no. 2 (March 2011) and are reprinted by permission of the publisher,
Taylor and Francis, Ltd., http://www.tandfonline.com.

A portion of chapter 4 previously appeared as "Parker Hitt's First Cylinder
Device and the Genesis of U.S. Army Cylinder and Strip Devices" in
Cryptologia 39, no. 4 (October 2015) and is reprinted by permission of the
publisher, Taylor and Francis, Ltd., http://www.tandfonline.com.

Library of Congress Cataloging-in-Publication Data

Names: Smoot, Betsy Rohaly, author.
Title: Parker Hitt : the father of American military cryptology /
    Betsy Rohaly Smoot.
Other titles: Father of American military cryptology
Description: Lexington, Kentucky : The University Press of Kentucky,
    [2022] | Series: American warrior series | Includes bibliographical
    references and index.
Identifiers: LCCN 2021049366 | ISBN 9780813182407 (hardcover) |
    ISBN 9780813182421 (epub)
Subjects: LCSH: Hitt, Parker, 1878– | Cryptography—United States—
    History—20th century | Cryptographers—United States—Biography. |
    United States. Army—Officers—Biography.
Classification: LCC UB290.H5 S66 2022 | DDC 358/.24—dc23/
    eng/20211013

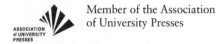

To my mother, Shirley Miller Hall,
who nurtured my interest in history

Conform and be dull.
—J. Frank Dobie, *The Voice of the Coyote*

Contents

Preface

Success in dealing with unknown ciphers is measured by these four things in the order named: perseverance, careful methods of analysis, intuition, luck.

Parker Hitt, 1916

Hitt's axiom for success with ciphers was equally applicable to my journey in writing this book. I first heard Parker Hitt's name during a talk by Dr. David A. Hatch in October 2007. My initial thought was to wonder whether Hitt was related to my husband's Hitt ancestors (he is). Then I grew curious; my intuition told me there was a story here. A careful reading of David Kahn's *The Codebreakers* revealed intriguing details, but I wanted to know more. Kahn had visited the Hitts in Front Royal, Virginia. I searched in vain for a grave site there and then asked Dr. Thomas A. Johnson, who lived nearby, if he knew where the Hitts were buried. As luck would have it, Tom was able to contact then-director of the Warren County Heritage Society, Patrick Farris. Some years earlier, Farris had helped a family organize and preserve some of Hitt's papers. David and Evie Moreman and their daughter and son-in-law, Jennifer and Kevin Mustain, were friends and heirs of Hitt's daughter, Mary Lueise. They kindly allowed me access to a trunk full of Parker Hitt's papers (to which I applied careful methods of analysis). I was now officially obsessed with telling his story.

Despite numerous obstacles, I persevered. More than a dozen years after first hearing his name, I now send Parker Hitt's story into the world. I hope this book brings much-needed light to the life of this extraordinary and ingenious man.

Note on Terminology

Cryptology broadly refers to the work required to extract information from secret or hidden communications or to protect the same. It involves all aspects of both signals intelligence, including *cryptanalysis* (breaking the codes and ciphers of adversaries), and communications security, including *cryptography* (making codes and ciphers to protect one's own communications). The term was coined by William F. Friedman,[1] and although it was not used by Parker Hitt, it neatly encompasses his work in that field and is in common use today. Hitt worked with both codes and ciphers: a *code* is a word or set of numbers representing a word or phrase, often presented in book form; a *cipher* is a system that uses one or more characters to replace individual letters and numbers in a message. Codes and ciphers require different methods of construction and analysis; Hitt had expertise in both but had more practical experience breaking ciphers.

Introduction

It gives us much pleasure to present this copy of our book
to Colonel Parker Hitt, USA, Ret., the father of modern
American military cryptology, whose Manual for the Solution
of Military Ciphers *guided our early, halting footsteps in the*
science and launched us upon our careers in the service of
our country.
                                        —William F. Friedman, 1957

As he lay dying, Parker Hitt's only regret was that he had not owned more dogs. The life of this extraordinary army officer had been full of opportunity, adventure, joy, and usefulness; Hitt had achieved success in life in much the same way he described the key to success in breaking ciphers—by using perseverance, analysis, intuition, and luck. At age ninety-two, though, his luck ran out. Hitt fell and broke his hip at home in Virginia in February 1971. On March 2, with his daughter, Mary Lue, at his bedside, Parker Hitt died.[1]

Colonel Hitt outlived the love of his life: a dark-eyed Texas beauty named Genevieve Young. He also outlasted two younger friends and admirers: Dwight D. Eisenhower and William F. Friedman. Hitt's army career was dedicated to clarity, invention, efficiency, progress, and modernity; his service spanned the US Army's critical transition from a small force focused on skirmishes—the "frontier constabulary"—to an organization ready to play a part in global conflict. Chances are you have never heard of Parker Hitt; the few memorials to him are obscure or difficult to visit, and there is no grave where one can pay tribute.[2]

Hitt, born into a middle-class, politically and socially active family in Indianapolis, Indiana, reached a turning point in his life in the summer of 1898, a few months shy of his twentieth birthday. Longing for adventure, Hitt answered his nation's call to fight the Spanish in Cuba, abandoning his studies at Purdue University and his ambitions for a career in journalism. Not yet old enough to become an officer, Hitt began his military career as a sergeant in the 2nd US Volunteer Engineers. Just days after he turned twenty-one, he became a second lieutenant in the infantry.

1

For more than ten years, Hitt traveled back and forth to the Philippines and crisscrossed the United States and the Alaska Territory with the 22nd Infantry Regiment. Lieutenant Hitt distinguished himself; some of his deeds made the newspapers, and he received a Silver Star for gallantry. While stationed at Fort Sam Houston, Texas, in 1910, Hitt reached a second turning point. The tall, scholarly, energetic, thirty-two-year-old Parker Hitt—seemingly committed to life as a bachelor—met and soon married Genevieve Young, seven years his junior.

Genevieve, a doctor's daughter, had lived most of her life in San Antonio, Texas. Upon completing her secondary education, she embarked on a pleasant existence of parties, card games, camping expeditions, and charitable work; she was undoubtedly pursued by many suitors. Parker and Genevieve married in July 1911. She knew she was becoming an army wife, but she had no idea she would become the first woman to break ciphers for the US government.[3]

In the fall of 1911 Parker and Genevieve arrived at Fort Leavenworth, Kansas, where Hitt was assigned to the Army Signal School. He quickly rose to star status as he developed an expertise in codes and ciphers and even invented cipher devices. Asked to stay on as an instructor, Hitt transformed the direction of the school's coursework. While at Leavenworth, he wrote *Manual for the Solution of Military Ciphers*, which lays down principles for establishing a code- and cipher-breaking effort—preliminary thoughts on what would become US signals intelligence operations. Hitt's work inspired early American scholars in the field of cryptology, particularly William F. Friedman. Using Hitt's ideas and those developed during World War I under Hitt's influence, Friedman created the US Army's Signal Intelligence Service (SIS) in 1930.

Though Captain Hitt was widely known in the army as a "shark on ciphers," he considered himself an infantryman first and eagerly accepted a teaching position at the School of Musketry at Fort Sill, Oklahoma. But code and cipher work followed him everywhere. When America entered World War I, Hitt was ordered to Washington; his skills were coveted by both the American Expeditionary Forces (AEF) and the army's new military intelligence organization. General John J. Pershing won the tug-of-war with Major Ralph Van Deman for Hitt's services, and Hitt traveled to Europe with Pershing on the RMS *Baltic* as assistant to the AEF's chief signal officer (CSO), Edgar Russel. As CSO of the First Army, Colonel Hitt was a strong advocate of the AEF's female telephone operators; he insisted on taking six of them to run the telephone exchange at army headquarters near the front. During the war he significantly influenced the development of the AEF's signals intelligence and communications security organizations, supplying guidance and support to the officers managing these efforts. While Hitt was overseas, Genevieve made a name for herself running the code room of the Southern Department's Intelligence Office at Fort Sam Houston.[4]

Hitt's promotions came regularly, but he was never plucked out of order and promoted ahead of his time. Unlike his AEF peers at similar levels of command, Hitt did not become a brigadier general while in France. He returned to the rank of major after the war but quickly rose to colonel in the summer of 1920. Despite his success, Hitt's military career was handicapped by his lack of an influential sponsor. His tendency to push for efficiency, practicality, and commonsense solutions was appreciated by many of his superior officers but certainly not all of them. Hitt was not afraid to ruffle feathers when he believed in his cause. Among the factors slowing or preventing his advancement were his lack of a combat command during the war and his age. By the end of World War I, Hitt was forty years old.

Disillusioned with the old guard of the Signal Corps at the end of the war, Hitt would have preferred an infantry assignment. Instead, his technical competence and effectiveness as an instructor led to a teaching post at the Army War College. This was followed by a brief stint as assistant chief of staff for military intelligence (G2) in the Second Corps Area, after which Hitt returned to the college. A tour as executive officer of the 23rd Infantry Regiment met with mixed reviews, and Hitt finished his career back in Washington with the General Staff.

When he retired from the army, Parker Hitt joined International Telephone and Telegraph (IT&T), where he was once again a cipher expert. A health crisis prompted his retirement from business, but by 1940 he had recovered and was recalled to duty by the army, at age sixty-two. He served for three years as CSO for the Fifth Corps Area at Fort Hayes in Columbus, Ohio. Hitt's daughter, Mary Lue, shared her parents' cipher aptitude. She worked briefly as a "code girl" at Arlington Hall Station during World War II.

In retirement, Hitt continued to advise and inspire others. For a short time, he was an active force in the American Cryptogram Association. Modern cryptologic expert Friedman (the spiritual grandfather of the National Security Agency) hero-worshipped Hitt and called him the "father of modern American military cryptology."[5]

Parker and Genevieve Hitt's personal story goes beyond that of a military family coping with frequent moves, inadequate quarters, and periods of separation. The trust, love, and respect they showed for each other reflect a very modern notion of equality between partners. They were not bound by traditions in lifestyle or child rearing but were influenced by their own free-spirited upbringings; they followed a path of their own choosing and enjoyed life in the moment, no matter what lay ahead.

Parker Hitt's career spanned a critical period in both the evolution of the modern army and the development of the American signals intelligence enterprise. Though acknowledged many times over—for his military gallantry in the Philippines, his cipher manual, and his service as First Army CSO—Hitt has disappeared from historical view, forgotten by all but the most devoted students of cryptology and military intelligence. Hitt stood out—both physically and intellectually—in the small pre–World War I officer corps. He displayed social skills, tact, personality, an innovative point of view, and a well-respected knack for teaching difficult subjects. He also had strong technical skills and a deep interest in technologies that were critical to the army's mission. Hitt's abilities made him a popular choice for difficult assignments and enabled a career of influence and accomplishment. Hitt was original, intelligent, clever, creative, skillful, and resourceful: he was ingenious by any definition of the word.

Hitt lived for the present and wanted no monument. He was a modest man. Fifty years after his death, this book looks beyond Hitt's modesty to reveal his life and legacy.

1

The Making of the Man

They all love to talk. They talk all the time. They are quick
energetic people. Want to know everything and do . . . Mother,
they are educated.

Genevieve Young Hitt, August 2, 1911

It was late summer 1878, and Indianapolis was abuzz with talk of the
yellow fever epidemic raging from New Orleans to Memphis. The world
was on the cusp of a technological and information revolution: Alexander Graham Bell's telephone had received a patent in 1876, and Thomas
Edison filed his first patent for electric lightbulbs in late 1878. Newlyweds George and Elizabeth Hitt welcomed a son into their multigenera-
tion household on August 27. They named him Parker, an unusual,
strong, and distinctive name derived from the Old English "park keeper."
It was a name that would carry their firstborn into a new age; little did
they realize the influence technology would have on his life.[1]

Never quite wealthy, but never entirely impoverished, the middle-class
Hitt family was full of energy and intellectual curiosity, romance and ideal-
ism, charity and accomplishment. George and Elizabeth raised their four
children (Parker, Muriel, Rodney, and Laurance) with Methodist principles
and a great deal of freedom, reflecting their own upbringings and beliefs.
Family had a significant influence on the direction of Parker Hitt's life,
loves, and career. He was the product of immigrants and soldiers, preachers
and craftsmen; they all sought education, and many served in the military.
A scion of Virginia's Germanna Colony, Parker's great-grandfather Martin
Hitt was an American Methodist Episcopal pioneer; he married the daughter of an officer of the Revolutionary War's Maryland Line before moving
to the Kentucky frontier. Unable to reconcile slavery with his religious
views, Martin moved to Urbana, Ohio, in 1815 and freed his slaves.
Martin's descendants became prominent citizens of the Midwest. His
son, William Washington Hitt, was a charter trustee of Indiana Asbury
College (now DePauw University). A grandson, Brigadier General William
H. L. Wallace, was mortally wounded at Shiloh; another grandson, Robert
R. Hitt of Illinois, was longtime chair of the House of Representatives'

5

Committee on Foreign Affairs. Martin's son John Wesley Hitt—Parker's grandfather—started the Brookville (Indiana) National Bank and was a founder and trustee of Brookville College. John Wesley Hitt and his wife, Maria John, raised three children to adulthood—Laura, Wilbur, and the doted-upon youngest, George Cooper Hitt, Parker's father.[2]

Parker's uncle Wilbur took up the family military tradition in 1862 at age nineteen, leaving Asbury College to enlist as a private in the 83rd Indiana Volunteer Infantry Regiment; he participated in the siege and assault on Vicksburg, Mississippi. In December 1863, newly commissioned in the 123rd Indiana Infantry Regiment, Wilbur fought at Kennesaw Mountain and in the siege of Atlanta. Disabled by pneumonia in early 1865, he was discharged as a first lieutenant but was brevetted to major in 1867. Wilbur was "a good soldier and a good man," and Parker spent time hunting and fishing with his uncle, for whom "fishing was an art." Wilbur's experience changed his brother George's view of war: it "stamped indelibly on my mind that war was an awful thing." In contrast, his uncle's war stories fascinated young Parker and lingered in his memory.[3]

While Wilbur was away at war, his mother indulged her younger son and let him run free. "She was liberal in her views, was not affected by the narrow mindedness of her time and allowed me many privileges that were forbidden to the boys of my acquaintance," George recalled. "I could play cards if I wanted to, I could smoke without concealment, I could ride or fish or hunt on Sunday and not be punished for it: consequently, I never overdid any of these things. A great mother was that!" George studied at the Brookville School and then left home at age sixteen for Ohio Wesleyan University; during his senior year, he was one of three editors of the student paper, the *Western Collegian*. Though George briefly clerked at his father's bank after graduation, he sought opportunities beyond the confines of small-town Brookville, and in 1872 he moved (with his parents) to the state capital, Indianapolis. A major rail hub during the Civil War, the city had more than doubled in population (to approximately 50,000 people) during the 1860s. But even Indianapolis was not enough for the young man: George took a civilian position as an army paymaster at Fort Platte, Nebraska, and got his chance for adventure. In May 1873 Captain William A. Jones, the chief of engineering in the Department of the Platte, hired George as secretary for an expedition to survey the headwaters of the Platte River and part of Yellowstone Park in northwestern Wyoming. Although there was some danger involved, the group was accompanied by the 2nd Cavalry and Shoshone guides and avoided the problems of a concurrent expedition (commanded by Colonel David S. Stanley and Lieutenant Colonel George A. Custer), which battled the Sioux.[4]

Upon his return to Omaha, George Hitt met Elizabeth Alice Barnett at a party. "She fascinated me," he recalled, but by the middle of November he was on his way back to Indianapolis and expected "never . . . to see her again." Barnett was the daughter of immigrants: her father, William, was a tinsmith and plumber from Fife, Scotland; her mother, Charlotte Busfield, was born in Yorkshire, England. The couple, both of whom loved literature, music, and learning, met, married, and raised their family in Andover, Massachusetts, where Elizabeth was born in 1853. Elizabeth studied classics and English, graduating from the Punchard Free School in 1870. She then began a course in physical culture at Dr. Diocletian Lewis's school in Boston before taking a job teaching physical culture at the new high school in Omaha, Nebraska. Traveling alone by train in September 1872, Elizabeth met Judge Elazier Wakeley, a member of the Omaha school board, who offered her a room in his home. While in Nebraska, Elizabeth developed strong religious feelings, and she was baptized at the Trinity Cathedral Episcopal Church, a Methodist Episcopal congregation.[5]

A fire at her hosts' home in January 1874 left Elizabeth with serious burns. George Hitt read of her injuries and began a correspondence. George returned to Omaha as a pay clerk later that year and professed his love for the young schoolteacher, calling her his "earthly paragon in whom there was no imperfection" and expressing his certainty that they would be "mated for life." Hoping to earn sufficient income to support a family, George returned to Indianapolis in early 1875 and became business manager at the *Indianapolis Journal*. The couple married in Massachusetts on September 27, 1877, and started their life together in Indianapolis, living with George's parents. George and Elizabeth set a high bar for marital bliss, and their son Parker, looking to emulate the perfect partnership of his parents, would not marry until he was nearly thirty-three.[6]

The Hitts had a happy, active household. Although George and Elizabeth never owned a home and the family moved frequently, they did not want for material things and usually had live-in household help. Both parents were risk takers. George endeavored to give his children the unconstrained, easygoing existence he had enjoyed in his youth, allowing them the freedom to explore, make choices, and express their individuality. The Hitts attended the Central Avenue United Methodist Church, and their moral life was infused with a strong belief in usefulness and charity. When John Wesley Hitt died, George said of his father, "a peaceful end had come to a useful life." George's mother, Maria, had filled Parker's head with stories of his Revolutionary War ancestors, and she was "a woman of fine intelligence, a cultivated mind and a strong and beautiful character." She maintained a presence in the lives of her grandchildren and moved back and forth between her sons' homes in Indianapolis and Washington, DC, where daughter Laura lived with her family. When his grandmother died in 1905 at age ninety-one after a "long life of usefulness," Parker, then in the Philippines, remarked, "it seems impossible that she has left us, for she has always taken such an interest in us all from the time we children were babies." Though Parker Hitt professed no religion in his adult life, he carried with him the admonition, emphasized in his youth, to be busy and useful.[7]

Parker's mother, Elizabeth, was a formidable force for good in Indianapolis; she actively encouraged community engagement and was known for her work on behalf of charity and the arts. Her causes included the Indianapolis Orphans Home, the symphony orchestra, and the Public Health Nursing Association. She served as president of a leading women's organization and also found time to write children's stories and give talks. For a time, she was disbursing treasurer of the local Red Cross. Her husband described her as "a feminist, but not a suffragist," for although she was progressive, she opposed giving the vote to women. Elizabeth's work illustrated the intellectual and organizational capabilities of women, and her example influenced both Parker's marriage and his army career. Parker had his mother's "striking personality and charm," but he did not resemble her physically, taking after his father instead.[8]

In addition to their liberal views on child rearing, George and Elizabeth Hitt shared a strong belief in the importance of education. Elizabeth regretted not attending college and wanted her children to have every possible educational opportunity. It was a talkative and inquiring household where everyone—not just the children—exhibited intellectual curiosity. "You know Parker's habit of looking things up. Well—they all have it and someone has the encyclopedia all the time," Parker's new wife would exclaim to her mother upon meeting the Hitt family.[9]

Parker Hitt was born during an age of technological innovation and increasing access to information. Journalism flourished with the advent of the telegraph (developed in the 1840s) and transatlantic submarine cables (developed in the 1860s); news rapidly circulated from all points of the country and even the world. It would not take long for Parker to learn of the eruption of the great volcano Krakatoa, which took place on his fifth birthday, and his father's work at the newspaper ensured that he developed an interest in world affairs and communications. Parker's political leanings were formed and hardened early, as George Hitt became a minor player in the Indiana Republican Party through his work at the *Indianapolis Journal*. Local attorney John C. New became chairman of the state Republican Party in 1880 and simultaneously bought the newspaper. A solidly progressive Republican instrument, the *Journal* boasted of its refusal "to put itself on a level with the cheap papers flooding the country" and insisted on presenting the news "in a decent and dignified manner." John's son, Harry S. New, employed by his father as a reporter and then editor, became good friends with George Hitt and served as an honorary uncle to the Hitt children. Harry New (fictionalized as Brainard Macauley in *The Gentleman from Indiana* by his friend and contemporary Booth Tarkington) would be an important connection for Parker, both as a US senator and later as postmaster general. New and his circle of politically influential men appreciated George Hitt's good humor and literary skill. An "informal club" met in the newspaper office to discuss the state of the world, literature, and the arts; it was a "political nerve center" for Indiana Republicans. Among the group were the News, Hitt, and Benjamin Harrison, a lawyer and Civil War officer with political aspirations. Added to the mix in 1876 was "Hoosier poet" James Whitcomb Riley. George Hitt became Riley's friend, confidant, and publisher, financing his first book. Riley was "ignorant of conventional forms" and often "went to Hitt, who knows how to do everything," to help him answer letters from schools and other organizations. Like father, like son: Parker Hitt would also be one of those people who seemed to know how to do everything.[10]

The *Indianapolis Journal* and, to a great degree, the informal club it gave rise to made Benjamin Harrison president of the United States. John New was the campaign's architect, and Harry New gave George Hitt a minor role in the campaign. George's college acquaintance, Indianapolis lawyer Charles Warren Fairbanks (who, a decade later, would be a US senator and would play a significant role in shaping Parker Hitt's military career), made speeches on behalf of Harrison. Even Riley, whose popularity in Indiana was greater than Harrison's, campaigned for the man. Harrison lost the popular vote to President Grover Cleveland but won the Electoral College, and the men of the *Journal* rejoiced. In February 1889 George and ten-year-old Parker traveled on Harrison's train to Washington; father and son had several days to explore the capital before the March 4 inauguration. They cheered Harrison as he took the oath of office and gave his address in the pouring rain.[11]

In 1890 the elder New, appointed by Harrison to be consul general at the American embassy in London, invited Hitt to be his vice–consul general. The ambassador (then called the minister) was Robert Todd Lincoln, the sole surviving son of Abraham Lincoln. Hitt took the job, and the family left Indianapolis on October 11 for New York. There they boarded the *City of New York,* the largest and fastest liner on the Atlantic, and arrived in London on October 25. New "provided an adequate salary for our support and bestowed on us many favors and delicate attentions that made our stay abroad delightful."[12]

The Hitts settled at 21 Montague Place in Bloomsbury, behind the British Museum. Twelve-year-old Parker attended the University College School, a boys' school then located on Gower Street, about half a mile from the Hitts' home. Boys went by their surnames and first initials, so Hitt never knew his schoolmates' first names. In the morning he studied English, Latin, French, and the history of England. Then the boys had an hour off for lunch: "some of us went home, others bought lunch off a man who brought in a supply of buns, cakes and every sort of unsubstantial food so dear to the average boy's heart." With their parents' consent, the boys had beer with lunch. Then they played soccer or other games. In the afternoon Hitt studied math, physics, and chemistry, and he noted that "arithmetic in English money was very hard at first." He recounted, "most boys knew nothing of America and asked . . . what language was spoken," as well as wondering whether he had ever shot a buffalo. "On the whole my experience at the University School was an exceedingly pleasant one. I received a good start in Latin, French and Algebra and the English work was equivalent to about two years' work in our school," he later wrote. As an adolescent, though, Hitt was already thinking analytically, commenting that it was "hardly a school to me but rather a place to study English ways and English boys."[13]

Elizabeth Hitt used her time abroad to seek out locales mentioned in books, attend musical events and plays, and visit art galleries. She also engaged in charitable work with both the Salvation Army and Toynbee Hall, part of the international settlement movement. The family took a trip to Paris and visited rural parts of England. The lively and engaged Hitt children enjoyed the works of Riley and often quoted his poems. They particularly loved his newest book, *Rhymes of Childhood,* and George Hitt informed Riley that "even the baby knows 'The Raggedy Man' by heart." The baby, four-year-old Laurance, was precocious; "at very embarrassing moments," he quoted Riley's poem to their nursemaid (who was in love with a policeman), saying, "'Take the hint, an' run,

Child; run! Er she cain't git no courtin' done!'" changing the pronoun and "pointing the finger of mischief at the blushing 'hired girl.'" Though the family enjoyed their time abroad, Hitt resigned his position on January 4, 1892, to return to the *Journal,* much to New's regret. They traveled home on the *City of Berlin;* on the passenger list, Parker is identified as a "scholar," while his siblings are listed as children.[14]

Back in Indianapolis, Parker joined the freshman class at High School #1, later renamed Shortridge High School. It was the oldest free public high school in Indiana, a racially integrated, progressive institution. During his sophomore year, Parker was the associate editor of the *Dawn,* a monthly paper edited by second-year students in the English Department; it featured letters and short items from prominent authors of the time, solicited by the student staff. It is quite possible that Hitt was responsible for the James Whitcomb Riley issue in 1893. At the end of his junior year, Hitt received Pass+ marks in English, physics, drawing, and mechanics. In June 1895 he finished his senior year with A+ grades in English and chemistry and As in advanced algebra and geometry. He was one of the editors of the "Prophecy" section of the senior yearbook, looking fifteen years into the future to predict what graduates would be doing on June 11, 1910. His prophecy read: "Parker Hitt is all the rage as a magazine illustrator."[15]

Eighty-four students graduated during an evening ceremony on June 11, 1895; fifty-five of them were female. Eight students spoke—two chosen by "reason of scholarship," three chosen by the teachers, and three chosen by the students. Hitt was in the last category and spoke on "The Opportunities of the Profession of Journalism." His essay "showed careful thought and study of his subject" and noted, if "men and women want to rise in their profession they must be tirelessly inquisitive and willing to work."[16]

After graduation, Parker spent time in the *Journal's* office thinking about a future career, but he was looking for adventure. Not yet seventeen, he and his slightly older friend Henry C. Churchman demonstrated persistence, independence, and physical strength when they set out on a bicycle ride from Indianapolis to New Haven, Connecticut. They probably followed the route of the National Road (now US Route 40) and what is now US Route 1. On June 30 they pedaled fifty miles from Cambridge, Ohio, to Wheeling, West Virginia. They found the road "very rough" and hilly, which "surprised the westerners, who are accustomed to riding on the smooth Indiana prairies." The pair left Wheeling on July 1 bound for Pittsburgh, where they planned to visit friends and then "wheel across the

Alleghanies" to Connecticut. Whether they made it to their destination is unknown.[17]

In the fall Hitt entered Purdue University, sixty-three miles from home in Lafayette, Indiana. A land-grant university established in 1869, Purdue (then as now) focused on science, technology, and agriculture. His freshman class, the class of 1899, was the largest the school had seen; the freshmen chose as their motto "row, not drift," a sentiment Hitt put into practice in his life. At Purdue he majored in civil engineering and aspired to be a "man of many broad qualities acquainted with nature and men," someone who was "profoundly familiar with mathematics, hydraulics, strength of materials and economic designing." He was mature and self-confident, possessed common sense, and was an outstanding student. Perhaps he was also a bit self-important, or at least he appeared so to others. Hitt was gently roasted twice in the yearbook as a member of the "Swell-Head Club" (motto: "so act that all men may notice") and the "Ego Club." In his first two years he served in the cadet corps (predecessor of the ROTC) on campus; he was in the corps' bicycle section and served as first sergeant as a sophomore. Cadets drilled two hours each week, attended weekly lectures on military sciences, and held a one-day "sham battle" each spring. According to university president James H. Smart, Hitt was "one of the best men in our cadet corps."[18]

Academically, Hitt excelled at Purdue, earning straight As in algebra, geometry, trigonometry, rhetoric, mechanical drawing, shop work, and theory of parts making. In Indianapolis for the summer, he spent time at the *Journal* office—hanging out, if not helping. He was young, strong, and unafraid. On his eighteenth birthday Parker was en route to a party when he encountered a would-be mugger. With a "hard fist and a strong arm," he knocked the man down "and escaped harm," walking "leisurely on to the party where he showed no nervousness whatever."[19]

Moving on to more advanced studies, Hitt again achieved straight As in his sophomore year, studying physics, analytic geometry, mechanical and architectural drawing, French, forging, calculus, and literature. He also learned surveying, and he and his fellow students developed "a mania for measuring the surrounding country, and on pleasant afternoons are frequently to be seen with their instruments ascertaining just how much land lies adjacent to Purdue." But he had fun too. In the fall of 1896 the sophomores painted "99" (their graduation year) on a large water tank a mile north of campus. Hitt may or may not have been involved in the initial painting, but he did help guard against attempts by the freshman class to paint "00" on the tank, and he may have been involved in repainting the

"99" after such an assault. He did not bury himself in books. In the spring Hitt's kite-handling skills attracted "much attention" from other students; no doubt he was learning practical lessons about aerodynamics.[20]

Though absorbed in engineering, Hitt had not entirely abandoned his literary interests. He worked for the *Exponent,* a semimonthly literary newspaper, in his freshman and sophomore years, and in his junior year he was the local editor for the class of 1899. He also served as corresponding secretary of the Civil Engineering Society for 1897–1898. Categorized as a "Persimmon Picker" (those trees can grow to sixty feet), "His Royal Highness" Hitt was teased by the yearbook, which described him as one of those who had a "lean and hungry look."[21]

In his junior year Tau Beta Pi, the engineering society, selected Hitt for membership, an honor bestowed on the upper quarter of each class. Academic ranking was not the only criterion for selection. Tau Beta Pi men possessed "those qualities of manliness and good-fellowship so desirable in every walk of life." Once again, Hitt had straight As in his coursework: calculus, chemistry (lecture and lab), field engineering, mechanics, French, and differential equations. At the end of the year, Hitt "commanded the confidence and respect of his instructors and showed himself to be a thoroughly reliable man." He was "one of the few students who has had the highest grade in every study throughout the entire three years." Despite his success, when he packed his bags in Lafayette in May 1898, Parker knew he would not be returning to Purdue. There were lives to be lived.[22]

The Indiana newspapers did not sensationalize the explosion on the USS *Maine* in Havana harbor on February 15, 1898. Unlike the "yellow press" of the era, they did not rush to promote war and recommended that readers remain calm. Though many advocated Cuban independence from Spanish colonial rule, the *Journal* supported President William McKinley's anti-interventionist views, advising readers to "maintain their present attitude of coolness and self-control." The paper continued to support McKinley even as his position shifted toward war. Congress authorized a volunteer army of 125,000 men on April 22. On the evening of April 25, the day Congress declared war, Indiana governor James A. Mount learned that the state needed to supply four regiments of infantry and two batteries of light artillery to fight what became known as the Spanish-American War.[23]

Hitt's reasons for leaving school to become a soldier were complex. He had been weaned on stories of his ancestors' service in the Revolutionary War, his uncle's adventures in the Civil War, the excitement of his father's Yellowstone expedition, and his mother's fortitude in leaving her home to teach school in distant Nebraska. He had an innate spirit of independence and had been raised to be useful; he was strong and not afraid of physical work. Hitt may have been bored with Purdue and unenthusiastic about his future as a civil engineer. The subtle societal signals that fighting for Cuban independence was a desirable course of action for a patriotic young man tipped the scales in favor of the army. In later years, Hitt gave an Armistice Day talk that sheds light on why this well-connected, well-educated young man from a progressive, middle-class family decided to be a soldier. With the prospect of another world war on the horizon in 1938, he told a crowd, "When the new generation begins to feel its oats and we have become the old fogeys doing our best to hold them back . . . and when *they,* not we, decide to have their war, we had better wish them Godspeed and help all we can." War "was a hard game," he said, "but now that you look back on it, I think all of you must agree that it made men out of you."[24]

Before enlisting, nineteen-year-old Hitt attempted to gain a commission, even though officers needed to be twenty-one and exceptions were rare. Senator Charles W. Fairbanks, who considered Hitt "an excellent young man educated in engineering," arranged to have Hitt examined by the Army Board of Engineers in Chicago; Parker missed a camping trip with friends to take the exam on June 16. He passed but was denied a commission because of his age. Still determined to serve, on June 20 he enlisted in the 2nd US Volunteer Engineers, his father signing the consent form (his mother was out of town at a convention). Hitt, who had dark brown hair, blue eyes, and a light complexion, was two months short of his twentieth birthday and stood six feet two-and-one-half inches tall, a few inches shy of what would eventually be his full height. He weighed 161 pounds stripped, had some small scars on his face and one on his wrist, and his teeth were good. He enrolled for two years of service and mustered in on July 1, 1898. Hitt did not want to miss the opportunity to fight; his energy and sense of adventure won out over the prospect of a college degree and a career. The accomplished young engineer went off to war to become a man.[25]

2

The Making of the Soldier

This boy of yours was raised to be a soldier and he is working at his trade.

Parker Hitt, May 30, 1942

Sergeant Parker Hitt of Company D of the 2nd US Volunteer Engineers, with three years of engineering studies and cadet corps experience behind him, was put in charge of older but equally new soldiers. The group—all men with mechanical and construction skills—mustered in on July 1, 1898, the day American forces fought battles at San Juan Hill and El Caney in Cuba. They were not a fighting force, but they were needed to build troop camps in the United States and in occupied Cuba. While the engineers were training at Fort Sheridan, Illinois, the war ended on July 17. In August the group hurried to Montauk Point, New York, at the eastern tip of Long Island, and built Camp Wikoff, a quarantine station for troops returning from Cuba to ensure that communicable tropical diseases did not spread throughout the general population. Even though the engineers arrived before most of their construction equipment (and after the first wave of troops), they quickly set to work. Soon roads, water and electrical plants, hospitals, and kitchens sprang up in the fields. Wikoff was a short-term venture: six weeks after the engineers arrived, they started to tear it down. The last troops left on October 28, and the engineers departed a few days later. Hitt, on leave in Indianapolis from October 18, missed the camp's shutdown and rejoined the unit in Savannah, Georgia, on November 5, where they waited to deploy to Cuba.[1]

On November 22 Hitt boarded the SS *Florida* in Tampa. Two days later he celebrated Thanksgiving Day on the ship, lunching on hardtack and cold canned tomatoes. It was the first of many Thanksgivings he would miss during his career. Company D began building Camp Columbia, soon to be the headquarters of VII Corps, the day they arrived in Havana. By December 10, when the Treaty of Paris officially ended the war, American occupation of the island was well under way. Hitt helped construct railroads, roads, and hospitals; the engineers also installed boilers and pumps and laid five miles of water pipes. Despite their work, the crowded camp had poor sanitation. "Most of the hardships of war are found off the battlefield," Hitt remarked much later, noting that he had gone "through the Spanish-American war as a kid under age and remember well the sanitary horrors of our camps and the inefficiency of our commanders and supply agencies in the field."[2]

Sanitation aside, Hitt enjoyed his time in Cuba, particularly the warm weather. Throughout his life he would be attracted by the prospect of a tropical retreat, and he maintained an intellectual interest in the island nation. In February 1899 his parents and youngest brother, Laurance, came for a visit, accompanied by Harry New's young second wife, Catherine (New served as a volunteer captain in VII Corps). Convinced that the army was his career, and not deterred by another war starting in the new American territory of the Philippine Islands, Hitt conferred with his father about becoming an officer when he turned twenty-one in August. Though he later referred to the commissioning process as easy—no more than an exam—in reality, it took the better part of a year and some political influence for Hitt to obtain one of the few officer billets available.[3]

At the beginning of March 1899 Congress authorized a regular army of 65,000 men; officers would be chosen from a pool of current regular officers and those volunteers who had excelled during the Spanish-American War. As soon as George Hitt returned to Indianapolis, he started to work his connections, and soon Parker's name topped Senator Charles W. Fairbanks's list of recommendations for appointment to second lieutenant. Fairbanks telegraphed Adjutant General Henry C. Corbin at the War Department on March 24 to adjust the timing of Hitt's commissioning exam (it was already scheduled to take place in Virginia, but Hitt was still in Cuba); Fairbanks asked that either Hitt be sent home or the examination be moved to Cuba. But Fairbanks had forgotten that Hitt was still underage, putting the appointment in jeopardy. The senator then requested that a place be held for the "faithful and deserving young man," and Fairbanks's good friend President William McKinley agreed. Meanwhile, on April 15 Company D left Havana; after two days at the Savannah River quarantine station, they spent a month in Augusta, Georgia, awaiting discharge. Hitt headed back to Indianapolis on May 16, with a detour to visit his aunt Laura and sister Muriel in Washington, DC. Upon his return to Indianapolis, Hitt worked nights in the *Journal*'s business office while waiting to turn twenty-one.[4]

That summer the army received two strong recommendations supporting Hitt's appointment. The first, from Purdue University president James H. Smart, commended Hitt as a "young man of fine personal character, and of conduct and habit above reproach . . . rather mature in his judgments," who "has, what is rare, a good deal of common sense." Smart insisted that Purdue could "send no better man to represent the institution as an officer in the regular army." A second endorsement came from Hitt's Company D commander, Christopher C. FitzGerald, who proclaimed that although all his men were "above the ordinary," Hitt "was one of the most willing ones and *the* most soldierly man in my company." FitzGerald was impressed that Hitt, though just a sergeant, had taken up the slack created by a shortfall of officers on the trip from Havana, acting "in a manner that showed him well fitted to look after the health and comfort of men."[5]

Nine days after his twenty-first birthday, on September 5, Hitt appeared at Washington Barracks (now Fort Lesley J. McNair) in Washington, DC, for his commissioning examination. He had no problem passing the tests, doing best in geography, with a score of 92, and worst in history, with a 67. But he failed the physical. Hitt was now six feet three inches tall but weighed only 164 pounds, below the army's minimum weight in relation to height. Aware that this might be a problem, Hitt was ready with an excuse, claiming that his night work kept him below his normal 175 pounds. The board recommended that the weight requirement be waived, and a few weeks later, Hitt was a commissioned officer, with a date of rank of September 1, 1899.[6]

Hitt joined the army just before Secretary of War Elihu Root's reforms led to its expansion in 1901. His two years in the Purdue cadet corps and brief enlisted service put him ahead of other young men commissioned during those years: of 2,000 line officers in 1902, 1,818, like Hitt, had joined after the start of the Spanish-American War in 1898. Only 20 percent (414) of the new officers came from the enlisted ranks; more than 75 percent (1,542) had no previous military education. The army was racially segregated, and Hitt was assigned to the 25th Infantry as a white officer in charge of African American troops. Fairbanks, who had pushed in the Senate for black soldiers to be commanded by black officers, intervened and recommended that Hitt be assigned elsewhere. Within days, Hitt belonged to the 22nd Infantry, a white unit, whose unofficial motto was "Regulars, by God"; he reported to the Presidio of San Francisco on October 16.[7]

After just a month of training in the duties of an officer, Hitt and First Lieutenant George D. Arrowsmith (destined for the 25th Infantry) took charge of a group of recruits bound for the Philippines on the RMS *Duke of Fife* on November 20, 1899. The ship encountered heavy headwinds leaving San Francisco but then enjoyed fine weather and smooth seas as it approached Honolulu, where it stopped on December 1. Hitt became ill a few weeks after leaving Hawaii and was (incorrectly) diagnosed with malaria. When the ship docked in Manila on December 28, he was transferred to the hospital ship *Relief,* where the doctors determined he was suffering from typhoid fever (although Hitt later insisted it was Malta fever). By the end of January 1900, Hitt was well enough to join the 22nd Infantry, which had been in the Philippines since March 1899. The regiment was commanded by Colonel John W. French; Hitt was assigned to Company H, stationed at Arayat in northern Luzon and led by Captain George A. Detchemendy. The first lieutenant in Company H, William H. Wassell, was on leave in the United States, so Hitt immediately became second in command.[8]

Spain occupied the Philippine Islands in the 1560s, and by the mid-1890s, the inhabitants were pushing back against colonial rule. Taking advantage of the conflict between Spain and the United States, the Philippine Revolutionary Army declared independence in June 1898, and General Emilio Aguinaldo became president of the politically disunited islands. The terms of the Treaty of Paris were anathema to the new Philippine government, as they allowed the United States to buy the islands from Spain. Tension between the small American force in Manila and the Philippine army and people developed into war in early February 1899, and American troops began a large-scale occupation of the islands, with the objective of quashing the nascent independent government and imposing American rule.[9]

There were many opportunities for a new second lieutenant to learn his trade. The regiment had eight companies spread across the Arayat district, north of Manila and east of Mount Arayat, and one of Hitt's first assignments was to prepare a detailed map of the area. In April and May 1900 he temporarily took command of Company G. On June 10 part of the regiment embarked on an expedition to the hills, and when they arrived at Sibul, Hitt became temporary commander of a garrison of men who were unfit to traverse the trail ahead. In July and August he went to San Antonio to fill in as second lieutenant for Company I in the place of Paul Draper, who had drowned at the end of June. Thomas Blatchford of Company I mentioned Hitt in a letter home, saying of his new lieutenant: "Parker Hitt is his name and he is a fine man."[10]

The weather was warm, the terrain was exotic, and disease was ever present. Hitt contracted malaria and suffered from dysentery but had recovered sufficiently to join Company H for an expedition to Pulang Buli in late August, and he remained with the company when it moved to Cabiao. In mid-November he spent a week carrying messages relating to the wrecked ship SS *Indiana* before rejoining Company H at its new station in Baler, to the northeast. Hitt evidently proved his mettle—or was a victim of circumstance, for the regiment was short three second lieutenants, two first lieutenants, and one captain—and received additional duties, serving as the post adjutant, commissary officer, quartermaster, and ordnance officer and on a summary court. In January 1901 he picked up the duties of assistant collector of internal revenue and began to keep a diary. There were more exciting, less administrative assignments to come.[11]

Baler, a coastal town, was the "only garrisoned place on the three hundred mile stretch of desolate and practically uninhabited coastline between Infanta to the south and Apari to the north." It was the northeastern outpost of the Fourth District, wedged between the shore and the mountains. A frequently washed-out mountain trail led forty miles west to Pantabangan and the nearest telegraph line. Company H remained in this lonely location for fourteen months, going "five months without mail and fourteen months without the sight of a white woman." Hitt and contract surgeon Dr. David D. Hogan arrived in Baler at the same time; Hogan became Hitt's preferred companion for excursions around the area.[12]

It was not an unpleasant life for the adventurous young outdoorsman from the Midwest. When not working on bridges or handling administrative business for his company, Hitt wrote letters to his parents and a handful of female acquaintances. Mail service was erratic—a Christmas 1900 package showed up on August 30, 1901, with "everything in good shape except one fruitcake"—but when letters did arrive, Hitt's evenings were spent catching up with the outside world. He bathed in the sea, played baseball and horseshoes, and socialized with the other officers. Hitt's height presented some difficulties, particularly with his cot and tent. "When he puts his head in the right place on his pillow his toes poke out at the other end, and when he draws them indoors his head bumps against the canvas," Detchemendy claimed.[13]

A proficient fisher and hunter, thanks to his uncle Wilbur's training, Hitt shot ducks, deer, and carabao (water buffalo), making him popular at camp, where fresh meat was at a premium. The ducks were "very good eating," and he brought in a carabao every few weeks to add to rations. Detchemendy, who called the towering Hitt "Shorty," recollected that he became the "hit of the hunting season" while on a fishing trip with four others. Three miles from shore, Hitt "caught and killed a fine big buck deer, evidently driven into the sea by a hunting party and swept out to sea." Everyone had venison for dinner. Hitt learned to speak Tagalog and cultivated a relationship with a local man who became his hunting guide.[14]

An action on February 6, 1901, demonstrated Hitt's command ability and poise under fire, and the event's significance to the Philippine-American war brought his name to the attention of military and civilian leadership. On the evening of February 4, Hitt's hunting guide visited his hut; Hitt offered him a chair, a drink, and a cigarette and heard an account of a band of "evil intentioned men" who had come ashore and forced the man's neighbor, Feliciano Rubio, to help them. Hitt took the story to his captain, and the next morning Detchemendy and thirty soldiers located the band's abandoned campsite on the beach. The only escape from the valley was the trail to Pantabangan, so Hitt persuaded Detchemendy to let him take twenty men to the trailhead at San Jose. They arrived at noon on February 6, and Hitt posted sentries to monitor the trail while he and the rest of his men hid. Late in the afternoon, "three men came out of the grass into the plaza clearing and we captured them neatly without a sound being made." One of the captured men was Rubio, who told Hitt that the group of thirteen men had two Remington rifles; they were resting in a coconut grove half a mile east of town and planned to take to the trail that night. Hitt's men crept down the trail, through high grass and a bamboo hedge, to an open field. Across the field they saw some small fires. "It was getting dark and we had not time to go around the open field and get at them. Our only chance was to make them come to us." Positioning his men along the hedge to the right and left of the trail, Hitt ordered them to hold their fire. Rubio called out to the group, saying that all was well and they should proceed. The man leading the group, dressed in white, could be seen in the dusk; he stopped halfway across the field and asked Rubio to guide him, but Rubio claimed to be tired and told the group to go straight ahead. Then, one of Hitt's soldiers "had his finger too close to the trigger, and a rifle cracked on the left." Hitt gave the order to fire, "and everything blazed loose." After three "ragged volleys," the soldiers rushed forward and found one dead, two wounded, a rifle, and many abandoned packs and hampers. In addition to rice, dried meat and fish, and twenty rounds of ammunition, they discovered more than 200 letters. The group had been carrying messages to President Aguinaldo.[15]

The dates and details of subsequent actions vary in both contemporary and modern accounts. Based on intelligence gained during Hitt's encounter, Lieutenant Joseph D. Taylor, leading Company C of the 24th Infantry in Pantabangan, arranged for the remainder of the group to surrender when they straggled off the mountain two days later. Among them was Aguinaldo's special courier, Cecilio Segismundo, carrying critical enciphered messages in "a tiny oilskin packet slung around his neck." Segismundo, who divulged information about Aguinaldo's location and forces, claimed not to "have the secret of Aguinaldo's cipher," and he stuck to that story, despite being deprived of food and sleep and possibly enduring the "water cure" (waterboarding). Frederick Funston, a journalist who had risen rapidly through the ranks to become a brigadier general in the volunteers, commanded the Fourth District of Luzon. Collaborating with a small team, Funston solved the critical enciphered message, which led to Aguinaldo's capture on March 23, 1901. This event was Hitt's first brush with the world of cryptology, but he was not aware of Aguinaldo's cipher at the time and had no role in its solution. Later in life Hitt disagreed with the cipher solution presented in Funston's *Memories of Two Wars;* by then, Hitt was a seasoned cipher expert, and he annotated his personal copy of Funston's book to explain how the cipher really worked. Hitt and Detchemendy received commendations for their part in Aguinaldo's capture.[16]

Hitt was surprised by the "rather sudden" arrival of a promotion board in the middle of March; with no time to prepare, he thought "they cannot expect too much." The board was pleased with Hitt's "general intelligence and adaptability for the military service," finding him to be "above the average civilian appointee to the army." These qualities made up for the fact that Hitt lacked "a proficient knowledge of the subject of administration," and Second Lieutenant Hitt was recommended for promotion. At about the same time, George Hitt and Senator Fairbanks were lobbying to get Parker promoted faster, but they learned that this might be possible only if he switched branches from the Infantry to the Artillery. George believed his son preferred the Infantry, so nothing was done to subvert the strict order of promotion (Hitt was twentieth on the list of second lieutenants in the Infantry).[17]

In September 1901 Hitt performed a second heroic act when he and his troops discovered the burial site of Apprentice Seaman Second Class Denzell George Arthur Venville, the victim of an April 1899 ambush of a party from the USS *Yorktown* (PG-1). Detchemendy and some men, accompanied by two prisoners, departed Baler just after noon on August 31 to search for Venville's remains. They located the approximate site of the grave and learned that one of the prisoners and another man had killed, dismembered, and buried the sailor; on the trip back to Baler, the guilty prisoner escaped. On the morning of September 3, Hitt and twenty soldiers went back to examine the site, where they found eight vertebrae, six and a half ribs, collar bones, the upper end of the sternum, some bones from the lower right arm, a finger bone, and two pieces of navy uniform cloth with two navy buttons. The group constructed a rock pyramid and a cross and cut an inscription on a nearby tree before making the four-and-a-half-hour walk back to Baler. Hitt put Venville's remains in a tin box, soldered it shut, and had a coffin prepared. He then drafted his report, including a sketch he had made of the site; he was sorry he had been unable to construct a better monument to Venville. By the end of 1901, Hitt's role in the Venville story had appeared in the newspapers back home, and the secretary of the navy commended him for his actions.[18]

A typhoon struck Baler on October 2, 1901; in the evening it was "blowing great guns," and Dr. Hogan came to spend the night in Hitt's more secure hut. But by 9:30 the two men fled the wrecked hut and took refuge in another dwelling, which was destroyed at about midnight. It was the worst storm since 1879; the roof nearly blew off the church, and every house in Baler was damaged. Hitt and Hogan set up a stove in a partially damaged hut and dried out a few things, but Hitt's papers were "all over town," and "even the safe was half full of water." The bridge he had helped construct in January was gone. Hitt moved into Sergeant Birkline's house the next night, where he cooked clam chowder for dinner. It would take weeks to rebuild, hampered by "another blow" on the evening of October 14 and another typhoon overnight on October 22. The first storm changed Hitt's career and life, for by the end of the month he was suffering from rheumatism in his left leg, later diagnosed as sciatica caused by exposure and rough living conditions. He received no treatment until January. Pain from sciatica would plague him for the rest of his life, especially in cold weather, and he was often temporarily unable to carry out his duties.[19]

A company of the 24th Infantry relieved Company H on January 13, 1902. Hitt departed Baler aboard the USAT *Lawton* on January 18 and, after many stops, arrived in Manila a week later. The men had a few days to shop, mail letters, and visit before boarding the USAT *Hancock*, which left port on the afternoon of February 1. Harsh weather made it a difficult trip, and it took a week to reach the coaling stop at Nagasaki, Japan. The weather did not improve as they crossed the Pacific; the ship encountered a ten-day-long gale during which two soldiers were washed overboard. On February 25, almost six weeks after leaving Baler, Hitt arrived at San Francisco.[20]

Back in the States, Hitt and Detchemendy faced a wave of publicity and praise for their role in both the capture of Aguinaldo and the repatriation of Venville's remains. But Hitt's "crazy captain" was upset. Detchemendy demanded promotion to brigadier general for his part in the Aguinaldo affair, equal to the (regular army) promotion Funston received. When it was clear that no promotion was forthcoming, Detchemendy resigned his commission, effective March 10.[21]

The men of the 22nd Infantry spent ten days in San Francisco before traveling by train to Fort Crook (now Offutt Air Force Base), Nebraska. On the last day of the trip, eight soldiers were injured when the train wrecked; Hitt was unhurt but lost his Cuban Occupation Medal in the chaos. He then took six weeks' leave to visit Indianapolis, where he shunned the local press. My "position forbids . . . being interviewed for publication," he told journalists eager to discuss his heroics. Hitt turned his attention to his social life, attending a variety of events; at a wedding in early May he met Evelyn Willis, whom he "rushed for a week." While on leave, he asked for permission to join the state encampment of the Indiana National Guard, at the request of Governor Winfred J. Durbin, but the War Department said no.[22]

Hitt's career took on the peripatetic nature of early-twentieth-century US Army regiments. Many regiments had companies based in multiple states—the 22nd was in both Nebraska and Arkansas—and a constant flow of men and officers moved from post to post on foot and by rail for training and drills. Hitt spent June at Camp Wood in the Omaha Indian Agency in Nebraska; during annual target practice there, he made rifleman first class. The companies marched the 180 miles out and back from Fort Crook; on the way, Hitt mapped the road, plotting distances with an odometer. In July he served as the assistant range officer for the Department Rifle Competition at Fort Leavenworth, Kansas, before returning to the regiment for about ten days in August 1902. While at Leavenworth, Hitt was promoted to first lieutenant, with a date of rank of March 21, 1901. Army promotions were characteristically slow; Hitt's first promotion took almost three years, despite his notable achievements, and it would be another nine years before he became a captain.[23]

Hitt spent a good deal of time pursuing women. After Evelyn Willis there was Janette Chambers at Crook; he spent a few weeks taking her to country club dances and on long walks. Then at Leavenworth he met Mabel Allen and May Evans, who lived in Kansas City. After returning to Crook, he resumed seeing Chambers but also began dating Marie

Pullman. After a "little row" with Marie, he was sent to Fort Logan H. Roots in Little Rock, Arkansas, where he commanded Company C and served as its adjutant, quartermaster, engineer, commissary officer, ordnance officer, and recruiting officer for four weeks. Of the women he met in Little Rock, Carrie Hempstead and Nan Wright were his "favorites." On September 17, 1902, the train carrying Hitt's unit north from Arkansas collided head-on with a freight train; two members of the regiment were hurt, and two trainmen were killed, but once again, Hitt was uninjured. Parker reconciled with Marie when he returned north and spent all his spare time with her until he had to return to Logan Roots. In November, on his way back to Nebraska from Arkansas, he met up with his father for a few hours in St. Louis and then looked up Mabel Allen as he passed through Kansas City.[24]

Hitt's sciatica flared again in October and worsened during the winter at Fort Crook; he felt no better after a week of leave in Indianapolis and was in acute pain from his upper pelvis to his ankle. The surgeon at Crook, Dr. William Corbusier, was an old Philippine hand and recommended two months of treatment in the milder climate of the Army and Navy Hospital in Hot Springs, Arkansas; he considered the prognosis for recovery good. Hitt was "hardly able to walk" and got "only temporary relief or none at all" from whatever remedies he was prescribed; he spent several weeks in his quarters at Crook before, with a tearful farewell from Marie Pullman, he left for Hot Springs.[25]

Once at the hospital, Hitt was found to have chronic articular rheumatism of the left hip in addition to sciatica. He was not confined to bed, however, and took his meals at nearby hotels. At first, Hitt did little socializing apart from standing around and watching others at the weekly dances in town. He met a few kindred spirits but thought "the rest of the officers are not my kind, somehow." In the midst of his treatment, Hitt met Melinda Weber "and rushed her for a week on a wager. Won it and she left." Then came Blanche Stearns, of whom he boasted in his diary, "The kid is mine from the start. We try all the roads and most of the walks around the Springs and keep disgraceful hours at her house." After three months of rest and relaxation, Hitt left the hospital and the Hot Springs social life, "with much regret," to rejoin his regiment in early July 1903.[26]

Just a few days after returning to Fort Crook, he was back on the range at the Omaha Agency, "working like a dog," yet he still had time to see Ruth Halford, the Casey girls, Miss Taylor, and Miss Newell. Hitt qualified as marksman with the best revolver score in the battalion and completed all but two miles of a long march before his leg gave out. In August 1903 he was well enough to participate in the Department of the Missouri's pistol competition, where he placed twenty-fourth out of fifty-two. Then he went back to Leavenworth (socializing with Mabel Allen in Kansas City) before a quick visit to Indianapolis. Lieutenant Hitt returned to Crook to take command of Company L, and in late September he was sent to Logan Roots to command Company C. While there, Hitt resumed his Arkansas social life and visited Hot Springs twice a week, having "several pleasant drives and some very good times" with Nan Wright. He was the best man at fellow officer Robert Whitfield's wedding to Eugenie Butler in mid-October and then rushed the bride's sister, Eva, "to the disgust of Mabel and Nan Wright." While at Hot Springs he also had lunch and supper each day with Blanche Stearns. While some "people had me married down there," Hitt's mind was elsewhere, as he prepared for the company's return to the Philippines.[27]

Hitt, now twenty-five, had spent a pleasant twenty months in the United States but, despite an active social life, had not yet found a wife. The regiment left Nebraska on October 20, 1903, bound for San Francisco and the USAT *Sheridan,* which sailed on October 31. Aboard ship, the days were filled with classes, lectures, clay pigeon shooting, and rifle practice over the stern. In the evening, the presence of officers' families meant there were dances and entertainment. A stop in Guam on November 23 permitted a hunting trip "through jungle and rice paddies"; Hitt returned with a few snipe and curlew. November 26 was Hitt's third Thanksgiving on the ocean in six years; a highlight of the day was a vaudeville show put on by the men. The ship stopped in Manila on November 28 and then continued to Iligan, Mindanao, where it arrived on December 1. After a few days at Camp Overton, the regiment took up station at Camp Marahui (or Marawi; renamed Camp Keithley in January 1905), on the north shore of Lake Lanao, on December 6.[28]

Although the United States had declared victory and established a military governorship for the Philippines in July 1902, armed conflict continued in remote areas and islands until June 1913. The colonial occupation exposed junior army officers to the realities of warfare in the decades before World War I. Mindanao had a majority Muslim population, the Moros, who fought American control, and much of this resistance occurred in the territory surrounding Lake Lanao. It was a dangerous place; the camp was ringed by barbed wire and heavily guarded. While some tribal leaders (*datus*) welcomed the American presence, others did not. Often the *datus* played both sides, making friendly overtures to the US Army while tolerating the presence of insurgents who attacked and harassed the American forces. Hitt was present during the peak of General Leonard Wood's aggressive counterinsurgency operations on the island between August 1903 and March 1906. The last battle between the Americans and the Moros would take place in June 1913, when General John J. Pershing achieved a clear victory at Bud Bagsak; this allowed the US Army to withdraw from Mindanao and Jolo and transfer responsibilities to the civil government and the Philippine Constabulary.[29]

Until the end of March 1904, Hitt served as the intelligence and engineering officer at Camp Marawi. He prepared maps showing march routes for the regiment's 3rd Battalion and spent time surveying the area, particularly the lake's shoreline. Though never in full-time command of a company, he intermittently filled in for absent officers, taking temporary charge of Companies I, K, L, and M. Marawi was different from lonely Luzon; the presence of officers' families provided the semblance of society. Hitt was also better prepared to entertain himself, or perhaps he was just more conscientious about recording his activities in his diary. A voracious reader, he had access to a regular supply of magazines and books from home and the camp library. At some point he acquired a banjo; it is unclear whether he had learned to play in his youth or this was a new hobby. There were frequent dances and dinner parties and regular baseball games. Along with Captain Frederick G. Stritzinger, Hitt conducted shotgun experiments. He remained an avid hunter and once again provided ducks to augment army fare. In addition to corresponding with many women, including his friends from Indianapolis, Omaha, and Little Rock, Hitt was a popular escort in camp. He often entertained Captain William H. Wassell's wife, Mary, and was her preferred companion from 1903 until Wassell's death in 1908. Hitt was well liked on post, and not just for his personality; he regularly used his engineering skills to repair sewing machines for the wives of his fellow officers.[30]

The bulk of Hitt's combat career took place in 1904. In mid-December 1903 a group of officers and men from Camp Marawi were duck hunting when they were fired upon. The shots came from the territory of the sultan of Ramaien, and the army asked the sultan to surrender the perpetrators; when he ignored the demand, an order went out for his arrest. Hitt, assigned to Company A of the 1st Battalion, spent the rainy evening of January 21 preparing for the expedition. At 3:00 the next morning, the battalion began the seven-mile trip across the lake in six Moro-built *vintas* (canoes) and ten "crude, flat bottom boats" left behind by the 28th Infantry. Companies B and D landed at 6:30, while the remainder of the battalion went upriver and engaged in a fight at a Moro *cotta* (fort). Hitt succinctly recorded the action in his diary: "[Campbell E.] Flake killed and [William E.] Roberts seriously wounded at a *cotta* 9:35. Many Moros killed. Burned all houses to the lake and returned arriving 4 PM. Very tired tonight and leg hurting badly." Thirty-two Moros died in the action. The sultan was not arrested, but he later came to Marawi asking for peace. Hitt's rheumatism flared up after the engagement; while he rested, he spent time using an Arabic alphabet to puzzle out the Koran, trying to better understand the people of the island.[31]

In March, General Wood invited the sultan of Taraca (also known as the sultan of Maciu) to a meeting. Wood's goal was to end the sultan's armed resistance and to free the Christian Filipinos he held in slavery. But the sultan, who had never acknowledged the sovereignty of the United States, refused to negotiate and continued to encourage hostilities and rebellion. Having failed at diplomacy, Wood launched a military campaign. Parts of the 14th Cavalry and the 17th and 23rd Infantries, accompanied by a platoon of the 17th Field Artillery, marched from Camp Vicars, on the south side of Lake Lanao; the 22nd Infantry came from Marawi by boat. Hitt was in command of Company K on April 2 when Wassell, commanding the 3rd Battalion, and Colonel Marion P. Maus, leading the expedition for the 22nd Infantry, started across the lake at 2:00 a.m. with two machine guns (a Gatling and a Vickers-Maxim) mounted in their boats.[32]

After four and a half hours, the force arrived at the mouth of the Taraca River, where there was a short firefight just after 7:00 a.m. When the boats reached the *cotta* upriver, Maus told the Moros he wanted to land and camp there and would not hurt them if they were friendly. The Moros talked to Maus, stalling for time as they readied for a fight. At 8:20 the American boats, arrayed in an arc broadsides to the *cotta*, took fire; they returned fire for more than thirty minutes. When Maus gave the order to rush the *cotta*, Hitt, Stritzinger, and Lieutenants Dean Halford, William S. Neely, and Max B. Garber "vied with each other to be the first to land," while "fearlessly" exposing themselves to fire. In April 1925 they were awarded Silver Stars for their gallantry that morning. It was all over by 11:00, and the Americans withdrew to prepare their landing point for defense. Hitt was not injured but was "very tired" and noted that his leg had "gone wrong"; he gathered data for a sketch of the area, while the soldiers buried some of the more than seventy Moro dead. Hitt's company, manning the ammunition and ration boats, departed at dawn on April 8, stopping on the coast at Dalama before returning to Marawi on April 10, where Hitt moved into bachelors' quarters.[33]

The US Army's collection of cobbled-together wooden boats and indigenous canoes was inadequate for combat and insufficient for regular travel between Marawi and Camp Vicars. Spain had faced a similar challenge on Lake Lanao. After ignoring the region for two centuries, the Spanish attempted to pacify the Moros after Christian Filipinos settled at nearby Iligan in the 1880s. In 1895 Spanish forces at Marawi received two disassembled ninety-two-foot steel gunboats, the *Lanao* and the *Blanco*. Once they were reassembled and armed, the boats kept peace on the lake. Two sixty-five-foot boats, the *Almonte* and the *Corcuera,* soon joined this inland fleet. In November 1898 the Spanish-American War was over, so Spanish troops disarmed and sank the boats and a few barges as they abandoned Mindanao. Gunboats of the US Navy's Asiatic Fleet now patrolled the coastal waters of Mindanao and helped the army transport men and material, but resources were limited. Although the Argus River connected Lake Lanao to the sea, waterfalls made it impassable. Consequently, the army set up its own small fleet to support counterinsurgency operations on the lake.[34]

Days after the Taraca engagement, Parker Hitt took charge of water transportation on Lake Lanao. He may have taken the initiative and suggested the assignment, given his leg problems. In a unit that was habitually short of officers, Hitt was a boon: he understood infantry operations, was a talented engineer, and had mastered the administrative work needed to keep an operation supplied. In early April a twenty-eight-foot steam launch acquired from the hospital ship *Relief* was hauled uphill from Camp Overton to Marawi on a rig drawn by eight mules; showing a distinct lack of imagination, the regiment christened the vessel *Relief.* On April 14, the day before the funeral of Captain David P. Wheeler (killed during the Taraca expedition), Hitt took charge of the boat and examined his new command. Just four days later, with engines and boilers installed, the *Relief* was running and had been "painted within an inch of her life." A formal trial run scheduled for April 19 was canceled by the arrival of General Wood at Marawi on the afternoon of April 18; Wood wanted to go to Taraca, so, according to Hitt, "we just got up steam and went." Hitt's ferry service was in business, and on most days he could be found making runs to Taraca and Camp Vicars, hauling supplies and transporting troops. The components of another boat arrived a few weeks later, accompanied by an engineer and 100 Chinese laborers. The new sixty-five-foot boat was christened the *Flake,* after Hitt's comrade Lieutenant

Flake, who had died in the January engagement against the sultan of Ramaien. Hitt mounted a Vickers-Maxim gun in the bow and a Gatling gun aft, and the *Flake* became the "dreadnaught" of the lake, running a daily scheduled round-trip between Marawi, Taraca, and Camp Vicars.[35]

When the army located the sunken Spanish gunboats in early 1904, Hitt was part of the effort to raise them. An attempt was made to lift the *Lanao,* but the equipment could not handle its weight. Attention turned to the smaller *Almonte,* and by mid-October, it was out of the water. Once it had been overhauled and painted, the *Almonte* replaced the *Flake* on the daily journey around the lake, and the *Flake* was used to tow logs and bamboo rafts for new construction. One of the four sunken Spanish barges brought up from the lake contained usable cargo; it joined Hitt's flotilla and could carry 200 men, allowing troops to land without small boats. The *Lanao* was finally floated in early October 1905. Even though there was no white paint available to cover the first coat of red lead, the ship's trial voyage proceeded on October 29. "When the Moros saw the resurrected *Lanao* steaming down the lake, painted in the Moro war color, and heard her gun being fired, they took to the hills by the hundreds," Hitt wrote. Although the civil governor sent a message reassuring them that they would not be attacked by the boat, according to Hitt, "it was not until the *Lanao* was painted white a week later that they felt safe again."[36]

Hitt's small fleet earned him the moniker "Admiral of Lake Lanao." He commanded operations and took turns captaining the boats, which were not just for transport. The boats—particularly the *Flake,* with its machine guns—were also for war. Hitt engaged in water battles multiple times over the next six months. On August 1 he took troops to Marantao to retaliate against the Moros who had attacked a sentry at Marawi on the night of July 10. A "vengeful assault" took place at dawn; many Moros were killed, and numerous forts were destroyed. Hitt brought 168 men from Marantao to Marawi in the late morning and then returned and brought back 96 more before heading to Vicars with a few passengers.[37]

The sultan of Oatu controlled an area on the western shore of the lake, where there was a small bay. He had initially welcomed the Americans and frequently visited Camp Marawi, but in September 1904 he changed his mind and told the army to stay away from his district. Lieutenant Colonel Henry E. Robinson, the new commander of the 22nd Infantry, decided to engage in a freedom-of-navigation exercise and sent Hitt to visit the bay on September 21. Hitt selected nine experienced riflemen, mounted a .30-caliber machine gun to supplement the other guns, and went out on the lake, first making the routine Marawi-Taraca-Vicars run. All was quiet when the *Flake* rounded the point to enter Oatu Bay. Then "long, red Moro streamers broke out from poles around the sultan's house and on the hillsides and fifty or sixty riflemen let go at the boat," just 600 yards away. It was 11:10 a.m. The crew of the *Flake* and the sultan's men exchanged fire; three shots hit the boat. The Moros then shot a six-inch muzzle-loading cannon that struck 200 yards behind the *Flake*. The ship cruised around the bay until the Moros were out of ammunition. The final cannon shot "barely hit the beach from lack of powder." It was all over by 11:45, and an hour later, the *Flake* pulled into Marawi. Four shots had hit the boat, the sultan's house was on fire, and two Moros had been wounded. It was, wrote Hitt, "a kind of opera bouffe battle." Robinson "was pretty mad" and sanctioned another expedition against the sultan. The *Flake* went by Oatu again on September 23, was shot at, and returned the next day to look around, but any retaliation was "indefinitely postponed on account of possible political significance." "Everyone sore," wrote Hitt of the postponement.[38]

A month later, the expedition was on again. The 2nd Battalion, on board the *Flake* and a towed barge, left Marawi before dawn on October 24 and landed at Oatu at 7:00 a.m., after first firing on the landing area. Hitt stayed on board all day and watched the long, slow advance. After six hours of combat and the capture of one fortress, there was a pause before the second assault. At last, a field battery marched around behind the bluff to join the companies that had climbed uphill from the bay, and a second fortress was captured without resistance. A "hard tiresome day without much results," observed Hitt, but the sultan had surrendered and given up his challenge to American sovereignty.[39]

In December the *Flake* and its guns were used against the Maciu Moros on the southeastern shore of the lake in what may have been the last action of Hitt's combat career. On the night of December 27 and the morning of December 28, the *Flake* shot at some canoes, and a landing party burned shacks before returning to camp.[40]

Robinson gave Hitt a positive efficiency report at the end of June 1905, calling him "an excellent man to place on any duty where a knowledge of machinery is necessary." Secretary of War (and former civilian governor of the Philippines) William Howard Taft and his entourage visited Marawi at the end of August on the Philippine portion of their diplomatic mission to Asia and stayed overnight. Hitt hosted Representative William Atkinson Jones of Virginia, and five of the party of thirty-five had meals with Hitt's mess. Hitt called Jones "a very charming fellow" but misjudged the congressman by describing him as "not much politically." Hitt noted, "I think we did ourselves proud and gave them a chance to see what the Army could do on a pinch." "Awful" Alice Roosevelt was on the trip too, and Hitt's disdain for Theodore Roosevelt's twenty-one-year-old daughter was clear: "Sweet Alice smoked cigarettes all the way coming across the lake and in every way behaved like a princess, or a hopelessly demoralized child in need of a spanking. She is the absolute limit."[41]

In June 1905 Hitt took a few weeks' leave, traveling to Manila and returning via Zamboanga; he made another short trip to Zamboanga in the fall. Hitt's last few months on Lake Lanao were busy. He made trips to Vicars for sand and gravel, assisted with surveying work, and completed construction of a big dock on the lake. The work was monotonous, but it gave him time for reading and study and let him rest his painful leg without going on sick report.[42]

Hitt left Mindanao on December 11, 1905. He spent a few days in Manila, where he went to a New Year's Eve function at the Delmonico Hotel and escorted Mrs. Wassell on her shopping trips, before boarding the USAT *Logan*. He had an overcoat made during the coaling stop in Nagasaki; he was measured on the morning of January 10, tried the coat on that afternoon, and picked it up on January 12. In the interim, he bought kimonos and other souvenirs and attended a hotel dance. The weather was cold, and his leg was bothering him. The ship left Japan in heavy seas and a cold northwest wind on January 13. Hitt spent the journey cleaning up Mrs. Wassell's sewing machine, reading, and playing cards and cribbage. As they passed Midway Island, he used binoculars to view the cable station there. His leg was still bothering him in Honolulu on January 26, but he went ashore in the rainy, windy weather. By the time the ship arrived in San Francisco, he was "very sick all day."[43]

The 22nd Infantry remained on the West Coast, setting up headquarters at Fort McDowell on Angel Island and scattering its companies across the San Francisco Bay area. Hitt went to the Department of California's rifle range, near Point Bonita on the Marin headlands. Created in 1904 by General Arthur MacArthur to improve the department's rifle target scores, the range was near the site of new Fort Barry and the beautiful coastline overlooking the Golden Gate of San Francisco Bay. Here, the troops camped in tents, and life was quiet. Going to town meant visiting Sausalito, but Hitt managed to travel to San Francisco—a bustling place for a single officer—several times a month via the ferry. He continued to escort Mrs. Wassell on shopping trips and walks. Target practice involved the newly issued Springfield model 1903 rifle, along with the model 1905 sight and knife bayonet. The US Army of this era allowed junior officers to demonstrate initiative, and once again Hitt took advantage of the situation; he gained his first practical experience with telephone lines in April when he helped install communications at the range. It was at Point Bonita that Hitt acquired two stray dogs while walking on the headlands one morning. They may not have been his first canine companions, but they are the first ones mentioned in his diary; they would not be his last.[44]

Hitt was on the range on the morning of April 18 when the great earthquake devastated San Francisco. It was a "very exciting day," but the units at Point Bonita stayed put and were not involved with the regiment's rescue and recovery efforts in the city. Four days later, Hitt went to the city and "looked at the ruins." In mid-May he was moved to Fort Mason, just east of the Presidio, but still spent time at the range. In early June his company moved to the Presidio and lived in barracks, rather than tents, for the first time since they had come ashore; Hitt occupied quarters 133 on the East Cantonment, next door to the Wassells. He was in charge of Refugee Camp 8, Harbor View, just east of the Presidio (part of the modern Marina District) for the month of June; he directed operations, ensured that refugees from camps in Oakland were properly settled, and resolved construction, supply, water, and sanitation issues for a population of nearly 1,400. The "moral tone of the camp is very good," he reported at the end of his term.[45]

In the middle of July the regiment left the devastated city for a maneuver camp at American Lake (Camp Tacoma), Washington. Companies C and D of the 1st Battalion of Engineers and Company H of the Signal Corps joined them there, and in early August units of the 3rd, 7th, 14th, and 20th Infantries, some cavalry and field artillery units, and several National Guard organizations arrived. Hitt was less concerned with military drills than he was with his social life. The camp was near a country club, and he bought a boat to explore the lake in his off-duty hours. Since 1905 Hitt had contemplated moving to another regiment, and it may have been his exposure to the 14th Infantry at American Lake that prompted him to ask for a transfer to that unit. Hitt never recorded his motivation for seeking the move; he might have wanted to get away from the troubled Captain Wassell, who was "drunk and nasty" on August 9. The regiment returned to California in mid-September, and a month later Hitt took a long leave and went home to Indianapolis; he did not return to duty until early January 1907. Upon his return, Hitt took command of Company L at the Presidio, where the regiment's unmarried officers hosted "the most brilliant military ball" in February. At the ball, in an odd coincidence of cryptologic history, Hitt may have met Frank Miller, a Sacramento banker who described the first known one-time pad cipher system in 1882.[46]

In 1906 the machine gun, a Civil War–era innovation, continued to be a point of major doctrinal contention for the cash-strapped military. That year the War Department attempted to make better use of the weapon by developing both doctrine and a permanent organization for the guns. The 22nd Infantry, stationed in San Francisco, was located near the Presidio of Monterey, where machine guns would be tested at the new School of Musketry. First Lieutenant Henry A. Ripley had charge of the regiment's new machine gun platoon. Hitt's Company D, ranked first in the regiment in target practice, was restless after living in "tents for seven months and in the so-called quarters at the Presidio for the remaining six months," so in late February 1907 Hitt requested that they be detailed to the school. But Company C and Ripley's machine gun platoon went to Monterey instead, as did one soldier from each company, two second lieutenants who were enrolled in the first three-month course, and Captain Stritzinger, who was chosen as an instructor. Hitt and his company moved to Fort McDowell on Angel Island.[47]

After more time on the range at Point Bonita and a few more weeks on Angel Island, Hitt was sent to Monterey in early July as part of the school's second course; through hard work and initiative, he soon became involved in the army's machine gun experiments. He found the school-work interesting but thought there was a "sad lack of the practical." He won a bronze medal at the 1907 Pacific Rifle Competition and participated in the armywide competition at Fort Sheridan in August, where the contest was "frightfully hard on my eyes. I will undoubtedly have to get glasses before finishing at the school." At the end of August he served as the range officer at the National Rifle Association meeting at Camp Perry, Ohio. When Hitt returned to the school in mid-September, his dog Slim (perhaps one of the two he picked up at Point Bonita) was so happy to see him that he "ran and fell on my neck when I arrived and he stays with me every minute." Before he finished the course, Hitt was recommended to be an instructor for the next term, but instead, he stayed on as a student. Stritzinger took advantage of the latitude allowed by the army and used Hitt as an unofficial teaching assistant.[48]

At a four-day field camp at the Laguna Seca range, ten miles from the school, Hitt directed problems in field firing, including shooting targets that jumped up on approach, and night shooting. After the exercise, his "analysis of volley fired at 2400 yards" took a mathematical approach to the problem of target size and accuracy. Using his range experience, he designed a new sort of target that fell when struck by a bullet but could stand in the wind; his target was eventually manufactured and used by the Ordnance Department. He also documented ideas for bobbing, beam disappearing, and sled targets. It was an exciting time for Hitt; he applied his academic training to field problems and also had the freedom to invent and submit ideas to Washington. The school "keeps me jumping to do all the work that is pushed in front of me," he told his mother. (When making a skirmish run in early October, he hurt his wrist; though not broken, it was wrapped so tightly he resorted to writing letters on a typewriter.) Hitt's efforts earned him a place on the school's experimental board, where he tested and reported on all new equipment forwarded to the school. In just three weeks, the board tested and reported on a muzzle rest, the subtarget machine rifle, and a new telescopic sight; it was also in the process of choosing a satisfactory target for pistol practice.[49]

Hitt's hard work paid off in an unexpected and unwanted way. He was "not agreeably surprised" to be given command of the regiment's machine gun platoon on November 5, after the unexpected removal of Ripley. He was not consulted about the assignment and was so busy with the school that he had "no time to monkey with the guns and saddles and mules and other toys that form the equipment of the platoon." Each platoon had two British Vickers-Maxim guns; each gun, including its tools and ammunition, weighed about 800 pounds. In addition, there were ten pack mules that needed care. Despite his initial reluctance to take on the new responsibility, Hitt threw himself into developing the platoon. He spent nine months working with machine guns; this put him on the cutting edge of military technology and innovation in a field that was not well understood by the service at large. Hitt was a natural innovator, and the army provided him with opportunities to build a technical skill set encompassing bridges, engines, telephones, and now machine guns. It was not the last time he would find himself developing expertise in a new subject.[50]

The pressure of his work was "outrageous." Hitt became the engineering officer for the school and had to set up experimental targets at the Laguna Seca range. The school's officers approved of his progress, for "Ripley made such a horrible botch of it last time that the guns were looked on as not much good." In late November 1907 he began to work on the problem of indirect fire. "I set the targets by using the machine gun and marking the points where the shots fell. This is the first time this has ever been attempted for infantry and it was such a success that we may be able to do something with it in time of war. Indirect fire of artillery is a recognized and approved method and our idea is to get at the artillery in their own way." In addition to writing his own reports, the school's commander, Major George M. McIver, and Captain Stritzinger both used Hitt to tabulate scores and make reports for other officers. Hitt could not say no. But at the end of November 1907, when his transfer to the 14th Infantry was denied, he applied for a transfer to the 10th Infantry instead, hoping it had a vacancy for a first lieutenant. The 10th was currently in Alaska but was scheduled to move to Fort Benjamin Harrison, the new army post in Indianapolis. It seemed like a good opportunity to leave the 22nd and return to his hometown.[51]

At 4:00 on the morning of Friday, December 6, the duty corporal woke Hitt and sent him to the post adjutant's office. The regiment was moving out; Hitt's machine gun platoon and the 2nd Battalion had to be on a train as close to 7:00 as possible. They were bound for Goldfield, Nevada, where a labor dispute between nearly 2,000 miners and the Goldfield Mine Operators Association had become a strike on November 27. Hitt had his men, guns, and property—including thirty days' rations and winter gear—on the train at 7:15; the rest of the battalion appeared a few minutes later. Despite a delay of five hours in Sacramento, they arrived in Goldfield on Friday night, just behind the companies sent from Angel Island. Hitt's platoon, along with Companies B, D, I, K, and M, camped on a plateau west of town; on the east side of town, near the mines, were Companies E, F, G, and H.[52]

The move to Nevada was unexpected. On December 5 a short article in a San Francisco newspaper had implied that troops might be sent to Goldfield, but Hitt did not think it would affect him. Unbeknownst to the rest of the regiment, its commander, Colonel Alfred Reynolds, had been directed to hold two companies in readiness on the night of December 4. But when orders arrived the next night, almost the entire regiment was headed to Nevada. There had been labor tensions at Goldfield for several years; the November strike was in reaction to miners being paid in scrip, a cash-saving move on the part of mine owners. Scrip could be converted to cash, but at a rate much lower than face value. This infuriated the Western Federation of Miners, an affiliate of the Industrial Workers of the World. When the mine owners threatened to bring in strikebreakers, Nevada governor John Sparks, anticipating violence from the unions, requested federal troops. President Theodore Roosevelt sent Brigadier General Frederick Funston, now commander of the Department of California, to investigate the situation; Funston agreed that federal troops were needed to keep the peace. This action required a careful understanding of the various parties' legal authority: Funston and Reynolds could not take orders from the governor but could consult him regarding local conditions. If Reynolds needed to use troops, army regulations required him to inform Roosevelt so that he could issue a presidential proclamation. Troops followed the 1904 regulations regarding mob control.[53]

The political balancing act and the players' contradictory assessment of the circumstances became clear to Hitt. He reported, "Everything is just as quiet as it can be and it does not seem at all like the lull before the storm. This place is a convent school in comparison to Frisco." By December 11, Reynolds informed Funston that there were no extensive disturbances requiring a military proclamation and the army was not needed; however, in his opinion, the mine owners were conspiring to deprive individuals of their civil rights. Funston disagreed with Reynolds's assessment and headed to Nevada, where the mines were set to reopen with strikebreakers on December 12. But on that day, Hitt reported, "Everything is as quiet as the day we arrived," and it was "the opinion of all the officers from the Colonel down that we were ordered in here with the expectation that we could smash the Federation, whether there was any violence or not and let the operators do as they pleased." Hitt was sure that any "outrages" would be traced to the "agitators among the operators who are sore because they want a fight between us and the miners and because we refuse to fight . . . we have been thrown very intimate with the operators and their disappointment at our course of action is very apparent." Hitt blamed Governor Sparks for misrepresenting the situation and President Roosevelt for being "glad to jump at a conclusion as usual." All the trouble had been stirred up by "a dozen rabid agitators, about evenly distributed on the two sides," but Hitt noted that Reynolds had persuaded some of them to leave camp. It was a "dull, cold time living in tents on the outskirts of town," but the 22nd was "satisfied with peace even at this price." Hitt enclosed a picture of his "babies" (machine guns) in the letter to his father.[54]

Meanwhile, Roosevelt—skeptical of Funston's intentions and trying to placate the mine owners without alienating labor groups—placed Elihu Root, the former secretary of war and now secretary of state, in charge of the crisis. Hitt assured his mother that Goldfield was a "graveyard of a place" and called the whole thing "the biggest fake trouble I have ever run into or ever hope to," but he did not know when the troops would go home. "We are having a perfectly peaceful and monotonous time with only the routine duties of drill and camp guard to occupy our time. We have no part whatever in the controversy and Gen. Funston leaves today, leaving us even more in the background, as the commissioners from Washington have the floor." The political machinations eventually resulted in the Nevada legislature asking Roosevelt to leave federal troops in place until they could be replaced with a state constabulary; federal troops were finally withdrawn on March 7, 1908, having fired not a single shot. The machine gun platoon left in early January. Hitt had not faced winter weather for five years, and his sciatica flared up while at Goldfield; he was glad to return to the milder climate of Monterey.[55]

Back in California, Hitt embarked on a six-month period of extreme busyness that would leave him physically and mentally exhausted. He calibrated the new rifles sent to the school and tested new types of range finders, hoping to "get something out of it later that will repay me for the time and labor spent." In March 1908 he picked up extra duty as acting secretary of the school. While at Monterey, Hitt formed a friendship with Lieutenant Thomas W. Brown of the 27th Infantry, "one of the greatest in the machine gun game"; the pair would meet again at Fort Sill and carry on the "cult of the machine gun." Hitt and Brown did much of the machine gun work at the school, but their efforts were overshadowed by Captain John Henry "Machine Gun" Parker, who commanded the provisional, independent machine gun company that was established in early 1907 and became part of the 20th Infantry. Hitt noted, "I am not to be mixed up in it. I have no particular desire to get in on this as Capt. Parker will be the whole thing anyhow and he works for no one but himself." Hitt's May 1908 memorandum on "Indirect Fire for Machine Guns," based on principles tested by his platoon on the range at Laguna Seca, summed up his work. Captain Parker used Hitt's material in a report he sent to the War Department on the same subject, but to his credit, Parker acknowledged Hitt's contributions in an article published in July 1908. Hitt could sometimes be found in the officers' club discussing guns with Parker; one such discussion on the relative merits of the Gatling and Maxim guns developed into an "accuracy firing test." Two of Hitt's men fired a new Benet-Mercier gun, and two others fired Maxims. Squads from the 20th Infantry fired two Gatling guns on artillery mounts under "Captain Parker's extremely personal supervision." Each gun fired 100 rounds at a target 200 yards away. By the time he wrote about the test, Hitt had forgotten the scores, but his Maxims "put every shot in the four ring," the Benet-Mercier put every shot in the target, "and the two Gatlings failed to account for about 50 of their 200 shots."[56]

Always the innovator, Hitt proposed in late March 1908 that the army adopt his device to eliminate steam coming from the water-cooled Vickers-Maxim machine gun. In certain atmospheric conditions and during sustained fire, this steam could obscure the gunner's vision, and in wartime, it could disclose the position of an otherwise well-covered gun. Hitt repurposed a five-foot rubber tube from a bathroom and adapted the wooden tip of a hat cord as a perforated plug to make an inexpensive, lightweight device that vented the telltale cloud of steam into a container away from the gun's position. Tests of the device at Sandy Hook Proving Ground in New Jersey in the summer of 1909 determined that the inconvenience was slight, the cost negligible, and the advantage great; as a result, all the army's water-cooled guns received Hitt's attachment. The device was unnecessary when the army switched to the Benét-Mercié (Hotchkiss) air-cooled gun, but it was used again with the Browning gun in 1918. Hitt believed that British and German military attachés had witnessed the test at Sandy Hook, as both armies began using similar tubes in 1909.[57]

In the spring of 1908 Hitt designed a logo to mark the equipment of his machine gun platoon, and Brown created a coat of arms for the 27th Infantry. The machine gun contingent at Monterey thought there should be one standard marking, and a squabble ensued. Captain Parker liked Brown's work; Maus, commander of the 20th Infantry and its provisional machine gun company, disliked the coat of arms and thought Hitt's design "neat." Washington questioned whether any marking was necessary at all. After three months, the Ordnance Department settled the matter, deciding that machine gun platoons should use the cavalry or infantry stencil with the letters MGP substituted for the company letter.[58]

While at the school, Hitt prepared and delivered an impressive number of lectures on a variety of topics, including "Physical Conditioning and Training for Shooting," "Musketry Schools of Foreign Nations," and "Trajectories and Their Variations"; no subject seemed beyond his capabilities. The school wanted Hitt to stay on at Monterey, for his "services could not well be spared," but the 22nd was scheduled to move to Alaska in the summer of 1908. Hitt would have been happy to stay, but he also wished to represent the regiment at the 1908 rifle competition; if he were working at the school, he would not be allowed to compete. In the end, he lost both battles: he was neither sent to the competition nor assigned to the school.[59]

Something happened in early June 1908. Maus, at Monterey, urgently requested that Reynolds order Hitt to report for duty at regimental headquarters: "Should not return here, situation may be dangerous for him," the telegram read. If Reynolds failed to act, Maus warned that he would take the matter to Brigadier General John J. Pershing, the new commander of the Department of California. Reynolds requested that an inspector from the department investigate the danger to Hitt. The exact nature of the situation remains a mystery; perhaps it had something to do with an allegation that Hitt had been involved in a "hair pulling match between two women," or perhaps there was merely some concern about his health and well-being. "I drove myself beyond reason or necessity in any work until my superiors felt obliged to call a halt and made me agree not to work in the office or shop after night," Hitt later wrote of the period. He slept only a few hours each night, doing "everything in my power to prove my efficiency and ability, in case any official trouble might arise." Hitt believed he had "succeeded in impressing all my superiors that I was not to blame for the things that happened," noting that his command had stood by him "in every way." Clearly, something unusual was happening in Hitt's life, but he and the official records are silent about what might have caused "any official trouble." Reynolds acted quickly; Hitt was relieved from command of the machine gun platoon on June 10 and transferred the next day to Fort McDowell on Angel Island and Company I.[60]

Hitt attributed the loss of his platoon to the fact that it was to be based with the regiment's new headquarters at Fort William H. Seward in Alaska, and Reynolds, who "picked his official family with care," wanted no bachelor officers at headquarters during the long winters. Lieutenant W. G. Doane, who arrived—with his wife—from a detail in the Judge Advocate General's Office, took command of the machine gun platoon. While at Fort Seward, Doane kept the guns packed and assigned the men to "special duty." Apart from Reynolds's social preferences, Hitt's mysterious troubles at Monterey may have deprived him of his platoon and led to his exile to Fort Davis at Nome. Despite all his troubles there, Hitt forever thought of California, from Monterey north to Marin, as one of his favorite "countries."[61]

Now in command of Company I, Hitt remarked, "A company is such an easy thing to manage, that if it were not for the eternal sameness of it, it would be the ideal lazy man's job." He was feeling "very worthless and lazy" but "in some ways glad" to be going to Alaska because he was "having a very curious time out here." As he scrambled to supply himself for two years in the north, Hitt ran short of money and had to borrow $150 from his father, and he apologized for not having time to visit Indianapolis before leaving the country (the army considered Alaska, a US territory, a foreign post). The 22nd Infantry left San Francisco aboard the

USAT *Crook* on June 20. Hitt's destination, Nome, was the last stop, and Company I arrived on the afternoon of July 12. Fog and masses of arctic ice caused the ship's captain to anchor several times to wait out the poor conditions, and after supper, the men were taken off the ship in lighters. The post made a good impression on Hitt: "The colors of sea, sky, and ice were like a stage picture, especially about the time of the ten o'clock sunset. It is midnight now and as light as a summer morning, with the mountains of Nome to the North and the ice to the south."[62]

Hitt, whose weight had plummeted to 165 pounds before leaving Monterey, was sick for four days after arriving in Alaska. He had a high fever and "some symptoms, obscure to the doctor, but plain enough to me as pure reaction from worry and mental strain." The doctor thought it was typhoid. Hitt slept for the better part of two days, which allowed him "to clear up my thinking machinery and now I am all right again." He wrote to his mother, "Thank God, I have at least a breathing spell and a chance to catch my mental balance although I have good reason to believe that there will be no more trouble at all," obliquely referring to his problems in California. He gained fifteen pounds in two weeks and had to have new uniforms made, as the old ones were "too tight for comfort." By August he weighed 185 pounds.[63]

Fort Davis, on a peninsula between the Nome River and the Bering Sea, was a quiet installation. Field training was impractical during the winter and limited at other times; during the brief summer, the tundra was boggy, and everyone had to work to store supplies for the harsh winter. Hitt had become interested in wireless telegraphy (radio) while in California; he brought a radio receiver to Alaska and spent hours studying the technology and learning to send and receive Morse code. He was a frequent visitor at the army's new Nome radio station, and he took advantage of every opportunity to visit the Signal Corps facility at Safety, twenty miles to the east. Hitt was soon a familiar presence to the radiomen, and when the station received new equipment, he persuaded them to let him have the old spark coils for his tests. "I am studying the theory and working out some special ideas with a view to simplification of the apparatus and increase of efficiency," he told his mother. He continued to expand his technical skills and dreamed of being sent to the army's Signal School, where he hoped to specialize in aviation, another new obsession. "It is certain that I cannot keep away from the 'birds' very long. I am about through with the humdrum of ordinary duty; there is nothing in it as I said years ago and believe more strongly now." Hitt's efficiency reports reflected the knowledge he had acquired through personal study;

his new expertise in radio would give the army an opportunity to use him in an entirely different manner in the not-too-distant future. The first documented mention of codes by Hitt is in a letter to his mother during this period, where he refers to his "old code" and the telegraph rates for using a code. This code was likely a system agreed on with his family to allow them to convey information privately and inexpensively.[64]

Between carrying out his company duties, studying for promotion, and doing his radio work, Hitt somehow found time for other tasks. He may have designed the addition to a building at the fort; at the very least, he prepared a study of the front and side elevations and a detailed plan of the interior. Hitt indulged his fondness for dogs in Alaska and became so interested in dog-sled racing that he spent $100 to join a syndicate supporting a team in the 1909 All-Alaska Sweepstakes, hoping for a piece of the $10,000 prize. He acclimated quickly to the winter weather, and while a shortage of officers' quarters meant that he shared a room with Lieutenant Solomon B. West, he was comfortable; the officers' mess was in the same building. He had plenty to read and got great pleasure from his subscriptions to *Colliers* and *Review of Reviews*, gifts from his parents. Nome had a lively winter social life, and the residents were hospitable; there was some sort of entertainment available every night. Hitt thought it "surprising" how well the townspeople danced, "until you realize that it is the one amusement of the winter that brings people together socially and that people must get together up here or go crazy." Another social outlet was the Arctic Brotherhood, an obscure fraternal order begun in 1899 by "eleven intoxicated men on a boat." Hitt, West, and the post doctor were invited to join the Camp Nome branch of "the most powerful secret order in Alaska and Northern Canada," which had 426 members in 1909. Membership gave them access to a social hall, entertainment, and dances. It seems unlikely that Hitt was interested in the Arctic Brotherhood's political efforts to support "home rule" for Alaska.[65]

After a year in Alaska, Hitt pronounced himself entirely content: "I do not remember a year for a long, long time that has passed so quickly and pleasantly." His new quarters were almost complete, and he was buying rugs and curtains and anticipating a great housewarming party. But he was "not in love with the Company Commander business" and was glad that a new captain would be arriving in October. "I have been on the job seven days a week for fifteen months and am ready for a change." As soon as his replacement arrived, he took a hunting trip and returned with thirty ptarmigans; the freedom from responsibility did him good. Hitt looked forward to the end of his tour, for he was "too much of a wanderer to enjoy being tied down in one place long." He noted that his service report showed twelve months' continuous service with troops for the first time ever and observed, "I do not want it to occur again." Hitt's apparent lack of ambition as a commander may be the key to understanding what he wanted out of his army career. He brought his engineering expertise and desire for innovation and efficiency to the service, and in exchange, the army helped satisfy his wanderlust and desire for adventure.[66]

The USAT *Buford* picked up units of the 22nd Infantry in July 1910. Nome was the second-to-last stop on July 15, but rough weather delayed the troops' boarding and cargo transfer. The ship headed south to Fort St. Michael on July 17, where severe weather delayed their departure until July 21. Ten days after leaving St. Michael, the regiment arrived in San Francisco. The "excellent appearing lot of soldiers" got to spend a few days in town before being hustled onto an afternoon train on August 2, 1910, bound for Fort Sam Houston in San Antonio, Texas.[67]

Hitt had been in the army for twelve years. The rough-and-tumble soldier's life of great excitement alternating with boredom had strained his health. When his physical problems hindered normal duty, Hitt adapted and used his technical skills to benefit his unit, aided by the army's willingness to encourage initiative in its junior officers. He survived the backcountry of the Philippines, the arctic tundra of Alaska, multiple ocean voyages, and innumerable train trips crisscrossing the American continent. Hitt had killed men in battle and taught students in school. He expressed no regrets about sacrificing his college degree and potential civilian career for twelve years of poorly paid adventure. Not quite thirty-two, he was still a first lieutenant—thanks to the army's archaic promotion system. These years had built both Hitt's character and his military expertise. The army was changing, and Hitt took advantage of opportunities for leadership and glory, but it was his interest in technology that would shape the rest of his career. Soon his life would change in ways he might not have believed possible. New adventures awaited Hitt in San Antonio; that was where he would find "the girl": Genevieve Young.[68]

3

Genevieve Young

You must not expect much of me, Mrs. Hitt. I am just an
ordinary girl—you can find hundreds like me every day.
                    Genevieve Young, May 31, 1911

Dr. Franklin Early Young was not in his office at Meyenberg's drugstore
on the main square in La Grange, Texas, on May 29, 1885. He was at
home with his wife, Mary Lueise, delivering his first daughter, Genevieve.
Known as Gee Gee to her friends and family, Genevieve joined her
brother, William Early, in a household that would eventually include
another brother, Flint Carter, and a sister, Louise Franklyn (later dubbed
"Tot" because of her small stature). Shortly after Genevieve was born,
the Youngs informally adopted Haidee Reichel, the daughter of a patient
in need, who was eight years older than Genevieve.[1]

Franklin Young's grandfather, Samuel, moved his family from Ten-
nessee to Texas in 1840 and received a Stephen Austin land grant west of
La Grange, the Fayette County seat. Franklin, born in 1854, graduated
from the Texas Military Institute in 1878 and from New York University's Bellevue Hospital Medical College in 1880. He returned to Texas to
establish his medical practice and in 1882 married Mary Lueise Franklyn
Carter, a descendant of Giles Carter, a seventeenth-century immigrant to
Virginia. Mary Lueise was born in Halifax County, Virginia, in 1858.
The Carters left Virginia after the Civil War, and by early 1867 they were
living in La Grange, where Mary Lueise's father was first a farmer and
then an innkeeper.[2]

Not long after Genevieve's birth, the Youngs moved to Brownwood,
Texas. Dr. Young kept up his medical knowledge by attending a "poly-
clinic" in New York in February 1891; he may have attended a medical
meeting in Berlin, Germany, as well. When Genevieve was seven or eight
years old, the family moved to San Antonio, where the "Doc" treated
tuberculosis and built up a surgical practice specializing in obstetrics and
gynecology. The "jolly old gentleman" had an erect figure and twinkling
eyes and made house calls by buggy. Young established hospitals in San
Antonio, Flatonia, and La Grange and served as president of the Bexar

County Medical Society. Genevieve's father exuded confidence: upon making his acquaintance, Parker Hitt remarked that Dr. Young was the only man he would allow to "put a knife in him."[3]

Genevieve considered herself a true southerner and led a privileged life compared with her parents and grandparents. She was an outdoors girl who enjoyed camping, fishing, and gardening. She sewed and made most of her own clothes. As a young girl she may have learned to crochet and knit as well. Genevieve also loved to read, cook, and bake. Although the Youngs had no expectations of their daughter beyond marriage and family, she received a good education. She first attended the Marshall Street School in San Antonio and later the Mulholland School. Sometime before 1897 she met Eleanor Rogers Onderdonk, from a family of talented painters, who became a lifelong friend. For her secondary education, Genevieve studied at St. Mary's Hall, a girls' school set up in 1879 by parishioners of St. Mark's Episcopal Church in San Antonio. The school, which had ninety-two pupils in 1899, offered "the very best advantages for the cultivation of a symmetrical womanhood," which included taking care of the students' physical health, training their minds "in accordance with the most approved methods," and providing spiritual guidance. The school also boasted that it cultivated "gracious manners, as a factor in a woman's influence." Graduates were required to complete coursework in mathematics through trigonometry, physics, chemistry, botany, psychology, Latin, history (ancient, medieval, modern European, and American), Bible studies, Shakespeare, and the English poets. There were optional courses in modern language, music, and art. The school's standards were high—one member of the class of 1900 noted that the school was the equivalent of a junior college and that graduates "could have entered as a junior at Smith or Vassar." The cost—$32 per term—was a small fraction of a surgeon's annual salary, and Dr. Young probably considered it money well spent. Genevieve graduated in 1903, and the principal remarked on her intelligence, "lady-like deportment, and Christian character."[4]

Though her life seemed placid, Genevieve experienced several challenges over the next few years. Dr. Young enjoyed financial speculation and was often insolvent. On August 22, 1903, the Youngs' house was destroyed by fire; thankfully, the family was unharmed. In March 1905 Genevieve's father was severely injured after falling between two carriages of a moving train. He received a $15,000 settlement, which may have gone toward supporting his hospital ventures.[5]

After graduating from St. Mary's Hall, Genevieve split her time between social and charitable activities; she did not attend college. As a member of the Young Ladies' Cotillion Club and the Debutante Club, she most likely had a formal debut in 1905 or 1906. Genevieve was free to travel; in 1907 she went on a weeks-long camping trip with "a lively crew of young people" in the Nueces Canyon and then spent the rest of the summer visiting friends in Uvalde, Texas. She was a whiz at cards, and when she was not assisting hostesses at luncheons and teas, she played euchre, 500, pitch, and bridge. The Friday Bridge Club was one of her favorite gatherings, and Genevieve won its first prize on March 5, 1909. Her charity work included the Travis Park United Methodist Church Philathea Class, which billed itself as "young women at work for young women"; its motto was "We do things." The club opened a "Girls' Rest and Lunch Room" in the church basement, offering lunch to female office and shop workers for fifteen cents. The success of the lunchroom led to the formation of the San Antonio YWCA. Genevieve was one of the hostesses for a fund-raising dinner at the church in October 1908 and helped at a party for the mothers' club in early 1909.[6]

Genevieve was in no hurry to marry. An avid reader who subscribed to the *Ladies' Home Journal,* she was aware of the increasing societal freedom for women and of the general desire to "participate in what men call 'the game of life'" as opposed to "the mere humdrum of household duties." In many ways, she conformed to the stereotype of the "new woman" of the Progressive Era, with more educational opportunities than her mother, an active interest in the outdoors, and strong self-confidence. Forthright and opinionated, she had great strength of character and "comprehension of whatever situation she found herself in." Somehow, "she always knew what to say or do and when to say or do it."[7]

Growing up so close to the large army post at Fort Sam Houston, Genevieve had frequent opportunities to socialize with young officers. She had "always vowed I would never marry an Army officer," but, she later admitted, "I didn't know Parker Hitt then." Parker, who was not a typical army officer, surely was not the first man who found Genevieve's dark beauty and adventurous spirit alluring. If Genevieve kept a diary with details about those who courted her in her youth, it has not been found. Men would continue to fall under her spell even after she married Hitt (including Lieutenant Walton H. Walker).[8]

Hitt arrived in San Antonio in early August 1910. He and his men, accustomed to the coolness of Alaska, suffered in the Texas heat. Just two days after reaching the city, they marched from Fort Sam Houston to the training area at Leon Springs for three weeks of maneuvers. Hitt was immediately immersed in exercises and administrative duties, including a board of officers investigating the death of a local man's horse during a "sham battle," a court-martial, and duty as a referee during the post's quarterly "field meet." The regiment somehow managed to avoid a 200-mile march, but there were other marches, target practice, and field exercises. Hitt was once again given command of the 22nd Infantry's machine gun platoon. When he learned of the assignment, Hitt asked George S. Simonds, the regiment's adjutant, what was left of the platoon, which just two years earlier been the best-trained machine gun platoon in the army. "The equipment, one corporal, and one private," Simonds replied.[9]

In September, when Hitt returned to Fort Sam Houston from Leon Springs, he took advantage of the social opportunities on the post and in the bustling city. Thirty-two and single, Hitt had danced with, escorted, and corresponded with many women over the years, looking "pretty much all over the world" for the right one. By 1905, he considered himself a "confirmed bachelor" and thought his brother Rodney, who had married that year, had "made a mistake not to wait longer."[10]

The dashing and elegant army officer and the tall, dark-eyed, dark-haired doctor's daughter met at a social event in October. The man who had "rushed" so many eligible women and squired other officers' wives when their husbands were away was smitten. William and Mary Syers invited Parker and Genevieve to a November 10 theater party at the Grand Opera House, where they attended the opening performance of *The Beauty Spot,* a musical comedy set in the south of France; Hitt was the only military officer in the group. After the show, the Syerses hosted a dinner at the new St. Anthony Hotel, the first luxury hotel in San Antonio.[11]

The couple's romance progressed quickly, but the timing could not have been worse for Hitt. On November 30 his transfer to the 10th Infantry became official. Hitt had been trying to leave the 22nd since 1905; this most recent transfer request had originated in his desire to attend the School of the Line (denied by the 22nd), and even though the 10th already had a candidate for the school, Hitt was glad to break free from the stale routine of his old regiment. With just a few weeks remaining before he had to report to Fort Benjamin Harrison in Indiana, Hitt made his move. He kissed Genevieve for the first time on December 10, 1910; seven years later, while on an overnight train in France, he would remember it as "the real anniversary of our love," reminding Genevieve of the day she "gave your lips to me for the first time." He recalled how she had "tried so hard to keep me away and yet at the end we forgot everyone else in the world."[12]

Once in Indiana, Hitt spent twenty days of leave with his parents in Indianapolis but, never one to advertise his private affairs, told them nothing about Genevieve. The couple apparently had no formal understanding at this point, and Parker probably did not know when he would be able to return to San Antonio. On December 29, with the School of the Line denied to him, Hitt asked to attend the Signal School. He still had dreams of aviation, which was under the control of the Signal Corps. The commander of the 10th Infantry, Colonel H. E. Green, wrote, "While I am reluctant to lose the services of this officer from the regiment, I am of [the] opinion from what I have heard of his mechanical tests and talents that more benefit would accrue to the Army by utilizing those gifts in specialized work in the Signal Corps than in keeping him on Infantry duty." By January 12, 1911, the request had reached the school and would be taken up for "consideration of the Academic Board of that school at the proper time."[13]

With Parker in Indiana, Genevieve resumed her usual social activities and charity work. Many of her friends were getting married. Genevieve served punch at the February wedding of her friend Eda Alma Westervelt. Another good friend, Susan (Sudie) Blocker, married an army officer, Robert H. Lewis, in April; years later, Lewis and Hitt would share a billet in France. If she corresponded with Parker during this period, their letters have not survived.[14]

Luck was with the couple, for just two months after Hitt returned from leave, the 10th Infantry moved to Fort Sam Houston to participate in the Maneuver Division. This unplanned, hastily assembled operation was an attempt to provide stability on the Mexican border and exercise a division-sized unit in peacetime. President William Howard Taft ordered the mobilization on March 6, 1911; the commander of the Department of Texas, Brigadier Joseph W. Duncan, learned that troops were coming his way in a telegram he received at midnight on Monday, March 7. Command and staff of the division came from a wide range of organizations, and multiple regiments from stations across the country moved to San Antonio. Twenty thousand troops arrived during the week of March 7, supplying the city with an unexpected economic benefit. Fort Sam Houston also gained some long-term infrastructure improvements as a result of the mobilization.[15]

As the men of the 10th Infantry marched from their barracks at Fort Benjamin Harrison to the trailers waiting to take them to the train on

March 9, the regimental band played "The Girl I Left behind Me." Hitt, however, was heading back to the girl he had left in Texas. When he arrived at Fort Sam Houston, he took his promotion exams; in May his promotion to captain became official, with an effective date of March 11. The pay of a first lieutenant with thirteen years of service was $200 a month; as a captain, he would earn $240 a month. He began to think that he could afford to marry.[16]

Hitt had a low opinion of the Maneuver Division, calling it "the worst grind I ever struck." He wrote, "The alleged maneuvers are wholly for the benefit of the various generals and we pawns get nothing from them." It was "thoroughly monotonous and unprofitable," and conditions at Leon Springs were dreadful. "We cannot stay out here more than a week or so at a time because we drink the tanks dry." The end "cannot come too soon," he complained. "I am sick and tired of it all." He added, "If it were not for the really vital and interesting things that have so taken up my time, these past two months would have driven me to drink." Those "vital and interesting" things were Genevieve and airplanes. After "thirteen years of more or less interesting drudgery," life was changing for Hitt. The prospect of marriage was exciting enough; then, in late April, Hitt joined the army's earliest aviation experiment. He had great expectations, telling his mother, "I expect a detail for permanent Aviation work and in that case we will go to Dayton, Ohio, for two or three months and then to Washington for an indefinite period."[17]

In early 1911 the Department of Texas allowed young officers to volunteer for "duty in learning to manipulate the aeroplane." In January three officers who had been taking lessons at the Curtiss Aeroplane Company's school in California traveled to Texas. Lieutenant Benjamin Foulois, who was rapidly becoming the most experienced army aviator, arrived in San Antonio with his modified Wright "Military Flyer" (designated Signal Corps Aircraft #1) on February 2, 1911. A new 1910 Wright Type B airplane, owned by Robert F. Collier and rented to the army for $1 per month, showed up on February 21. The first flights at the fort began a day later. Foulois did air reconnaissance of the Mexican border between Laredo and Eagle Pass before being detailed, with his plane, to the Maneuver Division on March 14. Frank T. Coffyn, the Wright Company's representative, arrived in town on April 18. Another plane, the Curtiss IV Model D (designated Signal Corps Aircraft #2), arrived on April 27, and a Wright Type B with wheels attached to the skids (designated Signal Corps Aircraft #3) arrived at about the same time. For a brief moment, most of army aviation's brain power and equipment were in San Antonio.[18]

Major George O. Squier, the chief signal officer of the Maneuver Division, ordered the immediate opening of an aeronautical school at Fort Sam Houston. It started on April 27 at "Government Hill," with Coffyn from Wright and Eugene Ely from Curtiss in charge. The officers who volunteered for the aeronautical school first met with Foulois and were offered their choice of training plane; they would take flying lessons at hours that did not interfere with their regular duties. Eighteen to twenty-two men (possibly including the three officers from California) volunteered to learn to fly, and Coffyn selected the men for further instruction. Hitt was one of this group.[19]

Approximately 500 flights took off from Fort Sam Houston between March 14 and May 10; some of them were as short as five minutes, and none were longer than two and a half hours. The number of flights made by the trainees is unclear. Hitt made at least two flights with Foulois, probably in one of the Wright aircraft, for he remembered that the plane had the original skids and was started from a catapult. His first flight reached an altitude of 1,000 feet, and the second achieved "a record" 2,000 feet. Hitt recalled that "landing . . . was the thrill. There was a wire from the throttle across in front of the pilot. When he got ready to land, he hit the wire with one hand—that killed the engine—and you slid in on the skids or else."[20]

On May 2 Lieutenant John C. Walker nearly crashed, but he managed to level off the Curtiss when it was just ten feet above the ground. He was shaken and asked to be relieved from flying. The next day, Paul W. Beck, in the same plane, experienced engine failure at 300 feet and crashed. Then, on May 10, 1911, George E. M. Kelly lost control of the Curtiss, crashed, and died. Major General William H. Carter, commander of the Maneuver Division, shut down flight training after Kelly's death, abruptly grounding Hitt's dreams of aviation. "I couldn't make the Air Corps then but if I was a young fellow and had it to do over I would burn up the world to get in."[21]

Hitt resumed his courtship of Genevieve when he returned to Texas. By mid-May, with his promotion official and his flying days over, the two had decided to marry as soon as Parker could find a place for them to live; he reckoned it would take two or three months, but certainly they would be married by autumn. Parker probably proposed to Genevieve in the days following Kelly's crash, for he told his mother on May 17 that he had "found the girl. She is Genevieve Young." He would not have waited too long to share the news with her. In 1918 he reminded Genevieve of "all the sweet love days back in May 1911," which "make May a very important month for me."[22]

Parker found the Youngs charming. The Youngs, in turn, loved Parker; Mrs. Young thought he was "the finest boy in the world next to her two." Their only objection to the match was that the army would take Gee Gee away from home and she would never be settled in one place. Parker knew they would be very happy together, and his only regret was "that she could not have come into my life before." Genevieve confided in her future mother-in-law that she was afraid Parker had "made a mistake in loving a Southern girl. They are such a lazy bunch and awfully poor housekeepers. But we can love our men even if we can't make them comfortable."[23]

On June 4 Hitt received orders to report to the Signal School at Fort Leavenworth on August 15. He evidently still expected to pursue aviation, for a newspaper article proclaimed that Hitt had "been in duty with the aeronautical corps in Texas and will continue that work after finishing the school at Leavenworth." Genevieve's wedding planning started in earnest, and the date was set for July. Hitt returned to Fort Benjamin Harrison on July 1; on July 12 he obtained a twenty-day leave of absence and dashed back to Texas to claim his bride.[24]

The couple married quickly and quietly to accommodate Parker's schedule. There were apparently no big parties for Genevieve. Hitt's family did not attend the wedding, and it is unclear whether he even had a friend by his side. The pastor of St. Mark's Church conducted the ceremony at the Youngs' home on the evening of Monday, July 17, 1911. It was a "nice and sensible" occasion, and the guests commented that Genevieve was "such a sensible girl" who "certainly did look swell." Genevieve told Parker's mother, "It was the funniest little wedding." Genevieve and Parker did not care what others thought. Hitt looked back fondly on that "night in July when we two went out into the world together. You were so fair and just a little afraid of me and yet—you kissed me at the end."[25]

The newlyweds traveled by train to Hot Springs, where they stayed at the Arlington Hotel. Genevieve was "a constant delight" to Parker, and they had "just the best time." The weather was cool, the town was pretty, and everything looked enchanting to the love-struck pair. Genevieve, who had been slightly ill before the wedding, recovered quickly; she could not get enough to eat and told her mother, "I have gotten disgracefully well and feel like a pig." Though Hitt hated the thought of "getting back to more packing and shifting around," his year of change was over. Fort Leavenworth and the Signal School were in his sights.[26]

4

The Making of the Expert

This field looks as if it had possibilities.
Parker Hitt, November 1912

Parker and Genevieve visited his family in Indianapolis on their way to Kansas. Genevieve, though initially shy, overwhelmed, and "awfully home sick," felt welcomed by the talkative Hitts. She was not intimidated by them; nor did she feel ignorant, despite realizing that they were better educated than she. Genevieve did find them a "little too affectionate," explaining that they "kiss too much for me who is not used to it." George Hitt, "a grand old gentleman," doted on his son's bride; she thought him "lovely," though he constantly nagged Parker to sit up straight. The Youngs missed Genevieve terribly. Her mother fainted the night she left home, and her sister Tot, who thought Parker "the grandest man on Earth," "felt like her heart would burst it ached so." Dr. Young claimed that he "never missed anyone as much in his life."[1]

The newlyweds arrived at Fort Leavenworth on August 11, 1911. Not far from Kansas City, Leavenworth sits on a bluff overlooking the Missouri River. This strategic strongpoint was, in the mid-nineteenth century, the last outpost of civilization for travelers along the Santa Fe and Oregon Trails. In the early twentieth century the fort remained a significant garrison post for the US Army. The presence of the Army Service Schools, including the School of the Line (later the Command and General Staff School), made it a bustling place; by early 1912, Leavenworth boasted more officers than any other army post. Post housing was filled to bursting; married officers crowded into bachelor officers' quarters, and single officers lived in former artillery barracks. Parker and Genevieve's first home consisted of two rooms in Root Hall, just off the main parade ground. Genevieve was "very courageous and clever" to try to cook without a kitchen, and her mother-in-law assured her the effort of "home cooking" would make Parker's work "both easy and successful."[2]

With Parker in school five days a week, Genevieve's days were monotonous. She soon tired of the all-female teas and bridge games, writing, "I like to listen to men as a rule. Women in general are such chatterers."

51

Parker quickly adapted to school life; he was the only student at the Signal School with "excellent marked on his papers and maps." Genevieve marveled, "I can't understand Parker Hitt. I can't see where he studies—in fact he does very little of it." The other wives "don't dare to speak" to their husbands, who studied until midnight and then started again at five in the morning. In contrast, the Hitts had "such a good time at home in the evenings," reading, talking, and entertaining visitors. But the best nights, according to Genevieve, were when they "shut our doors and pretend to these awful callers we are out," while she made fried chicken and Parker churned ice cream.[3]

The Signal School had moved to Leavenworth from Fort Myer, Virginia, in 1905, coincident with a redistribution of signal troops across the army; Major George O. Squier was its first director. All the schools were then housed in Grant, Sherman, and Sheridan Halls on what is known as Arsenal Hill (two of the buildings were once warehouses for the post arsenal). The early twentieth century was a period of great technological change in the field of communications, and officers not only needed to master traditional signaling techniques (visual, telegraph, telephone) but also required a firm grounding in aviation, electricity, and radio. In theory, graduates would provide the Signal Corps with a cohort of trained officers that it could not obtain through the commissioning process. It was the perfect situation for Hitt. He may have been disappointed about not attending the School of the Line, but he met and socialized with officers from many branches and made many personal and professional contacts at Leavenworth. Hitt brought his long-standing interests in radio and aircraft, as well as his engineering background and his bent for tinkering, to the Signal School. Perhaps he did not need to study because he already understood all the relevant subjects.[4]

Major Edgar Russel, "a quiet, soldierly, gentle-spoken man who was never known to raise his voice," led the school. An experienced signal officer, Russel had set up the army radio station at Safety, Alaska, in 1904; though he and Hitt were not in Alaska at the same time, the two men bonded over their arctic experience. Russel became Hitt's great champion and was crucial to the direction of his career. Hitt's instructors included Captain George E. Mitchell and First Lieutenant Joseph O. Mauborgne, a budding cipher expert destined to become the army's chief signal officer (CSO). First Lieutenant Charles F. Leonard instructed the students in gasoline engine management, Spanish-language instruction was provided by the Department of Languages at the School of the Line, and a topography and sketching course was run by Captain Laurence Halsted from the

School of the Line's Department of Engineering. Not one of the eleven officers in the 1911–1912 class had begun their careers in the Signal Corps. Of his classmates, Hitt would keep in touch with Captain Alvin Voris and Lieutenant Karl Truesdell, as well as Captain George S. Gibbs from the class of 1911; Gibbs, a Signal Corps officer and future CSO, joined Hitt's class in the spring of 1912 to make up missed lectures.[5]

The signal course was part theoretical and part practical; the students studied fourteen subjects, including electricity, engines, photography, telephones, telegraph, and radio. Codes and ciphers were also taught, but there was no standard text; just a few mimeographed pages supplemented lessons on how to use the army cipher disk. Once the essentials of a subject had been covered, the students engaged in independent research and presented their findings at "technical conferences," a system established by Squier. Hitt dug into the technical work and even brought it home. "I don't know what you call my front room," Genevieve remarked, "whether it is a wireless station, a telephone booth or telegraph station. Wires every where—I can't shut the window down tight as the wires would be mashed if I did. It's great to watch him and the fun he gets out of it."[6]

On the morning of Monday, October 2, the class started out on horseback for a mapping expedition. As Hitt mounted, with one foot in the stirrup and his right hand full of sketching boards, his horse bolted. Hitt was thrown into the air and landed behind the saddle. As the animal pitched and bucked, no one could get close enough to help. Then the horse took off, throwing Hitt off its back and dragging him down the road. Had the horse gone a few feet further, Parker's head would have encountered the stone curb of the sidewalk; as it was, he had a fractured left arm and was badly scratched and bruised. It was "a great wonder he was not killed," Genevieve observed. As a doctor's daughter, she was not impressed with the army's medical response: the "hospital wagon" took half an hour to go the four blocks to reach him, and the post x-ray machine was "very old-fashioned and out of date."[7]

A turning point for modern American cryptology came in the fall of 1911 as Hitt recovered from his accident. At the fourth technical conference of the year, Karl Truesdell read out portions of the article "Military Cryptography" by Captain Murray Muirhead of the British Army's Royal Field Artillery, which had just appeared in the *Journal of the Royal United Service Institute*. The discussion, led by Truesdell and Hitt, focused on Muirhead's method of polyalphabetic substitution. The pair had tested this method using both the standard army cipher disk and a disk with a mixed alphabet and proclaimed that the only safe cipher message was "one where the message itself is as short [as] or shorter than the keyword or phrase." These two junior officers had immediately grasped the cryptographic principle of a nonrepeating message key, sometimes called a "running key." The running key is a key longer than the message it enciphers; when used only once, it is known as a one-time pad, and it is unbreakable if used correctly. The concept of the running key and one-time pad would be improved and perfected a decade later by William F. Friedman, Joseph O. Mauborgne, and Gilbert Vernam. Hitt's imagination was spurred by this work, and he took on the task of inventing a practical device with a hard-to-break cipher. James G. Taylor was similarly inspired and postulated a device to easily decipher messages enciphered by the standard army cipher disk. Taylor's simplistic strip cipher and cylinder designs used a single alphabet in "true" order—that is, A, B, C, and so on. Hitt was quick to realize the potential for a device that could both encipher and decipher, and in his comments on Taylor's paper, he suggested some mechanical improvements.[8]

Schoolwork did not take up all of Hitt's time. His parents visited in late October, and on November 13 Secretary of War Henry L. Stimson and Army Chief of Staff Major General Leonard Wood made an inspection visit to the school. Parker and Genevieve met the visitors at a reception; it is possible that Wood remembered Hitt from the inaugural run of the *Relief* in the spring of 1904.[9]

The couple enjoyed their new life and were very much in love. One day they took a long walk across the river over the "old bridge," traveling about three miles into the woods. "Coming back it began to rain—but we didn't care. People looked at us as if we were crazy, walking along without an umbrella and the rain pouring off our heads." Genevieve noted, "It is so strange I don't get tired up here. I came home and cooked our dinner and wasn't the least bit tired. We had such a good discussion."[10]

Parker and Genevieve spent Christmas week in San Antonio with her family. When they returned to Kansas, they brought Genevieve's sister Tot and Genevieve's good friend Eleanor Onderdonk with them. Somehow, they managed to cram the visitors into their small makeshift home. The two young women were welcomed into Leavenworth's lively winter social scene; there was an informal dance in their honor, followed by a supper party at the home of Captain Hugh A. Drum on January 10. A highlight of the winter season was the Signal Corps Ball on February 19, where "heliograph men and 'thunder and lightning' experts and wireless sparkers provided light effects for the 'ladies choice' dance." Eleanor eventually went home, but Tot stayed on and had "the time of her young

life with the '57 varieties,' as they call the class of new 2nd Lieutenants."
Tot adored her older sister and often lived and traveled with Genevieve
and Parker until her marriage in 1927.[11]

On February 21, 1912, Captain Hitt presented a paper entitled "Enciphering and Deciphering Device," explaining a cylindrical device he had
constructed to improve on Taylor's inventions. Hitt had carved twelve
pairs of disks from apple wood for his prototype but believed a cylinder
with twenty-five or thirty pairs would be even more secure. Each pair of
disks, one with a forward alphabet and one with a reverse, mimicked the
army cipher disk; the device therefore did not increase message security,
but it made ciphering and deciphering faster. It was cumbersome and too
bulky for field operations, but if it were constructed from stamped metal
with interchangeable disks, Hitt thought it could be made portable. In the
summer of 1913 he made modifications to his cylinder design, creating
mixed alphabets for the disks. This change improved the device's cryptographic security, but there is no evidence Hitt built a prototype using this
design.[12]

Hitt's cylinder worked on the same principles as the nineteenth-
century cylinder devised by Frenchman Etienne Bazeries and a device
designed by Thomas Jefferson. Bazeries was unfamiliar to Hitt at the time,
and the Jefferson device was not discovered until 1922, ten years after
Hitt's invention. Hitt's 1913 design modification was the seed for the
army's M-94 cipher device. However, his mixed alphabets, dubbed the
"star cipher" by William F. Friedman, were not strong enough to with-
stand Friedman's analysis. During and just after World War I, Mauborgne
(Hitt's school colleague and friend) built stronger, more random alphabets
to use with the device; the M-94 was the result of Mauborgne's work
joined with Hitt's underlying principles. Despite vulnerabilities identified
by Friedman in 1918, the M-94, made of stamped metal (as Hitt had proposed) and using Mauborgne's alphabets on interchangeable disks (as
originally suggested by Hitt), was introduced in 1922; this compact, portable device was used until the mid-twentieth century. The cylinder cipher
and related sliding strip devices were the last mechanical steps toward the
development of electromechanical rotor devices, a post–World War I cryptologic leap forward in which Hitt would participate.[13]

Hitt was not the only student interested in codes and ciphers. Truesdell discussed the alphabetic frequencies of several languages at conference 6, and Captains Basil O. Lenoir and Alvin Voris discussed code issues
at conference 11. But of his classmates, Hitt was the only one remembered
for his cipher work.[14]

At the end of February, Leavenworth had the "heaviest fall of snow experienced here in many years." But the Hitts were rejoicing as if spring had arrived. Parker had been assigned to the Signal Corps, and it looked as if he might be sent to Fort Wood, New York. "We are both treading on air, we are so happy over it," wrote Genevieve. The couple were also celebrating their "little Hitt to be," "a lively young thing" expected in late July. Hitt told his father that the detail to the Signal Corps had come as a surprise, and all potential assignments were good ones, "except possibly Fort Gibbon on the Yukon," which seemed an unlikely destination for a married officer. Realistically, though, he believed he would be given Mitchell's job as a school instructor, "but I don't want that if I can get the New York station," he wrote. Hitt was correct in his judgment: in mid-April the Academic Board of the Service Schools, heavily influenced by Russel, recommended that he be assigned as an instructor, and by May, before Hitt had even graduated, the appointment was official. Parker and Genevieve were still living in Root Hall but hoped to have a house by late March; this was overly optimistic, as they would not move until August. Genevieve's mother visited in May and took Genevieve back to San Antonio in early June so Dr. Young could attend the birth of his grandchild.[15]

Hitt's year of study and invention went beyond cipher devices. He was rapidly becoming an expert in telephony, a subject he had first studied on the rifle range at Point Bonita in 1906. With help from classmates Gibbs, Voris, and Truesdell, he designed and constructed a small forty-line telephone switchboard for Signal Corps telegraph companies. Contained in a packing case, the switchboard had legs to support the equipment at a convenient height. Hitt used only standard telephone materials, so parts did not have to be specially manufactured, and he was proud that his unit was only one-fourth the size of commercial forty-line switchboards. The school shipped the model to Washington for evaluation; because Hitt had used only materials on hand at the school, he suggested some improvements— niceties such as reinforced corners and handles—should the Signal Corps accept his design. By late summer 1913, his switchboard, now called the "camp switchboard," was being tested, with most of Hitt's features retained and an improved iron framework. It was "about the most compact and efficient piece of apparatus of the kind that could be desired," according to Russel, who was now on duty in Washington. Hitt was encouraged by this news and hoped he might do more "toward improving our technical material." The switchboard was intended for division-sized headquarters, as it was still too bulky (and had too much capacity) for lower echelons; it was used extensively by the American forces in France during World War I. Hitt kept on inventing. His graduation thesis, "Testing of Dry Cells," included a new battery testing device he submitted for the Signal Corps' consideration.[16]

In May 1912 the class traveled to Fort Omaha, Nebraska, to learn about ballooning from Major Samuel Reber. Reber, a career Signal Corps officer who had an aptitude for ciphers and enjoyed a clever turn of phrase, took an interest in Hitt. When Reber moved on to lead the Signal Corps Aviation Section in Washington, he brought Hitt's cipher ability to the attention of the army bureaucracy. At the time, the service had a military intelligence effort in name only, and no cryptologic effort at all. Though Reber often filled the void by decrypting messages, he also furthered Hitt's reputation as a cipher whiz in 1915 and 1916. It may have been Reber who brought Hitt to the attention of Major Ralph Van Deman, who arrived in Washington in the summer of 1915 to wrestle with the army's intelligence shortfalls. It is possible that Reber was leveraging Hitt's work for his own purposes, but he served as Hitt's advocate, supporter, and quasi-mentor. Reber was not a particularly advantageous sponsor, though; his career crashed and burned when he suppressed a report critical of the Aviation Section and it was found that he had allowed the use of unsafe aircraft. Reber's support would not help Hitt get ahead, but it got him noticed.[17]

Hitt's aptitude for cipher work and his inventive nature went unremarked in his annual evaluation; instead, he was assessed as well suited to be a topographical officer, aide-de-camp, adjutant general, or line officer with volunteer signal troops. Taking six weeks of academic leave after graduation, Hitt hurried to San Antonio to see Genevieve. Almost immediately he was recalled to Leavenworth to evaluate a proposed infantry equipment manual on behalf of the Signal Corps; his suggestions heavily influenced the CSO's memo on the subject. As soon as he finished that task, he returned to Texas.[18]

Mary Lueise Hitt, named after her maternal grandmother, was born on August 12, 1912. It was a difficult birth, and Genevieve was unwell. Hitt requested an extension of his leave on the morning his daughter was born, and when he received no reply, he sent another urgent telegram the next afternoon; he was finally granted ten additional days of leave. The specific nature of Genevieve's illness is unknown, but she was in the capable hands of her father. Mary Lue would be the Hitts' only child, and her parents were completely devoted to her.[19]

While Genevieve recovered in Texas, Hitt moved from Root Hall to a spacious duplex house on Auger Avenue. There was a screened-in front porch, three bedrooms, a study, two bathrooms, and a large gallery hall. Before the furniture was set up and their belongings unpacked, Hitt had men from the signal laboratory install a radio antenna that ran from the top floor of the house to the top of the school's radio tower. He crowed that it would "be the finest one in all the post, even better in some ways (for receiving) than the big station on the Hill." He wrote to Genevieve, "Everything is still upside down at the house but I am solemnly promised two men from the Detachment for tomorrow and Cora is going to get a woman to scrub and sweep so it all ought to be cleaned up by evening." Parker wanted the baby's cradle to go in his den, where he would be able to rock her and listen to the radio while Genevieve slept. A prized addition to the house was a new bookcase containing the latest edition of the *Encyclopedia Britannica*, gifts from Genevieve and her father for Parker's thirty-fourth birthday.[20]

The Army Reorganization Act of 1901 established a system of rotation to ensure that officers did not spend their entire service on staff or in corps; staff time was limited to four years, followed by two years with line units. This practice did not help the Signal Corps, for few line officers had the technical aptitude or inclination to choose a signal detail. A provision in the Army Appropriation Bill of 1912 reinforced this practice by defining "detached service" as service away from an officer's primary branch or specialty, again limited to a period of four years. In army slang, the provision was known as the "Manchu law," and officers ineligible for detached service were called "Manchus." This system was "just about as efficacious as cutting off a leg in order to cure an ingrowing toenail," grumbled Brigadier General James Hagood in 1919. Schools outside an officer's own branch were also considered detached service. This negatively affected the Signal School because there were so few officers in the Signal Corps that all the students and most of the instructors came from other branches.[21]

Russel left the Signal School for Washington in the summer of 1912. Major Leonard D. Wildman was assigned to replace him, but Wildman was ill and could not report until late January 1913. Therefore, the just-graduated Hitt served as temporary director until Captain Arthur S. Cowan arrived from Omaha to cover for Wildman. When classes began in September, Hitt and Mauborgne shared teaching duties, and the post electrician, Junior Parrish, provided instruction on electric light equipment and meter testing. Hitt taught only seven days that month and urged Genevieve to "come as soon as you think best, sweetheart, and let's start real life again." He asked her to schedule her return for one of his "off days" so Mauborgne, "who has enough to do anyhow," did not have to cover for him. Mauborgne had to leave the school in mid-December because of the Manchu law, and Lieutenant Edmund R. Andrews took his place.[22]

Eighteen subjects were taught during the 1912–1913 school year. Hitt considered it an "unsatisfactory year," primarily because he had no time to do anything but teach; the school's annual report concurred, noting that the instructors "worked hard, faithfully, and continuously." Mauborgne's departure meant that Hitt delivered all the lectures except one, and he also had to keep an eye on the department office and the laboratory work. The graduating class of 1913, he lamented, "was very short on genius so that there was very little constructive or experimental work done." Hitt decided to increase the practical work and decrease theory next year, "teaching men to use their hands and common sense rather than their book knowledge."[23]

The Hitts had been in their house just a few months when they had to move to a nearly identical duplex on Meade Avenue, where they spent their first Christmas with Mary Lue. In the spring, Parker's parents traveled from Indianapolis to meet their granddaughter. The elder Hitts gave Parker and Genevieve $20 each, and Genevieve told her mother, "We feel like bloated bond holders." Tot urged her sister to buy a Victor Victrola with the windfall; Genevieve, who had "spent it twenty times in my mind," decided to save the money instead.[24]

It was fortunate that Tot was still with them because Genevieve found herself with a sudden child-care problem when their nursemaid, Myrtle, who was "so good to the baby," became entangled in a domestic dispute. It seems that Myrtle had an affair with a married soldier whose "wife had gone crazy," attacking Myrtle while she was walking Mary Lue in her carriage. The wronged wife grabbed the carriage and tried to throw the baby out of it, but Mary Lue was rescued when "a negro woman ran out of a home and took my baby away from her and ran into Captain Babcock's home." The post guard took the wife away, but the Hitts no longer felt safe having Myrtle in their employ. Genevieve recounted the drama to her mother in a letter, along with a plea for her mother's washing powder recipe.[25]

In August 1913, just before the school year began, the Hitts moved again, this time to a second-story apartment in a four-family building down the street. These apartments—two on the ground floor and two on the second—were not nearly as spacious as the duplexes. Because the Hitts had only one small child, they were likely bumped from the bigger houses by larger families arriving on post for the school year.[26]

Hitt and Andrews continued as instructors, and First Lieutenant F. E. Overholser, a June graduate of the school, stayed on to teach a signal course for enlisted men. Code and cipher instruction lasted only nine half-days, but it was more comprehensive with Hitt at the helm and included "various methods of enciphering and deciphering of messages when the key word and the manner in which the message was enciphered were both unknown." This was probably the year Hitt authored a short article titled "A Simple Transposition System," which began as a school lecture. In it, Hitt describes a method of using a zigzag line to scramble a message for transmission; he had read about this nineteenth-century technique in the army's *Manual of Optical Telegraphy*. Radio received far more attention than cipher at the school; the class dedicated the entire month of April and four full days in May to the subject, along with extra practice during the May and June field exercises. Hitt had great hopes of turning out "some real radio men" that year and encouraged students to take license examinations. To pass, students had to achieve a rate of fifteen words per minute in both International and American Morse code. Hitt collaborated with Andrews to eliminate "deep theory, obsolete ideas and apparatus" and to focus on radio equipment currently in use by the Signal Corps.[27]

Determined to find more time for his own experimental work in the new school year, Hitt began to keep a personal "idea book," and he made the book available to students who wished to conduct experiments. He made improvements to the 1912 service buzzer, with modifications that could be retrofitted to existing equipment, and the Signal Corps incorporated Hitt's work "as far as practicable" into future equipment purchases. Hitt also adapted the Doggett formula, which he learned about in *Electrical World,* into chart form; it was "surprisingly easy to use and you can get in five minutes what it would take an hour to do otherwise within an accuracy of one-half percent." But the formula, which was based on commercial radio circuits, did not work well with higher-frequency army equipment, and the Signal Corps declined to incorporate Hitt's chart into its standard material.[28]

More significantly, in a "natural evolution," Hitt took the principles of his cylinder cipher and built a strip cipher device better suited for tactical use. He constructed the first model in the spring of 1914, and in December the school sent the model, along with documentation and photographs, to the CSO. The device was a compact $7 \times 3.75 \times 0.5$-inch frame with twenty numbered sliding strips, each strip with a different mixed alphabet. The choice of a keyword determined the order of the strips. Decipherment entailed knowing the keyword, placing the strips in the correct order, and sliding the strips to produce a line that matched the enciphered text; the clear text message would be on another line. Hitt also designed a variant that was two frames wide, allowing forty letters to be enciphered or deciphered at one time. Although the strip system was more complex than the existing army cipher disk, Hitt thought it was more secure because the disk was slow to use and unsafe unless the keyword was the same length as the message, an impracticality for a hand-generated keyword that needed to be memorized.[29]

Wildman was enthusiastic about the strip cipher, calling Hitt "one of the best, if not the best, authority on ciphers in the Army today." He suggested that the device be submitted to State Department cipher experts, who might find it useful for diplomatic telegrams. Though the device was probably rejected in 1915, Hitt refined and updated his design the next year so he and Genevieve could send telegrams to each other. As he later remembered, "It was an upset time and Mrs. Hitt and I wanted a means for confidential communication in case we were separated." Genevieve Hitt demonstrated the 1916 model to both William Friedman (in 1917) and Herbert O. Yardley (in 1918), but it was never adopted for government use. However, in 1936, under the direction of Friedman, the US Army built a strip cipher device with twenty-five alphabetic strips, called the M-138; the US Navy's version of the device was called the CSP-488. A related thirty-strip device, the M-138/CSP-845, came into use in 1939 and was operational until the 1960s. Both devices were inspired by and derived from Hitt's original design.[30]

Hitt knew that, given the detached service regulation, he would have to leave the school in March 1915. He was already prepared to move on, and in February 1914 he requested reassignment in June, at the end of the school year. Wildman was sympathetic but unsupportive. There was no one at Leavenworth qualified to be a senior instructor, Wildman explained to the powers-that-be in Washington, and all the competent men who might replace Hitt were Manchus. Wildman claimed it was vital to the Signal Corps that Hitt stay, as he had "the gift to a high degree of imparting to others what he himself knows." Hitt, "one of the best-informed officers of the entire army on radio work" and "an expert in cipher work," was "thoroughly even tempered and clear headed" and had "used his good sound judgment in a number of cases where a lack of it would have caused friction." Wildman thought him irreplaceable. In Washington, Russel halfheartedly admitted that although they could probably relieve Hitt, there was no plausible replacement in sight. Hitt was not replaced.[31]

Making the best of a bad situation, Hitt leveraged his ability as an instructor to become a good public speaker. He gave speeches to civilian audiences and demonstrated his (and the army's) technical expertise in telephony and radio. Genevieve thought her husband was such a good speaker that he might one day beat renowned orator William Jennings Bryan "at his own game." On March 2, 1914, Hitt addressed twenty or more "telephone men" at a meeting of the Leavenworth People's Home Telephone Plan Society, speaking on the construction of the Nome, Alaska, telephone service. A few weeks later he "explained the mysteries of the wireless" to the Men's Club at the First Methodist Church. Captain Hitt demonstrated radio equipment and explained that radios allowed Fort Leavenworth to hear news days before it arrived via other means. In October Hitt gave three lectures to students at the School of the Line, explaining the Signal Corps' organization in peace and war; these talks were based on tables of organization and other material Russel sent from Washington. The lectures "were very fine," and Russel was impressed. He began to divert Signal Corps staff work to Hitt.[32]

Just a few months after war began in Europe, on November 9, 1914, Hitt was "tickled to death" by an opportunity to speak to the Missouri and Kansas Telephone Club in Kansas City. Genevieve was pleased that he wore his full-dress uniform with the shoulder boards for the occasion— "My! But he is handsome." The group first watched Lieutenant Colonel F. C. Waldon's demonstration of army communications equipment. Then it was Hitt's turn. His topic, "Nerves of an Army," discussed the technology used to gather information and issue orders, and the lecture was accompanied by stereopticon views taken in Texas and Alaska. Hitt informed the audience that both sides in the European conflict were using female telephone operators, which allowed men to be utilized "more advantageously" elsewhere. He stressed to the civilian telephone workers that, in wartime, it would "be up to you to furnish the nerves for the Army." The talk presaged themes Hitt would stress years later when he led a wartime signal force: the importance of teamwork, the use of the telephone in battle, the efficiency of female switchboard operators, and the need for skilled civilian telephone workers.[33]

In the spring of 1914 the army schools hastily graduated their students and closed early. The army needed all hands to respond to a crisis in Mexico. Mexico had been in a state of revolution for years and had an uneasy relationship (and ongoing border disputes) with the United States. President Woodrow Wilson refused to recognize Mexican president Victoriano

Huerta, who had come to power in a February 1913 coup, and imposed an arms embargo later that year. Tension between the nations escalated on April 9, 1914, when nine American sailors were arrested in an off-limits area of Tampico, Mexico. Though the sailors were released, the US Navy's demand of a formal apology accompanied by a twenty-one-gun salute was ignored. Mexico's noncompliance was used as a pretext to occupy the largest Mexican port, Veracruz. Brigadier General Frederick Funston's 5th Infantry Brigade deployed from Texas City, Texas, to Veracruz on April 30, occupied the city, and organized a military government; the US Navy interdicted a shipment of weapons intended for Huerta's forces.[34]

Hitt, in command of Signal Corps Company H, departed Leavenworth on April 26; the company left "amid the cheers of farewell from their friends, the kisses of wives and sweethearts—the caresses being intermingled with some tears." Company H, a telegraph company, lacked two of its six authorized sections but had been quickly beefed up with personnel, equipment, and transportation. It deployed as three telegraph sections and three telephone sections and "proceeded with great energy and enthusiasm on the part of the company commander" to Texas City to backfill the 2nd Division. Hitt's station of record was switched to Fort Sam Houston, and he was assigned to quarters 17G on the Infantry Post; Genevieve, Mary Lue, and possibly Tot took up residence there. It was a good opportunity for Genevieve to visit her family, who may not have seen Mary Lue since she was born. Parker was able to spend a few days in San Antonio with his family.[35]

Shortly after reporting to the 2nd Division, Hitt took it upon himself to inform the division chief of staff that the cipher they used, the Larrabee, was insecure and should be replaced with the Playfair cipher. Despite Hitt's status as one of the army's acknowledged cipher experts, the chief of staff ignored his advice and recommended no change. He explained to the division commander, Major General James Franklin Bell, that the Larrabee was what the War Department recommended, and Bell agreed.[36]

In June the division needed thirty enlisted Signal Corps men, experienced in visual signaling, to manage communications for ten Tampico-bound transports. When ordered to supply the men from Company H, Hitt raised objections. His exacting sense of detail and habit of truth-telling got Hitt in trouble with Bell, whose distinguished service included a term as commandant of the service schools and a stint as army chief of staff. Bell was a strong leader whose vigorous, enthusiastic style had been much appreciated at Leavenworth. Hitt explained that the assignment "calls for services for which Telegraph Company H, Signal Corps, is not equipped or trained" and that fulfilling the order would take 25 percent of the company's strength and break up its sections. Hitt claimed he had no objection to the men being used, as long as they were allowed to rejoin Company H as soon as the troops were landed, and he requested a detailed supply list because his company had "very limited" visual signaling equipment.[37]

Bell was not pleased. He spoke to Hitt "deliberately and with a purpose" to point out "the impropriety of the policy which inspired your objection," hoping to ensure that the younger officer "would never forget the lesson conveyed." Bell "was astonished and most unfavorably surprised" to receive Hitt's answer to the order and told him the objection to breaking up the sections had no merit, "as if one of the main purposes in organizing and maintaining the Signal companies was to maintain ideal sections and not for the service which the sections were expected to perform." Hitt's attitude, Bell noted, aroused "unfavorable impressions in my mind," and Bell pointed out that if the company was not trained or equipped, it was the fault of the company commander, though he admitted, "of course I recognize you had not had the time to train that company in everything it ought to know." Hitt's demand that the men return to the unit immediately after the journey was "perfectly legitimate," but it was not a reason to prevent the deployment.[38]

Not only did Bell chastise Hitt immediately; he also sent him a long letter in August while considering Hitt's efficiency rating. Bell was a fair man and had no wish to be unjust, but he wanted Hitt to understand the error of his ways. An aide had informed the general that Hitt was "a sick man" with a mental attitude "much influenced by an unfortunate physical condition." Bell therefore decided to give Hitt the rating that his "mental attainment, zeal, ability and character" deserved, for apart from the "incident," he had "formed a generally good impression" of Hitt as an officer. Bell then spent another page and a half counseling and chiding Hitt for his actions. No illness appears in Hitt's medical records for this time, but it is possible that his sciatica flared up or he suffered a relapse of malaria in the swampy environs of the Texas Gulf coast. Whatever the cause of his "mental attitude," Hitt survived this brush with authority, and while his propensity for speaking his mind in official channels may have been curbed by the incident, it never disappeared.[39]

As Hitt's time in Texas City came to an end, the tension that had been building in Europe since the assassination of Austrian archduke Franz Ferdinand in Sarajevo on June 28 exploded. Germany and Austria-Hungary aligned into one faction, and France, Russia, and Britain formed another. Between July 28 and August 4, 1914, European nations moved from military mobilization to declarations of war. The First World War had begun.

Back at Leavenworth on August 14, Hitt stepped in as acting director of the school while Wildman was on a detail in Panama. He instituted operational changes, first eliminating Squier's technical conference system and then realigning the coursework. The school shifted from "making all men in the class conform to the pace of the slowest and to recite a given number of pages" to a system in which "each man pursues a course along the lines of least resistance and with the greatest possible speed consistent with thoroughness." Two of Hitt's students that year would be colleagues during World War I: First Lieutenants Owen S. Albright and Frank Moorman. Moorman was the only student in the class commended for his academic work.[40]

Hitt juggled many priorities that autumn. The students for the enlisted men's signal course had arrived, but there was no instructor. Hitt improvised, starting the men in lessons on soldiering and augmenting this with practice in visual signaling, telegraph, and buzzer communications—"a very satisfactory beginning," according to Russel, who was still in Washington. Hitt continued to work long distance for Russel, examining and refining drill regulations for telegraph companies, a task he had begun in November 1913. This work came to an end only in January 1915, when Russel advised CSO General George P. Scriven of other organizational issues that needed attention. Russel also solicited Hitt's opinion on a talk he was giving to the War College, as the men had similar feelings about the "unsatisfactory character" of the existing Signal Corps tables of organization. Hitt, who thought it inevitable that the army would soon be fighting in Europe, continued to think about the wartime functions of the corps.[41]

Hitt's most important project, however, was the little book he was writing. He called it *Manual for the Solution of Military Ciphers.* He began writing the *Manual* before he deployed to Texas and meant it to be a textbook for the school, explaining "how to work out the simpler forms of ciphers that are in use in armies and among secret agents," based on his practical experience. Though not the first work on the subject used by the US Army, it was the most practical and accessible; its influence extended well into the middle of the twentieth century, long after it was out of print. Hitt believed it was the first book-length study on the subject in the United States. The *Manual* included a set of principles for establishing a code- and cipher-breaking effort—the first documented thoughts for an army signals intelligence operation. Hitt's book was William Friedman's introduction to cryptology, and he and his wife, Elizebeth, used it to instruct the army officers trained at Riverbank Laboratories in 1917 and 1918. Friedman used Hitt's principles and those established during World War I to develop the army's first true signals intelligence organization in the 1930s. Herbert O. Yardley, the State Department code clerk turned manager of the Military Intelligence Division's "Black Chamber" from 1917 until 1929, pooh-poohed the book, but it provided his first exposure to the subject. The *Manual* was the bible for members of the American Cryptogram Association until it was replaced in 1939 by Helen Fouché Gaines's *Elementary Cryptanalysis*.[42]

By the end of 1914, Hitt's book was substantially complete. Then, in January 1915, Reber sent him three Mexican telegrams that had been intercepted in June 1914. Reber asked Hitt to decipher them and explain his methodology, while keeping the matter "entirely confidential." Two of the messages were from Lazaro de la Garza, an agent for Mexican revolutionary leader Pancho Villa at Ciudad Juarez; they were intended for an associate of Villa's in New York, and at least one was thought to be in English. The third message was between two agents of the new Mexican president Venustiano Carranza. Despite his "fragmentary" Spanish, Hitt deciphered the garbled third message quickly. He then solved the other two messages and sent the information to Reber, thanking him for the challenge. Though Hitt would soon leave the Signal Corps, he remained "very much interested in cipher work of all kinds" and asked Reber to keep him in mind if he had more messages to break. Hitt continued to decipher foreign messages for the army for more than two years, as it had no formal cryptologic organization until the summer of 1917. In the interim, Hitt, Mauborgne, Moorman, and sometimes Genevieve filled the gap in the army's cryptologic capabilities.[43]

The three Mexican ciphers caused Hitt to make significant revisions to the *Manual*. He sought additional material and tried, without success, to locate copies of Mexican ciphers collected from the cable office at Veracruz during the American occupation. Reber urged the War Department to share everything it had that might support the book, for Hitt was "the best cipher expert in the army, with the possible exception of Lieut. J. O. Mauborgne." It was important, said Reber, to "lay a foundation for future cipher experts," who would be needed in wartime, as "cipher experts are not made in a day." Hitt incorporated so much of his subsequent work on Mexican ciphers—"hundreds of actual messages"—into the book that as late as 1917 it was said that "no Mexican cipher captured up to the present time has failed at analysis by the rules laid down" in the *Manual*.[44]

The *Manual* was complete in mid-May 1915, but Hitt wanted to rewrite the section on the Playfair cipher, as he was not completely satisfied with the material he had received from Mauborgne. He asked for his father's opinion, "to see how a technical exposition of the subject will strike you, for if you are like the average man, you will not have had very much experience with ciphers." The manuscript went to the Press of the Army Service Schools in October 1915, and when the book had not appeared by December, Hitt, feigning nonchalance, wrote to the press and learned that the delay was due to a higher-priority project: the 1915 edition of *Studies in Minor Tactics*. Hitt's *Manual* debuted in February 1916 and sold for twenty-five cents, with a press run of 1,000 to 2,000 copies. In 1918, unbeknownst to Hitt, the press issued a second edition of 40,000 to 50,000 copies.[45]

George Hitt, an experienced writer and publisher, had nothing but effusive praise for his son's work. "It is truly a mark of your patience and care in the unfolding of a very intricate and technical subject," he wrote. He urged Parker to "keep on with your writing. You know how—this book demonstrates that—and you ought further to exercise the talent you possess, whenever opportunity offers. Your mother and Aunt Kate and Muriel are quite as puffed up over your work as I am, and they join me in congratulations." Though perhaps "outdated at the moment of its birth," for World War I accelerated the development of new and more complicated ciphers, the *Manual*'s straightforward approach and charm, along with the lack of any other accessible material on ciphers in English, made it a popular, basic, comprehensible first volume for military officers and civilians.[46]

During the first half of 1915, Hitt's future was in limbo between his wishes and desires and the army's bureaucratic uncertainty about what to do with him. The detached service regulations required Hitt to return to the Infantry in March 1915. He continued to search for a convivial assignment, and in November 1914 he asked to go to the 10th Infantry in Panama "for personal reasons." He was not yet due for foreign service and did not want any foreign tour other than Panama; his request was denied as being contrary to the rules. By the end of January 1915, Hitt was still unsure where he would be going, but he knew he wanted to take his nearly four months of accrued leave when his stint at the Signal School ended in March.[47]

Hitt then made a stunning request to the War Department. He asked to use three months of his leave to travel to France, at his own expense and without official status, to "investigate systems of communication employed in wartime." The plan was endorsed by Wildman, who thought Hitt would be able to gather valuable information about the "methods by which the belligerents in the present war have provided for secrecy in their communications." Both Generals John J. Pershing (in command of the 8th Brigade) and Frederick Funston (in command of the Southern Department) signed off on the idea. But Major Peyton March in the Adjutant General's Office dismissed Hitt's request, as it was "not War Department policy to allow officers to go abroad on leave." Hitt's plan to wander about Europe might have been impracticable, but had the War Department supported the trip, perhaps the army could have better prepared signal and cryptologic support for its wartime force. Or perhaps Hitt, with no official cover, would have been arrested—or shot—as a spy.[48]

At the end of January Hitt received an assignment to the 6th Infantry in El Paso, Texas, effective the day after he finished at the school. At the same time, he was granted leave until June 19. There was no army housing at El Paso, so Parker would have to "live under canvas" much of the time; renting a house would cost $55 to $75 a month. Nothing was settled; despite his orders, there was still behind-the-scenes maneuvering going on. Russel sent Hitt some cipher work in February, and although Hitt did not reject it, he replied, "Cipher work is certainly the occupation for a man of leisure and that is far from being my status just at the present. I will therefore have to work on these ciphers at odd times and it may be some time before I can dig out the methods."[49]

In the middle of all this uncertainty about the future, a child living in the Hitts' building developed whooping cough, so they (along with Tot) quickly packed up their beds, dressers, and trunks and moved to the third floor of Root Hall. They left most of their belongings at the apartment, to be packed once they knew where and when they were going. Genevieve had an electric toaster and a percolator to cook breakfast and Mary Lue's supper, but they ate other meals at the mess, which was "a very good one and it is such a relief to me not to have to cook or even think about three meals a day," she wrote. Genevieve suspected they would end up at El Paso, and she was unsure whether Tot would accompany them. Parker wanted to take Genevieve to see California during his long leave, but because things were so unsettled, they stayed at Leavenworth. Genevieve used the time to pack and make new clothes. Hitt, who had been tinkering in the signal laboratory, submitted an innovative design for a signal lamp with a mounted sight that had a peephole and a cross-hair, making it easier to aim. The compact, space-saving lamp also had a telegraph key mounted on the lid of its box.[50]

Captain Henry E. Eames, who knew Hitt from the 10th Infantry and was now stationed in Washington, approached Hitt to gauge his interest in being assigned to the 19th Infantry at Fort Sill, Oklahoma, where the revived School of Musketry was scheduled to open in late 1915. Eames, author of the 1909 work *The Rifle in War,* was to be the assistant commandant of the school. Parker and Genevieve both thought this would be an ideal assignment, and Genevieve was pleased that they might "have a home for two years at least." Getting Hitt's orders switched to the School of Musketry was not simple, and plans almost fell through in the middle of May, but by the end of the month, he was ordered to report to Sill on July 1. Hitt belonged to the 6th Infantry until that date and was required to report to El Paso in June at the end of his leave.[51]

Genevieve was particularly upset when the Germans sank the passenger liner RMS *Lusitania* on May 7, 1915. Sensitive to the tension on post, she wrote, "Surely the people will demand an increase of our forces now. It is now or never." But she also sensed an opportunity and was pleased that Parker had made a good reputation for himself, for "it insures him a good position in time of war." Meanwhile, Tot went home to San Antonio. Hitt took advantage of the extra time at Leavenworth to design a code for field exercises and another cipher to protect the preamble, address, and signature in military radio messages. Though no longer an instructor, on June 11 he gave one last lecture on "Codes and Ciphers" and plugged his forthcoming book. Wildman was sorry to see him go, for he greatly appreciated the "knowledge, tact, and energy you have displayed as an instructor." He praised Hitt, stating he knew of "no officer in the army whose fund of general knowledge is so well-coordinated . . . and whose ability as an expositor and teacher is more marked." And Wildman expressed his personal appreciation for Hitt's willingness "to answer any unusual call with the greatest cheerfulness and enthusiasm." Hitt, however, was glad to go. Though he was now the army's "shark on ciphers," he considered himself an infantryman first.[52]

Hitt spent just under two weeks with the 6th Infantry at Del Rio, Texas; there is no evidence he did any cipher work there. Genevieve and Mary Lue may have visited San Antonio while Parker was in the field. The family traveled to Oklahoma in early July. Fort Sill, founded in 1869 near the confluence of the Medicine and Cache Creeks, had been the home of the

School of Fire for Field Artillery since 1911 and now added the School of Musketry. As a hunter, Hitt undoubtedly appreciated the countryside, which was known for its bountiful ducks, quails, and turkeys. A few weeks after the Hitts settled in, the 1st Aero Squadron arrived, commanded by Captain Benjamin Foulois, and Hitt saw how army aviation had evolved in the four years since his brief flying experience. In addition to his position in the school's Department of Machine Guns, Hitt commanded Company H of the 19th Infantry.[53]

Genevieve, who had initially been excited about the move, did not like Fort Sill. The housing was inadequate. She had a "makeshift kitchen" where it rained on the stove; she had to carry food to the dining room under an umbrella. "It is no joke cooking in rubbers and a raincoat," she told her mother-in-law. Though repairs were supposed to be finished in January, Genevieve did not believe they would happen. The following year was no better. The post began to replace all the windows and doors in the officers' quarters, and Hitt found it "hardly practicable to do much serious work at home under these conditions."[54]

The year also brought changes to the extended Hitt family. George Hitt, who had worked in several fields since leaving the *Indianapolis Journal,* faced a business setback, and he and Elizabeth were forced to economize. Parker could offer little financial aid, but he consoled his father and reassured him, "We are with you in your fight and, if the worst comes to the worst and the heavens fall, there is always a place for you and Mother here with us." But the senior Hitt was upbeat, telling his son that, "up until now, as Mr. Riley once said of the Hitt family, 'the hand of Providence has seemed to cover the whole flock.'" The family "had many blessings and we shall have many more, and for these we are and shall be grateful, whatever may happen." Later in the year, Parker's brother Laurance asked for a loan of $150 to support his plan to go to France and drive ambulances for the American Ambulance Corps. Laurance had been inspired by a fraternity brother, "a young chap named Childs," who had just returned from four months in France. "Dad said if he were my age and free to go, he would want to be there too, so I guess the streak runs in this family," Laurance told his brother. Parker was glad to lend him the money, writing, "It will be a great experience for you and, professionally, I envy you your chance to see some of the war at close range."[55]

The school's first four-month course was supposed to begin in late August, but it was delayed, so Hitt kept busy doing experimental work. He spent the fall going over the proofs of the *Manual* and preparing a speech on "Electricity in War" for a joint committee of the Chicago Section of the American Institute of Electrical Engineers and the Electrical Section of the Western Society of Engineers. It is not clear whether Hitt ever gave the talk, for there was some confusion in the Adjutant General's Office about the committee's request. Genevieve, in her expressive way, told Parker's mother, "You know his hair is never still and I am [as] confident that some day Parker Hitt will do some big thing as I am that another day is coming tomorrow." Genevieve was saving money—she thought she could save $1,000 a year while at Sill—"so that Parker would have capital to work on when the day comes and the idea." Hitt's inventions, however, belonged to the US Army. After examining telescopic rifle sights produced by the Warner & Swasey Company, Hitt designed one that he felt was superior. Genevieve was a bit put out that the Warner sight would earn the company $500,000 and Hitt would get nothing for his. He submitted for consideration in November 1915 modified slide caps and drift slides to confine the rifle fire of "untrained or excited men" to a zone between 100 and 600 yards; he believed this rear sight equaled the "leaf sight" for accuracy and enabled a shooter to aim at the target instead of two feet below it. Six slide caps and drift slides were manufactured by the Ordnance Department in December 1915, and in tests, the sights provided good results at 450 yards; forty more were constructed at the Springfield Armory in the spring of 1916. Although the sights increased efficiency, the cost—$1 million to adapt current rifles—was not worth the gain. And if the sights had been used only on new rifles, there would have been the problem of having to stock two different items.[56]

Hitt submitted a design to air-cool the Vickers-Maxim machine gun to the Ordnance Department in late 1915. He also recommended changing the "British type" of front and rear sights on the Vickers. Hitt claimed that the Lewis gun's similar sight caused "constant trouble," as men aimed over one of the side horns instead of over the sight itself. He recommended that the Vickers be equipped with the front sight from the Benét-Mercié gun and a modified version of that gun's rear sight. He also suggested graduating the windage scale to read in mils instead of points, adding a mils scale on the right edge of the sight leaf and redesigning the elevating screw so that one turn equaled one mil vertically. The school's commandant forwarded the latter suggestion to Washington because he liked the idea of the mil scale, but he saw no point in returning to the Benét-Mercié sight.[57]

In October 1915 the adjutant general formally tasked Hitt with a cryptologic assignment tangentially related to the war in Europe. The State Department was unable to decipher some papers associated with

German agent Franz van Papen, who in 1913 had become the military attaché for the German embassies in Washington and Mexico City. These documents may have come from the briefcase of German commercial attaché Dr. Heinrich Albert, which was recovered from a New York subway in July 1915, or they may have been obtained following that incident. The War Department's response to State's plea for help declared, "If anyone could succeed in translating the documents Captain Hitt was probably the person"; however, the memo also acknowledged the "difficulty of the task herein assigned" and stated that the department "is doubtful as to whether the documents are decipherable." Reber, who arranged for Hitt to work on the material, wrote to him a few days later and said he believed the messages were in an enciphered code. Reber also cautioned the secretary of the General Staff "not [to] expect the impossible." The task was so important that the commander at Fort Sill rearranged Hitt's duties so that he could focus on the documents. It was ten days of demanding work. On October 20 Hitt confirmed to Reber that the messages were in code, "with the exception of sixteen scattered words in one of the messages which were apparently in two different ciphers." Hitt prepared a memo so that someone with knowledge of German might be able to solve the cipher words, and he expressed his regret at being unable to complete the task. Genevieve told Parker's mother that, although he "did not solve the 'mystery' . . . the work he sent in on it will show that if it had been possible he would have found the answer."[58]

The people of the United States were divided on the question of US involvement in the European war. During the 1916 presidential election, Woodrow Wilson's campaign staff used the slogan "He kept us out of war" to appeal to those who favored American neutrality. George Hitt railed against his son's commander in chief, calling Wilson a "lovely, ladylike Cowardly president" who "watchfully waits" and is "too proud to fight." The elder Hitt despaired of the situation in January 1916 and pined for the days of Theodore Roosevelt, who "would do something, I know, to help us gain our self-respect. I am ashamed just now of my American citizenship." Parker likely shared his father's view of American neutrality and the political situation, but as a serving army officer, he kept his opinion to himself.[59]

The School of Musketry finally opened in February 1916, and Hitt was at last teaching his course in machine gunning. But a few weeks later, on March 9, Fort Sill and the United States were shocked when Mexican revolutionary Pancho Villa attacked and burned the border town of Columbus, New Mexico. Nineteen Americans died. For some time, President Wilson had supported Villa's efforts to remove Mexican president Carranza from power, but when Wilson changed his mind in late 1915 and supported Carranza, Villa was furious. He retaliated first by kidnapping and killing Americans on a Mexican train and then by attacking Columbus. In what would be a yearlong and ultimately unsuccessful attempt to capture Villa, the United States, initially with Carranza's permission, invaded Mexico, and General John J. Pershing led what became known as the Punitive Expedition. When Carranza changed his mind about having American forces in his country, Pershing's men had to avoid Mexican government troops while continuing their search for Villa. During the expedition, the Signal Corps used "radio tractors"—trucks fitted with radio gear—to communicate with one another and to intercept Mexican government communications. Two new US Army radio stations—one at Fort Huachuca, Arizona, and one at Fort MacIntosh, Texas—were built to provide reliable communications along the border and with Pershing. These stations also informally monitored Mexican communications, as radio operators were accustomed to "listening in" when not sending or receiving messages. Army radio stations and messages picked up by Pershing's signal troops were the source of the enciphered Mexican messages that Hitt, Mauborgne, and Moorman would break in the next year. Genevieve also worked on deciphering messages and would do so through 1918.[60]

Many US Army and National Guard units moved to defend the southern border. At Fort Sill, five batteries of the 5th Field Artillery and Companies E and H of the 19th Infantry prepared for deployment on the day of Villa's attack. The school was shut down. Official orders came on May 7, and Hitt, commanding Companies E and H, left at noon on May 9 for Fort Clark, Texas, thirty miles east of Del Rio. Hitt and his men were at Fort Clark for less than two weeks, moved to Del Rio for two months, and finally spent a few weeks at Fort Sam Houston. During these three months, the legend of Hitt—commanding an infantry company by day and code breaking by lantern light at night—was born. Cipher messages chased him from site to site. Captain Stephen O. Fuqua at Camp Stephen D. Little in Nogales, Arizona, sent Hitt intercepts obtained by tapping Mexican telegraph wires. Other posts forwarded him intercepted radio messages. The messages kept coming after he returned to Fort Sill. Some of the material Hitt received was not Mexican; in one case, a message intercepted from a Western Union telegraph wire was determined to be written in British Naval Code C, and he informed the Southern Department's intelligence officer that the message could be broken only with a codebook. In the midst of this activity, in June or July at Fort Sam Houston, Hitt made a new acquaintance—a young second lieutenant in the 19th Infantry named Dwight David Eisenhower. Neither man recorded their first encounter.[61]

When the school reopened in late September 1916, Hitt taught the fine points of the Benét-Mercié, Lewis, and Vickers-Maxim guns. Cipher work occupied the hours he was not teaching. While in the field, Hitt had received cablegrams believed to contain enciphered Japanese messages; he carried them home. By the end of September, despite having "practically no opportunity to work on these ciphers," he solved one of the simpler messages and had uncovered clues on the remaining two. He was making headway and vowed, "I will ultimately get this one." Hitt's feat was recounted in a September 1917 newspaper article telling the world that he had deciphered a Japanese message "written in a highly complex cipher" in less than an hour, "despite the fact that he did not know one word of Japanese." The occasional German cipher message slipped into the mix in early 1917, and Hitt admitted that the small message volume and his nonexistent German-language abilities kept him from providing solutions. In March 1917 Hitt told Reber about some messages he had received and specifically referenced Genevieve's work, noting, "Mrs. Hitt and I have done a fair amount of work on it and we think we begin to see the system behind it." Never one to be defeated by a cipher, he asked for more material in the same system and recounted the extreme pace of the musketry school's "intensive methods," which had "little consideration for the instructed and none whatever for the instructors." He cheerfully told Reber, "If a man really intends to do much at the cipher game he has to drop nearly everything else. Still, it is my hobby and if folks will not expect too much too quick, I am always glad to have material at hand to work on."[62]

Hitt did not neglect his machine gun work. With Thomas W. Brown, his friend from the school at Monterey, he developed a set of slide rules to mechanically calculate the percentage of accuracy for estimating distances; this made the process faster and free from arithmetical error. The pair combined these rules with mil and trajectory slide rules and packaged them into a compact device that included a wind table, protractor, and other features. This device became the Hitt-Brown fire control rule. The component parts of the rule were designed and adopted as the army standard for determining accuracy percentage and estimated distance in

1916; the Hitt-Brown rule and its instruction book were distributed by the US Infantry Association in 1917. Though the two men never obtained the patent they desired, they sold quite a few devices, providing some spending money for both households. In 1918 Hitt told Genevieve, "I used to say, when we were working in Fort Sill on it, that I would spend my share of the profit on shimmery, silky things for you and then Brown would laugh and talk about shoes for the baby."[63]

In the years between August 1911 and April 1917, Hitt's inventiveness was at its peak. He took advantage of the great latitude the army gave its junior officers to shape their own work. Hitt made advances in ciphers, signaling material, and machine guns, placing himself on the cutting edge of technological innovation in the army. His interactions with civilian experts in telephony helped bridge the divide between the military officer corps and the world of industry. Some people in the business world perceived soldiers as "a nonproductive social parasite, an expensive luxury, a waster of national resources," but Hitt proved otherwise in his quest for technological efficiency in the army. His background in engineering, despite his lack of a degree, made him an ideal signal officer in the mold desired by George Gibbs: the "'star' graduates of technical institutions" with the "attributes of a good army officer but also . . . a specialized aptitude that not every good officer possessed." These circumstances combined to make Hitt, still an infantryman, one of the few Americans who understood signal technology and cryptology—the underlying knowledge needed to conduct signals intelligence. His efficiency rating in the spring of 1916 assessed him as "fitted for promotion." During these same years, Genevieve evolved from a homesick newlywed to a confident young matron who not only ran an efficient household but also broke the cryptologic "glass ceiling," becoming the first woman to solve ciphers for the US government, albeit on an unpaid basis.[64]

In early 1917 German aggression, in the form of unrestricted submarine warfare and attempts to provoke conflict between the United States and Mexico, reached an intolerable level. President Wilson abandoned his policy of neutrality and called for a declaration of war against Germany, and Congress acted on April 6. An immediate scuffle began for Hitt's services, and he anxiously awaited orders. His future was still unclear when, on May 17, he received two different orders to report to Washington. He did not know what job he would have and when, if ever, he would get to France, but he was ready to go.[65]

On May 19 Hitt embraced his "really truly love baby" Mary Lue, who was just four and a half years old, kissed Genevieve, and left the house at Fort Sill. He looked back to see Genevieve standing there, "a picture of loveliness in your pink kimona [sic]," as he went off to Washington. It would be more than two years until Parker and Genevieve saw each other again.[66]

5

To France

*As you probably know, I was exceedingly sorry and disgusted
that General Pershing succeeded in stealing Captain Hitt from us.*
Lieutenant Colonel Ralph Van Deman, July 18, 1917

Hitt's years of thinking, writing, and speaking about radio, cipher, and war-time communications made him uniquely prepared to serve as a signal offi-cer or in some cryptologic capacity. Despite his experience with machine guns (a critical technology for the European war), he believed a detail to the Signal Corps would lead "to the kind of work that I like best." A delighted Samuel Reber, knowing the corps suffered from a lack of technical exper-tise, told Hitt, "We want you." Hitt's path to France was not straightfor-ward, however. The Signal Corps had a competitor for his services: Ralph Van Deman, head of the US Army's Military Intelligence Division (MID).[1]

The MID was formed in the weeks after the US declaration of war, and at the outset it had no formal organization for breaking codes and ciphers. Van Deman cobbled together a long-distance cryptologic team, farming out enciphered messages to Parker Hitt, Frank Moorman, and Joseph O. Mauborgne. Their assignments included coded German mes-sages intercepted in 1914 from the ships *Dresden* and *Sacramento*.[2]

Hitt was Van Deman's first choice to head a cipher bureau for the MID. After the declaration of war, Van Deman began maneuvering to have Hitt ordered to Washington "for work of this character," but he cautioned Hitt that it was "only a hope, so please say nothing about it and do not count on it." On May 16 Van Deman advised Hitt that he was to report to the MID for cipher work. Hitt immediately dashed off a letter to his father, asking him to keep an eye on the Washington newspa-pers for information because Fort Sill was "so out of the world" it could be days before orders arrived. Hitt was apparently unaware that his long-time mentor Edgar Russel was General John J. Pershing's choice to be chief signal officer (CSO) of the American Expeditionary Forces (AEF), and Russel wanted Hitt as his assistant. On paper, Hitt was the perfect choice to work with Van Deman. He had written *the* book on military ciphers, was well connected and mature, and outranked Moorman and

Mauborgne. But the qualities that made him ideal to head a cipher bureau, combined with his deep knowledge of telephony and radio and his close relationship with Russel, made him equally appealing to Pershing. Hitt was a hot commodity.[3]

Unfortunately for Van Deman, who had spent weeks working the system, one of Russel's first acts when he arrived in Washington was to rush telegraphic orders (under Pershing's name) to Hitt on May 17, 1917. Van Deman's orders arrived through routine channels later the same day. Unaware of Russel's order, Van Deman confidently told George Fabyan, the proprietor of Riverbank Laboratories, that Hitt was en route to Washington to take "charge of the cipher and sympathetic ink section" and would visit Riverbank (in Geneva, Illinois) to advise its small cryptologic force. Hitt did not stop at Riverbank. Traveling on Russel's orders, he left Oklahoma on May 19, briefly visited his father in Indianapolis, and arrived in Washington on Monday, May 21. He checked into the New Ebbitt Hotel, which was so near the War Department and so popular with officers that it was known as "Army and Navy Headquarters."[4]

Washington was "swarming with men after jobs in the expedition but few will get in the front rank," Hitt wrote to Genevieve. May 1917 was chillier than normal for Washington, and Tuesday was especially cold. Hitt breakfasted with his father's friend Senator Harry New, who "hoped he could do something for me . . . but I had nothing to ask for." Hitt checked in with Russel at the War Department, and at noon the two men visited Van Deman at the War College. Van Deman was "furious" and "not even civil"; he dismissed them and telephoned the Adjutant General's Office to launch a "vigorous protest" over Pershing's commandeering of Hitt. Russel and Hitt "beat it" back across town to the War Department, where Russel rushed to see Pershing while Hitt waited outside the office. "G-d the General Staff; my staff goes with me," Pershing told Russel. Then he stormed out of the office in search of General Tasker Bliss, the acting army chief of staff.[5]

Between meetings, Hitt petitioned for a change of station to Fort Sam Houston so Genevieve would not be stuck in Oklahoma, and he arranged for part of his pay to be deposited in their bank account so his wife "won't be penniless." In the evening he visited with his old machine gun colleague John Henry Parker, who was "just as wild as ever about everything." Back at the hotel, he penned a note to "his sweetheart," who had packed his trunk and sent it to New York (in anticipation of the voyage to France). He told Gee Gee not to worry about him "because my job is not going to be that kind."[6]

Once Van Deman had cooled down a bit, he explained to Fabyan that he did not know whether Hitt would stay in Washington or go to France, though "certainly, his greatest usefulness will be here." He promised Fabyan that if Hitt ended up with the MID, he would visit Riverbank. Months later, Van Deman acknowledged his dismay at losing Hitt and admitted that Hitt was "very glad to be stolen"; for this, Van Deman did not "blame him—we would all like to be over there, of course." Had Van Deman gotten his way, it would have been Parker Hitt, not Herbert O. Yardley, in charge of the MID's Code and Cipher Section (MI-8). Yardley claimed that, from his position at the State Department, he had schemed for a job in military intelligence, where he could "spring my plan for a Cipher Bureau upon the unsuspecting War Department." The hardly unsuspecting Van Deman had arranged for Riverbank Laboratories to do code and cipher work when he failed to get Hitt for the job; he did not hire Yardley until a few weeks later. Van Deman was still disconsolate about the loss of Hitt's expertise in September when he approached Professor John M. Manly and asked him to be MI-8's "cipher expert." Van Deman explained that Manly was needed because "General Pershing . . . knowing what Captain Hitt's abilities were . . . immediately grabbed him and took him away from me." MI-8 might have been more successful and efficient, particularly in constructing military codes, had Hitt been in charge, but without Hitt, the signals and cryptologic work of the AEF surely would have suffered. Hitt was a soldier; he would not have enjoyed being stuck in an office in Washington when the action was in France.[7]

Hitt was feeling "on the blink" on Thursday, May 24, recuperating from a typhoid shot and a late night working at the War Department. In 1914, while discussing tables of organization for the Signal Corps, Russel and Hitt had contemplated using civilian telephone workers in wartime; their theory became a reality when they arranged for two "$10,000 a year men from the Bell Company," experienced in heavy construction and telephone equipment, to join them. Hitt was busy, but his family was on his mind. He knew Genevieve would be all right in San Antonio, yet he was troubled that his hasty departure had left his wife alone to manage a move. Hitt asked his mother to keep in touch with her, for though "she is a game little woman . . . I am so afraid something will happen to her and she will not let me know for fear of worrying me."[8]

On May 28, just eleven days after leaving Fort Sill—breathtaking speed for the army—Hitt was aboard the RMS *Baltic* as it left New York, supposedly in secrecy. The artillery salute fired from Governors Island as the ship left the harbor gave the game away to those who had missed other clues. There were 191 officers and men of the AEF aboard, but only 40 of them were officers from the regular army. Hitt's shipmates included Russel, Pershing, Samuel D. Rockenbach, Fox Conner, Dennis Nolan, Hugh Drum, Arthur Conger, George S. Patton, and Eddie Rickenbacker—men Hitt would dine with nearly every May 28 in future years, commemorating their voyage to France and to war. On the ship, Hitt was responsible for the AEF message center and taught three field clerks how to use the War Department's telegraphic code. No messages could be sent while they zigzagged across the North Atlantic under radio silence, so the men spent time coding messages to send on arrival in Liverpool.[9]

With Parker on his way to France, Genevieve packed up and moved herself and Mary Lue to San Antonio. Over the course of the war, many army wives had the freedom to decide where they wanted to live while their husbands were away. Genevieve was lucky that she had family at her destination and the financial wherewithal to hire household help. She also had an interest beyond her domestic duties, for Genevieve continued to break code and cipher messages for the army. Parker sent her advice about her work from Washington, telling her that Van Deman knew of her efforts and would keep her in mind if he needed cipher assistance. While Hitt was crossing the Atlantic, Genevieve (with Mary Lue) traveled to Riverbank Laboratories, where she demonstrated Hitt's strip cipher device to William and Elizebeth Friedman and the other Riverbank staff. She set a challenge message for the group, offering a box of chocolates as a prize. William Friedman, who suspected Genevieve was not "wise to the quirks of inexperienced cryptographic clerks," won by guessing she had used "Riverbank Laboratories" as the keyword; he gave the chocolates to his wife, Elizebeth. Genevieve was "a good sort, and a mighty fine house guest, and we like her tremendously," Fabyan told Van Deman, but she was not as talented as her husband and could not fully explain Hitt's *Manual*. Genevieve had admitted to him that Riverbank was "way beyond her, and there was nothing that she could do to help us." Fabyan asked Van Deman to send Moorman to explain Hitt's *Manual* to his staff. Despite her failings, Fabyan was taken by Genevieve and Mary Lue and urged them to come to Riverbank for the duration of the war so he could look after them; perhaps he thought he might put Genevieve to work in his cipher unit. Genevieve declined. Upon her return to San Antonio, Genevieve, determined to contribute to the war effort, offered her cryptologic services to Van Deman. She told him, "Parker rather overestimates my ability along these lines," but there were "times when I have been 'lucky.'" Van Deman assured Genevieve he would not hesitate to use her if needed.[10]

The *Baltic* arrived in Liverpool on June 8, and the AEF staff traveled to London by train. Russel, Hitt, and their small contingent of signal men embarked on four hectic days of visits to the British army, where they learned about British equipment and made purchase decisions. After seeing the large signal depot at Woolwich Arsenal, where the British tested and inspected signal equipment going to France, and later the "remarkable" experimental plant in Paris created by the French army's CSO, Colonel Gustave-Auguste Ferrié, Hitt and Russel were convinced that the AEF required a similar facility. Together they concocted (and sent to Washington) a plan for what would be the AEF Research and Inspection Division. Colonel John J. Carty, an AT&T executive commissioned for wartime service in the CSO's office in Washington, was soon gathering specialists and equipment to staff the division in France. Hitt considered the new organization "one of the early triumphs" of his and Russel's work.[11]

Pershing's staff was welcomed in Paris by the French military and civilians and then embarked on months of often contentious consultation on how American forces would be used in battle. It took time to draft, train, and move American forces and material to Europe. The men on the *Baltic* were just the first drop in a great wave of troops: at the end of 1917, fewer than 200,000 Americans were on the ground, but by the end of 1918, more than 2 million men had crossed the Atlantic. Logistics constrained the AEF, and the Signal Corps would never have all the material it needed to do the job. Supplies began to arrive "properly" only after the armistice in November 1918, showing, Hitt said, "how long it takes to begin a war with nothing but money. We must keep the lesson in mind."[12]

"Very comfortably" billeted in a small hotel with two other officers, Hitt was tasked with setting up and supervising the first AEF code room at 31 Rue Constantine. The office was immediately "swamped" with communications to and from Washington, and Hitt was hugely relieved to abandon the "monotonous routine" of coding at the end of July when newly arrived Captain Frank Moorman was pressed into code-room duty. Hitt was charmed by France and wanted Genevieve to come over that summer, either to work or just to be closer to him. She might have been tempted into service in the G2A6 Code and Cipher Section had circumstances been different, but the US Army did not use female code breakers in France. Before the Hitts could organize her move—mail service was "abominable," and four of Genevieve's letters arrived in a bunch on August 8—the AEF prohibited officers from bringing their wives overseas.[13]

The AEF Signal Corps had to work quickly and efficiently to establish a network of telephone lines stretching from the Atlantic ports on the west coast of France to the front lines in the northeast. They could not spend years developing a communications infrastructure; American installations small and large needed dependable communications wherever they were located. Office hours began at 8:30 in the morning and continued until 7:00 or 8:00 in the evening; Hitt sometimes worked even later. Russel and Hitt had known each other for more than five years and worked well together; Russel was comfortable delegating complex tasks to his subordinate. Hitt's responsibilities included designing and managing American communications systems and conducting liaison with French and British signal authorities. Russel's office—which had a sign reading, "There is no place in the Signal Corps for the man who makes friction"—was moved to 64 Rue de la Boetie in mid-June and then to 10 Rue Sainte Anne in mid-July; Hitt spent his days traveling across the city between the code room and the main office. Under the guidance of the forward-thinking Russel, Hitt demonstrated an ability to solve supply problems and work with available material to get the job done.[14]

Hitt, Russel, and Major Alvin C. Voris, who arrived in late June, were continually on the move through the summer, investigating locations and meeting with Allied signal organizations. Hitt went to Meudon to see French ground telegraphy in action and to another facility to investigate sound detection and ranging equipment. Hitt and Russel spent five days at French General Headquarters in Compiègne during the first week of July, learning about French signal systems. Hitt and Voris then went to Nancy on the evening of July 9 to meet with officers of the French VIII Army's telegraphic service. This visit included many stops within French XX Corps, including the command post of a regiment with a carrier pigeon force and the French listening station in the Bois-le-Prêtre, "where we were able to overhear the telephonic and buzzer conversations in the German lines." They were the first members of the AEF to see the French radio intelligence system in action. The Americans were wined and dined by the French; a luncheon menu bearing "best wishes of welcome and prompt victory" was adorned with a drawing of a tall, pipe-smoking American *"au chapeau de cow-boy"* in chaps and spurs, striding across the Atlantic bearing weaponry, ships, and airplanes. Though Hitt had command of written French, he spoke the language "indifferently" but well enough "to get along."[15]

Hitt and Voris returned to Paris early on the morning of July 12 and left the same afternoon, along with Russel, for British headquarters at Abbeville. Hitt was back at the front for a week in August during the "big attack to the east of Ypres"—the August 10 assault by the British and French that took Langemarck and Saint-Julien as part of the Third Battle of Ypres/Passchendaele. He noted that it was both "wonderful and terrible to see at close range." When Hitt returned to Paris, he was examined for promotion; a month later, he was no longer Captain Hitt of the regular army but Lieutenant Colonel Hitt of the new national army; in November he was promoted to major in the regular army. There were two more quick trips to the front in late August "for special purposes" (possibly related to radio intelligence), and Hitt celebrated his thirty-ninth birthday on the road "in the desolation of the front."[16]

Pershing, in consultation with the commander in chief of the French army, General Henri Philippe Pétain, decided to take responsibility for the Lorraine sector, which stretched from south of Verdun to the Vosges mountains. On September 1 AEF headquarters moved from Paris to the "large and airy" nineteenth-century buildings of the Caserne de Damrémont in Chaumont, about 170 miles southeast of the capital. Here, headquarters was well positioned to serve the AEF's area of operations. The caserne had three main buildings: building A on the left, building B in the center, and building C on the right. Pershing's carpeted office was on the second floor of building B, at the head of the main stairway. "Like most French barracks they were alive with vermin of every loathsome description" and had to be fumigated for three days prior to the AEF's arrival; Hitt believed "we will make it livable after a while," helped by new "electric lights and good American telephones." Hitt's quarters on Rue du Commandant Hugueny were an easy walk from headquarters. It was a "dandy house and mess for the eight of us with a cook and a maid." Twenty francs per month covered maid service, shoe cleaning, clothes brushing, and electric light; heat cost extra. The sheets were changed every fifteen days, and pillowcases and two towels were changed weekly.[17]

Hitt stayed on the move, traveling to Gondrecourt with Captain Robert B. Owens to inspect the Signal Corps school and other installations on September 19 and 20. As Russel's "right hand man" and his eyes and ears, Hitt's duties were wide ranging. In late September he went on the road to plan telephone lines and examine the areas to be occupied by American troops. For his pains, Russel promised to make Hitt CSO of First Army once it formed. In late September Russel suggested to AEF chief of staff General James Harbord that it would be beneficial if the signal officer supporting AEF headquarters (and later each subordinate headquarters) were an "ex officio" member of the G3 Operations Section. This officer, possessing "the ideas of a specialist," could supply precise technical information on communications in support of operational planning. The acting G3, Colonel Kirby Walker, liked the idea and requested that an officer "familiar with codes, lines of information, aviation, and organization of equipment and signal units" be assigned to him. Hitt was that officer. By October, it was clear that he would stay on at Chaumont, serving as the Signal Corps' representative to the General Staff, when Signal Corps headquarters moved to Tours with the Services of Supply. Hitt might have hoped to be named Russel's assistant, but his friend and Signal School classmate Colonel George S. Gibbs, a career Signal Corps officer, arrived in France and took that job. Hitt was, after all, an infantryman on a detail. At the end of October his detail to G3 became official; he spent his mornings on signal work and his afternoons at G3, assisting with signal and machine gun matters. These two assignments demonstrate his superiors' high regard for Hitt's capabilities, the lack of qualified Signal Corps officers, and the AEF's indecision as to what to do with Hitt, whose skills did not neatly fit into signals, staff, or infantry.[18]

Russel may have been "a bit of a gad-about since we got our new limousines for winter work," but Hitt was no slouch in the travel department. In early November he was in the Belfort sector "on the edge of Switzerland" on one of many inspection trips. November 12 found him at the heavy artillery camp at La Valdahon; then he was off for a few days to the British front "to see the latest things and verify some arrangements." He spent four "wonderful" days between Ypres and Cambrai, "picking up new ideas and renewing old friendships among the British Signal folks." He was at the front at the start of the Battle of Cambrai on November 20.[19]

There was a foot of snow on the ground in Chaumont on December 30. Hitt, who told Genevieve he was suffering from "too much popularity," believed his afternoons at G3 would soon turn into a full-time job, although Russel seemed to think he needed Hitt too. Still, as the snow continued in January, Hitt was more often on the road for the Signal Corps than in Chaumont in the Operations Section. "I am no office man and it irks me to be in this kind of a job but,—c'est la guerre,—and as long as I stay well and can smile a bit and growl a bit everything will be all right. Maybe I get me a real job someday." He made time to keep in touch with his "dearest girl," even though there was "so much in sight to do that it is really stealing government money to stop for a personal letter."[20]

The G3 assigned Hitt to Committee 1 with General Fox Conner; Colonels LeRoy Eltinge, Stuart Heintzelman, and Hugh Drum; and Major Price. Hitt's focus was "operations codes" and lines of information. Edgar S. Gorrell was added to this committee to handle aviation issues in February 1918. Hitt also served on Committee 5 for signal matters and shared an office with his friend George Simonds and Walter S. Grant.[21]

Signal work sent Hitt back to La Valdahon in January to open a telegraph office there. Ten days later he traveled through Paris to Brest, Saint-Nazaire, and Bordeaux, inspecting the progress of telephone line construction. "Things are coming on wonderfully," he reported, "and the Signal Corps will be in fine shape in a few weeks." Hitt was the obvious choice to be the senior member of a board charged with examining the security of codes and ciphers used by the AEF to communicate with Washington (the other members were newly promoted Major Frank Moorman and Second Lieutenant Wallace B. Chambers). Although the AEF operated on a relatively autonomous basis, secure and reliable communication with the United States was necessary and was accomplished telegraphically, via undersea cables. Moorman made inquiries and found that Washington considered the code in use, the War Department Telegraphic Code of 1915, to be insecure. Once the United States entered the war, the British (who had been monitoring American cable traffic and breaking American codes) informed their new ally that the code was "a menace to secrecy." The board members did not meet again; there was nothing for them to do but wait for a new code from MI-8.[22]

Hitt had been promised leave in January, but the date was shifted to the end of February, and he never managed to get away. He did have time to greet and dine with friends who were trickling into France, some of them bearing letters and packages from Genevieve, and some of them carrying messages from his father. One of those friends was Dr. David Hogan, Hitt's companion during his days at Baler in the Philippines.[23]

In late February 1918 Hitt realized that the day was coming when he would be detailed full time and indefinitely to the Operations Section. Once again, he was reassured that there would be a Signal Corps position for him at some future date, perhaps as CSO for II Corps (a step down from the First Army job). Until the Signal Corps left Chaumont, Hitt continued to spend mornings there and afternoons with G3. When the Signal Corps departed for Tours in March, Hitt found himself in a difficult position, and not just because his mail ended up in Tours. He hated being separated from Russel, who wanted Hitt to stay in Chaumont, trusting him to be "his representative near the throne." Once again, Hitt's services were very much in demand, as other sections, anticipating Russel's departure, clamored to employ him. The G3 made it clear that its understanding with Russel was for Hitt to "eventually devote all of his time to the Operations Section," for there was "no other officer known who has sufficient understanding of all the matters relative to the transmission of information, etc. and also the military education" to do the job. Eltinge told AEF chief of staff Harbord that Hitt's assignment to Operations should be "complete and final." Russel pushed back, unwilling to completely give up Hitt's services. "There are so few officers experienced in Signal Corps work," Russel pointed out, and he hoped Hitt might be "kept specialized as far as possible in Signals Corps work so his service may, when practicable, continue to be available for occasional consultation with the Chief Signal Officer."[24]

Meanwhile, Hitt stayed connected with his infantry roots. He carried 100 Hitt-Brown rules with him to France and sold them for $2.50 each. The government ordered 2,000 rules, and army organization tables called for twelve to be issued per infantry company and sixteen per machine gun company, though it is not clear whether this actually happened or how much money Hitt earned from his "toy." In December 1917 his collaborator, Brown, sent Genevieve a check for Hitt's share of that year's sales.[25]

In March Hitt made a one-day inspection trip to Paris, "missing the air raid by one night just as I missed the January 30th one." More Signal Corps officers were en route to France, and this news cheered Hitt, for "we have been awfully handicapped for want of people who speak our Army and signal corps language." By later winter 1918, the American 1st Division had set up operations on the southern side of the Saint-Mihiel salient. The salient, a wedge of land northeast of the city of Saint-Mihiel, was French territory captured by the Germans in September 1914. Hitt visited the division in March. While there, he probably saw the work being done by the Radio Section in that area, including the new listening stations installed near the front lines at Marvoisin and Bois de Remières. In early April Hitt traveled to Montreuil, where II Corps headquarters was located along with British forces; the sector had been the target of new German offensives since March. Simonds, II Corps' chief of staff, advised Hitt to bring his bedding roll just in case they went on the road. He hoped Hitt would stay with II Corps permanently, writing, "I know you will enjoy it up here and we will be glad to see you."[26]

By July 1917, Russel's team in the Signal Corps office on the Rue de la Boetie was "sick enough" of the terrible service they received from "French *téléphonistes* and soldier operators." Hitt's subordinate, Robert B. Owens, suggested bringing American women to France to run the AEF's switchboards. Hitt, who had spoken of using female telephone operators in 1914, agreed; he convinced Russel to do so during a trip to the British front. There was no formal study or recommendation; Hitt quickly calculated the number of operators required, drafted a message for Washington, and turned the matter over to Russel, who sold the idea to Pershing. After the war, Hitt, not Owens, was credited as the "moving spirit" behind the idea. The AEF's willingness to use women as switchboard operators but not as cryptologists can be attributed to women's well-established role as operators in the United States and the newness of the cryptologic profession for either men or women.[27]

The women began to arrive in France in March 1918. On April 20 Hitt was the guest of honor at a dinner given by the younger Signal Corps officers for the fifteen "telephone girls" stationed at Chaumont; the women reciprocated with an invitation to a party and dancing on May 4 at the YWCA Hostess House. Hitt and some of his fellow officers updated their wives at the end of April with a lighthearted "Monthly Report of the Association of Husbands of San Antonio Wives," which claimed that "information about the dance at the Hospital and the Telephone Girls' dinner is vague and conflicting" but reassured readers that the group's conduct "has been beyond reproach." The Association of Husbands also urged that the "automatic supply of knitted socks, sweaters, etc., if any, should cease. Present supply sufficient for all needs; . . . such garments appear from the result of present experience in this war to be not well adapted to hot weather use." They assured the wives that there was no truth to the rumor that one member had used a homemade sweater to polish his boots or that another had soaked a hand-knitted sock in oil to use as a rustproof pistol holder. Although the house full of women had "an attraction of sorts," and "a friendly voice is *pas mal* if it is that of a *jolie femme americaine*," the novelty had worn off and the women had "become just a part of the big machine." Hitt mused that Genevieve could get a job with them, if only "you were not married to an Army officer and could talk French and work a switchboard."[28]

The G3 had originally planned to send Hitt to the British front for six weeks or longer in late March, but Robert Lewis, the husband of Genevieve's friend Sudie Blocker, went instead. Hitt kept traveling, moving through Paris "in the midst of the daily bombardment" to the Verdun sector (where he heard mention of his brother Laurance, who was with the 40th Engineers, but missed seeing him), then over to the Saint-Mihiel sector to inspect communications, and finally to Toul to see the work of the air service. On one of his trips, "the boche was on the rampage with H.E. (high explosives) and gas and it was no Sunday morning stroll to get back to the artillery positions. So we got through our business without haste but with considerable speed and dispatch and left a part of the world that was none too healthy that morning." The traveling continued through May, but Hitt missed a trip with Gibbs because he was "too busy" preparing for an upcoming detail. "I am like a small boy who is afraid of missing something," he told his mother, while reassuring her that he was healthy and working hard to earn his salary. When in Chaumont, Hitt now shared an office with Hugh Drum, who would soon be chief of staff of First Army.[29]

In the spring of 1918 a German offensive moving in the direction of Paris caught the French with few available reserves and presented the AEF with an opportunity to fight. The 1st Division moved into the French reserve in May 1918 to support an attack near the village of Cantigny; on May 28, 1918, it fought the first American battle on French soil, demonstrating its ability to execute an attack with a limited objective, despite inexperienced, poorly trained, and badly supplied troops. A few days later, the 3rd Division moved to occupy the town of Château-Thierry on the Marne. Hitt, with his own car and driver and a "roving commission to go anywhere and see anything," arrived on May 31 as the division's G3 liaison officer. Arriving in Chateauvillian, a "funny little French farm town," he reported to the division commander, General Joseph T. Dickman, before settling into a little billet where "madam even goes so far as to bring me hot water and has taken good care of me and my things." He reported that "madam" was "glad to have me here because I am an American and she is afraid of the territorials and colonials." Hitt was astonished to find that "this whole country for twenty miles south of the Marne is stripped of food, wine, and the petty valuables of house and shop," all plundered by friendly troops. The 3rd Division helped hold the southern bank of the Marne, halting the German offensive that had started on May 27. At some point during the first week of June, Hitt got too close to the action; a shell fragment struck his helmet, and he suffered a concussion. It was "only a dent in my tin hat and a most undignified 'sit down,'" he told Genevieve, adding, "if anyone mentions that I was wounded, it is not so." Hitt did not tell Genevieve about the concussion.[30]

Hitt's routine mirrored that of division staff—to bed at 3:00 or 4:00 in the morning and up at 8:00 or 9:00, "then a nap in the afternoon and up for the night." But he enjoyed the "open air life after being caged up in an office for so long." He noted, "Our forces are getting in such shape that we have become a real and most formidable factor in the war." Hitt had once again been promised the position of First Army CSO, and he reassured his wife that he was "being careful and taking no unnecessary chances for I love you." While in the field, Hitt lost the few pounds he had gained while in the comfort of Chaumont.[31]

Returning to Chaumont, Hitt prepared an after-action analysis of 1st Division's communications during the Cantigny engagement; that assessment informed the choices and adaptations he made later in the war. Battalions used telephones to talk with units in the rear and with the artillery. Despite the fact that wires were almost always cut during heavy shelling, the phone remained the most reliable method of carrying out critical front-line communications. Hitt recommended that, in the future, wire be buried in shallow trenches by using a trench-cutting attachment on the cart carrying the reel of wire. Front-line, short-distance voice and Morse code communications transmitted using ground induction (ground telegraphy) could not be electronically located by the Germans, but these messages were not secure because the enemy could "copy everything that is sent." Radio was available as an emergency method, but it was not needed at Cantigny. Visual signaling methods "were quite useless owing to the fog and the dust." Runners were slow "but sure," and despite the "usual heavy losses," they were used extensively during the battle when visual signaling failed. "As it has always been," the link between front-line troops and the battalion command post was the greatest point of failure. Hitt hoped that new radios, still in development, would "become the normal means of front-line communications," but until they were available, units had to depend on runners, visual signals, and pigeons. He believed "training and more training" would alleviate communication difficulties. The war ended before the new radios were ready for use, but as Hitt had anticipated, this communications technology was essential along the front lines during World War II.[32]

Hitt next went to the headquarters of French I Corps at La-Ferté-sous-Jouarre to observe the Second Battle of the Marne, particularly the Aisne-Marne offensive. His daily afternoon situation reports provided details of the French counterattack, which gained, then lost, then regained the town of Saint-Agnan. Hitt reported that the 3rd Division was operating well and showing a "really fine spirit of 'hold on,'" despite the difficult situation the 38th Infantry found itself in on July 15 when the French withdrew "without any attempt to notify anyone of the movement." On July 18 he declared, "The 3rd Division is ready to cross the river if the drive from the west makes it practicable."[33]

The sheer number of activities Hitt took on during his first year in France is overwhelming, and his productivity is astonishing; one wonders when he slept. Hitt cranked out work at a rapid pace, and throughout it all he remained patient, gracious, and pleasant to colleagues and subordinates alike. It is no surprise that many organizations wanted Hitt to join them. While Hitt accomplished his many assigned duties, he also played a critical role in the successful operation of the three interlocking AEF cryptologic organizations: the Radio Section, the G2A6 Radio Intelligence Section, and the Code Compilation Section.

During World War I, and for some time afterward, what is now known as signals intelligence was called "radio intelligence." The US Army had little experience with the systematic collection and processing of signals in wartime and spent months learning techniques employed by its British and French allies. Americans were colocated with French collectors, and initially, much of their equipment was supplied by the French. Both the British and French shared methods of cryptanalysis and code breaking, and the British advised on the sensitive subject of code making.[34]

In the AEF, both the Signal Corps and the G2 Intelligence Section engaged in aspects of radio intelligence. The Signal Corps' Radio Section collected communications from electromagnetic sources: radio, telephone lines, and ground telegraphy. It also determined the location of radio stations using goniometry, now known as direction finding. Major (later Colonel) Robert Loghry ran the Radio Section. When the United States entered the war, Loghry, a high-ranking Signal Corps enlisted man with extensive radio experience, was commissioned and sent to France from Alaska (someone, perhaps Russel, recognized that Loghry's radio knowledge exceeded that of any current Signal Corps officer). To analyze the signals collected by the Radio Section, the G2A6 Radio Intelligence Section broke codes and ciphers, read plaintext messages, interpreted direction-finding results, and reported this information to other G2 elements, particularly the Order of Battle Section. Hitt's friend and former pupil Major (later Colonel) Frank Moorman oversaw the G2A6. The Code Compilation Section (CCS), part of the AEF Signal Corps, was run by Captain (later Major) Howard R. Barnes, who had worked in the State Department's code office. As its name suggests, the CCS produced codes, primarily the trench codes used by the AEF. These three organizations worked closely together under the unofficial leadership of Moorman, and each of them was heavily influenced by Hitt. Hitt's role in making this three-part cryptologic organization work had a long-lasting impact on the postwar structure of army cryptology. At the time, the men running these organizations did not realize they were devising the principles of a future American cryptologic system; Hitt considered their work part of the routine duties of the Signal Corps.[35]

When Moorman took charge of the G2A6, he called on Hitt for advice and consulted with him on the design of the many blank forms needed for intercept operations. In March Hitt checked and commented on Moorman's "Instructions for Use of Code and Cipher in Armies and Lower Units" and his later "Use of Code and Cipher by A.E.F." Hitt, who had worked with the French on signals collection, helped Loghry plan Radio Section activities in the summer of 1917, visited the section's collection sites in the 1st Division's area in March 1918, and supervised collection efforts later in 1918. But Hitt was most involved with the Code Compilation Section. The development of codes and ciphers was a traditional Signal Corps concern and an area in which Hitt was highly skilled. The CCS built codes but did not assess the efficacy of codes or ciphers, so Hitt frequently performed that task. While he was working in Operations, he volunteered his thoughts about a simple substitution cipher submitted to the AEF adjutant general by the commander of the 9th Infantry, condemning the system as "worse than useless because it takes time to use and gives an entirely false idea of security to the user. Its use should be disapproved at once before something serious happens. Any messages sent in a cipher of this general character must be classed as DANGEROUS ENGLISH."[36]

Because of his expertise, Hitt sometimes developed cipher material for use in his own work. In April 1918 Major Sosthenes Behn was supervising the construction of telephone lines for the Signal Corps, so he and Hitt developed the Behn-Hitt code, a very simple system that substituted one English word or phrase for another, so "officer" became "switchboard" and "radio detachment" became "amplifier." Hitt also created a spelling code to disguise place names. There is no evidence that this system was used in any other capacity beyond communications between the two men.[37]

In the summer of 1917 Hitt had briefly managed the AEF's Code and Cipher Section, which was responsible for coding AEF message traffic. He also had an administrative role in the CCS, serving in loco parentis for the Signal Corps. He arranged for the section to work in a private room that could be locked at night for the sake of security. Hitt frequently consulted with CCS head Barnes and chipped in by developing some minor systems, such as a code used on the telephone and nicknamed the "female code" because it consisted of a female first name to designate a position (e.g., commander or chief of staff) and a surname to identify a unit.[38]

Hitt was a minor player in the American evaluation of the British Pletts's cipher device, invented by John St. Vincent Pletts of the British War Office's cryptologic organization MI1(b). He was probably present when Britain's Major Malcolm Hay and Captain Oswald Hitchings demonstrated the device to Moorman in early May 1918. "Neither Col. Hitt nor myself have been able to find a quick solution for messages enciphered by its use," Moorman reported to the G2. The device was concurrently analyzed in Washington and solved by William Friedman at Riverbank Laboratories. The AEF rejected the device and advised the British of its vulnerabilities in June.[39]

The extent of Hitt's influence on AEF codes is best illustrated by the test of the first American trench code. Trench codes were for front-line use and thus vulnerable to capture. Hitt, visiting the CCS in building A at Chaumont on May 17, was "appalled" by the new code's simplicity, and he rushed across the courtyard to building C to see Moorman. The two men devised a test for the code and picked Moorman's subordinate, J. Rives Childs, as their guinea pig. If Childs, who had almost no experience with codes, could break it, the code was not going to stop the Germans. The code was "superenciphered," meaning that a codebook was used to code messages, and then the code words were enciphered using a substitution table. Childs was given the codebook but received no information about the encipherment system. Hitt wanted to know whether the system was secure should the codebook be captured. Moorman and Hitt composed forty-four messages for Childs to break; he had the assistance of one of G2A6's field clerks.[40]

As they got to work, the clerk made frequency counts of the letters in the messages, and after just ninety minutes, the pair had identified the first letters of the cipher; three hours in, they had solved a word— "killed." It took them five hours to recover the cipher alphabet and another five hours to break the messages and type them up. The trench code had been broken, "to the consternation of the code section and the great satisfaction" of Moorman and Hitt. Herbert O. Yardley twisted the truth when he wrote about this event in *The American Black Chamber*, claiming that Childs "induced" his superiors to intercept American coded messages, solved the code in hours, and found that the messages revealed the disposition of troops in the Saint-Mihiel salient and the start time for that operation. The test had nothing to do with intercepting American radio traffic or the still-to-come Saint-Mihiel operation.[41]

Meanwhile, Barnes did not wait for the test to finish. Alarmed by Hitt's initial reaction and abrupt departure from the CCS office, his team reexamined the code and decided that the system was too difficult to use at the front, whatever the outcome of the test. Hitt's quick action thus led to the development of the Potomac code, the first of the River trench code series issued in late June 1918. When the British tested the Potomac code, they reported, "We have not been able to solve them or even to get any light. The security appears of a high order." Hitt complimented the CCS on its work and informed Russel, "We believe that this code system will be better than anything now in use on either side, and that messages intelligently sent will be perfectly safe."[42]

In September 1918 the American high-power radio transmitter at Bordeaux, dubbed Radio Lafayette, was nearly complete. Barnes consulted with Hitt, and they agreed that a secure code—a problem Hitt had examined earlier in the year—was still needed for AEF transatlantic communications. Barnes was prepared to have the CCS work on the code when he learned of Military Intelligence Code Number 5, which had been issued in July. Without seeing the code, Hitt and Barnes agreed that it should solve the problem. But in mid-November, after examining the new code and finding it inadequate, Barnes approached Russel and proposed that the CCS prepare a proper replacement for the War Department Telegraphic Code of 1915. Russel, after a lengthy discussion with Hitt, agreed, and work began in December, with Hitt assisting. Hitt's illness in February 1919 briefly delayed its completion, but on April 1 the code was finished; it became the War Department Telegraphic Code of 1919 and was eventually issued in September 1921. Barnes profusely thanked Hitt for his assistance, his "unflagging industry," and his "never-failing courtesy," which had lightened Barnes's load. Barnes's final tribute to Hitt hints at how strongly his ideas influenced the CCS: "to him more than to any other officer of the American Army is due whatever success the American codes may have obtained."[43]

Perhaps the most important meeting for the future of army cryptology took place on a street in Chaumont on July 12, 1918. Second Lieutenant William F. Friedman, who would become the most famed American cryptologist of the twentieth century for his theoretical and practical work before and during World War II, had just arrived in France from Riverbank Laboratories to work in G2A6. Parker Hitt was Friedman's idol. He had learned about military ciphers from Hitt's *Manual* and had used the book to train military students at Riverbank. Hitt knew of Friedman by reputation through his contact with Fabyan and Van Deman. On July 12 Friedman was out with his friend Lieutenant Edwin Woellner when he spotted Hitt walking down the street with a colonel. He immediately went up to Hitt and introduced himself. "Well, I am indeed very glad to meet you and to see that you are here. I have heard a great deal about you," said Hitt. Friedman, flustered by the "very tall" man who "towered above" him, told Hitt he had brought some messages and a package (a box of candy) from Genevieve. Hitt again expressed his delight at meeting Friedman as the men parted. Friedman delivered the package to Hitt's office "at the first opportunity," but Hitt was away observing the Aisne-Marne offensive. They did not meet again until after the war.[44]

The AEF's cobbled-together cryptologic organization resembled a modern matrix-managed system. Against all odds, it worked well. The American radio intelligence effort took advice and supplies from its British and French allies without rancor, in contrast to the disagreements Pershing and his staff had with Allied commands regarding doctrine and methods. The three commanders—Moorman, Loghry, and Barnes— had a good rapport and communicated well, surmounting any issues of cross-organizational management. The obscure and mysterious nature of the work prevented too much outside interference from superior officers. But it was Parker Hitt who tied these men together. Moorman had been his pupil at Leavenworth, and he likely knew Loghry, who had been in a signal company at the same post. Barnes was an outsider to these army veterans, but he fit in and sought their advice and guidance. Working in the background and semiofficially, Hitt made this machine work.[45]

Back in the United States, Genevieve was happy to be away from her "pet aversion," Fort Sill. Though the Hitts had a house in San Antonio, she moved into quarters 18 on the Infantry Post at Fort Sam Houston. Genevieve had a monthly allotment from Hitt's pay and received an occasional check from sales of "the toy" (the Hitt-Brown rule). In March 1918 post officials began to evict families of officers serving overseas; Hitt was confident Genevieve could handle the situation, writing, "I feel reasonably safe about you these days. You seem to be so perfectly able to take care of yourself . . . and you have the little house if there is no place else left to lay your darling head." Genevieve enjoyed investing in real estate and bought other houses in 1918. When Hitt returned a power of attorney to her, he remarked, "It looks as if a Philadelphia lawyer had drawn it up but possibly it was only a Texas one. I seem to have signed away everything I have or am ever going to have but I trust you to do the right thing by me and leave me my tobacco money." Hitt suggested using the profits from the Hitt-Brown rule to pay off one of the houses, but he was happy to leave the decision to his wife, for "that is your business to run the family financial affairs." Genevieve had demonstrated an aptitude for managing the family finances from the early days of their marriage. Parker—whether at home or at war—expressed no preconceived ideas about which gender should manage money and was happy to leave the tedious paperwork to her.[46]

While at Fort Sam Houston, Genevieve met Captain Dwight D. Eisenhower and his wife, Mamie, who lived nearby in quarters 17H. Because Genevieve was the wife of a higher-ranking officer assigned to the post, Mamie would have paid a formal social call on her. Mrs. Eisenhower almost certainly knew Genevieve's sister Tot, for Mamie's family, the Douds, had wintered in San Antonio for many years, and the women had common acquaintances. The Eisenhowers' first son, Doud Dwight (Ikky), was born September 24, 1917; as the Eisenhowers did not leave Fort Sam Houston until February 1918, Genevieve was a presence during his infanthood.[47]

Genevieve may have been unaware that she was the first woman to do cipher work for the government, and when America entered the war, other women joined in the task. Riverbank Laboratories, which employed a substantial number of women in its Department of Ciphers, began working for the MID and the Department of Justice in 1917; Fabyan told Van Deman, "Women are particularly adapted to this kind of work." MI-8 in Washington hired at least twelve women for cryptanalytic jobs by the spring of 1918, and the US Navy used "yeomanettes" in its Code and Signal Section. Although women were a significant factor in government cryptologic efforts on the home front, this was not true in the AEF. Elizebeth Friedman and Genevieve Hitt never worked in France, despite some unofficial speculation on the subject. In August 1918 William Friedman overheard an officer named Van Horn speaking with Moorman about women and code breaking; specifically, he wanted to know whether Mrs. Hitt was working in G2A6. Despite widespread agreement that women—or at least certain women—might be usefully employed for cryptology, the AEF never attempted to do so.[48]

By August 1, 1917, the Southern Department's Intelligence Office at Fort Sam Houston was routinely sending Genevieve intercepted enciphered messages to work on at home. At first, the messages were routed to her with a penciled note, but by the end of August, the process became more formal, and her address was typed on each message. In late August she remarked to her mother-in-law, "Here we are, Parker and I, spending the best years of our lives fighting the Dammed [sic] Huns." She was not getting paid and acknowledged, "It is not worth a pay check."[49]

Genevieve was not sitting at home fretting and deciphering messages. She had a busy social life and often engaged in flirtations with officers passing through on their way to France. Hitt knew "fairly well about all your coming and goings," and Genevieve had his "heartiest support in keeping the post gossips supplied with material." Hitt knew that flirting was fun and commented, "[I] used to do it myself." He wrote, "It covers up that real love affair with the man in France who adores you and would like to eat you up this minute." Genevieve was in demand as a chaperone at military dances, and a parade of young officers who knew the Hitts clustered around the "glamor girl," seeking attention and advice.[50]

Notable among this group was Captain (soon Major) Walton Walker; years later, he would be commanding general of the Eighth Army in Korea. As a fellow Texan who knew Eisenhower (and perhaps Hitt) from Mexican border service, Walker probably met Genevieve through the Eisenhowers or perhaps her sister Tot. Genevieve became "Buddy" Walker's confidante and adviser, and the younger man fell in love with her. From the time they met until his departure for France, Walker brought Genevieve his "thoughts, disasters, hopes and discouragements," and he felt as comfortable talking to her as he did confiding in his best friend "Gee" Gerow. When he left for France, Walker told Genevieve he would "lay a DSC [Distinguished Service Cross] in your lap." This was a flirtation that had gone too far, but there is no indication they were lovers. Genevieve did not answer the letters Walker wrote from France. In 1919 Walker sent her copies of two commendations he had received for his combat service, and the accompanying letter wondered at the silence of the woman "to whom I've given the love of a kid and a man." Walker finally realized, after many unanswered letters, that Genevieve "[didn't] want to hear from me, that you aren't interested in me, and that you won't write to me." He sent his love to Tot and Mary Lue and concluded, "Know, Genevieve, that now as always, I love you."[51]

Mary Lue, who turned five in 1917, was "just like Parker in every way," down to her walk, but she laughed like her grandmother Hitt. Genevieve and Parker had a shared point of view on child raising: "we stand together on things, and you can not have discipline if you do not." The couple's views included having young Mary Lue address them as Gee Gee and Parker rather than Mother and Father. With Parker away at war, Mary Lue was "far from an angel child," but she was sweet and affectionate. She enjoyed post life and charmed the bachelor officers, who gave her rides on their backs while pretending to be wild ponies. Genevieve employed both a nurse-housekeeper and a cook to look after their needs.[52]

Because she had household help, Genevieve was able to accept an offer of full-time work in the Alien Enemy Section of the Southern Department's Intelligence Office at the end of April 1918. Major Robert L. Barnes, the department's intelligence officer, hired her for a position variously titled code clerk or cryptographer. Though she mostly coded and decoded army messages, Genevieve also broke messages intercepted by radio or by the postal censorship office. It was a short walk from her home to the ground-floor offices on the east side of the post's Quadrangle, where peacocks roamed the area. She worked five and a half days per week (Saturdays from 9:00 a.m. to 1:00 p.m.), and there was plenty of overtime. Genevieve earned $85 a month ($1,000 per year); she was determined to spend her pay on a Liberty Bond, despite Parker's wish that she spend the money on herself.[53]

Genevieve traveled to Washington in May 1918 for meetings at MID headquarters; it was a four-day train ride each way. She received "quite a welcome," noting that "everyone was lovely to me from the Chief [Yardley] on down." During her stay, she demonstrated Hitt's sliding strip device to Yardley and proposed that it be used for emergency encipherment of communications between San Antonio and Mexico City because the codebooks had been compromised. Yardley refused, adamant that a new codebook with an "unbreakable enciphering system" would soon be available. While in Washington, Genevieve had a "very long conference" with Dr. Edith Rickert, one of the women working in MI-8. Rickert told Genevieve about Lothar Witzke, who, using the name Pablo Waberski, had been arrested at the Mexican border near Nogales, Arizona, on February 1. Witzke claimed to be a Russian American returning to San Francisco, but sewn into the left sleeve of his jacket was a 424-letter cryptogram that, when broken by MI-8 on May 18, revealed that Witzke was a German agent. Rickert explained that she, not John M. Manly (Yardley's deputy) or Yardley, had broken the message. Rickert and Manly traveled to Witzke's trial at Fort Sam Houston later in the year and visited Genevieve there. After the trial, Robert Altendorf, the military intelligence agent who had brought Witzke to San Antonio, reportedly gave Genevieve Witzke's pearl-handled revolver.[54]

Bemused by the circumstances in which she found herself, Genevieve told Parker's mother, "It is all so foreign to my training, to my family's old-fashioned notions about what and where a woman's place in this world is, etc., yet none of these things seem to shock the family now." The war necessitated a loosening of strict gender roles for gently bred middle- and upper-middle-class women. Genevieve perceived the change in her expectations and feared "I will never be contented to sit down with out something to do, even when this war is over and we are all home again." She imagined Parker would be both pleased and amused to hear that she was doing "a man's size job."[55]

Parker was pleased and amused, but he was also solicitous of Genevieve's health and well-being. Her letter from Washington prompted him to joke that she would soon be the chief of staff of the Southern Department. He had been puzzled after receiving a telegram about the commutation of quarters, but her letter made the situation clear and he wrote, "You are evidently holding quarters again, probably in your own name. Good work, old girl!" Parker bragged of Genevieve's work to his envious colleagues, who thought it "splendid that you are able to handle your own office and many officers have said they wished their wives had the energy and ability to do something instead of loafing and worrying about their perfectly safe husbands." Walker, who had arrived in France and saw Hitt on July 2, was very interested to hear news of Genevieve and sent his love via Parker, who reported, "Walker said you had neglected him." Genevieve's efforts caused Fabyan to modify his view of her abilities; he directed William Friedman to "give my compliments to Colonel Hitt and tell him that Mrs. Hitt is doing damn good work in the Southern Department and she is entitled to a lot of credit for it. It has been a long, hard, tiresome drag and I think she has won out."[56]

Genevieve enjoyed her job, but after six months with only three Saturday afternoons off, she was tired, and the novelty of office work had worn off. She complained that the "atmosphere of this office is not what I have lived in all my life, and I do not think it has improved my disposition at all." The influenza epidemic struck Fort Sam Houston in early October 1918; Mary Lue did not get ill, but Genevieve did. She was "so afraid for a while that I *wouldn't* die I did not know what to do." Aware that her family needed her, she called in a female osteopath who gave her two "rubbings," after which she "was up and going." As the end of the war approached, Genevieve decided she could stop working without being considered a slacker. "I am glad I stayed it out, but I am so tired I will gladly quit."[57]

Barnes had recommended Genevieve for promotion to an annual salary of $1,140 in September 1918, for she had "performed her duties most faithfully and efficiently." The promotion was meant to take effect on October 1, but the paperwork was lost and had to be resubmitted, and by the time it was straightened out on November 25, Genevieve was already gone. She left her job in mid-November, resigning "as soon as the Armistice was signed as she did not want to stand in the way of other clerks when the necessary dismissals would be considered."[58]

While Genevieve was making her wartime contribution in Texas, Parker's military career was advancing. For a year he had been promised a Signal Corps job, and on July 14, 1918, it finally became official: Hitt was CSO of First Army. He was "at last cut loose from GHQ with a real job . . . Russel has been to visit, has given me a wonderful staff and everything I asked for." Though excited about his new position, he took time to write to Mary Lue, telling her, "I have not forgotten your sixth birthday and I would send you a present if I was not at the war."[59]

6

Chief Signal Officer

If anyone had told me at Leavenworth that someday I would
be in charge of the battle communications from the Argonne to
the Moselle I would have thought him crazy. But today I am
and so far, am getting away with it.

Parker Hitt, 1918

The Americans prepared for battle. Pershing, determined to have the American Expeditionary Forces (AEF) fight as a national unit rather than subordinate to the French or British army, wanted the first American-run offensive to be against the Saint-Mihiel salient. After heated discussion, Allied Supreme Commander Ferdinand Foch and French Army Commander in Chief Pétain allowed Pershing to proceed at Saint-Mihiel, on the condition that American forces would fight on the Meuse-Argonne front two weeks later.

Major Bruce Wedgwood, Hitt's new executive officer, found him at French VI Army headquarters at La Ferté-sous-Jouarre on July 28, as the Second Battle of the Marne was winding down. The men ordered supplies and supervised the installation of telephone equipment before returning to Chaumont. Hitt was "a work machine, running from eight in the morning to midnight and sleeping like a baby the rest of the night," conscious that he was responsible for all communications forward "to the barbed wire" of the front. US First Army was officially formed on August 10, a few weeks before Hitt's fortieth birthday. Two days later, trucks lined up in the courtyard of AEF headquarters in Chaumont before dawn to collect office equipment. As the sun rose, the staff climbed into waiting automobiles to travel the thirty-five miles to First Army headquarters at Neufchâteau.[1]

Army communications followed a specific pecking order in the years leading up to World War I. The preferred method was wire—telegraph, buzzer, or telephone—followed by visual—flags, heliograph, or night lamp. Radio, not yet a mature technology, was next in the hierarchy. Other, less technological options filled out the Signal Corps' repertoire: human messengers (on foot, horseback, motorcycle, bicycle, automobile, or "flying machine") or pigeons could be used to get messages through. In theory, radio's advantage was that it required no physical connection between two locations and did not endanger any personnel. But "wireless" did not yet provide telephone-like voice communication; instead, like the telegraph, it used Morse code. Radio antennas broadcast in all directions, making transmissions vulnerable to interception by adversaries, so messages had to be encrypted—slowly, by hand—before being sent. The disadvantages of radio were clear to commanders, who preferred the immediacy of a telephone call.[2]

The telephone was thus a critical tool for planning operations and a crucial method of battlefield communication. But phone installation was supply-, time-, and labor-intensive, for as the army moved, poles had to be erected and wires strung before individual users were connected to the network. And telephone lines did not have an unlimited capacity. When telephone lines at headquarters became congested in August 1918, Hitt refused to put time limits on calls and instead established more circuits by stringing more wire. He advised First Army command that the "only immediate remedy is in the hands of the users," and he suggested sending telegrams whenever possible to cut down on phone calls, for "every second you can save is a second for someone who may need the line badly." A month later, Hitt still believed that officers were using telephones as a convenience rather than a necessity, jamming the lines when the "judicious use of the telegraph" or a courier would suffice. He threatened to take drastic action by cutting off telephone service except for operations and intelligence, which had been the French practice at the start of active operations. Every wire he installed depleted an "extremely limited" supply, and Hitt wanted to reserve equipment for the battles ahead. First Army never had adequate telephone capacity: during both the Saint-Mihiel and Meuse-Argonne operations, Hitt denied commanders' requests for additional telephone wire and directed them to use radios instead, protecting the wire supply for critical long-distance communications. The supply problem had security ramifications. Telephone communications were not as easily intercepted as radio transmissions, but the telephone wire was vulnerable to shelling; radios were less vulnerable to shelling (except for a direct hit), but radio communications were easily overheard by the enemy. Although Hitt was concerned about the security of communications, he knew there were occasions when the use of radios made logistical sense.[3]

Hitt shared his plans in a "personal and confidential" letter to his mentor, AEF chief signal officer (CSO) Russel, and took advantage of the fact that he was Russel's "one chick," the lone army CSO. He asked that the boundary of the zone of advance be adjusted north to a line through Bar-le-Duc–Ligny–Void–Toul–Nancy; this would allow the 407th Telegraph Battalion, an AEF asset under Russel's command, to prepare the rear. First Army signal units could then work north of the line, freeing corps and division signal organizations to prepare for battle. Splitting the effort in this way was efficient, but it diverged from normal Signal Corps practice and doctrine; this presaged changes made after the war ended. Hitt warned Russel that he was stocking two forward depots with material and pleaded, "When the requisitions begin to pour in please do not think I have gone crazy."[4]

Code names, used in communications to mask the identity of American units, received little centralized attention before Hitt took charge. Divisions devised their own confusing, duplicative, and insecure naming systems. American units often used towns and cities from their home states as code names, making it easy for German radio intelligence personnel to identify them. For example, the 32nd Division (composed of men from Michigan and Wisconsin) used Detroit, Battle Creek, Milwaukee, and Green Bay as code names. Hitt halted the disorder in mid-August by assigning each corps and division either a one-letter or two-letter designation for its exclusive use in composing code names. Division signal officers devised their lists of code names and sent them to Hitt a week later; these lists took effect when First Army assumed tactical command of the corps. Hitt urged that care be taken not to duplicate code names within a unit, and he forbade the use of geographic names and female first names—the former because they could be confused with actual locations, and the latter because female names were already used in the AEF telephone code. Hitt's system was praised as "the most expeditious and the only one that will eliminate duplications of the code names used by the different divisions and corps."[5]

When Hitt became CSO of First Army, he had already decided to use female telephone operators on the army headquarters switchboard for "maximum efficiency." He requested six operators, and competition for the positions was fierce; one woman complained, "We were all just dying for a chance to go up forward and the mean things would let only six of us go." Hitt had been working with the women since their arrival in France, and his "sweet young things" had acclimated to "regular military discipline" by late April 1918. Hitt enjoyed their company; he attended a "merry little dance" at the operators' house in the spring, and although he did not dance, he found it "refreshing to hear U.S. talk from somebody with skirts on." Parker assured Genevieve, "I shall not lose my heart over any of them but am very likely to go out there whenever invited." Hitt's admiration for the operators came from both his understanding of the intellectual and organizational capabilities of women—learned firsthand from watching his mother with her committees and Genevieve's success at the Southern Department—and his personal command philosophy of comradeship and cooperation. He maintained a solicitous concern for their well-being while they were under his command. Though some of the operators thought Suzanne Prevot was Hitt's "particular friend," Parker remained devoted to Genevieve, despite his flirtatious nature.[6]

On August 19, while official channels were still churning with his request, Hitt penciled a "secret order" for chief operator Grace Banker, Ester Fresnel, and Suzanne Prevot. "Kiss your happy home goodbye and get ready for a roving life," he told them, for "with luck," they would be with First Army by August 26 or 27. That left one week to prepare: Hitt told them to acquire helmets and sent them to George Gibbs for the new American-type gas masks, which allowed the wearer to talk. "When you get the masks, learn how to put them on and wear them," Hitt ordered. He also advised them to obtain "regular soldier mess kits" and directed them to "bring all your worldly goods . . . I will send a truck to Chaumont for your things and a car for you." Several days later, still waiting for a decision, Hitt met with Banker to go over his plans. On August 26 Banker, Fresnel, Prevot, Helen E. Hill, Berthe M. Hunt, and Marie Lange were ordered to First Army headquarters in Neufchâteau, arriving the day before the organization moved thirty-six miles northwest to Ligny-en-Barrois. Julia Russell, the "fearless" woman who ran the YWCA in Chaumont and supervised the telephone operators' house there, accompanied them and arranged for their quarters in Ligny. The "living reminders" of the previous tenants made the first night there "exceeding[ly] interesting, if sleepless," but "stern sanitary measures next day obliterated the unwelcome pests and the billet became habitable."[7]

First Army had two battalions of signal troops, each with about 500 men; most of them were volunteers from American communications companies such as Bell Telephone and Western Electric. They began to build telephone lines between army headquarters in Ligny and the cities of Void, Toul, and Saizerais just two weeks before the planned attack in the Saint-Mihiel salient. With the roads clear of traffic and supplies nearby, construction averaged four to five miles per day; as the roads became jammed and supplies more distant, construction fell to one to two miles a day. Hitt's radio officer, Captain George C. Pratt, a Western Electric employee, set up radio stations at Ligny on August 28 and at Toul on August 29. These stations remained silent until the assault began on September 12, to prevent German direction finding from "locat[ing] the units of our Army."[8]

Ligny's location was a difficult one in the French signal plan. The town was situated along a boundary between French II and VIII Armies and was completely cut off from II Army's telephone system. Long-distance lines in Ligny were controlled by the French second line, apart from three independent circuits that ran to Bar-le-Duc, French VIII Army in Toul, and the city of Toul. Complicating matters, the fortress commander in Toul, not French VIII Army, controlled all other phone lines into that city. The area occupied by American forces north of the road between Ligny and Toul had no telephone circuits at all. Hitt had two weeks to take over existing French circuits and adapt them to American requirements, take control of all available circuits between Ligny and Toul, and build more telephone lines. Though construction began "as energetically as the arrival of material would permit," by September 5, Hitt knew he needed six to ten additional circuits, more than could be built in the next week.[9]

On September 7 Hitt convened a meeting at Ligny between the French and American signal organizations and presented his requirement for more circuits to Colonels Fatout and Gaston Tongas of French General Headquarters. Lieutenant Colonel Becq (French II Army's signal officer) and Major Torquebue (French VIII Army's signal officer) spoke in support of Hitt's request. Together, the group painstakingly reviewed the status of every telephone circuit in the area. It took three hours, but Hitt succeeded in extracting nine additional circuits from the French, running along three different routes between Ligny and Toul. It was a "slender foundation" of communications to support the Saint-Mihiel operation, but it was sufficient. The conference also "cleared the atmosphere" between the French and American signal officers, enhancing their ability to work together in the months ahead.[10]

Four telephone switchboards were set up at headquarters to manage the telephone lines. The female operators ran the main operations board, which controlled two lines from each corps headquarters. Three other switchboards—one each for the Air Service, Army Artillery, and French Mission—used male operators. Telegraph communications were handled from a trailer until a larger system could be moved into the main signal office. The Pigeon Service had twenty cotes—fourteen American and six French—connected by telephone to the units employing the birds.[11]

After an extended period of preparation and coordination with Colonel Willey Howell, head of First Army's Intelligence Section (G2), Hitt took over AEF Signal Corps' radio intercept, direction finding, and listening stations in the First Army area on September 1. Hitt understood the significance of the intelligence derived from signal collection, the differences between the types of collection stations, and the principles of their work. He provided technical, administrative, and material support for the intelligence mission and received intercept reports. The radio intelligence effort, jointly managed by Hitt and Howell, made a key contribution in the lead-up to the American attack on the Saint-Mihiel salient. A week before "D-day," airplane reconnaissance and prisoner debriefing indicated that the Germans were preparing a withdrawal from the salient. The signal collectors and analysts in the field, at Ligny, and at G2A6 in Chaumont worked to support or refute this conclusion, knowing that intelligence would influence Pershing's decisions about the attack. Weeks of monitoring German radio traffic revealed changes in messages, including an increase in some types of coded messages. Listening to German communications near the front line, intercept operators identified different voices, new accents, and speakers who seemed unfamiliar with the area—an indication of fresh troops. Along the southern side of the salient, German operators were increasingly nervous, afraid of a surprise attack, and their stations moved back slightly from the front line. German radio stations usually moved a day or more before a withdrawal, but on September 11, the day before the planned American attack, direction-finding analysis found the stations holding their positions. Lieutenant Charles H. Matz, trained by Frank Moorman to lead Howell's First Army G2A6, prepared a map; it was the only direct intelligence that showed the Germans were still in place.[12]

Howell brought the map to the First Army staff meeting on the afternoon of September 11. Hitt, promoted that day to full colonel, was there; his Radio Section believed the Germans had not yet withdrawn. Pershing was "urged by almost every one present to call off the attack, as the terrific artillery barrages which were scheduled were likely to result in only a needless waste of ammunition"; it would be easier to take the salient once the German forces were gone. One dissenter was Colonel George C. Marshall (then assigned to First Army chief of staff Hugh Drum), who privately appealed to Pershing to precede the attack with an artillery barrage. Howell presented the overwhelming radio intelligence evidence showing that three lines of German radio stations were still in place; his argument helped convince the group that the attack should proceed as planned. The bombardment began at 1:00 a.m. on September 12, and the attack commenced four hours later. It was successful: by the evening of September 13, American troops controlled most of the salient. Though some German units were preparing to withdraw, most were still present. Approximately 4,500 Americans died during the Saint-Mihiel offensive, and 2,500 men were wounded; had the attacked proceeded without preparatory artillery fire, many more might have been lost. The value of radio intelligence as a battlefield tool was proved at Saint-Mihiel. The combined Signal Corps–G2 system had worked.[13]

For the Signal Corps, most of the work related to the battle involved preparation. Hitt and his officers, sitting in Ligny twenty-five miles from the front, were not sure how much telephone traffic to expect once the attack began. On September 8 the switchboards had been at their limits; volume began to drop off the next day, and by the morning of September 12, as American forces pushed forward, the number of calls was "quite insignificant." Urgent front-line communications traveled on local, lower-echelon lines; although the staff could hear the guns booming, the signal office in Ligny was quiet. Assuming that calls would swamp the switchboard that first evening, Hitt had put the female operators on the night shift, "with the idea that the men operators, who had been handling the night shift, would not be able to handle the rush of business." But there were no calls all night, followed by "one of the quietest mornings the First Army ever knew"; no one had time to call headquarters as the battle raged. On September 14, however, calls began to pick up, and for the next week, the switchboard was busier than in the period before the battle. Units then began the forty-mile move to the next front. Hitt found that the "curve of telephone business" demonstrated at Saint-Mihiel held true during the Meuse-Argonne operation.[14]

Hitt, Suzanne Prevot, and Helen Hill traveled to the liberated city of Saint-Mihiel on September 14 in Hitt's black Cadillac with his faithful chauffeur, Loyal Bunnell, at the wheel. "The poor civils who have lived there for four years, 2000 of them, were wild with joy. You never saw such a sight." That night there was a party in Ligny celebrating Hitt's promotion. A few days later, Hitt was walking through town with Pershing when the pair spotted three female telephone operators; they crossed the street to speak with the women. When Pershing wondered whether "they were happy so near the front," the women insisted they were and said they "wanted to be nearer." Pershing, convinced of their dedication, directed Hitt to "take them where they want to go." Hitt, of course, had already planned to do so.[15]

On September 20 First Army headquarters moved to Souilly, a small town on the French Voie Sacrée (sacred way), just south of the line where

American troops were massed for the impending Meuse-Argonne offensive. The town had been General Pétain's command post during the 1916 Verdun operation, and First Army took charge of a sea of hard-used French wooden barracks north of town. Hitt's office (dubbed the "sacred precincts" by the telephone operators) was set up at one end of a long building; at the other end were the operators' living quarters. The offices were separated from the quarters by the telephone exchange and a common mess. When his schedule allowed, Hitt demonstrated his collegial leadership style by sitting at the head of the long table where his officers and the telephone operators ate their meals family style. Captain George D. Beaumont, First Army's telegraph officer, remembered that he "worked hard" under Hitt and his assistant Sosthenes Behn at Souilly, "but with these two officers, looking after our interests, the way they did, it was a pleasure to work hard, and we were glad to do it." The enlisted men, too, were fond of Hitt; Private Weiklin, who worked in one of the supply depots, told his parents that he had "many pleasant chats" with Hitt.[16]

Radio deception—sending false radio messages to mislead an adversary—had been a minor part of the Belfort ruse, an operation run in August and early September to make the German army think the upcoming American attack would come in the Belfort sector rather than at the Saint-Mihiel salient. It seems that Hitt did not take part in the Belfort effort, but he was deeply involved with planning and implementing an operation that took place just after the Saint-Mihiel offensive. The Lorraine deception focused on the territory near the cities of Nancy and Lunéville and intended to slow the movement of German reserves to the Meuse-Argonne front. Pershing, Drum, Howell, and Hitt planned the operation during a First Army conference in Ligny. On September 18 Hitt ordered a radio network installed east of Nancy to make the Germans believe that an American corps had moved there. The radio effort was accompanied by diversionary tank maneuvers. German observers almost immediately remarked on increased air and artillery activity in the region.[17]

The rapid move north and west from the Saint-Mihiel salient to the start line for the Meuse-Argonne offensive was logistically difficult for the AEF, and the Signal Corps was no exception. Under pressure to move, units did not have time to recover wire and equipment, and they arrived at the new front without the necessary gear. Telephone wire remained a critical and scarce resource; Hitt calculated that an army consisting of three corps needed a minimum daily supply of 2,500 miles of twisted pair wire of varying composition and gauges, depending on where and how it would be used. In addition to wire, hundreds of pounds of tape, hundreds of dry batteries (of two distinct types), telephones, switchboards, telegraph instruments, and radio equipment were required to keep communications running. Hitt took over telephone lines from French II Army about a week before the operation began, but they were "far from being up to our standard," and the control center had to be shifted from Laheycourt to Souilly. A single switchboard was not big enough to handle all the traffic. The operations board, run by the six female telephone operators, handled lines to the corps and back to Ligny, all G2 and G3 business, and communications for the commander in chief and chief of staff. A commandeered French switchboard provided direct lines to hospitals, ammunition dumps, railheads, supply, and G1 and G4. Switchboards for artillery communications and the Air Service were installed in their respective headquarters. A separate telegraph trailer had dedicated lines for each corps. Hitt was also responsible for pigeon lofts installed along the line of departure, the Meteorological Service, and the Photographic Service. As he had before the Saint-Mihiel offensive, Hitt asked Russel to take over signal activity south of a line through Ligny and Toul; this allowed Hitt to put all First Army signal troops (apart from a small supply depot detachment at Toul) into the battle area.[18]

In the days before the Meuse-Argonne operation, the telegraph battalions set poles and strung wire. Their best rate of advance was ten miles per day with 300 men on the job, but on average, 250 men could construct four to six miles of line per day. By September 26, the day the American attack began, the central army communications axis was within a mile of the front line. Setting up poles and wire was difficult and dangerous in combat conditions. After the first attack, 250 men, "working practically day and night to the limit of their endurance," spent four days carefully picking their way across the former no-man's-land to the abandoned German first position. Over the course of the war, Signal Corps casualties were second only to those of the Infantry. Though Hitt's command included a radio company, he took pride in knowing that First Army radio stations "never sent an official message except that announcing the armistice and that was merely to give it the widest publicity." After November 11, 1918, when uncoded messages were allowed, "the increase in the use of the radio was very remarkable." The Radio Section moved radio collection and direction-finding stations to the new front, installing direction-finding gear in three trucks that could move forward as the line advanced. Listening stations were attached to the French Colonial Corps and 35th and 79th Divisions, but this technique, developed during a period of little operational movement, proved ineffective as the front line changed quickly.[19]

There were short pauses in activity during the forty-seven-day Meuse-Argonne offensive. By November 1, when the third phase of the battle began, First Army's signal units had constructed two additional axes of communication that reached to within a few miles of the line between Grandpré and Brieulles. Hitt admitted that this could not have been done "against a determined enemy with heavy artillery, but it was well that we did so in view of the tremendous jump ahead in the few days following" the new attack. Persistent supply problems frustrated Hitt. Many divisions, often those in combat for the first time, "did not appreciate the value of Signal Corps material" and left equipment in the field. This meant that Hitt's men had to completely reequip these divisions each time they returned to the rear; Hitt identified the 35th and 79th Divisions as particular offenders.[20]

The telephone operators tried to make life at headquarters as enjoyable as possible; they held frequent celebrations, and the officers often joined in the fun. But the party held on Sunday, October 20, during a lull in the battle was especially important. Everyone worked to prepare a special dinner to celebrate the upcoming birthdays of Bruce Wedgwood, "Tootsie" Fresnel, Marie Lang, and Grace Banker. Wedgwood went to Paris searching for special delicacies, and Berthe Hunt "begged" some yellow flowers from a nearby French barracks. Menu cards, with a "little verse" specific to each individual, were drawn up. Hitt supplied signal flags for decoration. Hunt borrowed a cook from the French aviation camp. The meal included fruit—fresh, not dried—celery, nuts, lobster salad, caviar, "roast potatoes, roast goose with stuffing and mushroom sauce and cauliflower," cheese, and cakes, all served on an assortment of dishes and tin plates. And there was champagne. In a photograph commemorating the happy event, Hitt sits at the far right; in the center hangs a "wire dome with eight lights"—constructed by men of the signal battalion—decorated with signal flags and celery greens. Though a hard rain fell all day, everyone had a wonderful time.[21]

A new radio deception operation cooked up by Howell, Hitt, and Matz began on October 23. A dummy radio network, manned by Radio Section personnel as if they were a mythical "X Army," sprang up along the front from Beaumont to Fresnes, east of Verdun. Matz played the role of army commander in chief; his assistant in First Army's Radio Intelligence Section, Lieutenant John A. Graham, was christened the chief of troop movements. Their work succeeded: two German divisions were held in reserve rather than being sent to the front lines because they were fooled into thinking that the AEF planned to attack in the other direction.[22]

Near noon on October 30, disaster struck at Souilly. Whether an accident or an act of sabotage by a German prisoner working as an orderly, a stove overturned in the wooden barracks occupied by the G2. The fire ignited nearby Signal Corps buildings, including the telegraph office, Hitt's office, the mess, the building containing the telephone switchboard (where it had been moved just days before), and the recently improved telephone operators' quarters. Hitt immediately directed efforts to extinguish the fire, while Behn told the operators to grab whatever they could from their quarters. The operators on duty remained at the switchboard until Hitt ordered them out so the engineers could save the board from destruction. Once the fire was extinguished, Hitt made sure everyone was safe and then ordered the 401st Telegraph Battalion from the front to Souilly. Within a few hours, the switchboard and the telegraph office were up and running in temporary quarters; full service was restored, and Hitt's team was ready to support the next phase of the battle. The fire destroyed not only the official records of First Army's signal office but also Hitt's personal papers and his wooden sliding strip cipher device. First Army's G2A6, run by Matz, was apparently not disrupted by the fire; nor was the work of the Radio Section intercept facilities, which were located some distance away from regular operations to avoid electronic interference.[23]

Momentum was with the AEF; on November 5 Drum asked Hitt to recommend the best location for a new First Army headquarters, based on available communication lines. Drum expected to move from Souilly on November 9 or 10. Hitt proposed Chatel-Chéhéry, northwest of Exermont, and hurried there to make preliminary arrangements. He was back in Souilly on November 6 as American troops reached the bluffs over the Meuse River near Brandeville and found themselves under friendly fire from 5th Division artillery. Acting First Army chief of staff George C. Marshall worked quickly to stop the inadvertent attack and placed a call to the chief of artillery. But the phone line was busy, and the switchboard operator refused to override the connection, unaware that Marshall had the authority to do so. Frustrated, Marshall asked to be connected to Hitt instead and told him to run to artillery headquarters and deliver the order in person. Hitt did so. The upset telephone operator immediately called and apologized to Marshall; she later visited his office "to learn in person how much damage her action might have caused."[24]

The move to Chatel Chehery never happened. The armistice took effect on November 11, 1918, halting the shooting and the movement of troops. The war appeared to be over, but the armistice was a truce, not a treaty, and the AEF had to be prepared to resume hostilities if the temporary peace failed. Hitt spent ten days "wandering around Longwy and Conflans" in mid-November, which persuaded him that the war was "entirely over and done with." He buckled down to prepare his final reports and took a break to write to his father. Hitt firmly believed the United States was now "a real world power . . . in spite of anything we may do," and he declared the country "must not fall back into that disgraceful attitude of mind of 1916." He admitted, "Frankly, I would rather fight the war than write the report," but now that the war was "done and over with, we must fix up the material for the hysterical research cranks to paw over in after years."[25]

Hitt's wartime experience convinced him that battle communications were an art rather than a science—too complicated to have fixed rules or formulas. He advised future signal officers to make the most of what they had, economize, and "somehow, some way, provide the means of command." The relationship between the army's CSO and the signal officers for each corps was not one of command, he thought, but one of cooperation, "friends, all bent on achieving the same military end"; this was the approach he took within his own command.[26]

Lapses of blunt honesty punctuated Hitt's reputation for wisdom and tact. He sometimes employed language considered too harsh for formal army communications; he was not always deferential and sometimes appeared to be a know-it-all. Hitt's exasperation with inefficiency and his occasional tendency to use acerbic phrasing had gotten him in trouble before, and late in the war he ruffled Russel's feathers by commenting that the "thick veil of secrecy surrounding the photographic work" was "not conducive to stimulating an interest in the output." Russel was Hitt's mentor and greatest admirer, but he was also keen on the Photographic Service and thought the criticism unwarranted; he could not help but snap back. While admitting his "unfortunate" choice of phrase, Hitt did not back down on his complaint.[27]

Hitt was "thin and not altogether in as good shape as I could wish," and he hoped to go home before too long. As soon as he could, he dashed to Paris to buy a doll for Mary Lue, "the cutest French thing I ever saw . . . although it may not appeal to Mary Lue's sense of beauty," as well as a "little remembrance" for Mary Lue's mother. Genevieve had finally had a photograph taken in October but had not yet mailed it to him; Hitt mused that he would soon be home, "and then I shall love you to death instead of just looking at your picture." Alternatively, he suggested that he might get a position that allowed him to settle down in a French town, and Genevieve could come to stay. This was wishful thinking, and he knew it.

France was both unsettled and expensive, and the AEF was unlikely to assign Hitt to a permanent location.[28]

First Army moved to Bar-sur-Aube on November 25, 1918, where Hitt expected to get some rest and return to "soldierly shape." During his downtime, he worked on an "important lecture" about the Signal Corps' performance in recent operations. He spent Thanksgiving with his officers, the telephone operators, and Julia Russell; they enjoyed a festive meal of olives, cream of celery soup, turkey, chicken salad, mashed potatoes, cauliflower, pumpkin pie, cheese, raisins, nuts, and coffee. A Christmas box from Genevieve, full of much-appreciated "goodies and sweet things," reached Parker early in the new year. Hitt's future was unclear; officers of the regular army were not supposed to leave Europe, but many were going home. The quiet holiday interlude ended when Hitt was sent (in Russel's place) to the Interallied Radiotelegraphic Conference; he hoped this would lead to a more permanent position and told Genevieve it might "mean that we can have our flat in Paris soon." General Russel also wanted Hitt in Tours to help with the Signal Corps' "special services"—the Radio Section, the Photographic Section, and the pigeons—and Hitt suspected this would be his fate when First Army disbanded. His hopes of returning to the United States dimmed, as did the idea that he could stay in one place; he knew the Signal Corps would be needed until the very end "because the last two members of the AEF will want to talk to each other over the phone just before their transports sail."[29]

Understandably, the long separation caused by the war took a toll on the Hitts' marriage. During his absence, Parker missed three of Genevieve's birthdays, three of their anniversaries, and two of Mary Lue's birthdays. Consequently, the time between the armistice and Parker's return to the United States in July 1919 was a difficult one for the couple. Without work to keep her mind occupied, Genevieve was depressed and hated the world. She was particularly bothered when other wives received more mail from their husbands than she did. "I write when I can and you must not be too hard on me dearest," Parker responded. He explained that he was "one of the few men who has personally had more than he could do for the past two months," and he found it "hard to be compared with the gentlemen letter writers of our AEF who have to find something to do." Hitt traveled 600 miles by car one week in January, "over the same old roads that no longer are interesting to write about." It took time to shut things down, and "everybody is ready to drop everything and beat it for the US but it can't be done that way." Parker still nurtured the hope that Genevieve could come to France, perhaps once the Peace Conference was over. In some ways, he missed the war; if it had kept up, "it would have kept down the chorus of 'when do we go home.'" Hitt reported that he had a cold, but he hoped Genevieve was "at least keeping warm and a little bit contented these trying days, even if I am not."[30]

Genevieve was also concerned that Hitt would lose rank and be bumped back to captain. Parker assured her it would not happen, explaining, "We need the money too badly and you will find that I have lots more fun out of life as a colonel." He told her if "anyone hands me any stars, I will grab at them—for the same reason. I hate money but we have to have it to get along." It was difficult to cheer Genevieve from the other side of the ocean, but Hitt tried. "Please get over the blues, my dear, and be a soldier with the rest of us. I know it isn't easy for you . . . but the war isn't over yet—by a whole lot—for us regulars. It is absolutely impossible for me to even think of going back now except sick and I don't want that."[31]

In late January 1919 Genevieve abruptly moved to New York City, where she initially planned to stay "for months and months." Perhaps she had tired of life on an army post, where other women's husbands were returning from France. Parker learned of the move on February 11 when he received her formal change-of-address card. He had no clue whether she had left Mary Lue in Texas or taken her to New York. Just a few weeks later, Genevieve, her sister Tot, and Mary Lue moved to Winchester, Virginia. Parker carefully couched his puzzlement and wished her well, hoping she would find the change "delightful" and asking to be kept informed of her whereabouts. Genevieve expected Parker back from France imminently, but he chided her about that "funny idea" and told her he might be away until August. Another letter from Genevieve apparently shed more light on her moves, but that letter does not survive, and Parker's reply is mysterious. He wrote, "Your second reason for leaving San Antonio is a bit remarkable. Be careful about *trying* to hide anything no matter what, if the proper people want to know in the proper way." Hitt hurried to fix problems with his payroll allotments to Genevieve, which had been missed in January and February. "You know I would not wittingly starve you to death," he wrote, though he was "still at sea about why you picked out Winchester, sight unseen, but you will probably let me know." By May, Genevieve had become disenchanted with Winchester and was back in Midtown Manhattan with Mary Lue.[32]

Hitt had his own struggles in February. He was not feeling well and had lost so much weight that his clothes hung on him. A persistent cold (perhaps influenza) had gotten worse with his constant travel; he no longer enjoyed visiting "cold and expensive" Paris. Hitt stayed in bed one Sunday to see if that would help, but it only made his cough worse. His illness slowed the work of the Code Compilation Section, which he was assisting with the new code for transatlantic communications.[33]

On February 11 (the same day he received Genevieve's change-of-address card) Hitt attended the last First Army conference, held at Montigny-le-Roi, east of Chaumont. Drum "wound it up in a blaze of glory that took the edge off of much that had looked like severe criticizm [sic] before." But the war was not over. Back in Bar-sur-Aube, after a long drive from the conference, he penned a note to Genevieve. "Here is a formal card announcing my residence for the time being," he mildly rebuked his wife; he signed off by wishing that he could be with her in New York, but without his usual endearments. Hitt wanted to go home, and he was a bit miffed that Russel had just ordered Alvin Voris, CSO of Third Army, back to the United States. Voris had been having an affair, and Russel expressed his disapproval by sending him back to his wife. When Hitt learned of Voris's fate, he joked to Genevieve, "Look out, I may start something at any moment" so Russel would send him home to her.[34]

Hitt's bad week only got worse. On February 12, while traveling from Bar-sur-Aube to Paris, his car (driven by Bunnell) hit a young woman. Obscured from view by a passing goods wagon, she had run into the street, crossed in front of Hitt's Cadillac, and then inexplicably turned back to recross the road. Hitt, riding in the front seat, bundled the woman into the car, and Bunnell drove them to a nearby military hospital, where she was given first aid and then transferred to a local hospital for treatment of a compound fracture of her left leg and head injuries.[35]

Drum finally insisted that Hitt take leave at the end of February, his first time off in nearly two years. Two weeks on the French Riviera put him "quite on my feet again." Bunnell drove him to Nice in the Cadillac, but the car, "after being such a wonder during the war," broke down and needed expensive repairs. Hitt enjoyed the sunshine and had time to see the sights on the Italian border. Upon his return, he attended a "gorgeous motor and horse show" put on to entertain the troops. Baseball and rifle shooting competitions were beginning, and he thought he might participate in the shooting match to kill time. Hitt's leave in the sun had restored his mood; he was once again able to work at full power "without wanting to lie down, mentally and physically." Laurance Hitt was sent home in February, and Parker was glad to hear it, telling their mother, "The

Army is not his métier: he did not begin early enough with habits of self discipline, if I may put it that way."[36]

Hitt returned to the grind of travel, and the third week of March was the "most strenuous weeks of 'after the war.'" He was in Paris on Sunday, March 16; Le Mans on Monday; Paris again on Tuesday; and Bar-sur-Aube on Wednesday. He spent Thursday and Friday on an inspection trip and at a conference with new Third Army CSO Colonel Irving Carr, traveling from Bar-sur-Aube to Coblenz via Trier. An urgent telegram reached him in Coblenz, directing him back to Chaumont, where, on Sunday, March 23, Hitt and his First Army comrades Generals Hunter Liggett and Hugh Drum, Colonels John L. Dewitt and Willey Howell, and Lieutenant Colonel Sosthenes Behn received the Distinguished Service Medal from Pershing. After the ceremony, he went back to Germany and had little news for Genevieve other than tales of the "bad roads of France and the good roads of Germany" and the delight of staying in a steam-heated hotel.[37]

Apart from shutting down First Army's signal business, Hitt was in demand for "other duties as assigned." "I have to take these extra jobs on just to keep from being absolutely idle," he explained to Genevieve. His January assignment to the Interallied Radiotelegraphic Conference was testimony to Hitt's technological knowledge and skill; it is telling that the AEF still did not have a regular Signal Corps officer it could trust with this critical assignment. The group met for a few days at a time at irregular intervals in Paris, which added to Hitt's travels. In March he joined a board on Allied radio telegraphy services, part of a subcommission on economic treaties of the Peace Conference. April found him "busy as a bird dog" with committee work, which, he believed, was "better than sitting at Bar-sur-Aube waiting for something to happen." In early April Hitt met with French CSO Colonel Ferrié; he was back to Paris in the middle of the month for the radio conference and remarked, "We have done a really enormous amount of work and I think we are entitled to some compliments for it." In May he went to Paris twice for meetings. It was seventeen hours from Coblenz to Paris by train; the car trip was shorter—only twelve hours—but still "no picnic." He arrived just after noon on May 17 "and had to go direct to the Commission meeting without anything but a sandwich picked up at the hotel. We sat until nearly eight o'clock." By the time the meeting finished, the stores had closed, foiling Hitt's intention to buy Genevieve a birthday present. He promised her a special birthday next year.[38]

On April 8 Hitt received "a most complimentary assignment" to serve on Pershing's board to study the lessons of the war "with reference to tactics and organization"—the so-called Superior Board or Organization Board. Some consider it "the most significant military committee to meet in Europe after the war." It was chaired by Major General Joseph T. Dickman; Hitt and Colonel George R. Spaulding (First Army's chief of engineers), chosen for their technical expertise, were the only non–general officers in the group. The board reviewed the findings of a multitude of committees that had examined the AEF experience and considered the operation of infantry divisions. After their first meeting in Chaumont on April 21, Hitt declared, "We have a large proposition on our hands but the thing will be worth while and is sure to make a professional reputation for all the members of the board if it is well done." He was less sanguine after a week of meetings in Trier in May, for the board was "moving a bit slowly but it is moving." There had been "a lot of thinking and talking and a little very valuable writing," as well as a decision on the report's format and underlying principles. But the group had yet "to study the subsidiary boards and see how they fit our scheme." Another week of work was scheduled for the middle of June, and Hitt was sure the group would be finished by July 1.[39]

Hitt most certainly wrote the Signal Corps' section of the report, which declared communications "absolutely vital to military success" and praised the "brilliant work done by individual officers and organizations" but concluded that the system was "makeshift" and needed improvement. Though the corps had gotten the job done by using initiative to mold material and organizations to the situation, Hitt knew the AEF had suffered from a lack of supplies, technology, and training. Board recommendations influenced a later change to Signal Corps doctrine by making the Infantry and Artillery responsible for their own communications from division level to the front line; the Signal Corps would no longer control communications to the barbed wire, to the displeasure of CSO George O. Squier. Whatever the hopes of Superior Board members, their report was not a great success. Pershing disagreed with their conclusions, believing they had been overly influenced by wartime operations. He held the report for a year before forwarding it to the War Department.[40]

Hitt had thought long and hard about the Signal Corps' problems after the armistice and before his Superior Board service. Russel had summoned him for a "personal conference" in November 1918, and Hitt remarked that Russel "takes my advice and views more readily than those of anyone in the Signal Corps." For his part, Russel hoped to convince

Hitt to help him reorganize the corps and clean out the "dead wood." Hitt believed "the old Signal Corps is as dead as a door nail and has got to go if we are going to keep things moving after the war," and he thought the "fighting Signal Corps" would be the ones to reform the service; however, he cautioned that "Generals Squier and [Charles M.] Saltzman are strong in Washington and not inclined to do anything for those who have been 'over here.'" Russel made Hitt an attractive offer, but in the end, he was not disposed to make the move; "the Infantry or the Machine Gun game may be the better games," he mused, though "a decision as to what to do in the future is not an easy one to arrive at." Genevieve was "positively disgusted" with the Signal Corps, which had promoted George Gibbs and William "Billy" Mitchell (both career Signal Corps officers) to brigadier general and bypassed Hitt; she told her mother-in-law that another officer had shared the opinion that, "as usual Hitt is holding the bag for the Signal Corps."[41]

In May 1919 Hitt prepared an assessment for Russel, touching on the many ways he thought the larger Signal Corps could be improved; this was probably done in concert with his Superior Board work. Hitt believed that moving the AEF's CSO from Chaumont to Tours had been a mistake, calling it a "grave error" to consider signals a supply department. The "highly successful system" in First Army, where Hitt served as technical adviser to the army chief of staff and staff officers, was the model to emulate, not the "more or less unsatisfactory" situation in the divisions, where the CSO reported to the G1 or G3. It was "absolutely vital" to the success of operations that communications be laid and maintained, even at the expense of other traffic on the roads; Hitt pointed out that the army plan for the Meuse-Argonne had given the Signal Corps the right-of-way, but individual division orders had not. The slow progress of signal construction before the battle was, however, "more or less inevitable," given the number of divisions that had to move at great speed from the Saint-Mihiel salient.[42]

Hitt fought against the institutionalization of complacency, for he knew the army needed to learn from the mistakes of the war. One of his pet peeves was the difficulty of getting commanders and staff officers to use codes and ciphers. Even if this was a function of the message center, "it will always be necessary for commanders and staff officers to understand and use these accessories to secrecy." The solution was education, and according to Hitt, the G5 had not assisted the Signal Corps sufficiently "in this most important matter." Hitt was also frustrated with the Motor Transport Section, which did not understand the Signal Corps' work and its requirements. It was bad enough that the signal units' vehicles had been taken away upon their arrival in France, but when they tried to obtain more transportation, they found it "common practice to issue one 5-ton truck when a requisition called for five 1-ton trucks, because the tonnage was the same." Hitt thought this a "perfectly ridiculous condition," noting that "it would have been as sensible for the Ordnance Department to issue one 12-inch gun when the requisition called for four 3-inch guns."[43]

Third Army was created in early November, and by mid-December 1918, it was headquartered in Coblenz, Germany. Hitt's old traveling companion Alvin Voris was Third Army's first CSO, but after he was sent home in disgrace in February 1919, Colonel Irving Carr took the job. When Carr became ill almost immediately and returned to the United States, Hitt replaced him on April 20. Hitt was a good soldier and extremely conscientious, but he probably wondered once again why he, who had been in the first group to arrive in France, had to stay, while Carr, who had arrived much later, was allowed to leave. He was beginning to believe that he might end up as CSO of the entire AEF in a few months, when everyone else was gone. Hitt, however, was uniquely qualified to accomplish some important tasks. In May 1919 he turned an informal discussion with the deputy signal officer of the British Army of the Rhine into a formal proposal for code and cipher communications between the two national forces. Hitt suggested that messages from the Americans to the British first be sent to the British Mission at Third Army headquarters to be enciphered using British systems; messages from the British to the Americans would likewise be sent to the American Mission at Cologne to be coded or enciphered using American systems before transmission to the recipient.[44]

The Allies planned a combined advance from the Rhine to Berlin should the Germans be reluctant to sign the peace treaty. Hitt, examining the route American forces would take to advance through Montauber, realized that the telephone lines along the way could carry only two circuits; he proposed an alternative route via Limburg that had a better communications infrastructure. The French army had "strenuous objections" to changing the route, but Hitt prevailed, and Third Army's zone of advance eventually included Limburg. Hitt later stressed the importance of the CSO having detailed information about wire lines, including route maps and circuit diagrams, to properly advise his commander. "A real communication plan can be drawn up in advance and the Command Posts definitely located" if the right sort of information was available.[45]

Despite these satisfying tasks, serving as CSO in occupied Germany did not compare to serving as CSO in battle. The job was more akin to commanding a large peacetime organization. The Signal Corps ran the AEF Courier Service, and from his first to his last day in Coblenz, Hitt had to deal with a variety of complaints and problems surrounding it. These included couriers carrying bulky packages containing German helmets and even typewriters (they were supposed to handle only official first-class mail); an indiscreet chaplain, on courier duty to Berlin, who regaled a commander with stories about his visits to dance halls and theaters (officially off-limits); and a drunk officer who made profane and insulting remarks to passersby on the Unter den Linden. One of Hitt's more pleasurable administrative jobs was obtaining authorization for telephone operators Banker and Prevot to wear the Victory Medal Service Ribbon. These annoying administrative issues might have driven Hitt crazy had he not been constantly on the move between Coblenz, Chaumont, Trier, Bar-sur-Aube, and Paris for his work on various boards and committees and other consultations.[46]

Things were winding down by early June; Parker told Genevieve that he might be able to sail on July 1, "as soon as the organization board completes its work." Hitt might have come home sooner, for Russel was finally willing to release him in mid-June, but he stayed on and finished his work with the board. His only excitement was a trip to Trier, where advance general headquarters closed down amid "loud howls from the multitude of hangers on, [as] I removed ninety-one telephones in one morning." Hitt was "glad, in a way, to close out this Signal job. It has been wonderful but I am getting to the stage where I never want to see a telephone again. We are too much 'jacks of all trades' in the Army to stick to anything very long."[47]

Another unexpected assignment came his way when, at the end of May, Hitt participated in Major General James W. McAndrew's War College Planning Conference in Trier. McAndrew was to be commandant of the college and was selecting his faculty; nineteen of the chosen twenty-four had been stationed in France and Germany, and Hitt was surprised to be one of them. He thought the "caliber of this group is perhaps best shown by the fact that nine of the officers held temporary general officer rank during the war." He told Genevieve that he felt "all swelled up on myself to be in a crowd like that, especially when the *students* are considered"; he remarked to his mother that it was "some assignment for a man who hasn't even been to the Line School!" Hitt was especially pleased that he would soon be able to give Genevieve an idea of when he would be home and where they would live. His detail to the War College became official on June 14, and he was relieved from duty with Third Army on June 20, giving him time to wind up his work with the Superior Board.[48]

Hitt wrote to Genevieve, "General [John L.] Hines and I will have to put some days in with the Third Army on its move forward" if the Germans did not sign the peace treaty, but he still hoped to be home for their eighth wedding anniversary on July 17. On June 29, the day after the Treaty of Versailles was signed, he believed he could leave immediately after the Superior Board's report was completed, on July 6 or 7. He now hoped to be in New York between July 18 and 25, "unless something entirely unforeseen comes up."[49]

Once the board had finished its work and signed its report, Hitt hurriedly left Trier for Coblenz, where he packed and sent his baggage off to Brest. He told Genevieve that he would cable his brother Rodney's office to let her know when he would arrive in New York. Three boxes of war relics, "which I detest but which were wished on me by friends," were already waiting for him at Hoboken, including a machine gun, a range-finder, and "a lot of other boche stuff," but he assured Genevieve they would be able to give it all away. "It certainly will be good to be home with you once more, sweetheart," he wrote. "I shall probably be worthless for a while but I shall do my best to get back to a fair compromise of work and play, if you will only play with me. Kiss my baby for me and tell her I am coming soon. I adore you." Hitt departed Coblenz on July 9 and arrived in Brest on July 13, ready to go home.[50]

Parker Hitt had the proverbial "good war," suffering only a slight concussion in early June 1918. He spent more than two years in France, where he played a significant role in the development of army code making and signal collection. He worked hard and did exceptional work. But his name is rarely mentioned in histories of the war or in the recollections of senior officers, and the work of the AEF Signal Corps is similarly neglected. Hitt's wartime efficiency reports—written by Generals Edgar Russel, Fox Conner, Hugh Drum, Malin Craig, and Joseph Dickman—were uniformly excellent and superior. Russel called him "simply invaluable . . . displaying in the highest degree foresight, energy and tact." According to Conner, Hitt was "superior in all categories including capacity for command." Drum, who had known Hitt since their Leavenworth days, thought him "the best Army Signal Officer I know," for he was "capable, energetic, painstaking and well-educated in his profession." Hitt was "progressive, very active, tactful and thoroughly able and conscientious," in Craig's judgment, and Dickman thought Hitt was "able and zealous." Russel's July 1919 letter of appreciation praised Hitt for his "labor and your loyalty, devotion, and talents," which made the AEF's signal work a success; the write-up for Hitt's Distinguished Service Medal noted his "sound judgment and untiring efforts." Hitt was named an *officier* of the *Légion d'honneur*, France's highest order of merit for military or civilian achievement.[51]

Hitt's reputation for professional courtesy and generosity solidified during the war. Unlike many of his peers in similar levels of command, however, he was not promoted to general officer, despite Pershing's recommendation at the end of September 1918 and again at the end of December 1918. Had the war continued until early 1919, he would have been promoted. Any hopes Hitt had of commanding troops, though, were dashed by Pershing's evaluation at the end of September, which declared him "fitted for duty with troops but better in staff duty." Hitt expressed no disappointment in his circumstances or discouragement about his failure to obtain rank.[52]

Few were "over there" longer than Hitt, who traveled with Pershing at the end of May 1917 and did not see the United States again until the RMS *Aquitania* arrived in New York Harbor on July 20, 1919. Genevieve and Mary Lue were waiting for him on the docks. He had been away for two years, one month, and twenty-seven days.

7

Jack-of-All-Trades

There is no other officer known who has sufficient
understanding of all the matters relative to the transmission
of information, etc., and also the military education to be
able to relieve Lt. Col. Hitt as a member of this Section.

LeRoy Eltinge, 1918

The technical expertise that made Hitt such a valuable commodity during the war earned him a teaching position at the Army War College. He was flattered by the assignment, and it gave him a reason to resist Edgar Russel's plea for him to transfer to the Signal Corps. But postwar fatigue and work on the General Staff affected the forward progression of his career: Hitt began to drift, not row (in juxtaposition to his old college motto "row, not drift").[1]

While in France, Hitt rose from a captain in the regular army to a colonel in the national army. Once the war was over, Hitt, like most returning officers, reverted to his highest rank in the peacetime army: he was now a forty-one-year-old major. Parker, Genevieve, and Mary Lue had a few weeks to get reacquainted before reporting to Washington Barracks in mid-August. They probably visited the Hitt family in Indianapolis. Hitt had lost weight while in France, and he looks tired in a photograph taken in July 1919, but when he reported to Washington, he weighed 185 pounds, 5 pounds heavier than when he sailed on the *Baltic* in May 1917. With a return to regular exercise and military drills, he dropped 15 pounds in the next year.[2]

General Pershing arrived by train at Washington's Union Station on September 12, the anniversary of the Saint-Mihiel offensive; the ceremony and reception offered some closure to Hitt and the other officers of First Army and the General Staff who greeted their commander and witnessed a seventeen-gun salute. It was hard for Hitt to adjust to being home after the excitement of the war. He sometimes felt blue; he got slightly "homesick" when he saw the telephone operators "tripping into the picture" in the AEF films he reviewed at the college. It comforted him to know that the films were in the vault if he needed cheering up.[3]

At the confluence of the Potomac and Anacostia Rivers on Greenleaf Point, Washington Barracks stood where an earthen fort and solitary cannon had protected the city in the early 1790s. On the west side of the post lay Washington Channel, created as part of the massive Army Corps of Engineers project to drain and reshape the marshy land in the 1890s. The post had many roles over the years, and it had changed considerably since Hitt's 1899 commissioning exam. In 1919 the War College was the post's primary tenant. The Hitt family settled into quarters 30B on the east side, awaiting the arrival of the 4,000 pounds of household goods coming from San Antonio and Genevieve's New York hideaway. Hitt's bedding roll, which had traveled with him on the *Aquitania,* had to be chased down and arrived in Washington in October. The three boxes of gifted "war prizes" were misplaced in Hoboken and finally turned up in December.[4]

An imposing granite, limestone, and brick building at the southern tip of the post housed the War College; a flight of stairs led to a large, vaulted rotunda. After an orientation to the General Staff, the students studied (and solved) problems related to intelligence, operations, supply, and training. The faculty presided over conferences run by parliamentary procedure. Lectures took place in the mornings, and afternoons were reserved for independent work; Wednesday afternoons and Sundays were free time. In the spring and early summer there were staff rides, war games, "and reconnaissance of strategic areas." Social life was not neglected. Army officers and their wives were expected to make "first calls" when they arrived on post, and the college mess hosted frequent dinner dances and informal hops. Tennis, golf, and horseback riding were available to fill any leisure hours, and Washington culture and society were just a short electric streetcar ride away.[5]

Hitt, still recuperating from his years at war, did not demonstrate his usual verve that autumn. It is unclear how many lectures he presented, but he probably gave his talk on AEF Signal Corps operations. At the end of 1919 McAndrew gave him only an "average" evaluation, although he noted that Hitt was an "excellent officer of good judgment and common sense." It was the lowest rating of his career.[6]

The college did not occupy all his time. In late 1919 Hitt participated peripherally in a test of a printing telegraph cipher device designed by Gilbert Vernam at the American Telephone and Telegraph Company (AT&T). The test was organized on behalf of the Signal Corps and the Military Intelligence Division (MID) by Hitt's old teacher and friend Joseph Mauborgne, and it was carried out at George Fabyan's Riverbank Laboratories, where

William and Elizebeth Friedman examined the cipher. Although Hitt corresponded with Fabyan during the test and may have suggested some methods of exploitation, William Friedman broke the cipher without substantial input from Hitt. Hitt later congratulated Fabyan on Riverbank's success and asked him to "please give my kindest regards to Friedman and tell him that we are very proud of his work."[7]

That fall, Fabyan reprised his 1917 offer and invited Genevieve and Mary Lue to stay at Riverbank while Hitt was in Washington, suggesting that he would "adopt Mary Lue" and Hitt could "go down and pound the hell out of those damn Mexicans without being worried where your family is." There was no chance of Fabyan separating Hitt from his family, although Mary Lue enjoyed the short musical cipher puzzle (composed by Elizebeth Friedman) Fabyan had sent to entertain her.[8]

Hitt always had time for those who had served with him in France, and he went out of his way to aid his First Army family. In December 1919 he obtained a pier pass for Suzanne Prevot's mother so that she could meet her daughter's ship. Prevot, the "wild cat of First Army signals," thanked him and noted, "One could expect nothing else from our Col. Hitt." When Captain John L. Carney, who had been in charge of First Army's pigeon lofts, told Hitt that he was having difficulty getting credit for his battlefield service, Hitt quickly wrote a detailed account of Carney's role, apparently from memory. He apologized to Carney for issuing only verbal orders and thus creating the paperwork problem. Hitt also wrote a recommendation for Captain Mark J. Ryan; Ryan had served in the Code Compilation Section and desired to do the same work in the United States.[9]

After more than two years apart, Parker and Genevieve wanted to spend some time together and took a ten-day trip to Havana, Cuba, in December. The couple stayed with Sosthenes Behn and his brother Hernand and enjoyed the amenities at El Habana Yacht Club's Casa Club Playa de Marianao. Parker likely took Genevieve to see the site of Camp Columbia, where he had been stationed over the winter of 1898–1899. Sun, good friends, and the high life were welcome balms and helped blunt the annoyance the Hitts felt when Prohibition began on January 17, 1920. Hitt, who had a tradition of writing letters on New Year's Day, told Fabyan that the Cuba trip had been "most satisfactory," though he joked that it might have been "just a trifle too lurid for staid Genevieve who is now recovering from the effects of having her champagne ration cut off too suddenly. She hopes to be able to write to you tomorrow but it may be a bit unintelligible as she is talking something about 'diamonds, cut or uncut' just now."[10]

Early in 1920 Hitt, still an irrepressible inventor, sent the Signal Corps' Engineering and Research Division an idea for a device to automatically take signals from telegraph machines, transmit them over radio (rather than telegraph wire), and print the message on a telegraph machine at the receiving end. This was similar to AT&T's work in carrier telegraphy that was already under way; by 1922, the corporation had a system operating from coast to coast. Mauborgne thought Hitt's idea had merit and asked him to conduct experiments in the Signal Corps laboratory. Although his duties at the War College were relatively light, Hitt may not have had the opportunity to work on his device; there is no evidence that he conducted experiments or developed his idea any further.[11]

The college sent Hitt on two investigatory trips in 1920—one in February to his old haunt, the Signal School at Fort Leavenworth, and the other in April to the new Signal School at Camp Alfred Vail (later Fort Monmouth), New Jersey. In late May the college class was divided into three sections for a three-week reconnaissance exercise in New York and Vermont. One group went to Fort Ethan Allen in Vermont, another to Plattsburgh Barracks (later Plattsburgh Air Force Base) in New York, and the third, including Hitt, to Watervliet Arsenal, near Albany, New York. Before the group left Washington, Hitt attempted to organize communications for the exercise in the form of three radio tractors from Camp Vail. McAndrew declined to sign the order for men and equipment, killing Hitt's plan. At the end of the academic year, as was customary for instructors who were not already graduates of the school, Hitt received a War College degree with the class of 1920.[12]

Genevieve was immersed in all things domestic. Her mother-in-law exclaimed, "What a wonder" she was, "with her ability to keep house, to make clothes and put up preserves, jams, jellies, pickles, etc. It quite takes my breath away to think of all the things she accomplishes." Elizabeth Hitt was not an idle woman, but she preferred business and committee work to housekeeping. Money was tight for most military families in Washington in 1920, particularly for men who had lost rank after the war. Hitt's income had gone from a full colonel's pay of $500 per month to a major's pay of $333 per month. In March Genevieve applied for a position as an abstractor in the Department of Justice's Bureau of Investigation (BOI). Abstractors indexed documents for the massive file system developed by J. Edgar Hoover, the young Justice Department lawyer who ran the BOI's Radical Division. It is possible that Genevieve was looking for something to occupy her time other than housework, but it seems more likely that, as the household's financial manager, she wanted to cover the salary shortfall. On April

20 Genevieve began working in Hoover's office at a salary of $1,200 per year, plus a $240 bonus for accepting the job. One hundred dollars a month did not close the gap, but it helped considerably. But at the end of June, with Parker's promotion to lieutenant colonel due on July 1, Genevieve quit, telling Hoover her duties at home prevented her from staying on. Her last day in the office was July 5.[13]

The day after Genevieve submitted her resignation, the Hitts moved into quarters 7, one of the houses built in 1905 on the west side of Washington Barracks. With twenty rooms, it was one of the largest houses on post, and the two-story rear porch overlooked Washington Channel and East Potomac Park. The spacious home was partially furnished with heavy mahogany furniture, and it even had a refrigerator; it was the most luxurious house the Hitts had ever lived in, and there was plenty of room to entertain. Genevieve reconnected with her friends from Fort Sam Houston, Dwight and Mamie Eisenhower, who were just a short train ride away at Camp Meade, Maryland. Genevieve made a "lovely birthday cake" for little Ikky's third birthday in September 1920. That fall, the Eisenhowers attended a weekend house party at the Hitts' "wonderful" new quarters and had a "dandy good time" playing bridge and socializing. During the party, Hitt issued mock "special orders," in proper military format, from "Headquarters Watchthescore" and signed by "Play Rubbers, Chief of Staff." The orders read: "By command of 'Generally BIDHIGH,'" Major "Hering" (almost certainly Charles D. Herron) was directed "to locate Mrs. Eisenhower and accompany her without undue delay to a point known as Table No. 2 and will proceed to engage opponents in auction Bridge." The party was the first time Parker had seen Ike (who had been promoted to major in July) since their time with the 19th Infantry on the Texas-Mexico border in 1916. During the long weekend, discussion likely touched on Eisenhower's 1919 transcontinental motor train and Hitt's wartime experiences; Ike, who had not been in France, surely wanted to hear Parker's war stories. It is easy to believe that Eisenhower learned something of Hitt's work with radio intelligence and codes and ciphers, but neither party kept a record of their conversation. If so, Eisenhower's education in signals intelligence started long before World War II. The two families saw a good deal of each other in 1920. Genevieve's mother, visiting from Texas, looked after Mary Lue and Ikky so the couples could attend a football game. New assignments for both officers outside of Washington would limit future social opportunities, but the bonds of friendship and the memories of fun times in San Antonio and Washington kept the families connected.[14]

Hitt was due for a change of station in August 1920 but asked to stay at the college, as he expected to be a section director in the next school year. After that, he hoped for an assignment with an infantry organization; other than commanding a company at Fort Sill, Hitt had not been with infantry troops since June 1911. Hitt was "strongly opposed" to taking a detail in the Signal Corps "under any circumstances," largely because of what he perceived as "dead wood" in the corps, which in 1920 was still being run by George O. Squier. Hitt's antipathy to Squier—who was, like Hitt, technologically innovative and forward-thinking—probably stemmed from discussions with Russel. In addition, Hitt almost certainly felt betrayed by Squier's October 1919 testimony to Congress, which intimated that the Signal Corps' wartime use of officers from other branches had been "an absolute failure." Hitt had been one of those officers, and he had trained many of the others. Whatever Squier's intent, Hitt interpreted it as a personal attack on his work. He believed that, despite his technical expertise, he would never get a fair shake in the postwar Signal Corps. Squier, despite his congressional testimony, valued Hitt's abilities and, in the fall of 1920, picked Hitt to serve as an adviser to the American commissioners attending the International Communications Conference in Washington. This did not change Hitt's view; he remained a loyal supporter of Russel. In a rare attempt to use his political connections, in March 1921 Hitt petitioned Senator Harry New to support Russel's appointment as chief signal officer (CSO), claiming that "a very real injustice will be done if he is passed over this time." But Squier was not dislodged from the position, and Russel, who was ill, soon retired.[15]

Genevieve and her mother-in-law, Elizabeth, exercised their newly won voting rights in the autumn of 1920. George Hitt filed Genevieve's registration papers, in absentia, in Indianapolis, the Hitts' home of record. Elizabeth registered "after much hesitation, her sense of duty having prevailed over her reluctance to have anything whatever to do with the suffrage for women." The elder Mrs. Hitt might have had no inclination to become involved in political affairs, but Genevieve and later Mary Lue reveled in politics.[16]

That year, Hitt took charge of the G1 course. At the end of 1920 he was put on the General Staff "eligible" list, and his efficiency rating was raised to "superior." His new boss, Colonel H. A. Smith, had known him for a dozen years and described Hitt as "a most industrious, painstaking, capable officer . . . a student of great capacity and wonderful retentive memory. Invaluable in research work." These qualities contributed to his selection for a detail with the General Staff, which, in Hitt's opinion, made him one of the "lucky ones."[17]

On January 31, 1921, Hitt began what is the most troublesome and controversial portion of his career. In his first assignment as a General Staff officer, Hitt became assistant chief of staff for military intelligence (G2) under the command of General Robert L. Bullard (whom Hitt knew from his days in the Philippines) in Second Corps Area headquarters in New York City. Stephen Fuqua tried to swap his Third Corps Area (Baltimore, Maryland) assignment with Hitt, but Hitt was unwilling to give up New York, even for a friend. Hitt received his orders with "much satisfaction" and told Bullard he had access to the MID in Washington, should anything be needed before he reported to New York. Precisely why Hitt was selected for this position is unknown, but he was a good fit, and not just because he was already assigned to the G2 and was known to General Dennis Nolan, chief of the MID. Lieutenant Colonel Hitt had a reputation for industriousness, intelligence, and good judgment, and he was socially comfortable in culturally complex situations. The family left their lovely house in Washington and moved to Fort Jay on Governors Island in New York Harbor, a short ferry ride from Lower Manhattan. They found it "delightful to live in this quiet place, ten minutes from the Battery and twenty from 42nd Street." Both of Hitt's brothers were nearby—Rodney worked in Manhattan and lived in Westchester County, and Laurance lived in the city. It was a wonderful opportunity for eight-year-old Mary Lue to get to know her father's family.[18]

After the war, the United States was beset by unrest and perceived threats from labor activists, Bolsheviks, and African Americans; the year 1919 was marked by race riots, strikes, and bombings. In September 1920 an explosion on Wall Street in front of the headquarters of J. P. Morgan—said to be the work of anticapitalists—killed 30 and injured 300. The blast was certainly heard at Second Corps Area headquarters, and troops from Governors Island responded to provide security for the nearby Treasury office; the need for intelligence must have been acutely felt by the corps area commander. Duties for military intelligence officers in corps areas were poorly defined, and the relationship between these officers and the MID in Washington was similarly unclear, creating an unfortunate situation for all involved. A hasty revision of a wartime pamphlet titled *Provisional Instructions for the Operations of the Military Intelligence Service in Corps Areas and Departments,* originally intended for field information officers, contained methods of investigating persons and organizations that might become involved in "domestic disorders." But these methods were not designed for peacetime, and they became and remain controversial.[19]

Hitt attempted to establish his organization, despite a lack of clear guidelines from Washington. He had only one assistant; the two men served as the main office and staff of both the Research Section and the War Plans Section. Hitt, "trying to fix the principle of the thing rather than an immediate practical application of the diagram," postulated a workflow where routine and daily work passed through the main office to the Research Section, which took what it needed to prepare information for the War Plans Section. War Plans, in turn, would suggest problems to the Research Section and keep war plans up to date. By separating routine day-to-day problems from real General Staff matters, he hoped "the former can, slowly but surely, atrophy where necessary and the latter can expand when Washington has developed the War Plans to the point where Corps Area Commanders can take a real interest in them." Hitt told the MID, "I think I am going to enjoy the work, as it is new to me and there are many elements of real interest in it." In February he had not yet received the revised pamphlet of instructions; while waiting for guidance, he chose to conduct research on war plans from a corps area standpoint as his first project, thinking it more important (though less urgent) than day-to-day intelligence gathering. Nolan's executive officer, Major James Lawton Collins, thought Hitt's plan was overkill for such a small office and assured him that instructions were on the way. Administrative matters and army bureaucracy frustrated the precise and efficient Hitt, who wrote to Collins complaining about the "cumbersome and extravagant system" of trying to obtain a "symbol number" so that financial matters for the office could be handled properly—a process that had taken more than a week and countless man hours and involved an expensive coded telegram (which arrived garbled). Coded telegrams from the MID, he found, caused trouble with the corps area's assistant adjutant, "a rather excitable young man" who had a way of stirring everybody up; to avoid the fuss, he asked Washington to send material by mail instead.[20]

The mission of this nascent domestic military intelligence effort was to surveil not just foreign interests but also those domestic organizations suspected of receiving support from hostile powers or threatening the stability of the US government. In 1920 General Marlborough Churchill, Ralph Van Deman's successor and Nolan's immediate predecessor at the MID, observed that "secret service methods carried on by military agencies cannot be justified in time of peace" and that such work during the "current unrest" required a "very sincere" effort to comply with the "spirit and letter of our laws as full as is possible." Churchill thought only three general classes of investigation should concern intelligence officers: disloyalty and sedition, enemy activity, and graft and fraud in War Department contracts. But in 1921, as the MID expanded its reach to the corps areas, Churchill's categories were stretched to their limits, and the MID began targeting American minorities. Soviet Russia, the ongoing Russian civil war, and the Communist Internationale were considered threats to the nation; many American Jews belonged to domestic factions associated with the Internationale and were therefore targets of investigation. Organizations campaigning for civil rights for African Americans were also perceived as domestic threats, and many leaders of this movement were similarly targeted.[21]

When Hitt received guidance from the MID, he did his best to satisfy Washington's requests. He implemented orders to surveil domestic organizations and individual citizens. This work was not limited to minorities and included the Industrial Workers of the World, a group Hitt had first encountered in Goldfield, Nevada, in 1907. In New York he was ideally positioned to supply Washington with books, pamphlets, and papers available only in that city, including Theodore Hertzl's *The Commonwealth of the Jews* and the weekly newspaper *Dos Yiddisher Folk*. The ever-frugal Hitt, whose office had limited funding, was always careful to request reimbursement from the MID for the books and subscriptions he procured. Budget issues plagued him throughout his tour, and by July, there was no money for investigations or newspaper subscriptions. Hitt's office also handled the MID allotments that paid the salaries of some of the employees of Herbert O. Yardley's "Black Chamber," operating in Manhattan under cover of a private code-making company. When one employee's salary was not included in the April allotment, Hitt intervened and took the money from his own accounts to pay the man; he then requested reimbursement from Washington. Hitt apparently had no personal association with Yardley while in New York.[22]

In addition to domestic surveillance, a good deal of Hitt's intelligence work involved the activities of foreign nations. He personally gathered information at social events and tasked the BOI's New York office to conduct subsequent surveillance. At an event in April, Hitt met a group connected with American businesses in Cuba; they believed the United States would soon have to intervene against the growing nationalism on the island. Most of the people at the event did not want to talk about politics, but Hitt was able to gather some tidbits about the New York branch of the Cuban Banco Nacional, which he passed directly to Nolan. Hitt's grace, tact, and congeniality undoubtedly made him successful at this work. Washington also needed intelligence on Japan, a growing economic and military power with a desire to control Asia. Hitt frequently received information on Japanese sources of copper from Claude T. Rice, a reporter for the *Wall Street Journal*. Rice's editor was not happy about this, but Rice considered himself at "perfect liberty" to help the army, as he was violating no confidences and was not helping a competing news agency. "What the managing editor does not know will not hurt him," Rice said, and he arranged to meet Hitt outside the financial district in the evenings, on his own time. Hitt directed other inquiries into Japanese business interests, including an investigation into whether Joseph F. Starr of the Starr-Arnell Company was actually a "consulting engineer for the Japanese government, Army, Navy, and Imperial Dockyards."[23]

On August 9 John W. Hartfield, a manufacturer of codes, informed Hitt that a man named Harris (possibly a former employee of the State Department's Code Section) had offered to sell Hartfield a government code for $5,000; apparently, Harris had already tried to sell the code to J. P. Morgan and the Guarantee Trust Company. The next day, Hitt arranged for a BOI agent to surveil Hartfield's meeting with Harris, where they learned the code consisted of a single typed sheet in a small black book or folder. Hitt then supplied Hartfield with an address (belonging to a sergeant in the MID) and had him inform Harris that an agent of a foreign government wanted to meet him there the next day. A BOI agent waited at the address at the appointed time to negotiate with Harris, but the man did not appear. Hitt concluded that Harris did not want to sell the code to a foreigner, and he turned the matter over to the State Department.[24]

Hitt made several trips to Washington during his New York assignment and attended the first dinner of the Baltic Society on May 28, 1921, celebrating the fourth anniversary of the sailing of Pershing's staff. He combined that pleasurable event with a visit to the MID office. Just a few days later, he served as an usher at Sosthenes Behn's wedding in Philadelphia. He visited the MID again at the end of June. Due to a period of rapid command turnover at Fort Jay, Hitt received three evaluations between January 31 and August 24, 1921; he was uniformly rated superior and was described as "one of the best-equipped staff officers in the service" and "an able and experienced officer of the highest professional attainments." Hitt's reputation for excellent staff work was solidly established at this point, and he would have a tough time shaking off administrative jobs in the future. He maintained his reputation as a jack-of-all-trades, a quality that put him in demand but did not aid his advancement in the army.[25]

Hitt's six months of MID service should be neither minimized nor exaggerated. In hindsight, the army's monitoring of domestic minority groups was an infringement of civil rights. Time has also uncovered the extent of racism and anti-Semitism in the army. Hitt, a freethinking, principled man with broad experience, apparently did not share these views; his greatest prejudices were against inefficiency and incompetence.[26]

In July the General Staff ordered Hitt back to Washington as an instructor; there is no indication that the move was due to a request on Hitt's part or any dissatisfaction with his work at the MID. Though he disliked having to move again, he thought it "a real compliment" to be recalled. The Hitt family departed Fort Jay on August 24, and he returned to duty at the War College the next day. This short detail in military intelligence now garners Hitt more attention from historians than any other part of his noncryptologic career. Once again, happenstance made the man famous for something outside his area of expertise.[27]

By the early 1920s, the American signals intelligence effort had declined significantly from its wartime peak. Though cryptology had made small contributions to the conduct of AEF operations, there had been no spectacular successes to spur the creation of a permanent peacetime effort. Instead of capitalizing on wartime gains, the MID rapidly divested itself of cryptologic assets. Yardley's Black Chamber, a scaled-down version of the MI-8 Code and Cipher Section, was technically subordinate to the MID but was funded largely by the State Department. The organization moved from Washington to New York in 1919 and concentrated on breaking diplomatic communications; commercial telegraph companies supplied the needed "intercepts." Similarly, MID's wartime radio collection sites along the Mexican border and in Maine were downsized and eventually turned over to the Signal Corps, which intercepted long-distance radio communications primarily for technological rather than intelligence purposes. In Washington, the Signal Corps employed William Friedman to make codes and ciphers and investigate cipher machines. Working alone, he kept abreast of radio developments, documented principles of cryptanalysis, and preserved the legacy of the AEF's cryptologic work. The US Navy established a small communications intelligence effort by 1925, but the US Army spent a decade struggling to decide whether cryptology belonged in the MID or the Signal Corps.

This bureaucratic dysfunction meant that Hitt was the most well-known code and cipher expert in the government in the early 1920s, but by the end of the decade, William and Elizebeth Friedman eclipsed him in prominence. Apart from his *Manual,* much of Hitt's fame derived from newspaper articles written about his work during World War I. The army failed to capitalize on the critical cryptologic skills Hitt had acquired. He understood (and directed) signal collection and radio deception, he excelled at creating codes and ciphers, and he demonstrated expertise at breaking enciphered communications to exploit the intelligence they contained. He had the management skills to run a complicated organization, and he was well known to those who ran both the MID and the Signal Corps. Had Hitt been inclined to move his career in this direction, and had he possessed the foresight to push for a unified cryptologic organization, the army may have made better use of his skills. By not creating a consolidated signals intelligence organization at the close of World War I, the army wasted much of the energy it had invested in cryptology (and Hitt). And the United States fell behind in technological and intellectual progress in signals intelligence, particularly when compared with the United Kingdom, which established the Government Code and Cipher School (later called the Government Communications Headquarters, or GCHQ) in 1919.

The lack of a single cryptologic organization left Hitt (officially and unofficially) evaluating cipher systems devised by others. These requests started after publication of his *Manual* in 1916, and they were still coming when he returned from France. Inventors usually bypassed army channels and contacted him directly. In 1916, perhaps recognizing that his real work could be overwhelmed by such requests, Hitt tried to head off the problem. He drew up specific criteria for government cipher methods and devices that could be sent to amateurs who contacted the CSO, and he submitted the guidelines to George Gibbs in the CSO's office, but his advice was never taken. Hitt graciously answered queries and briefly examined each suggestion. He made no effort to turn this work into a full-time career and directed serious (or persistent) correspondents to Frank Moorman and William Friedman at Signal Corps headquarters. Friedman began to receive direct solicitations after his code-related work in the Teapot Dome scandal was publicized in 1924; Yardley received queries that had reached the MID in Washington, but he was not publicly known as an expert until *The American Black Chamber* was published in 1931. Though the government did not lack experts whose duties included examining suggestions by civilians, the public believed Hitt to be their man; this perception held true well into the 1950s.[28]

Hitt and Friedman kept up a sporadic correspondence and saw each other from time to time. When John M. Manly discovered Thomas Jefferson's design for a cylinder cipher device in the Library of Congress in 1922, Friedman and Manly marveled at its resemblance to Hitt's 1912 cylinder. Aware of his interest in teleprinter ciphers, Friedman invited Hitt to look at the modifications he had made to the War Department's printing telegraph. Hitt wrote a favorable review of Friedman's book *Elements of Cryptanalysis;* the review appeared in the May 1924 issue of the *Signal Corps Bulletin.*[29]

Albert S. Osborn, an "examiner of questioned documents," was among those who received Hitt's assistance. In 1924 author B. E. Brigman acknowledged Hitt's solution to a cipher he had sent him and promised to praise Hitt's work in an upcoming issue of *Real Detective Tales.* These were simple requests; other correspondents were more persistent and became ongoing irritants. Dr. Edwin Lunn Miller, the pastor of St. Mark's Evangelical Lutheran Church in Roxbury, Massachusetts, was one such nuisance. For more than a year, he attempted to interest Hitt in a home-grown encipherment system, asking Hitt to fully evaluate his work or refer him to "some particularly competent cipher enthusiast." Hitt's patience wore out from the constant back-and-forth with Miller, for he had "neither the time nor the inclination, at present, to work on puzzles." Hitt scoffed at Miller's idea that another enthusiast would evaluate his work for free, commenting, "You might get an examination for $1000 with a guarantee of $500 more when, (note I do not say if), they broke out the secret." Those who charged money laughed at Hitt because, he wrote, "I do things for love so I think we will not ask them to do likewise." Miller was incensed with Hitt's attempt to get rid of him and called his replies "unbecoming a government official of your standing." The reverend thought Hitt's conclusions and sarcasm were "quite gratuitous, because you have no ground for declaring that a knowledge of operation deprives my system of value, nor for putting it summarily in the puzzle class." Hitt never heard from Miller again, and he was undoubtedly relieved.[30]

Hitt's understandable impatience with Miller may have been heightened by his exasperation with another correspondent, John F. Byrne, an inventor whose 1918 device, called the Chaocipher, consisted of a "cigar box, a few bits of string, and odds and ends." In thirty-five years of trying, Byrne never got anyone in the US government to go beyond watching a demonstration of the machine. Hitt refused to endorse Byrne's work "in the interest of my own liberty of action. I am a free lance at this game and expect to remain one." Instead, he introduced Byrne to Moorman and

Friedman in March 1922. But Byrne was not impressed by his new acquaintances and told Hitt that he had "no hesitation, however, in saying at once that so far as their competence to pass judgement on my principle is concerned, they are *not* in the class of Colonel Hitt." Byrne repeatedly used feedback from Hitt out of context, including in an article he wrote for the *New York Herald* and in his 1953 autobiography. Hitt was also unhappy when a letter he had sent to Byrne in August 1921 was reproduced in an advertisement. Though annoyed that Byrne kept contacting him instead of the War Department, the harassed Hitt remained gracious but stern, telling Byrne, "The commercialization of my friendly interest would be a matter of great regret to me." Noting that he had given Byrne so much time and "explained to you fully my attitude toward the commercial end of cipher matters," he asked to be left out of "your future arrangement for the exploitation of your device." "It would be a great favor to me," Hitt wrote. He did not hear from Byrne again until 1937.[31]

When the Hitts returned to Washington Barracks, they moved into another large house, quarters 11, which had seventeen rooms and a magnificent springtime view of the cherry blossoms along the riverfront. Nine-year-old Mary Lue attended the Georgetown Visitation Convent because the nearby public schools did not have room to accommodate all the children on post. The Hitts practiced no religion, but Parker's high school friend from Indianapolis, now Sister Margaret Mary Sheerin, was the school's director. Mary Lue took "the catechism with a good many grains of salt" and told her father, "I think the man who wrote that catechism had never read the *Encyclopedia Britannica*." "I fear she will not make a good catholic," Parker told his father, "although, in fact, they don't force the religious side at all." Mary Lue's marks were generally very good and good, but she was only fair in physical culture and just tolerable in plain sewing. When her class presented *Snow White* in December 1921, Mary Lue played the Queen Stepmother. She was learning to play tennis and had the run of the post; commissary receipts show that Miss Hitt frequently bought pop or gum on her father's account. In the spring of 1922, however, Mary Lue was kicked out of the convent school for smoking on the roof. A place was found for her in public school, where she maintained strong views on her education and life. She wrote in 1923 that school was "as bad as ever" and said of Washington Barracks, "I swear this is the dumbest post ever."[32]

Hitt was once again teaching the G1 course and gave a lecture on replacements in the fall of 1921 and again in the spring. He directed the heavily data-driven work of the conference on replacements and also lectured students on "Some Peculiarities of the Japanese Language." For the school's summer 1922 excursion to Nova Scotia, Hitt prepared a paper titled "The Attack and Defense of Halifax, Nova Scotia," which included his assessment of the terrain. He was given a "superior" rating as an instructor, and Major General Edward McGlachlin, who had been First Army's chief of artillery, noted Hitt's "attractive and driving power, common sense, understanding of men, executive ability, high capacity and attainment," and "very good presence."[33]

In the autumn, as the 1922–1923 school year began, Hitt presented what would become one of his standard lectures on the topic of "Graphic Presentation." He stressed the importance of preparing and rehearsing graphic presentations as carefully as verbal ones and advised that, when using slides, the view should be checked from all areas of the audience in advance; if the slides could not be seen, it was "worse than useless as it only aggravates a part of your audience." Blackboards were "an emergency expedient" and should be used only when no other method was available. Hitt provided practical advice on the preparation of slides, the college's existing collection of slides, and the "entirely adequate" equipment available to students; this did not include "an excellent moving picture projector," which was available only to lecturers.[34]

During the G2 course, Hitt's comments on the work of the student committee on the British Empire revealed his consciousness of British signals intelligence efforts. Hitt informed the students that the British government not only supervised cable traffic coming into and leaving the country but also made "copies . . . which are unblushingly used in the promotion of British trade and commerce." He noted, "History backs me up when I say that the British Empire will make war on any nation that threatens its commercial supremacy."[35]

Parker's mother, Elizabeth Barnett Hitt, died on March 3, 1923, in Worcester, Massachusetts, where she and George had moved when he took a job with the New England Daily Newspaper Association. A graveside service took place on June 16 at Crown Hill Cemetery in Indianapolis; of her children, only Muriel was there. George Hitt told his son, "The day was lovely, the surroundings, as perfect as Nature could make them, were soothing, and the ceremony was dignified. I am sure it was just what your Mother would have approved. There was sadness there and some tears, but the thought that was uppermost in the mind of each person present was, What a life of service she had led and how useful she had proved in her day and generation!" Elizabeth was remembered for traits she shared with her son—"a vivid personality, an active mind, and a sympathetic nature."[36]

The year had started badly: Hitt suffered from acute bronchitis in late January, his mother died in March, and then in May he fractured a finger playing indoor baseball. He attended the Baltic Society banquet at the Racquet Club in Washington on May 28, after which he and George Simonds went to the Naval War College for four days in June to arrange the next war game between the two schools. The strain of these months seemingly robbed Hitt of some of his flare as an instructor. In his June appraisal he was rated only "average" for his instructional duties, although he was rated "superior" as an exercise umpire. When the new school year began in the autumn of 1923, Hitt was aware that it was his last year at the War College; his formal assignment to the General Staff would expire in late 1924. That summer he expressed a preference for the Infantry, based on a desire to be near family and a compromise with Genevieve: his request was heavily weighted in favor of Fort Sam Houston (his first, third, and fifth choices—the 1st, 9th, and 23rd Infantries) or a midwestern post near Indianapolis (his second and fourth choices—the 2nd and 3rd Infantries). Hitt also asked to attend the refresher course at the Infantry School at Fort Benning, Georgia.[37]

Hitt's September 1923 lecture for the command course, "Signal Communication for Higher Command," provides significant insight into his war experience and the importance of communications to command. Commanders, he said, "must know the powers and limitations" of communications, and he opined that radio "is a last resort that no prudent commander . . . will use as long as any other means remains." He warned of the danger of radio interception; if this occurred, "not only would the radio station be located but the type of headquarters the station served would be clear to the enemy." To Hitt, a lesson of the war was that "every successful commander in the future" must understand communications "before he takes hold in war." The signal officers of major units "must be soldiers first and technicians afterward," for the signal officer's staff and subordinates will be the technicians supporting his decisions. This was a subtle criticism of retiring CSO Squier, who insisted that signal officers be members of the Signal Corps.[38]

The chief of Infantry, Major General Charles S. Farnsworth, wanted Hitt to attend the Command and General Staff School (CGSS) for the 1924–1925 school year. He believed Hitt would do well, and his attendance would "reflect credit not only on yourself but on the Infantry arm as well." There was some urgency to Farnsworth's request; the maximum age for attendance at the school was forty-eight for the class starting in 1923, and it decreased by one year each subsequent year, until no one older than thirty-eight would be allowed to attend. Hitt would be forty-six in 1924, so this would be his last chance—by 1925, he would be too old. Hitt declined Farnsworth's suggestion with thanks, observing that he was "professionally stale" from too much time in school and needed duty with troops. Apart from his time in France, Hitt had been assigned to schools since 1911. His rejection of the opportunity to attend the CGSS, whether a conscious career decision or one based on weariness with the army's education system, surely doomed any hope of a higher command. Hitt's career planning was haphazard at best; he advanced through the army in whatever direction his interests and abilities pulled him. It is possible Hitt was already contemplating retirement and wished to close out his career as he had started it: as an infantryman.[39]

Harry New was no longer a senator; he had been appointed postmaster general, which was then a cabinet-level position. New's wife, Catherine, was close to Genevieve and frequently invited her to events attended by the wives of cabinet members and other prominent Washingtonians. In December 1923 Genevieve attended a small "ladies' dinner" for President Coolidge's wife, Grace, while the men went off to the Gridiron Club for their meal. Genevieve asked her father-in-law to tell Parker's sister Muriel about the invitation and hoped she would be "duly impressed." She also begged the widower to visit Washington for Christmas, as she planned to cook a "great big fat turkey," and he would be needed to eat some of it.[40]

In January 1924, while still managing the G1 course, Hitt gave the introductory lecture for the "course of informative studies," a four-week period of study focusing on the personnel requirements for four hypothetical war plans. Hitt advised his students, "We give you ample time to achieve quality at the expense of quantity and will appreciate your efforts along that line." Lieutenant Colonel Henry Dickinson, a National Guard officer who attended the course that semester, noted, "No grass grows under the feet of that faculty, no dilly-dallying; just a welcome, and then a run into the loading shoot [sic] for a trip through many labyrinths of military lore." He remembered that Hitt rode "herd on us for our entire drive through."[41]

As soon as the four-week course was over in February 1924, Parker, Genevieve, and Mary Lue, along with Tot Young, took a month's leave and journeyed to Panama. They were met at the dock by General and Mrs. John Palmer (Palmer was commander of the 19th Infantry Brigade) and saw the canal locks. They took the train to Panama City, where they stayed at the Hotel Central. Many old friends were there, including the Eisenhowers and Generals Fox Conner (commander of the 20th Infantry Brigade), William Lassiter (commander of the US Army's Panama Canal Division), and Meriwether Lewis Walker (governor of the Panama Canal Zone). Captain Manley of the US Navy took them golfing; Hitt had known Manley's wife as a girl in Nome. They were "all brown from living outside for a month." It was a "perfect trip," Hitt told his father, despite having to leave the ship at Charleston and dash to Washington on the train before his leave expired. "We are plumb wore out resting," Genevieve remarked. The family had spent "ungrudgingly and with pleasure all the money we could afford and now we must sit still for a while." They returned to Washington, where the weather was awful and there was no news about Hitt's next assignment.[42]

"The cherry blossoms have turned the parks into a mass of pink and white so that it is hard to keep one's mind on any serious work," Hitt wrote to his father. It was the middle of April 1924, and Hitt now knew he would be going to the 2nd Division in San Antonio, but he did not know which of the three infantry regiments he would be assigned to. George and Florence Gruenert moved into the Hitts' house in May; the two families had become close, and the Gruenerts, who were en route to Fort Huachuca, had packed up and relinquished their apartment, so they needed a place to stay. Both families had to camp out because the Hitts' belongings were already on their way to San Antonio. The mess was available for meals "as a last resort," but they usually ate at home or went downtown. "We are all well and feel like a lot of gypsies," Hitt informed his father. He also mentioned that he had escorted Catherine New to a White House garden party, for "I always have fun going out with her."[43]

After a staff ride to Gettysburg, Hitt supervised the summer exercise at Fort Ethan Allen in late June. Before leaving the college, he wrote a memorandum for his successor in which he stressed the importance of developing a good relationship with the G1 in the War Department, for "personal contact is by all means the best way to do business with this division." Hitt also made suggestions about the content of the course and the importance of record keeping; he advised "religiously" keeping a private record for each student, including "everything that you pick up about each individual in connection with his work . . . [as] it will save you a great deal of time throughout the course."[44]

If the Hitts were fans of the Washington Senators in their World Series–winning year, they missed the opportunity to celebrate with the rest of the District of Columbia when the team clinched the pennant at the end of September, for they had departed on July 2, 1924. They spent some of their leave "with Genevieve's people" in West Point, Texas, before Hitt reported to Fort Sam Houston on July 13.[45]

"I have turned soldier once more and the change is not bad at all," Hitt reported. His heart had always been with the Infantry, and his assignment as executive officer of the 23rd Infantry at Fort Sam Houston was a dream come true. For Genevieve, though, the post housing situation was a nightmare. In contrast to their lovely house in Washington, the family moved into quarters 109 on the Cavalry Post, a "second lieutenant's set in the old days," with three bedrooms and only one bathroom. Hitt proclaimed it "infinitely better than the cantonment quarters, so we have no growl," but it was a tight fit for the 9,200 pounds of property and 1,000 pounds of professional books shipped from Washington. They employed a Mexican American manservant "who does everything but put us to bed." And they bought an automobile, which all three of them—even twelve-year-old Mary Lue—drove. Parker used the car to commute the few miles to regimental headquarters. Despite her age, Mary Lue started high school at Incarnate World Convent.[46]

Colonel Lincoln F. Kilbourne, Hitt's new commander, had fallen from his horse in June and would be incapacitated for the entire summer, so Hitt immediately took command of the regiment. "I am about the busiest little bee you ever saw," he told his father. But Hitt was not entirely well himself, suffering from "an old trouble—too much acid in his system," probably aggravated by the heat and hard work. Genevieve insisted that she would send for her father if Parker did not feel better soon, "and he will fix him up, I know." Hitt's relationship with the newly promoted Kilbourne began well; the colonel appreciated Hitt's technical skills and, at least at first, the many suggestions he offered.[47]

Hitt was soon off to the Infantry School's refresher course at Fort Benning, Georgia. He left Texas, alone, on September 30 for the two-month assignment. The idea for a refresher class had been implemented just after the war to ensure that all colonels who had been selected or were due to be selected to command regiments were brought up to speed. Though Hitt was not in command of a regiment, he was of the right grade, he served as an executive officer, and he had specifically requested the course to update his infantry knowledge. At Benning, Hitt joined eleven other colonels and lieutenant colonels—"all old friends"—who were newly assigned to regiments after service in Washington. It is fortunate they were friends, for it seems that nine of the twelve shared the same quarters. Hitt was glad to see Leonard T. "Gee" Gerow, who was attending the advanced infantry class; Omar N. Bradley was in Gerow's class, but Hitt makes no mention of meeting him. The work of the class was leavened by social events, including a party given on November 23 by Colonel and Mrs. Ephraim G. Peyton, the school's director of experiment, and a larger party at the Columbus Country Club hosted by the Gerows the following weekend. Fort Benning was "not exactly the best place to spend Thanksgiving," but Hitt admitted having "no luck" with this particular holiday and reminisced about the times he had been out of the country or on duty. While at the Infantry School, Hitt could not help but invent. He designed a device to make panoramas from contoured maps for the Military History Section; the school was still trying to construct a working model the following February.[48]

Hitt made such a good impression at the Infantry School that the commandant, General Briant H. Wells, asked that he be reassigned there as director of the Department of Experiment, which was responsible for testing ideas for weapons and other gear needed by the infantry. It was the perfect job for him. Even though Hitt was "not surplus at his present station," the chief of Infantry believed the move was necessary "because this officer is well qualified for the detail proposed and because of the great difficulty in finding a qualified and available officer for this particular duty." The Infantry School wanted Hitt to start by late June 1925, and it "understood [that] Colonel Hitt very much desires duty at Fort Benning." When the request arrived in the adjutant general's office in Washington in January 1925, a worksheet was prepared showing that Hitt was eligible for detached service in July 1925, was not currently eligible for the General Staff, and was number eighty-seven on the foreign service roster. No decision was made at that time, and the request was put in the "suspended" file to be considered after March 1. The school did not wait to use Hitt's expertise, however. In February Captain W. A. Dumas in the Military History Section solicited Hitt's opinion on the expansion of the "Methods of Instruction course" and forwarded him a package containing all the lectures and materials, which he hoped would be "the best short course in pedagogy in the country." Dumas desired Hitt's "very frank (even harsh, if you choose) criticism, whether constructive or destructive." There is no record of a reply.[49]

When the request to reassign Hitt was reviewed in early March, the adjutant general had no objection and passed the paperwork to the deputy chief of staff, with the recommendation that his office examine the number of officers who would be available for the General Staff in the next couple of years, as Hitt would be eligible in the summer of 1926. The only duty that could delay a General Staff assignment was the command of troops, and the school was not a command. The numbers were crunched, and the acting assistant chief of staff in G1 concluded, "There seems to be no reason why" Hitt could not be released to the school. Yet the office of the chief of staff stamped the request "disapproved" on March 14, and several days later the school received a memo to this effect, with no explanation. Wells informed Hitt that the request had been disapproved, and because he had not been told why, he assumed "your services have been requisitioned in some other position that was deemed more important." Hitt was disappointed but resigned himself to staying in Texas until he had two years of duty with troops, after which he expected to return to Washington for a four-year stint on the General Staff.[50]

While Hitt was at school, Genevieve added to her San Antonio real estate empire and visited with her hometown friends. Mary Lue was doing well in school; she played tennis, swam at the country club pool, and took up horseback riding at the Remount Depot. Parker returned from Georgia on December 7, and the Hitts expected to have a "simple but satisfactory Christmas," despite a malfunctioning furnace in their quarters.[51]

The spring brought a new home, quarters 102 on the Cavalry Post, which had "no more room but a working furnace!" And then it was time for a vacation. The family set out in late May to spend a month with the Gruenerts at Fort Huachuca, where they enjoyed long horseback rides in the canyon, moonlight picnics, and the beauty of the mountains. Genevieve found the houses at Huachuca large and spacious compared with their quarters at Fort Sam Houston. She loved the post and told her father-in-law, "It's more than interesting in the day time and at night it is like fairy land." Parker was "downright crazy about riding . . . worse than Mary Lue. I wouldn't be surprised if the Hitts joined the Cavalry." Parker returned to San Antonio on June 30 and immediately went off to Camp Stanley for target practice, while Genevieve and Mary Lue traveled by train to Los Angeles, San Francisco, Yellowstone Park, Colorado Springs, and Denver before returning to San Antonio, "dead tired of trains and scenery, I have no doubt."[52]

Kilbourne appreciated the technical training Hitt contributed to the regiment but thought him "better adapted to staff than line duty." Hitt had a positive influence on at least one officer of the 23rd, a young lieutenant fresh out of the US Military Academy named Clyde Davis Eddleman. Eddleman, who would be promoted to brigadier general on the

Leyte beachhead in 1944 and later serve as vice chief of staff of the army, recalled the "splendid training" he received under Hitt's guidance and how kind both Hitts were to him. Hitt, for his part, remembered the "fine impression" Eddleman made on him "among the rather motley crew of officers of the regiment."[53]

Hitt continued to perform tasks outside his remit. In February 1925 he devised a small codebook for an exercise. In September, apparently on his own initiative, he wrote a long memo to the chief of Infantry about a plan for reorganizing infantry regiments, though it appears that he never sent it; in 1927 he finally shared his idea with a General Staff colleague. Hitt's plan provided a "war strength" regiment with a minimum of manpower and a "maximum of ability to meet and destroy an opponent," while providing the means for "radical economy in maintaining Infantry regiments in time of peace." He included a design concept for a "power cart," inspired by the recent development of power-driven lawn mowers. The cart could serve as a firing mount for a Browning machine gun, making it "as mobile as the riflemen"; alternatively, it could carry ammunition, supplies, or even communications equipment. His idea was to reduce manpower, increase the number of machine guns (while reducing the number of effective rifles), eliminate the need for animals (along with their forage and sanitary problems), and increase firepower. Hitt envisioned the army putting a whole regiment into trucks, without having to depend on animals.[54]

Brigadier General Paul B. Malone, commander of both the 2nd Division and Fort Sam Houston, thought Hitt "should be given the opportunity of extended service with troops." In mid-September 1925, when Hitt's tenure as executive officer for the 23rd Infantry ended, Malone assigned him command of the division's special troops—signals, tanks, police, ordnance, maintenance, and personnel at division headquarters. The move gave Hitt an independent command but made him feel "very much like the man who complained of the dictionary because it does not stick to any one subject long enough," for all the odds and ends of the division fell to him. For instance, the position made him provost marshal, "which I do not care for much." By early 1926, Hitt had "about lost all faith in modern civilization" as a result of his service as provost marshal, for despite weeding the recruits of criminals "of every kind and variety," hardly a day passed without a soldier committing "some crime of violence." He bemoaned the "ruin" of the military court system after the war, which he attributed to revisions by "a lot of civilian lawyers who were taken into the Army with a high rank."[55]

Meanwhile, the Hitt family was "living very quietly and trying to keep well and not eat too much." It was a busy, happy household. Parker and Mary Lue often rode horses together in the early morning before he went to work. Their small quarters grew even tighter when Florence Gruenert and her daughter "Sis" came for a visit; they stayed so long that Sis enrolled in first grade at the post school. Genevieve's sister Tot was also living with them again; she attended classes at Incarnate World College and convinced Genevieve, who had always wanted to better express her thoughts on paper, to take a journalism course. Thirteen-year-old Mary Lue was now so skilled at tennis that she was the runner-up in a citywide tournament, winning over girls five and six years her senior. In December the Hitts let their manservant go, for he had become "too much of an autocrat around the place." Genevieve loved running the house herself, but they expected to hire a cook in the new year. Christmas 1925, though devoid of a tree and trimmings, was particularly enjoyable. Mary Lue, with all the ambition of a teenager, had many ideas for how to spend her school holiday, although her father doubted she would carry through with any of them. The family had "almost everything we want all the time," so they were "not much on the conventional Christmas." All the gifts received from friends were opened immediately because Genevieve, Mary Lue, and Tot did not "believe in [do not open] signs when their curiosity is aroused." George Hitt sent a check, and the money was spent on a joint family present. Parker arranged for a Santa Claus and a tree for the troops' forty or fifty children, as many of them would not have a tree in their quarters. Snow fell overnight on December 26, giving the next morning a wintry feel, even though it turned to slush and mud by afternoon.[56]

The family's plans were on-again, off-again at the whim of the army bureaucracy. In mid-December they were thrilled to learn that Hitt would begin a four-year General Staff detail in Washington the following July, and they began to mentally prepare for the move. It had been a wonderful experience, but two years in Texas was "quite enough"; Genevieve sold all the houses they owned in San Antonio, for she did not expect to live there again. But in February 1926 the Morrow Board, tasked with examining how to develop and use aircraft in national defense, recommended that Air Service officers be represented on the General Staff; as a result, Hitt's job was given away. Instead, he would be leading the Fifth Corps Area General Staff at Fort Hayes in Columbus, Ohio. The collapse of Hitt's plans for a four-month detail with the post's field artillery unit was an added disappointment; all the artillery colonels had been sent to school for three months, and the army was not amenable to leaving an infantry officer in command of the entire Artillery Brigade.[57]

Just a week later, new orders were issued, and the Hitts were again Washington bound. Almost immediately, Hitt was relieved of command of special troops and received only an average rating from Malone; he thought the "unusually intelligent" Hitt liked "his own point of view very much" and was better suited for "an independent job in which he can create his own policies and carry out his own ideas." Malone suggested that Hitt might make a good military attaché. At the end of June, Hitt's final evaluation (by the division's chief of staff) was much improved; he commended Hitt's single-handed preparation of the division's mobilization plans as "splendidly done," while agreeing that Hitt was "essentially a staff officer type." Malone eventually came around, praising the "superior manner" in which Hitt had prepared the mobilization plans.[58]

Hitt twisted his ankle stepping off a sidewalk in June; he was just off bed rest and still limping when the packers arrived on July 6 to crate the family's furniture. Genevieve and Parker tried to determine the "exact amount of stuff that will fill a hypothetical apartment in Washington" so they could dispose of or store the remainder. The trip east was an opportunity for a vacation. The family said good-bye to Genevieve's family in West Point, stopped in to see Parker's father in Indianapolis, and then boarded a ship in Chicago for a five-day journey to Buffalo. After a quick look at Niagara Falls, the Hitts traveled to Quebec City and then to Washington, where Hitt was to report for duty with the General Staff on August 1, 1926.[59]

The end of July found the Hitts occupying a spacious duplex in the Cordova, an apartment complex on the corner of Twentieth Street and Florida Avenue NW. There were four big rooms downstairs, three bedrooms and a bath upstairs, and a good-sized gallery on each floor; it was much more space than they anticipated. Sleeping on cots supplied by the quartermaster, they camped out while waiting for their household goods to arrive. Many of their army friends were in Washington that year, and Harry and Catherine New entertained the Hitts for several evenings that first week. The Gruenerts were also residents of the Cordova and may have arranged the Hitts' lease. The apartments were comfortable, but Genevieve and Florence Gruenert decided they were paying too much for too little. The women explored the housing market, and that fall they embarked on an unconventional arrangement, convincing their husbands to rent a three-story house at 1723 Nineteenth Street NW for the two families to share. The house cost $100 a month, less than either of them had been paying at the Cordova, which pleased the thrifty Hitts. The first floor contained a modern kitchen, living room, and dining room, and each of the two upper floors had three bedrooms and a bath; the Gruenerts occupied the second floor and the Hitts the third. The Hitts paid for a servant to cook and clean. It was "a curious experiment," but the families had been stationed together and had been close friends for eight years, so they believed it would work out. Parker boasted to his father that they were across the street from Secretary of State Kellogg and Senator Sheppard of Texas. George Hitt joked that his son had been influenced by President Calvin Coolidge's "infectious" policy of frugality. He suggested that because Parker now lived closer to the War Department, his shorter walk could result in savings on shoe repair. And if he were Parker, George continued, he would make further economies and "quit cigarettes, street-cars, and maybe get Gee-Gee to cut my hair, thus improving the chance for advancement and influence in the Army."[60]

Despite the honor of serving in the Office of the Chief of Staff, the work was not exciting; Hitt described it as just a "grind against the pinch of poverty, trying to make one dollar do the work of two in true New England style." Hitt worked in G3, the Operations and Training Section, which controlled the organization of branches, tables of allowances, and training publications and had oversight of the military schools. Hitt had some expertise in all these areas, but there was little room for innovation and invention. Major General John L. Hines was the chief of staff, and Major General Frank Parker was the G3; General Charles P. Summerall would replace Hines in late November 1926. Hitt found that Summerall brought busyness but little change to the office, and he told his father, "We just have the work of preparing new plans and revamping old ones and the inertia of the machine prevent their being carried out."[61]

The Hitts spent Christmas Eve with the News; Christmas Day dinner, in the tradition of military families everywhere, included George Simonds's daughter Marjorie and other waifs and strays who could not be home for the holidays. On New Year's Eve, they welcomed in 1927 in Front Royal, Virginia; Genevieve and Florence had visited the town in the fall, and a celebration there was cheaper than a pricey Washington event. In January, Mary Lue, who had not attended school since they arrived in Washington, was enrolled at the nearby Gunston Hall School, located at 1906 Florida Avenue, for the winter term. The Hitts and Gruenerts enjoyed their communal life and planned to spend the summer at Sherwood Forest, a community of cottages near Annapolis, Maryland; the men would stay in Washington during the week and visit on the weekends.[62]

But come June, instead of going east to the shore, the Hitts and Gruenerts went west to the mountains. The women and children established themselves at the Ricketts Hotel in Flint Hill, Virginia. Parker stayed in Washington for a conference that had brought most of the army's generals to town. Mary Lue returned to the city and joined him at the June 11 festivities celebrating Charles Lindbergh's triumphant return from his transatlantic flight. That evening, father and daughter traveled to Flint Hill, where Hitt enjoyed a few days of horseback riding. Upon his return to bachelor life in Washington, he faced a promotion board on July 27 and had his annual physical.[63]

Hitt was back on solid ground professionally at the General Staff, and he was rated "superior" for the remainder of his career. Assisted by a newly arrived major, Hitt had charge of the Operations Branch when his boss, Colonel Otho B. Rosenbaum, and Rosenbaum's deputy both took leave; they were "getting away with" the strenuous pace of work in the absence of management. Parker assured his father that the family was well and enjoying life. There is no hint that Hitt was thinking about retirement; in fact, he had submitted his statement of preference for foreign service, listing the Philippines, Panama, and Hawaii as his preferred assignments once his four years on the General Staff were complete in 1930. But in late 1927 and early 1928, Hitt began taking more frequent leave, indulging Genevieve's desire to get away from the city.[64]

Genevieve loved the Shenandoah Valley and began to look for a more permanent residence there. In early August 1927 Genevieve, Mary Lue, and Florence were ensconced in a furnished house (with ninety-six acres of land) Genevieve had purchased for $6,875. It sat a few miles outside of Front Royal on Browntown Road. Parker had not seen the house, but Genevieve called him before she bought it, and he made the financial arrangements from Washington. The telephone was hooked up by August 22, and Genevieve obtained estimates from roofers, painters, and carpenters. In an excited letter to her husband, Genevieve admitted she could not remember what she had told him on the phone and asked for his approval to install a green tin roof, as she could not get "good old-fashioned shingles and the fireproof ones look funny on an old farm house." One of the property's attractions was the proximity of the Shenandoah River with its good bass fishing; she believed Parker would also enjoy some winter hunting on the extensive property. Genevieve could "hardly wait" until Parker saw it all for himself. Meanwhile, she made herself at home, gathering fruit and making jam. Parker bemusedly informed his father that Genevieve, who was "not at all in love with Washington," had "inherited the farm instinct" from her forebearers. He admitted he did not know how it would work out, but in any event, it would not break them financially. And with six trains a day, travel between Front Royal and Washington was not inconvenient.[65]

A few weeks later, on September 2, Genevieve's sister Tot married Lieutenant Edgar W. King, an army officer she had met in Panama during the family's 1924 trip. King had been at Fort Monroe, Virginia, in early 1927 and had spent many weekends with the family in Washington; they all enjoyed his company. Genevieve's mother traveled from Texas for the ceremony in Washington. After the wedding, the couple were off to New York, where King was stationed at Fort Jay.[66]

The Browntown Road house, christened Genlue Park (a clever blend of names), had been constructed of logs in 1824 and later covered with weatherboard. It now had a new roof and new paint and had been weatherproofed. Genevieve soon acquired an addition, buying a room from the old Lane's Tavern in Front Royal and moving it to the property; the tavern had served as the first Warren County courthouse. Front Royal was near the spot where immigrant Peter Hitt had settled in 1714, and it was closer still to the farm where Parker's grandfather had spent his young adult years. George Hitt found this coincidence quite striking. Among the Hitts' furnishings was the grandfather clock that Parker's great-grandfather Martin had transported from Maryland to Kentucky, Ohio, and Indiana in the early nineteenth century. They may not have realized it in 1927, but the Hitts were home.[67]

Mary Lue changed schools again in the fall of 1927 and became a boarder at Briarcliff, near Ossining, New York. Parker had heard it was a "fine, healthy school," and he and Genevieve believed their daughter needed "to get away from grownups for a while," even though it was difficult for Genevieve to be apart from Mary Lue. In October, after attending the Army-Yale football game in New Haven, Connecticut, Genevieve made a quick visit to the school and found that something was not right. A few days later, the Hitts pulled Mary Lue out of Briarcliff, telling the headmistress they had made a mistake placing her there. Parker sent Mary Lue a copy of the letter with a penciled note telling her to "pack your trunk" and remarking, "the war is over"; he cautioned her to say nothing at the school, as this was "our decision, you had nothing to do with it." Genevieve brought Mary Lue back to Washington on November 4 and reenrolled her at Gunston Hall.[68]

With Mary Lue back home, Genevieve was content to spend the winter in Washington. Ike and Mamie Eisenhower were in town, as was Gee Gerow (both men were at the War College), and she had many friends to visit. Hitt remained busy at work, and he thought Summerall was irked by the "legal and bureaucratic limitations which surround his job." The General Staff was still preparing all kinds of plans "which we know beforehand are impossible of realization," but "that is what we are for I suppose." The hardworking Hitt was bored with his position, which provided little opportunity to use his ingenuity. He actively followed college football (particularly Purdue) and took the family to the Army-Navy game in New York that year, watching Army beat Navy 14–9. Hitt delighted in having a quiet Christmas in Washington, a Sunday–Tuesday holiday from the grind of the War Department.[69]

Genevieve hurried back to Front Royal in April 1928. She and Mary Lue, who was on spring break, camped out in the house and got it ready for the summer season, while Parker stayed behind in cold, rainy Washington. Genevieve had thirty acres plowed so she could plant corn, and she and Mary Lue planned to start a kitchen garden at the end of the school year. In the middle of May, however, plans changed. Parker and Genevieve decided to send Mary Lue to Europe for the summer, depositing $100 with Beaux-Arts Tours to guarantee the trip.[70]

In March 1928 Hitt congratulated his old friend Sosthenes Behn when Behn's International Telephone and Telegraph (IT&T) acquired the Mackay Company—the largest telecommunications merger to date. He asked Behn to keep him in mind for a job, as he was thinking of leaving the army and going into "some more constructive business." Behn's reply was quick and positive: "it would give me great pleasure to have you in the international family." Hitt's desire for something "constructive" grew out of his increasing dissatisfaction with his General Staff work and the realization that, after thirty years in the army, he needed to make some real money to support his family. Just shy of his fiftieth birthday, Hitt was not ready to renounce a cosmopolitan lifestyle and the society of the workplace for rural life on the farm outside Front Royal. His army pension would be $4,500 per year (more than $67,000 in 2020 dollars), and Behn offered a starting salary of $10,000 (about $150,000 in 2020 dollars). By taking the job—"a fine executive position"—in New York, Hitt would be able to support Genevieve's farm, provide for Mary Lue's future, and afford some degree of indulgence.[71]

Hitt's decision to retire was a considered one. Under the army's promotion system, he had just a slim chance of reaching the rank of major general in the next ten years; he had effectively reached the top of the pay scale. His retirement pay of $375 a month would be no higher even if he were promoted to brigadier general. Hitt's mind was made up; in June 1928 he accepted the job with IT&T and requested that his retirement from the army become effective November 6, 1928. Because he had months of accrued leave, he left Washington on full pay on July 6. Of the new position, Hitt told his father, "I will probably stay with it for a long time," for he was "sure it is going to suit me exactly."[72]

During the years 1919–1928, Hitt reaped the rewards of his World War I success, holding positions of responsibility that required political skill, discretion, and tact. They were not, however, jobs that would advance his army career. He was a good instructor, but his technical skills were largely wasted at the War College. His position with the MID required some panache, but it was not a job that would propel him to higher command. Hitt's work with troops at Fort Sam Houston failed for many reasons, and although his position on the General Staff was a tribute to his ability to deal with bureaucracy, Hitt found the work boring. The time had come to leave the army behind and use his talents in the world of industry.

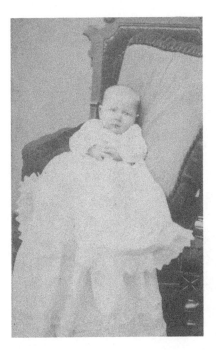

Parker Hitt as a baby, 1878. (Parker Hitt Photograph Collection, Philippine Photographs Digital Archive, Special Collections Library, University of Michigan)

Parker Hitt as a small child, circa 1880. (Parker Hitt Photograph Collection, Philippine Photographs Digital Archive, Special Collections Library, University of Michigan)

Parker Hitt as a young man. (Parker Hitt Photograph Collection, Philippine Photographs Digital Archive, Special Collections Library, University of Michigan)

Sergeant Parker Hitt in Cuba, 1899. (Parker Hitt Photograph Collection, Philippine Photographs Digital Archive, Special Collections Library, University of Michigan)

Second Lieutenant Parker Hitt, October 1899. (National Archives and Records Administration, Parker Hitt, Official Military Personnel File)

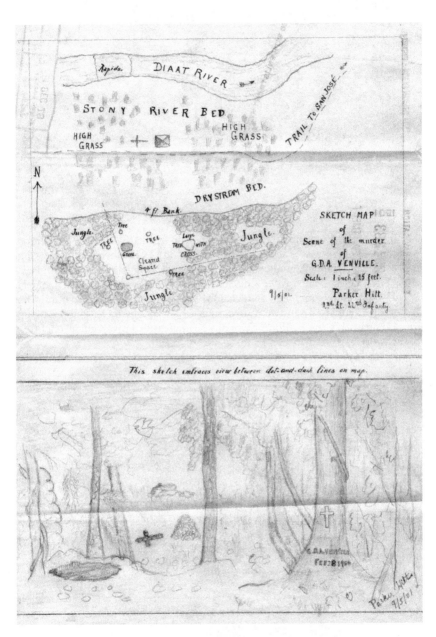

Map and sketch of the grave of Denzell Venville, drawn by Parker Hitt. (National Archives and Records Administration, RG 395, entry 3031)

Members of the 22nd Infantry, possibly after the April 1904 Taraca Expedition, Mindanao, Philippines. Front, left to right: Captain J.L. Donovan, adjutant; Captain John R.R. Hannay, gunboats; John J. Burleigh, Company M; Captain Frederick Stritzinger, Company L; Colonel Marion P. Maus; Captain William H. Wassell; Battalion Commander Gregg, QMQ Company. Back, left to right: Max P. Garber, Company L; Justice, Company M; Hitt, Company K; Philip Remington, Company I; Dean Halford, Company K; unidentified Moro guide. (Courtesy of the Moreman and Mustain family)

Illustration of Parker Hitt as the admiral of Lake Lanao, 1906. The artist is unknown (possibly Hitt). (Parker Hitt Photograph Collection, Philippine Photographs Digital Archive, Special Collections Library, University of Michigan)

Hitt (behind machine gun), Laguna Seca Range, US Army School of Musketry, 1908. (National Archives and Records Administration, RG 156, entry 28, box 2139)

Officers of the 22nd Infantry at the Fort Davis, Alaska, Officers' Club. Front row: Dr. Inman, Major Jacob F. Krepps, Captain George M. Bowford. Back row: Hitt, Captain William E. Hunt, Lieutenant Soloman B. West, Lieutenant Thomas W. Hammond, Lieutenant John J. Burleigh. (Seiffert Family Photographs, Alaska and Polar Regions Collections, Elmer E. Rasmuson Library, University of Alaska–Fairbanks)

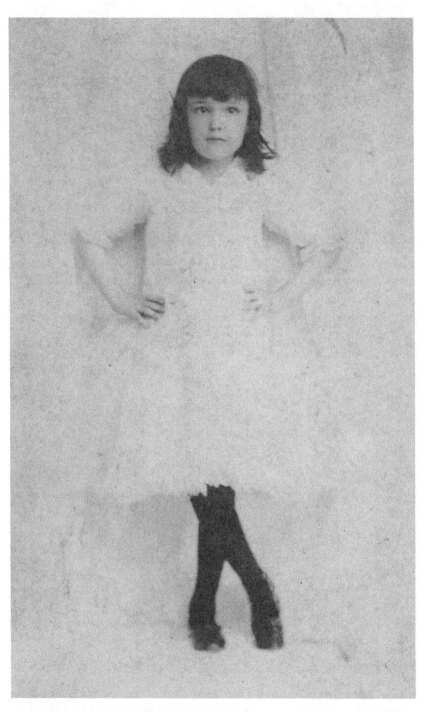

Genevieve Young as a child, circa 1892. (Courtesy of the Moreman and Mustain family)

Genevieve Young, circa 1911, possibly her wedding photograph. (Courtesy of the Moreman and Mustain family)

"Glamor girl" Genevieve Young Hitt, date unknown. (Courtesy of the Moreman and Mustain family)

Parker and Genevieve Young Hitt, Fort Leavenworth, circa 1912. (Courtesy of the Moreman and Mustain family)

Parker Hitt's portable telephone switchboard, 1912. (Courtesy of the Moreman and Mustain family; also available at National Archives and Records Administration, RG 111, entry 44, box 387)

Mary Lueise Hitt, date unknown. (Courtesy of the Moreman and Mustain family)

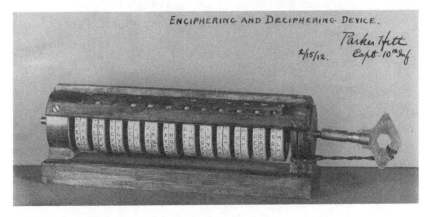

Parker Hitt's first cylinder cipher device, 1912. (National Archives and Records Administration, RG 111, entry 44, box 387)

Parker Hitt on his front porch at Fort Leavenworth, 1913. (Courtesy of the Moreman and Mustain family)

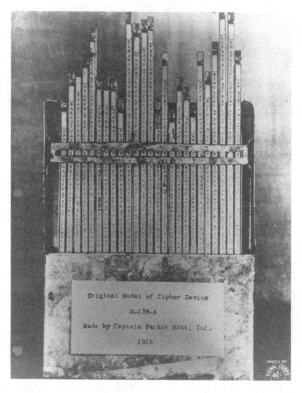

Parker Hitt's 1916 sliding strip device. (US Army)

Colonel Parker Hitt, Chief Signal Officer, AEF First Army, 1918. (National Archives and Records Administration, College Park, RG 111, photo 23349)

Parker Hitt at Souilly, France, 1918. (National Cryptologic Museum Library, David Kahn Collection, Parker Hitt Papers)

Celebration at Souilly, France, attended by officers of the First Army Signal Corps and the female telephone operators, October 20, 1918. Parker Hitt is at the far right. (Courtesy of US Army Intelligence Center of Excellence, Fort Huachuca, Arizona)

Parker Hitt and officers of the First Army Signal Corps. Left to right: Lieutenant Colonel Sosthenes Behn, Captain Ralph H. Keller, Hitt, Lieutenant Burgess, Major Bruce Wedgwood, Lieutenant George Pratt, Major Carroll O. Bickel-haupt, Captain Roy S. Bowland, Lieutenant Ira P. Gillette. (Courtesy of US Army Communications-Electronics Command History Office)

Mary Lue Hitt on a motorcycle, Fort Sam Houston, December 22, 1918. (Courtesy of the Moreman and Mustain family)

Colonel Parker Hitt, Superior Board, 1919. (National Archives and Records Administration, College Park, RG 111, photo 162060)

Parker Hitt, 1923. (National Archives and Records Administration, Parker Hitt, Official Military Personnel File)

Colonel Parker Hitt, Fort Hayes, Ohio, 1940. (National Archives and Records Administration, Parker Hitt, Official Military Personnel File)

Genevieve Hitt, circa late 1940s. (Courtesy of the Moreman and Mustain family)

The Hitt family—Genevieve, Mary Lue, and Parker—circa 1950s. (Courtesy of the Moreman and Mustain family)

8

Commerce

It will seem strange to us all to think of you hereafter as a civilian rather than a soldier.

George Cooper Hitt, 1928

Colonel Louis Richard Sosthenes Behn, a forceful man who rarely took second place to anyone, served as Parker Hitt's assistant during World War I. The two shared a deep interest in communications and ciphers. Though their postwar lives diverged—Hitt remaining in the army and Behn becoming a captain of the commercial telecommunications industry—they kept in touch. The Hitts visited Behn in Cuba in December 1919, and Hitt served as an usher at Behn's May 1921 wedding.[1]

Behn was born on St. Thomas, when it was still a Danish possession. In 1914 he bought a small telephone company, and after the war, he and his brother Hernand formed the Puerto Rican and Cuban Telephone Companies. From this venture grew the International Telephone and Telegraph Company (IT&T). By 1928, IT&T was a corporate giant with cable and telephone companies around the world, a growing stable of associated telecommunications businesses, and a corporate research center. Behn called this his "international family," and he modeled his business on his competitor American Telephone and Telegraph (AT&T). It is not surprising that Behn was interested in cipher development and that, when given the opportunity, he would hire his friend Hitt. He may have believed that having Hitt on his team would give him an advantage in marketing cipher machines to the military.[2]

Before formal orders for his retirement were issued, and before he signed his IT&T employment paperwork, Hitt offered Behn the design for a printing cipher telegraph system. Hitt's design was an outgrowth of his 1920 efforts to combine a printing telegraph and a radio signal, and it may have been influenced by Gilbert Vernam's work. Hitt was enthusiastic and believed his machine would be "safe, simple and inexpensive to construct"; he promised Behn, "We can make such a spectacular demonstration of its security that your idea will practically sell itself." Hitt was ready to immerse himself in the world of commerce and directed his lively and inventive mind toward improving the efficiency and security of commercial telecommunications systems.[3]

At the end of June 1928, Parker put Mary Lue on the train to New York, where she boarded a ship and spent the next eight weeks with her friend Evelyn on a lightly chaperoned European tour. Parker and Genevieve had a month alone together at Genlue Park—a "honeymoon" that their daughter urged them to enjoy. Mary Lue, who turned sixteen while traveling, faithfully wrote to her parents from Paris (twice), Interlaken, Munich, Venice, Florence, Rome, Naples, Basel, and London, sometimes illustrating her letters with little drawings. She vowed to smuggle home four "darling little bottles of Scotch and Cognac" in her garter belt for her Prohibition-deprived parents, so they could each have one drink. "I think you'll find that I've improved lots when I get home—I'm ever so much nicer than I used to be and don't take myself nearly so seriously either. I honestly believe I'm really growing up now," she wrote. When she returned, Parker wanted her to wait and start school in January, but Mary Lue was determined to attend classes, believing she had "wasted entirely too much time already." She entered Friends Seminary, a coeducational day school at 222 East Sixteenth Street in New York, and also took art classes to learn to draw "properly."[4]

While Mary Lue was in Europe, Genevieve tended her crops in Virginia and drove herself around in her car, "Clarice." Parker moved to New York in late July, first staying with his sister-in-law Tot at Fort Jay on Governors Island and then at a hotel. He soon took an apartment at 15 East Tenth Street in Greenwich Village, a short subway ride from the new skyscraper that housed IT&T corporate headquarters at 67 Broad Street in Lower Manhattan. There, on August 1, he settled into his tenth-floor office. In New York, the Hitts had the company of Parker's brothers Rodney and Laurance, as well as Tot and her husband, Edgar. But Genevieve's heart remained in the country, and she split her time between her farm in Virginia and her husband in New York. Mary Lue stayed with Parker in New York during the school year. Parker and Genevieve had the financial means to maintain two residences, and their strong relationship allowed them to give each other space to pursue their divergent interests.[5]

Hitt was assigned to an IT&T subsidiary, International Communications Laboratories (ICL), its version of AT&T's esteemed Bell Laboratories. He made rapid progress there. In early August he signed an inventor's agreement; the next month he submitted patent specifications for a cipher machine "particularly adapted for use in enciphering and deciphering messages sent and received by means of telegraphic or signaling alphabets." By mid-September, his machines had "passed the gauntlet of some of the experts of the Engineering Division, who are very much pleased with them." The company initially planned for Hitt to finish the cipher device that winter in IT&T's London office—a trip the family eagerly anticipated—but then decided to make the model in Newark, New Jersey, instead. Behn was pleased with the pace of Hitt's work and increased his annual salary to $11,000. More important than the money was the fact that Hitt was enjoying his work. William Friedman's Christmas 1928 "grille" cipher puzzle found the Hitt family enjoying the season in New York. There was just one shadow on Hitt's success: in late 1928 or early 1929 he suffered the first bout of what he later referred to as pseudo-angina. He visited a doctor who, after studying an electrocardiogram, proclaimed that Hitt suffered from "no disease whatever," but his heart had low voltage "due in all probability to . . . a heart proportionately small for your body." The doctor warned against heavy physical exercise, despite the fact that Hitt had no specific circulatory problem or disease.[6]

Inventions were just one part of the job, and Hitt spent a great deal of time evaluating cipher systems and machines devised by people who wanted IT&T to buy or invest in their inventions. In August 1928 and again in June 1929, he gave a negative assessment of an unidentified cipher machine developed by AB Cryptograph of Stockholm. This was a bit of a doddle for Hitt, who had been doing this type of evaluation for free since the publication of his *Manual*. In early December 1929 Hitt deciphered messages produced by the Kryha machine and recommended that IT&T not buy the system. In January 1930 he broke the ciphers of two other machines offered to the corporation—one in just a few hours, and the other over several days. "As a result, we will not buy them or be responsible for them to the public, so I have earned my pay this month," he told his father. IT&T had no one else who could deliver such frank and pithy evaluations of cipher equipment; Hitt prevented the company from acquiring inferior devices or patent rights and thus saved it a great deal of money. He also investigated a variety of codes, including the 1923 private code compiled on the "Atomic System" for Western Electric and used by IT&T to protect company communications; he found the code to be unsecure and "dangerous . . . for business use," recommending the use of a new private five-letter code instead. Behn increased Hitt's salary again on April 1, 1929; he was now earning $12,000 a year, nearly triple his army pension.[7]

Cryptographic technology changed dramatically in the decade between Hitt's experience with the American Expeditionary Forces (AEF) Code

Compilation Section and his time at IT&T. Electromechanical devices using rotors were independently created between 1917 and 1922 by at least four inventors—Edward Hebern, Hugo Koch, Arthur Scherbius, and Arvid Damm. Rotor-based machines (such as Scherbius's Enigma) enciphered messages more efficiently than hand-operated mechanical devices (disks, sliding strips, cylinders) and dominated the encryption field by the middle of the twentieth century. Hitt stayed current with these technological innovations, and the most significant of his inventions at IT&T was a rotor-based machine.[8]

Hitt invented seven devices while at IT&T, but only four received patents. The model of his ciphering and deciphering apparatus, a rotor-based "scrambler," was nearly complete in the summer of 1929. It was being constructed at the ICL facility in Newark, New Jersey, and Parker did not enjoy the hassle of traveling across the Hudson River in the heat to supervise the final adjustments. The system included a teleprinter transmitter and receiver. The cipher device had ten rotors that moved one step at a time to apply a running key to the plaintext of the message. Each rotor had a different number of "teeth" on the edge (the first had 96; the tenth had 105), as well as irregular "notchings" corresponding to an engraved alphabet. Output from the device was Baudot code. Hitt's printing telegraph system automatically deciphered the messages with a minimum of expense and delay. A companion device to ensure the privacy of telegram messages attached to the printer and wound the printed tape in such a way that it could not be read; the tape was then back-wound into a container for delivery to the addressee, ensuring privacy and security. The device included a "telltale" mark to show if portions of the message had been exposed to view by the machine operator.[9]

In early October 1929 Hitt demonstrated another new device very similar to his original sliding strip cipher of 1914: it consisted of a piece of paper with slits, "through which twenty strips of paper, each bearing an individually arranged alphabet, are slipped to provide twenty letters in a horizontal line." This "device" enciphered plaintext to produce code words of ten letters, meeting the requirements of the September 1928 International Telegraph Conference; it also remedied a weak feature of his original sliding strips by hiding the keyword used to arrange the strips. By October 16, he had found two ways to use this type of cipher with a typewriter keyboard, and he believed the device would "have a wide field of usefulness for firms which require secrecy and rapidity of handling for their cable, radio and telegraph business." Hitt's resulting cipher typewriter produced and formatted a message in either five- or ten-character groups, but unlike the scrambler, the device contained no means of transmission; decipherment was accomplished on another machine (with identical settings to the first one), where the cipher was entered and the plaintext message printed.[10]

The stock market crashed on Tuesday, October 29, but it had no immediate effect on ICL or IT&T. Hitt was aware of the gloom and despair in the city but was absorbed in his work, which was progressing slowly due to the "sometimes very exasperating . . . perversity of inanimate things." At the end of January 1930, when the machine models were shown to upper management, they worked "as well as first models usually do. Not perfect yet, but that takes time." The machines' automatic ciphering and deciphering feature was working by the end of May. When Genevieve saw them in action for the first time, she remarked that they could have "saved her hours and days of time" in 1918 while she was working in the Southern Department. Perhaps inspired by her husband's work, Genevieve invented a device to illuminate a telephone dial and received a patent in February 1930. Parker forwarded the patent to Behn, who sent his "congratulations to your good wife" but did not purchase the device.[11]

"Why did I take the 10 o'clock train instead of the 11 o'clock," Genevieve despaired in November 1929. While traveling from New York to Washington, she found herself on the train with retired chief signal officer George O. Squier. Squier, proclaiming the coincidence an "act of God," pitched Genevieve his latest invention: the Monophone (later renamed Muzak), which used telephone wires rather than radio waves to broadcast music and other programming to homes. Knowing that her husband was both an engineer and a businessman, Squier thought that Parker Hitt was "the one man in this world" to market the device. He wanted to have lunch with Hitt a few days later at the Metropolitan Club in Washington, where he intended to ask Hitt to convince IT&T to buy the invention. Genevieve thought she might be willing to use Squier's device (if it worked) instead of a radio, and she advised Parker that it "might not be a bad idea not to ignore him on this," as "your ole chief thinks pretty well of you." There is no evidence that Genevieve's gentle persuasion convinced Hitt to meet with Squier. Hitt's loyalty to Behn, his lingering distrust of Squier, and his self-identification as an engineer rather than a salesman meant that he missed what might have been a career-changing lunch.[12]

There were blizzards in Indiana during the winter of 1929–1930, and in Virginia, the ice on the Shenandoah River was a foot thick. Genevieve spent the winter in New York, where, strangely, there were "very few days when an overcoat was essential and practically no snow." By late January, though, she was "itching" to get back to Genlue Park. Mary Lue shared an interest in poultry with her mother, and her rooster "The General" won first prize at a show in January in North Carolina. There was a striking similarity between the traits Mary Lue attributed to her prize bird and those of her father: "The General" had "more brains than lots of people. He knows his business, guards his flock, and always looks the part of a monarch. He is a very proud gentleman, gracious and all that, but he tolerates no familiarity by strangers." In February Genevieve traveled by herself to Virginia for a few weeks, as Mary Lue was "too interested in school to think of much else until June when she gets her coveted diploma." But once school was finished, Hitt knew, "she too will be off for the valley for the summer."[13]

Genevieve spent the spring of 1930 in Virginia. She returned to New York only for Mary Lue's graduation and the birth of her sister's baby. With his entire nuclear family in town, and despite Prohibition, Parker celebrated his father's seventy-ninth birthday on May 27 with a mint julep "with real Virginia mint and other 'fixin's.'" May 28 was the thirteenth anniversary of the sailing of the *Baltic,* and the ship was in port in New York. Parker planned to "go down tomorrow and make a call for auld lang syne," but he made no mention of attending the Baltic Society dinner.[14]

Despite the state of the economy, IT&T moved forward with Behn's plan for worldwide expansion, buying nearly all of a medium-sized German radio manufacturer, C. Lorenz AG, from the Philips Corporation in May 1930. Economic conditions seemed to improve in May, but the boom was only temporary. The reality of the Depression caught up with both the company and Hitt. New York was "too hot," and there was "too much gloom." Business was "awful." Cable and telegraph companies were floundering, and ICL, a nonprofit arm of IT&T, had been "cut to the bone." Hitt still had a job and, he assured his father, "it looks as if I will keep it," but his work had slowed "almost to a standstill" because the company had laid off draftsmen and mechanics. He believed the company was holding on to its engineers only because it would be difficult to build up the workforce again if they were let go.[15]

The summer of 1930 was disastrous in the Shenandoah Valley as well. Genlue Park had no rain between April 2 and the end of July, and it looked "like the Arizona desert." Fortunately, the Hitts' well and spring were still running, but many of their neighbors had resorted to hauling water in barrels from the Shenandoah River. "Our grass is burned to a crisp. I am trying to save some of our new trees and that's about all I can do. Mary Lue enjoys the river swimming," Genevieve told George Hitt. The drought of 1930 destroyed many crops and damaged the valley's apple orchards. Although they had water at Genlue Park, "We could not think of [having] city visitors while the drought lasts; they, one and all, are water wasters." The next year, federal drought relief to the area funded the construction of Skyline Drive; noise from the machinery could be heard at Genlue Park, near the drive's northern entrance. Parker was able to visit only once during the summer. "Young Stephen Reynolds" was sharing his apartment, but Parker remarked, "I certainly miss my women-folks," who were better off in Virginia, as "I want them to be as comfortable as possible."[16]

Hitt's scrambler began a series of shakedown tests in September, including enciphering telegrams between IT&T's New York and London offices. Some were concerned because the format of the machine's messages was unconventional and ineligible for the cheapest per-word transmission rate. Hitt was confident that the additional cost would be more than offset by the decreased time spent coding and decoding messages. As a result of these tests, operational procedures were implemented to require dividing messages longer than 300 words into two or more messages of 200 words or less and resetting the encipherment keyword for each message.[17]

By late autumn 1930, Hitt was placed in charge of "Traffic and Special Studies," subordinate to vice president and chief engineer Allison Andrew Clokey. On the organizational chart, his was the only box without any subordinate organizations. In October Hitt took a six-month lease on apartment 1219 at the four-year-old Fifth Avenue Hotel, just around the corner from his old place. That same month, Genevieve and Mary Lue set out by car to visit Genevieve's ailing father in Texas. Harry New provided a set of American Automobile Association strip maps—the predecessor of AAA's "triptiks"—and recommended the northern route via Memphis and Texarkana rather than the southern one via New Orleans. He advised the women to not "pick up any hitchhikers and get to the towns and put up at respectable hotels. . . . Be good girls and come back to them as loves you as soon as you can." By November 17, they were on their way home and telegraphed Parker from Clarksville, Mississippi.[18]

From New York, Mary Lue traveled to Front Royal on her own to host the family's traditional outdoor Christmas party for the "mountain people" near Genlue Park; these parties, complete with a decorated tree and presents, made a great impression on the community. Mary Lue served hot chocolate, sandwiches, and candy and handed out gifts to the twenty or twenty-five attendees. Parker and Genevieve hated to miss the celebration, but Hitt was needed at work, and Genevieve decided to spend the holiday with him. The couple had dinner with Tot, Ed, and baby Edgar on Governors Island on December 23, and they visited Rodney's family in Westchester, New York, on Christmas Day. That evening, they prepared their own Christmas dinner in their kitchenette at the hotel. It was "wonderful what can be done with electric stoves and a Frigidaire," Parker told his father. Genevieve, of course, had long experience cooking under less-than-ideal conditions.[19]

IT&T cut its workforce again in early 1931, and those who were still employed had to juggle multiple jobs. Hitt's machines were still in development, and his position was secure; in fact, the company authorized him to design a new machine, which would keep the drafting and model shop employed. It was a "strenuous time and not a particularly happy one from a business standpoint," but Hitt thought things were looking up a bit. In February 1931 IT&T began using Hitt's scrambler and printing telegraph for its own international communications, and it was soon ready to market the system. The first client Behn had in mind was the US government. Lieutenant Joseph N. Wenger, of the Navy Department's Bureau of Engineering, came to New York to see the scrambler in late January and told Hitt the navy wanted to study the device. A demonstration of the machine was scheduled for late summer, but whether this happened is unknown, as is Wenger's ultimate evaluation. Herbert O. Yardley's tell-all book *The American Black Chamber* had just been published, and Hitt opined that the navy, which traditionally focused on codes, had "developed a great interest in ciphers since Yardley had his say about codebooks."[20]

By the end of February 1931, Genevieve and Mary Lue were anxious to return to the farm, as "chickens, gardens and the life there make an interest for them that they cannot get in New York." Parker planned to stay in New York through the summer, making "as many trips south as I can squeeze in." Genevieve and Mary Lue left New York at the end of March and arrived in Front Royal in a heavy rain, which, they hoped, had broken the drought. Hitt showed up a few days later and, upon viewing the general conditions in the area, told his father, "Thank God we don't have to make a living down there. It is all right for a summer loafing place but that is all." Still, he hoped for a "pleasant summer with lots of flowers and chickens for Gee Gee and plenty of tennis and swimming for Mary Lue." Genevieve "is a great farmer," Parker proclaimed. She had planted new fruit trees—apricots, nectarines, and three varieties each of plums, peaches, and cherries—to supplement the old trees, and everything had started to bloom during his visit.[21]

Genevieve returned to the "dreadful city" in late May to check up on Parker and Tot, while Mary Lue went to Virginia Beach with friends. Parker accompanied Genevieve back to Virginia for Memorial Day. At Genlue Park, everything was green and growing. Parker, who had never seen his wife "so happy and well," thought Genevieve might be able to "bookkeep" her flock of 250 Black Jersey Giant chickens into a profit "if she makes a reasonable allowance for the good it has done her to have an interest that keeps her out of doors and busy." Parker spent most of the hot and humid summer of 1931 in New York, with only the occasional weekend away. His plans for the fall and winter were still up in the air; he thought he might have to move closer to IT&T's Newark plant to oversee production. His old friend from Leavenworth and the AEF, General George Gibbs, retired from the army as chief signal officer that summer and immediately came to work for IT&T, filled with ideas for expanding Hitt's work.[22]

Despite the navy's apparent lack of interest in the scrambler, there were other potential clients in Washington. Both the US Army and the Department of State needed to secure their communications. In September 1931 Hitt invited Signal Corps personnel to examine the machine in New York, and William Friedman and Major David M. Crawford, Friedman's immediate superior, saw the device in action in New York in late October. The State Department also asked IT&T to demonstrate the system in Washington, and the company installed two sets of equipment in two separate rooms at the department's communications center. Friedman, representing the Signal Corps at the State Department demonstration, thought the machine "performed splendidly and that the State Department communicators were greatly impressed by it." Friedman asked for, and Hitt supplied, additional information about the arrangement of the machine's notched wheels, along with a complete set of circuit diagrams.[23]

After the demonstration, the State Department asked the Signal Corps' Signal Intelligence Service (SIS), headed by Friedman, to evaluate the scrambler for cryptographic security. Friedman and his team—young mathematicians Frank Rowlett, Solomon Kullback, and Abraham Sinkov—conducted a series of tests on November 11 and 12, 1931. They first studied the material and diagrams provided by Hitt; then, once they understood how the machine worked, they devised principles for solving the cipher even before they conducted a physical test. An adversary may or may not have access to the same information, and although Friedman and his team had the advantage of knowing the machine's operating principles before beginning their evaluation, they did not have the keys used for the cipher messages. Their goal was to recover both the keys and the original plaintext of the test messages.[24]

Signal Corps offices were located in the Munitions Building, constructed during World War I to house the War Department. On November 11 Hitt delivered one of the machines to the SIS offices there; he showed the team how the scrambler worked and explained the procedure for setting a key. As soon as Hitt left the room, the team planned their attack. Hitt then went to the State Department to pick up the test messages; under his guidance, State Department employees had drawn up twelve typical diplomatic messages and enciphered them, each with a different key. Friedman telephoned Hitt when the team was ready to begin, and Hitt delivered the messages shortly after lunch. The SIS team assumed the key would be an ordinary word found in a dictionary; this proved to be true.[25]

The flaws in Hitt's machine were immediately apparent to Friedman and his team. Three characters were generated when the machine came out of cipher mode, and the team (correctly) assumed that the preceding set of three characters must represent a period. They discovered two ways to solve the messages: by knowing or assuming some of the message's content (using what is known as a crib), and by analyzing a frequency count of the cipher characters. By examining the machine's blueprints and the machine itself, the mathematicians discovered "extremely structured" patterns in the wheels; these patterns assisted their solution. Friedman halted the first test when four of the twelve messages had been solved, as "there seemed no point in solving all the messages of this set, it being deemed satisfactory to demonstrate, by solving any four of them, the possibility of solving any messages of this category . . . it may be stated that, with practice, any message of this type may be solved within an hour or less."[26]

For the second part of the test, conducted on November 12, State Department communicators composed four messages representing the third, fourth, fifth, and sixth in a set of six messages enciphered from an unknown initial key. The purpose of this test was to evaluate a sequence of messages transmitted without resetting the key when some of the messages had not been intercepted. Friedman's team, with their knowledge of the machine's physical characteristics, quickly reduced the number of potential initial settings for each wheel from ninety-six to twenty-six, which enabled them to solve all four messages. The SIS team assumed that an adversary with either good intelligence or a stolen copy of the machine would have the same information used in the test and concluded that Hitt's machine was not cryptographically secure.[27]

Once the test was complete, Friedman telephoned Hitt, who returned to SIS to hear the verdict. In the outer office, Friedman showed him the keys and the decipherments. Hitt's reaction was "amazement and awe," and he asked permission to congratulate Friedman's team. True to form, Hitt was gracious in the face of defeat. Rowlett tells the story best: "When we had assembled, Colonel Hitt made a short and somewhat formal speech of congratulations, in which he stated that while he was disappointed that his invention did not offer the high degree of security that he had expected of it, he was personally gratified to learn that the War Department had developed a cryptanalytic capability powerful enough to solve in such a short time a cipher machine that he had considered to be impregnable." Hitt "must have felt a great disappointment at having his invention proved to be unsatisfactory in such a short time," but "he never let it show for an instant."[28]

Hitt's machine had been solved by some of the best cryptologists of the twentieth century. SIS's analysis could have been used to increase the security of what was otherwise a practical and efficient machine, but as a government agency, it could not supply specific advice to a corporation, even if those suggestions would improve a machine the government wanted to use. Kullback thought this was "unfortunate." At the time, the development of secure communications for the army took place largely at Fort Monmouth, and "some of their notions about cryptographic security were not too good"; in retrospect, Kullback believed the government would have benefited if SIS had been permitted to work with Hitt and IT&T in the early 1930s. A few hours of work had "completely ruined" IT&T's chance of a government sale; it lost years of Hitt's effort and at least $100,000 (about $1.7 million in 2020 dollars) in production costs. In Friedman's opinion, the IT&T machine embodied principles that might have been developed to produce an unbreakable cipher. One stumbling block, even for Friedman, was adding complexity to the ciphering mechanism without unduly complicating the operator's use of the machine.[29]

Friedman gave Hitt some official feedback, and he may have revealed other technical details of the SIS analysis in a face-to-face confidential meeting with the man he so admired. Hitt "guessed" that one problem with the scrambler was the three-character sequence that took the machine out of cipher. He was working on a new and more portable machine that had eight irregularly notched, interchangeable wheels and no termination signal. He was convinced that the SIS method of attack would not work on this new device. The fact that his new design specifically remedied problems identified by SIS but not officially shared supports the supposition that Friedman took Hitt into his confidence. Hitt was anxious to have two models of his new device built because both Friedman and Wenger wanted to see it in operation. Work on the new machine was halted in 1932, although George Gibbs recommended that detailed drawings be completed so efforts could resume if the faults were resolved. Nothing more is known about the last machine Hitt would make for IT&T.[30]

For a decade, Friedman had investigated and invented rotor-based cipher machines. He first conceived the idea for his M-134 converter in the mid-1920s. In mid-1930 the army set aside a small amount of money for its construction, and after much delay, the M-134-T1 was evaluated in March 1932. Given his limited budget and the progress under way on the M-134, Friedman would have resisted any urge he had to purchase and improve on the IT&T machine. Still, Hitt's ideas stuck with him, and in April 1932 Friedman wrote of the "inherent weakness of all such devices" and outlined his thoughts on a machine that separated keying material from the cipher device. SIS and the navy worked on the problem through the 1930s; by early 1940, a prototype of the Electric Cipher Machine Mark II/SIGABA (designated M-134C by the army) had been designed. SIGABA was the most successful American military encipherment machine of the mid-twentieth century. In a small way, Hitt's machine contributed to Friedman's thinking.[31]

In an odd twist of history, Hitt's ciphering and deciphering apparatus was also a direct predecessor to the Lorenz Company's Schlüsselzusatz (SZ) cipher device, more commonly known in cryptologic history as TUNNY. The German government used this device for high-level communications during World War II. Friedman and his team did not learn of this connection until after the war; however, knowing how to solve Hitt's machine would not have helped solve TUNNY, for the two machines did not share the same weakness. Lorenz, an IT&T subsidiary since 1930, legally obtained the details of Hitt's scrambler and used his ideas in the earliest versions of the SZ. In December 1930, nearly a year before Friedman's team assessed Hitt's machine, Lorenz asked IT&T about the "automatic code and decoding system," but IT&T did not share any details until the patent had been approved. By May 1931, Hitt knew of plans to manufacture his machine at one of IT&T's German plants. In 1937 Lorenz produced a machine with ten wheels that was largely identical to

Hitt's scrambler. The 1937 machine was quickly succeeded by the twelve-wheel SZ-40, which was later supplanted by the improved SZ-42a and SZ-42b.[32]

Kullback discussed the similarities and differences between Hitt's scrambler and TUNNY in 1976 but was unaware of the corporate link between IT&T and Lorenz; he believed Hitt's device had been sold to the Germans. Hitt never knew—and would have been appalled to learn—that his work had led to a device used by the Third Reich. At some point, Hitt was told (probably by Friedman) that "the principles covered by my patents were used in the design of the supersecret teletype cipher machine which was widely used both on land lines and radio circuits during the last two or three years of the war." Friedman may have been referring to TUNNY, but he was more likely crediting Hitt with contributing to the development of SIGABA. Friedman's high opinion of Hitt's work had not been damaged by the failure of the scrambler, and he was probably trying to reassure Hitt of the importance of his work at a time when the older man needed an ego boost. This revelation was extremely indiscreet on Friedman's part, but he was familiar with the pain of being marginalized and felt empathy for Hitt.[33]

A few months before the government tests, Hitt became a stockholder in IT&T. In September 1931 he received credit for an additional five years of service (at his initial rate of pay) for purposes of the company's pension plan. This was Behn's attempt to recognize the experience of "employees who entered the System service at higher than normal age." Even though Friedman and his team had broken Hitt's cipher device, costing IT&T a lucrative government sale, Behn was loyal to his friend; he made Hitt (perhaps at the urging of Gibbs) a director of the corporation and appointed him acting administrative director of ICL on November 27, 1931. The year had been a good one for Hitt professionally; by any measure, he was successfully building his second career. But work-related stress, a lack of sleep, and the general economic conditions took a toll on Hitt's health. On Tuesday, January 26, 1932, he suffered a so-called heart attack, and the doctor sent him home to Front Royal to recuperate for ten days.[34]

No description of Hitt's symptoms can be found. Some correspondents called it an "indisposition" or an "attack of illness." It might have been an anxiety attack or stress-related gastroesophageal reflux disease (GERD). After Parker's attack, George Hitt remarked on two earlier "warning attacks." In any case, his recovery was rapid, with minimal medical intervention. During a 1940 physical, it was noted that he had suffered from "pseudo-angina" after physical strain in 1928, 1931, 1935, 1938, and 1940, but Hitt did not mention a heart attack during this exam, and he did not include the January 1932 attack as one of his pseudo-angina incidents. Physical and mental exhaustion had slowed Hitt in the past: he had suffered a stress-related physical collapse in 1908 after overwork at the School of Musketry, experienced illness and weight loss in early 1919 after the war, and been plagued by recurrent "acid problems" at Fort Sam Houston in the 1920s.[35]

Parker's father blamed his illness on "the strenuous life of New York . . . with its heavy responsibilities" and gave his son a pep talk, telling him to "keep your courage up and remember that you have years of usefulness yet, provided you exercise care in your daily life . . . you can, if you will it, beat this enemy to your health and continue to use your splendid mind for yet greater accomplishments" and "regain your former vigor and resume your joy of living." A few weeks later, George Hitt sent two parcels to Front Royal—one contained Parker's army sword, and the other had letters, papers, and photographs Parker and Genevieve had sent to his parents over the years. "What a thrilling life you have had!" George told his son.[36]

As he recuperated, Hitt documented, at great length, his worries about ICL, sharing his thoughts with Colonel Augustus H. Griswold, IT&T's executive vice president for postal telegraph and cable. Hitt was acutely aware of the need to retain key personnel to maintain IT&T's research and development efforts in the coming years. But money was a problem. The lab's budget of $436,300 for 1932 (more than $8 million in 2020 dollars) could not be properly allocated for development, as each IT&T subsidiary demanded equal sums, despite having unequal investments in the laboratory. Expenses in the budget were not aligned with actual requirements, and because ICL was not designed to make a profit, there was no permanent plan of financial support. Hitt thought the problems could be rectified if the corporation set up a support system similar to AT&T's arrangement for Bell Laboratories. ICL had a "ruinous" policy of hiring and firing trained research and development personnel each year to fit a "freak" situation caused by working for wire and cable companies one year and radio companies the next. Hitt proposed moving radio functions to the engineering department and allowing the laboratory to remain the corporation's patent holding company; it could then bill the various subsidiaries for patent services. He also suggested selling or licensing newly developed cable printers and other equipment to provide income directly to ICL. Hitt followed up his memo with a personal note to Behn, writing, "I think you will see that the present financial and technical domination of the laboratories by the operating companies had put me in a most difficult administrative position."[37]

Though Hitt was feeling better by March, Behn suggested that he take more leave "so that you can come back strong and relieve your friends of the feeling of responsibility should you come back too quickly." Behn proposed that, on his return, Hitt could be reinstated to his current job or something less "exacting," and he put Hitt on a four-month convalescence at half pay. Parker and Genevieve traveled to New York for a few days, and while they were away, Mary Lue kept things running on the farm during a blizzard. George Hitt praised his granddaughter's "self-reliance," reminding her parents that their nineteen-year-old "isn't a little girl anymore."[38]

Although IT&T management told Hitt the company would be glad to have him back, 1932 was a terrible year for both IT&T and Behn. A combination of the Depression and bad business decisions was to blame. Behn's acquisition of a majority share of the Ericsson Company went badly wrong. At the end of April IT&T's chief engineer, Clokey, told Hitt there was little chance of resuming construction on his scrambler for "some time to come"; the company had been forced to "discontinue other activities which were formerly considered to be essential." In June 1932 IT&T's laboratories were shuttered when research and development efforts were halted to save money. Hitt was terminated. He took the news with his customary equanimity, expressing gratitude to Behn for his "thoughtful and considerate" provision of sick leave on half pay, writing, "I shall always appreciate that final courtesy even above the many others which I have received." Hitt would have intermittent communications with Gibbs and others at IT&T through mid-1934; Gibbs continued to seek out his opinion on cipher matters.[39]

Hitt's work at IT&T brought no profound change to the company or to the progress of American cryptologic efforts, although it may have influenced Friedman's thinking and contributed to the development of SIGABA. What began as a challenging and profitable postmilitary career ended in a health crisis and a lack of practical achievement. Hitt displayed no remorse or regret at the abrupt end of his business career. He began a long and interesting period of semiretirement, during which he still wielded some influence in the cryptologic world.

9

Retreat

*I am delighted to report that Parker Hitt is in fine shape. I have
never seen him in such health. He is helping me to run this
place but I do not think he enjoys it so very much. It is hard
to make an idle man of him.*

Genevieve Hitt, 1932

The Hitts hunkered down in Front Royal as the Depression deepened.
Hitt's only income was his retirement pay, which would soon be reduced
in line with cuts to military pay. Retirement did not suit Hitt, who had
apparently recovered completely from his ailment by mid-1932. He was
well enough to attend the fifteenth anniversary dinner of the Baltic Society,
held at the home of Major George S. Patton that spring. Genevieve and
Mary Lue were delighted to have him in Virginia, but Parker, only fifty-
three years old and restless, wanted something to do. Harry New attempted
to come to the rescue. In August 1932 New became a commissioner for the
1934 Chicago World's Fair—dubbed a "Century of Progress"—and tried
to find a job for Hitt within his committee, telling the younger man, "Any
place or in any way I can ever help you know I want to do it." The open
positions were funded by the State Department, which meant that Hitt
would have to surrender his military retirement pay; he demurred.[1]

In June 1933 Hitt requested active duty with the Public Works Administration (PWA) created under the National Industrial Recovery Act. Colonel George R. Spaulding, the retired army engineer who had served with
Hitt on the Superior Board at the end of the war, took charge of the PWA
in advance of congressional authorization. Though unable to offer Hitt a
permanent position or salary, Spaulding used him on a temporary basis
for communications work before the authorization bill was passed. Hitt
spent a few weeks at PWA offices in Washington at his own expense before
finding that his services were no longer required. He enjoyed his short stint
there and in 1937 attended a small reunion at the Army and Navy Club
on the fourth anniversary of the PWA's birth. Recording the PWA's early
history was one of the activities at the reunion, and Hitt came prepared
with short remarks about his role and documents for the files. He hoped

the event would avoid "comment or criticism of anything which occurred after we had done our part."[2]

While looking for work, Hitt stepped up austerity measures at home. He entered into negotiations with the local telephone company to reduce the rental cost for the 2.1 miles of line (sixty-three poles) from town to his house. He had paid more than $300 for line rental over the years; at $6 a month, this exceeded his combined monthly telephone rental and long-distance charges. He had not complained about the "exorbitant" price in the past, but now he believed "there should be a sharp reduction in the charge" for the circuit, which had been "cheaply built" with wires strung on existing poles. The matter remained unresolved in November, but Hitt hoped the company would see reason. Always frugal and a stickler for accuracy, he now paid closer attention to his bills and regularly questioned and disputed certain items. In December 1932 he received a notice from the New York State Department of Taxation, which claimed that his tax installment for October 1931 had not been paid; Hitt asked International Telephone and Telegraph (IT&T) to resolve the matter, as the company had deducted the tax from his pay, but it had not been recorded by the state.[3]

The Depression brought some hardship to the extended Hitt family: Laurance had inconsistent work, Muriel suffered some loss of income from investments, and Parker's aunt Kate lost her job and was unable to access savings tied up in a building and loan association. Parker and Genevieve had the farm and his retirement pay, even though it was not as much money as they were accustomed to. The family cut down on travel, and it appears they did not go to Texas when Genevieve's father, Dr. Young, died in December 1932. Genevieve and Mary Lue visited Tot and her family in Panama in the spring of 1933, but Parker stayed home. This may have been when Genevieve gave Parker a membership card in the "Protective Association for Married Men," granting him permission "to go where he pleases, drink what he pleases and when he pleases," and "keep and enjoy the company of any lady or ladies he sees fit, as I know he is a good judge. I want him to enjoy life in this world for he will be a long time Dead." Hitt's one personal indulgence during these years was spending $143.75, paid in monthly installments, on a new set of the *Encyclopedia Britannica* in 1936. It replaced the set Genevieve and Dr. Young had given him for his birthday in 1912.[4]

The farm fed the family and provided a small income. Genevieve planted raspberries, strawberries, and fruit trees, including figs; the Hitts loved figs and may have distilled the fruit. In the summer of 1932

Genevieve and Mary Lue had 200 chicks and were getting about seventeen eggs a day from their brood hens. Genevieve longed to have ducks too, which would have been "such a nice change for the table." Although the garden was coming along, she had only cherries in the orchard and no peaches, for "you have to work hard to keep things growing and to keep something from eating everything up." In late 1934 she had a plan to make and sell marmalade. In the spring of 1937, with the ever-bearing strawberries "going great guns," the family sold forty-five quarts on one day alone, netting $6.75.[5]

By 1938, the Hitts had about 170 acres of land. More than half was the original Genlue Park acreage, and the rest was adjacent or nearby. Genevieve, who had always been interested in real estate, became something of a land speculator; she bought several parcels of land bordering the new Shenandoah National Park between 1933 and 1935. She may have received advice on the purchase from her lawyer, Aubrey G. Weaver, a member of the Virginia senate and director of the organization that had worked to establish the park. Genevieve did not intend to farm this land; she wanted it to provide financial security for Mary Lue's future. The Hitts were undoubtedly aware (perhaps through Weaver) of Virginia's efforts (starting in 1929) to take private land through condemnation and augment the park. In February 1937 the State Commission on Conservation and Development filed a condemnation suit involving a parcel of Genevieve's land. After a hearing in July 1938, Genevieve challenged the valuation of the property, which had initially been set at $1,056 and then at $1,850; she received $2,000 for the parcel in September. The state's taking of land was a sad event for many mountain residents, but it was a successful business deal for Genevieve Hitt.[6]

Apart from farming and investing, Genevieve maintained a lively interest in politics in her adopted home of Virginia. Though very much a Republican, she somehow found herself elected as a delegate to the Democratic Convention in Richmond in 1932, which she did not attend. "Can you imagine any man wanting to be President! I can't imagine four years of Hell. I may lack ambition but I do love peace," she told her mother in June. She was a member of the Women's Organization for National Prohibition Reform (WONPR) and may have joined during her time in New York. She supported the repeal of Prohibition, observing that "a saloon on every corner would be better than the present condition." When a man in Front Royal told her there had been five saloons in town before Prohibition, she responded, "And now you have 38 and not one cent of revenue, and the county can't afford to feed the men on the road and in your jails." She became the Warren County chair of WONPR and found it a "hard uphill job as I have the Methodists and Baptists to contend with"; the only rational argument that worked was an appeal to their pocketbooks. In 1933 Genevieve represented Virginia's Seventh Congressional District at the state constitutional convention, which voted on repeal of the Eighteenth Amendment and ratification of the Twenty-First Amendment. The convention met on Wednesday, October 25, 1933, in the Old Hall of the House of Delegates in Richmond. Genevieve brought her father-in-law as her guest and voted with the majority to end Prohibition. Pauline Sabin, head of the WONPR, congratulated Genevieve for her role in the "gallant fight for a righteous cause." The Hitt family celebrated the end of Prohibition on December 5, 1933.[7]

Parker did not enjoy winters on the mountainside. He was tempted by an invitation from George Gruenert to visit the Philippines one winter but was reluctant to venture so far from home. A car trip to Key West, Florida, where the family could stay at Fort Zachary Taylor, was an economical solution to the winter blues. The Hitts spent at least two weeks in Key West, soaking up sunshine, in March 1935. Mary Lue played tennis every day and won a ladies' singles tournament at the Casa Marina hotel. During their visit, Parker reportedly made the acquaintance of Key West's most famous resident, Ernest Hemingway; in later years, Mary Lue Hitt would tell of encounters with the author. While there is no evidence of anything more than a casual acquaintance, the two men may have enjoyed discussing Cuba and World War I.[8]

Harry New, Hitt's friend, benefactor, and "honorary uncle," died on May 10, 1937. Parker and Genevieve were at his hospital bedside and escorted his body and his widow to Indianapolis by train. Parker made the funeral arrangements and was one of the honorary pallbearers. Genevieve spent the entire spring and early summer in Washington with the grieving Catherine New, leaving Mary Lue to tend the farm.[9]

In 1937 the Hitts splurged and headed south in mid-November, making their way to Key West. During a stay at Fort Barrancas, Florida, part of Pensacola Naval Air Station, Hitt, as a retired senior army officer, paid a courtesy call on the station's commander, Captain William Halsey. When they arrived in Key West, Hitt found a letter from cipher developer J. F. Byrne waiting for him. Hitt warned Byrne, "Do not expect to get too much work out of me," for "[I am] on a vacation and all my cipher books and apparatus for work are at home. . . . This is a delightful place but there is not much incentive to do anything but loaf." The family had been in town for at least a week when the front page of the *Key West Citizen* announced that they were staying in a cottage at Fort Taylor. Key West society was full of retired army officers who had homes there, and it attracted many more visiting officers during the season. Parker, Genevieve, and Mary Lue enjoyed the sun and socializing and took advantage of the opportunity to be lazy; Mary Lue in particular loved tennis and swimming. Hitt's former company commander from the 2nd Volunteer Engineers, Christopher FitzGerald, ran an engineering firm in Havana. When the captain of the SS *Florida* told FitzGerald that an officer of his old unit, "a very tall man," was in Key West, FitzGerald guessed it was Hitt. He invited the family to visit for a "a pow-wow and you can look over the old camp ground." Hitt declined the offer, and FitzGerald contemplated sending him a bottle of Cuban rum to help him enjoy his vacation. The family stayed in Key West at least until the end of January; it may have been their last visit to the island.[10]

Hitt had aspired to be a journalist in his youth, and now that he had time on his hands, he pursued some literary and quasi-literary ideas related to both his army service and his cipher skills. In 1931, while still at IT&T, he had been asked by Thomas M. Johnson, a war correspondent who specialized in intelligence matters, to appear on an NBC radio program discussing codes and ciphers. Hitt declined because of IT&T's work in foreign countries, but he told Johnson he had lots of stories about the nongovernmental use of ciphers that might be of interest. Nothing came of this. In 1933 Hitt offered an article titled "A Side Light on the Capture of Aguinaldo" to *Liberty,* a general-interest weekly magazine, but there is no evidence it was published.[11]

Early in 1932, while still recovering from his illness, Hitt told George Fabyan that he and Genevieve were gathering material for an "exciting book" on ciphers. This was the beginning of *The ABC of Secret Writing.* As Hitt's health improved, however, he abandoned the project. The book was resurrected in 1934 when Roy Paulus of Puck Publishing approached Hitt looking for a "recognized authority" to author a short book to accompany a game he had developed. Hitt was interested in Paulus's proposal but wanted to know more before he made a commitment. He arranged to meet Paulus on April 24, 1934, at the Army War College in the office of his old friend and college commandant General George S. Simonds.[12]

Energized by the meeting, Hitt wrote a short "cipher story" for Paulus to send, on speculation, to a publishing syndicate. Hitt contemplated other ways, including radio broadcasts, to share cipher skills with the public, and he developed an idea for a monthly puzzle subscription that would include a short story, a cipher, suggestions, and a sealed envelope containing the solution. Hitt told Paulus he had enough material to issue one puzzle a month for a "practically indefinite period if we can work up a demand for it." Paulus was excited by the idea of a cipher game, which he considered an improvement on his original idea. Paulus drew up a marketing plan and, unaware of the book project Hitt had abandoned, asked him to prepare a small, "semi-technical" booklet on methods of solving ciphers to accompany the game. By July, Paulus had the "ABC manuscript" typeset, and the proofs went to Hitt in November; then progress stopped. George Hitt, with his publishing experience, advised that if the book was a bit too technical for the average reader, Parker could add a chapter on cipher oddities, noting, "It may be mere journalism but it is something that the fool public likes to read. Anything mysterious is attractive. Try it!"[13]

Meanwhile, in May 1934 Paulus approached the Scripps-Howard newspaper chain, the McClure Syndicate, and the United Features Syndicate and proposed a series of articles about an unnamed officer (Hitt) and ciphers, intended to publicize what Paulus now called "Cryptogame." Hitt objected to the series being part of United Features' proposed "Sunday Supplement," fearing that it was the wrong outlet for the "class of people who will be interested in cryptography as a game"; in addition, he did not want "to be associated with sensational publicity of this type if it can possibly be avoided." Hitt also balked at a stipulation that the anecdotes be based on "authentic cases" with actual names and places; he wanted to use fictional tales. United Features expressed interest in a daily item short enough for a commuter to complete in twenty minutes, built around a fictitious investigator. At the same time, the McClure Syndicate showed interest in a weekly cipher-related short story. To avoid potential conflict over the two syndicates "sharing" an author, Paulus proposed that Hitt use a pen name for one of the features. Hitt enthusiastically proposed a daily feature "that I can keep going until kingdom come" and suggested using the nom de plume "Cooper," his father's middle name. He agreed to payment of 15 percent of gross sales and thought they should copyright the idea of a "Write-Down Cipher." Hitt was happy to let Paulus handle the business arrangements.[14]

Whether Hitt and Paulus were too slow to respond or United Features changed its mind, by August 1934, the syndicate had lost interest in a daily cipher puzzle. Plans for the game continued, however, and Hitt gave Paulus six different Cryptogames. He also provided a new proposal for a daily "Secret News Item" for United Features, but Paulus was unable to close the deal. Sets of Cryptogame cards were printed on specu-lation by Puck Publishing, and Hitt tested them out on some Boy Scouts from the Front Royal area, as well as some friends, who all had fun with the cards.[15]

In January 1935, as his work with Paulus stalled, Hitt started look-ing for an outlet for a new book he called *Ciphers and Their Solutions*. He planned fourteen chapters, expanding on his *Manual* and going beyond the limited scope of *The ABC of Secret Writing*; the book would cover machine ciphers, codes, and examples of famous ciphers. Hitt approached Jerome S. Meyer, managing editor of Heyday House (a sub-sidiary of Doubleday) in New York with his book proposal; they met in New York in late January. Meyer thought the material was "too difficult and complicated to warrant the risk of publication." Hitt was somewhat surprised at this, as he had feared the work was too simple. He informed Meyer that he was "no judge at all of the capabilities of the general read-ing public along these lines." It seems that Hitt abandoned the manu-script after Meyer's rejection.[16]

Paulus realized in June 1935 that he had not heard from Hitt for six months, so he wrote to request further revisions to the *ABC* manuscript; Hitt sent eight additional exercises for the book in July. The publishing process dragged on through the autumn. Hitt believed that, with "war excitement in the air," the public's interest in spies and ciphers would increase. By mid-December, he had twelve copies of the book in hand. *The ABC of Secret Writing*, which sold for $1, was an extremely simpli-fied version of Hitt's *Manual*; it was intended for a lay audience and pro-vided simple instructions for those new to codes and ciphers. For instance, it focused on how to distinguish between substitution and transposition ciphers and how to solve simple examples of each. Although most of the exercises were taken from civilian life (banking, crime, and romance), one example used Mexican general Trevino's cipher. The book did not sell well, and Paulus still had more than half the copies of the first edition available in October 1937. Cryptogame never found a market, and Puck went out of business in 1936. One of Hitt's stories, "A Tale of the Rio Grande," was published in the *New York National Guardsman* in 1936; it might have started out as one of his prospective columns for Paulus. Hitt hoped to exploit the market for cipher stories created by the publi-cation of Herbert O. Yardley's *The American Black Chamber* in 1931, but he was unable to do so.[17]

Hitt gave up on writing about ciphers, but he did not give up writing. In 1936 he started to pull together material for an article about the Spanish gunboats on Lake Lanao and his time as "admiral" of that fleet, working from his diaries and other papers. When he needed more information, Hitt asked his old friend Eisenhower, then stationed in the Philippines, to dig up some material. Eisenhower's hasty telegram in November 1936 indicated that he was having trouble finding worthwhile information, and he passed along news of their mutual friends the Gruenerts. In January 1937 Hitt wrote to Eisenhower again, asking Ike to answer four questions about the boats' current operations, as he hoped to round out his article with a link to the present day. Ike came through a few months later and sent three pages of material he had tracked down from the adjutant general, as well as a 1916 monograph about Lake Lanao province.[18]

While waiting to hear from Eisenhower, Hitt contacted Gruenert, now a brigadier general commanding the 23rd Brigade of the Philippines Division and then the division itself at Fort William McKinley. Gruenert had his chief of staff, Colonel Edwin Butcher, do some research for Hitt. Working from leads provided by Butcher, Hitt wrote to a few other retired officers. Gruenert's inquiries to the *Manila Bulletin* prompted the editor of that newspaper to assign a member of the editorial staff to help Hitt. Although Hitt felt the story was still incomplete, "Amphibious Infantry" was published in February 1938.[19]

After the Lake Lanao article appeared, Hitt's desire to write was exhausted. He found a new hobby in the American Cryptogram Association (ACA), an organization formed in September 1929 by a group of friends whose interest in ciphers was quickened by a recurring column on cryptography in *Detective Fiction Weekly*. Hitt had known of the organization since at least September 1933, when Donald Millikin, a former army officer who had worked in the G2A6 Radio Intelligence Section in France, sent Hitt an issue of the ACA publication the *Cryptogram*. Almost five years later, Hitt joined the organization. ACA members used "noms"—cryptic nicknames—to identify themselves to other members; Hitt chose PHERTIKRAT, a simple anagram of PARKER HITT.[20]

Another famous cryptologist, Yardley (nom BOZO), was the first vice president of the ACA at the time of Millikin's 1933 letter. Yardley's participation may have been a factor in Hitt's decision not to join the ACA until 1938, for he had no desire to be associated with the man. George Lamb reassured Hitt, "There is no reason why your paths should ever cross, in the Association or in the pages of the *Cryptogram*. Just between you and me, he [Yardley] is not well-liked by members." Yardley's book and related articles in the *Saturday Evening Post* had upset many cryptologists. William Friedman was particularly outraged by the inaccuracies and untruths, and when Yardley's first article was published, he wrote a long memo to Hitt, whose work, he felt, had been slighted and misrepresented. Hitt responded that he had "never seen in a reputable magazine any series of articles so full of misstatement of fact, uncalled for criticism and innuendo as those by Yardley." Of the *Saturday Evening Post,* Hitt lamented, "A great national weekly has permitted him to pose before its readers as one of the outstanding heroes of the war, poor fellow, and he had to lie to do it." In September 1931 Hitt provided George Gibbs, the army's chief signal officer, with a long negative commentary about *The American Black Chamber.* Yardley "always was a skunk," Hitt told an ACA friend in 1940, and in 1963 he informed David Kahn that he "disliked him [Yardley] so much that I would rather have you consult someone else about anything in the 'Black Chamber.'" Mary Lue continued the animus toward Yardley long after her father's death, saying he was "one of the most thoroughly disliked people that it was my good fortune never to run into."[21]

The members of the ACA knew Hitt by reputation; many owned his *Manual* and were deliriously happy to have him among their number. George C. Lamb (DAMON), editor of the *Cryptogram,* welcomed Hitt and said the members "hail your arrival amongst them with great joy." O. D. Williamson (SAHIB), who ran a "friendly" group for those interested in military ciphers and advanced problems, immediately invited Hitt to join. Helen Fouché Gaines (PICCOLA), first vice president of the organization, wrote, "Well-well! So the Parker Hitt is really a person and not a manual which somebody is always borrowing or making me copy!" Thus began a delightful correspondence between Gaines and Hitt. It is doubtful that Yardley received such effusive praise from the ACA community.[22]

Hitt's extensive correspondence with Gaines before her premature death of a heart attack in April 1940 included advice on her forthcoming book *Elementary Cryptanalysis.* He declined to prepare a glossary for the book but agreed to review the draft and discuss definitions, and he eventually wrote a positive review for *American Photographer* magazine. In October 1939 he told Gaines, "Your new book is appearing just in the nick of time from a sales standpoint and will probably be a best seller if reasonably advertised. Funny how people are impressed with spies and secrets and codes and ciphers just as soon as war breaks out. Bet you make big money out of it." Sadly, Gaines died before she could profit from her work, which was published without a glossary.[23]

Discussions with Gaines about her book's glossary reveal Hitt's strong views on correct cryptologic terminology. He told Gaines, "I detest BIG-

RAM and prefer DIGRAM. As you say, DIGRAPH is not a good word, and DYAD, TRIAD, etc. are completely out, as far as I am concerned." Hitt felt particularly strongly about the word "decrypt"; he and Friedman had discussed this term and were in agreement. In a letter to Lamb, Hitt shared Friedman's views:

> Your [Hitt's] objection to the word "DECRYPT" is a perfectly valid one and I [Friedman] have never liked it nor have I used it in any of my writings. I cannot at the moment verify the state- ment but I am under a very distinct impression that I have men- tioned the word once, and only once, in a section of a publication entitled *Elementary Military Cryptography,* a section devoted to definitions. I believe that I said that the term is used by the French and that certain English writers have an inclination to adopt it. I prefer to use the word "Solve" as being simpler and without the objections you note.

Hitt criticized the word and its variations "as a bastard Latin-Greek com- bination, bad from a philological standpoint and unnecessary in view of the available synonyms."[24]

Drawing had been one of the pastimes of his adolescence, and Hitt returned to art in his involuntary retirement. He designed a cover for the *Cryptogram,* but it was never used. It depicted a stone with a runic inscrip- tion that, when solved, read: "The Official Publication of the American Cryptogram Association they raised this stone to say so but PH made these runes." A scribbled list on the back of an undated envelope indicates that he bought an easel, charcoals, watercolors, canvas, and paper in sup- port of his hobby. In 1938 one of his Key West associates passed along information about buying a small (twelve-inch) etching press. Hitt likely never made the purchase, as the press does not appear on the inventory of items the family moved in 1940, but it shows he was taking his hobby seriously.[25]

Hitt spent years looking for work, writing, and guiding the nascent ACA, while Genevieve worked on the farm and dabbled in politics. But Hitt's time of retreat was ending. On November 11, 1938, he spoke at a veterans' luncheon in Winchester, Virginia, marking the twentieth anni- versary of the armistice. Hitt noted that, on average, wars came along every thirty years, or "one a generation." This meant that the next one was due in 1948, and he urged the audience not to be surprised by it and not to cry for peace when there was no peace. "Make sure that the nation has your support," he said, and he noted, "It was the proudest day of my mother's life when her three sons went off to war in 1917." He closed by saying, "When the time comes, we'll all be Americans together." His estimate of 1948 was wrong. Less than a year later, the US Army would start preparing for the next war, and Hitt was determined to participate in the war effort.[26]

10

Return to Service

If the Signal Corps had more Hitts it would make a better hit with the Army.

Samuel Reber, 1917

By the summer of 1939, it was clear that there would soon be another war in Europe. Hitt, who had not held a full-time job since 1932, turned sixty-one that August, but he still wished to serve. He stayed connected with his army friends, and earlier that year he gave a talk at William Friedman's Signal Intelligence Service (SIS); Friedman had showed him around the office and invited him to drop in again.[1]

To keep occupied, Hitt had been leading a "friendly group" of American Cryptogram Association (ACA) members, setting advanced cipher problems for those looking for a challenge. "The personnel of the group was chosen hastily and blindly, and while I got some peaches like you," he told Helen Gaines, "I also got some dreadful lemons." The members tried his patience; everyone wanted to correspond with him, but their skill levels were low. Hitt could not keep up with their demands for assistance while maintaining his work on the farm, so he abandoned the group that summer. The ACA's secretary, Oscar Phelps Meaker (POPPY), had something else in mind for Hitt. Meaker was looking for ways that this group of amateur cryptanalysts (with wildly varying abilities) might offer their talents to the War Department. One member prepared an "examination" for ACA members who wanted to study military cryptography and asked for Hitt's opinion; Meaker also asked Hitt to leverage his standing in Washington on behalf of the organization. Unfortunately, the ACA had once inadvertently upset William Friedman, and this complicated its attempts to contribute to the war effort. A December 1935 article in the *Cryptogram,* "The Unsolved Benjamin Franklin Cipher," recounted how Ernest Berkel (SUO MYNONA) had "devoted five years of his spare time in an effort to solve this cipher before locating the text which proved to be the key." But Berkel did not do the work himself; he used an official connection to contact the army's chief signal officer (CSO), who ordered Friedman, his civilian employee, to solve the cipher.

Friedman located the solution in the Library of Congress, and Berkel publicly took credit for Friedman's find. Understandably, Friedman felt aggrieved and was not predisposed to accept cryptologic assistance from the ACA.[2]

Hitt drafted a resolution regarding potential wartime work for consideration at the ACA's 1939 convention, which he did not attend. Acknowledging that the organization had "many persons willing and capable of serving the government in a cryptographic capacity," the resolution conceded that it was "impracticable and undesirable" for individual members to offer their services to the government. Therefore, the ACA proposed to serve as a coordinating agency through which the government could reach qualified talent. Hitt asked that his name not be publicly linked to the resolution, for it "should appear to the War Department as a spontaneous action of this association." In late September 1939 Friedman approached Hitt about using the services of ACA members; whether this was because of the resolution or because Hitt had personally smoothed things over is unknown.[3]

The Hitts likely tuned in to hear President Franklin D. Roosevelt's fourteenth fireside chat "On the European War" on September 3, 1939. The United States declared its neutrality on September 5; three days later, Roosevelt instituted a state of "limited national emergency." In reaction, Hitt traveled to Washington and met with his old Signal School colleague and friend, CSO General Joseph O. Mauborgne. He asked Mauborgne to call him to active duty in the Signal Corps and specifically suggested that he be assigned to evaluate signal-related inventions offered to the army. Hitt said he would be happy to serve as a Signal Corps representative on any board that might be established by the War Department to consider new ideas and devices, but he was open to any duties Mauborgne might offer. On September 9, 1939, Hitt requested assignment to active duty; he received an acknowledgment of his request on September 16. Then he waited.[4]

In January 1940 Friedman asked Hitt to sign two copies of his *Manual.* Hitt took the opportunity to advise Friedman that he had obtained five German radio messages, intercepted by an amateur radio operator in mid-December; he turned them over to Friedman for analysis. In his "spare time," Friedman was writing a history of the codes and ciphers used by the American Expeditionary Forces during World War I, and he had some questions for Hitt about the Code Compilation Section. The men exchanged thoughts on cryptology for a few months.[5]

The winter of 1939–1940, which began with a freak twelve-inch snowstorm on November 4, was a tough one in Front Royal. Parker told his brother Rodney, "This has been about the most rotten winter we have ever been through hereabouts. Snow, cold and flu have played the devil with the family and the community. I am the only one out here who has not been sick but I stay away from town by preference." His frustration over his prolonged period of retreat on the mountain was evident, and he proclaimed, "This is, (unless something unforeseen comes up) positively our last winter at Genlue Park. We don't have to stay here and we are not going to." That winter, Parker's aunt Katherine Barnett, his mother's youngest sister, died, and his father began to exhibit symptoms of dementia. Hitt, snowed in at Genlue Park, was unable to travel to Indianapolis, so his sister Muriel Hitt Brandon became George's guardian. Parker was concerned but hoped "the poor old fellow will not drag on the way Katherine did, much as I love and admire him." Their father's illness spurred more frequent correspondence among the siblings; Muriel sent documents to Rodney in New York, who forwarded them to Parker, who then passed the information on to Laurance in Florida.[6]

In July 1940 Genevieve, who had always regretted giving up her job with the Bureau of Investigation, visited its successor—the FBI—to offer her services "in any way needed." She may have been motivated by world events, restlessness, or a desire to earn money. She met with FBI agent Fred Hallford, whose meeting notes acknowledged that although Genevieve "seems to be intelligent," she would not be of any "material assistance in any emergency situation"; no further action was taken. Mary Lue, perhaps feeling as restless as her parents that summer, took a long trip to Canada with a friend.[7]

The War Department took a long time to process the numerous requests from retired officers who wanted to return to duty. Hitt probably commiserated on the delay with his comrades at the Baltic Society dinner that June. It took just over a year for Hitt to receive a response. In September 1940 Mauborgne's executive officer, Colonel Clyde L. Eastman, advised Hitt to have a physical examination "at your earliest convenience" and tipped him off that Mauborgne "may possibly want to use you as Corps Area Signal Officer somewhere."[8]

When Parker got the news, Genevieve was in the hospital in Charlottesville, with Mary Lue at her bedside. She had been there since September 2, recovering from surgery, leaving Hitt on his own to take care of the house and the family dog, Big Boy. He told Genevieve the news either by phone or in person, and he assured Eastman that his wife was cheered by the prospect of an assignment, for "she is still an Army woman, after being away from it all these years," and she still had "one foot in the road." Hitt wasted no time in reporting to the Front Royal Quartermaster Depot (the old Remount Station) for a physical.[9]

The sixty-two-year-old Hitt was shorter (six feet three inches) and heavier (198 pounds) than he had been at his retirement in 1928. His blood pressure was 140/80, and he claimed that both his pseudo-angina and recurrent sciatica were painful but not disabling. Immediately after the exam, Hitt wrote an enthusiastic letter to Eastman, claiming he had passed his physical "with flying colors." He said he could easily take the bus from Front Royal to Washington anytime in the next ten days should Eastman or Mauborgne need him immediately. "It gives me a thrill to think that the chances are so good of getting into the old Signal Corps harness again," Hitt enthused, and he asked Eastman to thank Mauborgne for the opportunity. Hitt's first choice for assignment was Eighth Corps Area (at Fort Sam Houston); his last choice was First Corps Area (in Boston).[10]

In truth, Hitt had *not* passed his medical examination, and there were no "flying colors" about it. The office of the surgeon for Third Corps Area deemed him physically disqualified on September 27. But the old-boy network pressed on, and on October 5 Mauborgne's office recommended that Hitt's recall become effective at the earliest practicable date; he was assigned to Fifth Corps Area, headquartered at Fort Hayes in Columbus, Ohio (his fifth choice). The assignment date was set for November 1. Anxious to get moving but eternally cost-conscious, Hitt requested that several army policies on moves be modified because they were a "decided hardship on retired offers under existing conditions." Hitt noted that, as the War Department was getting his services as a colonel for $225 a month (the difference between retired and active-duty pay), he should receive the same allowances as an active-duty officer for a change of station. After all, he explained, he needed to buy uniforms, close his current home, and establish himself in a distant city; it was only fair that the government pay for the cost of the move. In the end, the army agreed to pay.[11]

There was still the question of his medical status. On October 18 an informal action sheet from the adjutant general to the Medical Corps asked if Hitt could be passed for limited duty, as he was "especially desired for a particular assignment." Three days later, a medical officer relented, reiterating Hitt's disqualification due to his pseudo-angina and sciatica but agreeing to certify him for limited duty "if the need for this officer is such that his services are desired even though he is likely to be temporarily incapacitated from time to time by the above-mentioned defects." Hitt's orders were issued on October 21, and he reported to

Fort Hayes on November 1, having left Genevieve and Mary Lue at home to oversee the packing. Before returning to active duty, Hitt broke off regular contact with the ACA, although he received an occasional letter from his old friends in the organization. But as he told William S. Warford (BOBHITE), he was "a very busy man these days and have had to lay aside all my hobbies." Hitt immediately got to work, and a week later he made a quick visit, by military aircraft, to Fort Knox. It was the first time Hitt had been in a plane since his two flights in a Wright aircraft at Fort Sam Houston in 1911.[12]

Hitt saw his return to the military as an opportunity to leave Genlue Park and the terrible winters on the mountain behind; he and Genevieve decided to sell the house and two parcels of land. They retained thirty acres across the road from the house, probably at Genevieve's insistence; she hoped that someday they could build another house there, after, as her sister-in-law said, "Hitler gets through wrecking the world." Sad as she might have been to leave her fruit trees and the house she had purchased so impulsively in 1927, Genevieve was an army wife and was ready to move; her prolonged illness may have made the decision easier. A local doctor and his wife—Lewis K. and Fannie Mae Woodward—bought the house just four days after Hitt's orders came through. Parker's sister Muriel was glad the family retained some of the land and advised her sister-in-law to let the "young and strong" do the hard work. Muriel was delighted ("Hip Hip Hooray and Three Cheers!" she wrote) when she learned that Parker and Genevieve would be so close to her own home in Indiana; she became a regular guest in Columbus.[13]

Parker commandeered a noncommissioned officer from the Front Royal Quartermaster Depot to supervise the move, as Genevieve was not strong enough after her surgery to handle the job alone. On November 11 everything the family owned—including Parker's drawing table, power saw, and drill; three ice cream freezers; a typewriter; Genevieve's electric sewing machine; their Victrola; and Martin Hitt's grandfather clock—was loaded into two vans. Genevieve, Mary Lue, their housekeeper Viola Martin (who would help Genevieve unpack in Columbus), and, of course, Big Boy set out in the car and headed west, with Mary Lue at the wheel. When the vans arrived, Hitt was so pleased with the drivers' professionalism that he wrote the company a letter of commendation. Viola Martin went back to Virginia on a Greyhound bus, carrying a letter from Hitt that asked the driver to make sure she got home safely.[14]

The Fifth Corps Area encompassed territory that was familiar to Hitt and his ancestors: the states of Indiana, Kentucky, Ohio, and West Virginia.

As CSO, Hitt ensured that all aspects of communications were efficient and carried out according to regulations. Hitt immediately had a chance to use the army's newest cipher devices and supplied feedback on them. It was a great job, Hitt told one of his ACA pals, for it involved telegraph, radio, photography, the army's amateur radio system, and many other things, but otherwise, he noted, it was "just the old Army game and I have fallen into the groove with little trouble."[15]

The Hitts first occupied quarters 52, "one of the best" at Columbus Army Depot, about six miles from Parker's office at Fort Hayes proper. The first floor contained a living room, dining room, kitchen, three small bedrooms with a bath, and a maid's room with its own bath. Upstairs there was one large bedroom and bath. When he arrived in Columbus, Hitt wired Genevieve to let her know that the quarters were wonderful and that the neighbors had "dogs on both sides"; he camped out there, waiting for the furniture and his family. As was typical with the army, they were not in one house for long; they later moved to quarters 21 at Fort Hayes, possibly so Hitt could be closer to work, and then to quarters 13.[16]

Restored to the rank of colonel (with a date of rank of September 23, 1938), Hitt was surrounded by old friends, including Generals Clement A. Trott and John McCauley Eager, as well as quite a few other officers who had been Hitt's students at various service schools. Though thankful for Mauborgne's "kindness in giving me this very desirable station," he was cautious and told Eastman, "If I am putting my foot through any of the policies and customs of the Corps, please jump on me gently but firmly. I am not trying to be a radical but even with the fine staff I have here I may go wrong in questions of policy and if I do, I want to be pulled up short." After his trip to Fort Knox, he alerted Eastman to the "amazing proportions" of the unauthorized telephone installations there.[17]

Hitt expressed curiosity about a "beautiful piece of equipment lying idle": this was Friedman's M-134 converter, predecessor to the SIGABA machine, which would not arrive at Fort Hayes until mid-1941. Eastman and Mauborgne urged Hitt to write to them or to Colonel Spencer B. Akin, who had taken charge of the SIS, to discuss confidential matters. Akin welcomed Hitt's suggestions for improvements to the M-134 and its follow-on machine (which were certainly shared with Friedman and his team). Hitt also had some ideas about how to ensure security and simplify day-to-day cipher operations. He had a positive reaction to the Hagelin C-38 device (later modified and renamed the M-209), despite thinking that it generated some "disconcerting repetitions" in its ciphertext. Akin, gratified by Hitt's feedback, informed him that this was likely due to the fact that the keying elements had not been completely set up, and he reassured Hitt that it was "quite safe for the time limits required for tactical communications."[18]

In December 1940 Hitt traveled around the corps area by automobile, investigating the communications situation at Wright Field, Fort Benjamin Harrison, and Fort Knox. In April 1941 he made several trips to Fort Benjamin Harrison and a longer journey that took him around Ohio (to Ravenna, Cleveland, Sandusky, Fostoria, and Erie Ordnance Depot) and then onward to La Porte and Fort Wayne, Indiana. The unrelenting pace of travel kept up until the end of his assignment. He visited Jefferson Proving Grounds and Jeffersonville Quartermaster Depot in Indiana; Fort Thomas, Lexington, Fort Knox, and Blue Grass Ordnance Deport in Kentucky; and Middletown, Westerville, and Patterson Field in Ohio. He took leave to attend the May 1941 Baltic Society dinner in Washington, where Pershing, against doctors' orders, appeared for ten minutes before returning to Walter Reed Hospital. There was no dinner in 1942, and Hitt declined the invitation in 1943, as he was unable to get away from work. He asked to be remembered to the attendees and requested that Pershing be told he was doing his "best to live up to the ideal that he set up for his staff in the other war."[19]

Although cryptology was only a small part of his job, in December 1940 Hitt responded to a query from Colonel John F. Landis, professor of military science and tactics at Indiana University, concerning correspondence courses in the subject. Hitt answered Landis's questions and noted, "As you see, I am back on the job after twelve years retirement. The game is about the same and I am enjoying it." Hitt's public reputation as a cipher expert led to a request for him to speak to the Ohio State University post of the Society of Military Engineers in early 1941. His talk, titled "Codes and Cryptographs or Mechanism of the Written Word in Relation to Communication in War," emphasized that it was best to use machine encipherment because it was harder to decipher. In addition, the army sometimes directed issues to Hitt that normally would have been managed by the post communications center. General George Luberoff, commander of the Jeffersonville Depot, asked Hitt to unofficially investigate an error-riddled cipher message he had received. Hitt was able to decipher the message correctly (except for one letter); he told Luberoff he would attempt to make sure future messages were more accurate but noted that messages sent via long-distance radio were prone to transmission error.[20]

The Signal Corps had reclaimed Parker Hitt, and the US Army now gained another Hitt: twenty-eight-year-old Mary Lueise. She had graduated from high school in 1930 but had no specific career aspirations. And as she was completely devoted to her parents, she had accompanied them to Fort Hayes. The colonel's daughter first worked in the Columbus Engineer Depot, where she operated a mimeograph machine and served as a file clerk from November 1940 until August 1941 at a salary of $1,260 per year. On her own initiative, she took on supervising confidential systems for Fifth Corps Area's Military Intelligence Office, but she resigned in August 1941, as Genevieve was ill again. In December 1941 Mary Lue became a confidential clerk and teleprinter operator in the Military Intelligence Office; however, the job required more than the usual civil service qualifications. The corps area commander testified that the position and the applicant were of such "exceptional character" that an exemption from normal processes was warranted; the work required absolute loyalty and discretion, which "Miss Hitt possesses in a high degree due to her Regular Army background." This position also paid $1,260 a year; Mary Lue's job performance was rated very good, and she taught teleprinter operation to more than 100 counterintelligence agents and handled the dissemination of confidential material. Mary Lue became ill in March 1942 and went on leave without pay until mid-July, when she was well enough to return. But at the end of October she resigned to accept a better position with advancement potential. On January 1, 1943, she began working as a clerk in the Adjutant General Depot, earning $1,440 annually. She was promoted on March 1, with a salary increase to $1,620 a year. On June 1 she was promoted to principal clerk at $1,800 a year, which meant that she was "bossing fifteen employees and working six days a week." She remained at this job until early October 1943.[21]

While Parker and Mary Lue did their war work, Genevieve kept the household running, managed their social life, and entertained visitors. These included Mary Lue's suitors, for she was popular with the young signal officers under her father's command. Many of them corresponded with her when posted elsewhere, respectfully sending their regards to "the Colonel" and "Jenny" (Genevieve) and the occasional virtual pat on the head for Big Boy. As time went on, Genevieve began to regret selling Genlue Park and fretted over no longer having a home. She wanted her own roof over her head. Real estate prices were soaring, and she thought they might be "out of luck" if Parker lost his job, as he was now sixty-four, the normal military retirement age. Genevieve also kept a long-distance eye on her widowed mother, "Marmee," in West Point, Texas. At age eighty-four, Mrs. Young managed her own financial affairs and farm business, which included a herd of cattle and fig trees. In her spare time, she crocheted.

Conscious of her age and the passing of time, Marmee planned for Gene-vieve and Tot to have some of the family land.[22]

Hitt had been on duty for just over one year when the Japanese attacked Pearl Harbor on December 7, 1941. He preserved the decoded copy of the message his office received from the War Department after the attack, which ordered the command, in cooperation with the FBI, to "round up all suspicious characters on your list" and to coordinate with area industries to protect against sabotage. This message was ordered to be destroyed later in the day. With the nation officially at war, Hitt engaged with local civil defense authorities; he approved the Canton, Ohio, civil defense program, praised the training of civil defense radio operators in Zanesville, Ohio, and encouraged qualified people to join the Signal Corps. Nearly 150 people worked for Hitt by May 1942. In addition to normal Signal Corps operations, the office was responsible for providing and operating telephone systems at war manufacturing plants, army stations, and schools in the Fifth Corps Area.[23]

Though busy, Hitt had not lost his desire to chronicle his early army career. In March 1942 he wrote to the Army Historical Section at the War College in Washington for background information about the situation in Cuba in 1898–1899 and the specific units comprising VII Corps at Camp Columbia, as well as information on signal units associated with the command. He received a prompt and comprehensive reply but appar-ently did not use the material in his writing. In September 1943 he sent photographs of his cylinder and strip cipher devices to the CSO's office, asking that they be passed on to the Signal Security Agency for "histori-cal purposes."[24]

Mary Lue spent much of November 1942 visiting Catherine New in Washington. Parker accompanied her to the train station and hitched a ride back to the post on a truck because the taxi line was so long. "Can't you see him coming in the gate on a truck! I told him I bet he was only sav-ing the taxi fare," Genevieve told Mary Lue. Genevieve missed her daugh-ter "more even than I thought I would," and her letters were peppered with news of the happenings at home and on post. She hoped Mary Lue would come home for Thanksgiving and bring Catherine with her, for she had invited "two boys" (probably young officers who were acquainted with Mary Lue), and Parker's sister Muriel was coming for a long visit. Muriel stayed in Columbus through Christmas; her son John Brandon was "on a boat somewhere in the Pacific," and her daughter Barbara was overseas "with a field unit with the Red Cross." Genevieve felt a great deal of sympathy for her widowed sister-in-law, who also bore the burden of looking after George Hitt. She told Mary Lue, "If it had been *my* only daughter [in an unknown location] I think I could not have stood it. But Muriel does. I imagine she has some very hard hours at night, alone, in her room. I am glad she is here with us. Parker is so good to her."[25]

Genevieve's wartime letters to Mary Lue and to her mother in late 1942 are like a time capsule of the day-to-day concerns of an army family, from the blessings of "fake cloth" that did not need ironing to the tunneling taking place in their backyard for "unknown reasons." Genevieve loaned her Spode Pink Tower teacups to her neighbor Catherine Eager for a get-together she was having for her brother, Senator Milliard Evelyn Tydings of Maryland. The family also speculated about the movements of their friends the Eisenhowers; Genevieve "told Parker this morning that I didn't think Ike had ever come back to Washington and he said he didn't think he had ever intended to." Mrs. Young, who knew Mamie Eisenhower, wondered if the General Eisenhower in the news was "Mamie's husband and do you know where Mamie is now? The last I heard of her she was in San Antonio." Mrs. Young was "getting her house in order," and Genevieve admitted she did "not like to think of living on without" her mother, "the Queen Bee around who we all revolve." She urged Marmee to "take good care of yourself as you are most necessary," and the "entire family needs you for an anchor." Genevieve's thoughts were with Mary Lue just before Thanksgiving; while Parker took Big Boy, "the sweetest dog," out for a run, she wrote to her daughter, "If home is where the heart is you are at home with me this minute, or rather I am there with you." December 1942 was cold and snowy, and Genevieve thought it was too cold to go Christmas shopping in the stores, which were "full of the most awful trash and you stand for hours waiting to be helped." Instead of shopping for her mother, she sent her subscriptions to *Reader's Digest, Saturday Evening Post, Good Housekeeping, Ladies' Home Journal,* and *Women's at Home Companion.*[26]

In 1943 Hitt began his largest wartime project, establishing a communications relay center for corps area headquarters; this may have been the reason for his trip to Washington in March. While there, Hitt called on his friend George Gruenert at Services of Supply headquarters and took care of some paperwork for his sister-in-law Tot. Due to the difficulty of obtaining equipment, the relay center was not complete until August 1944, months after Hitt left the service. Once it was operational, the center handled approximately 175,000 messages per month—an increase of 450 percent over January 1944.[27]

Hitt's performance ratings were consistently superior. Trott described him as "an engaging, serene, highly distinguished in appearance, versatile, cultured, industrious, reliable, co-operative, trustworthy, original thinking retired officer of the highest type." The next year, General Daniel Van Voorhis tried to find different words to say the same thing; he described Hitt as "a frank, distinguished, helpful, intelligent, sound, discerning, self-reliant, accomplished, effective officer." General Fred C. Wallace cut to the chase, saying Hitt "knows his present job and likes it. Efficient and energetic . . . an officer of outstanding personal and professional qualities." In Hitt's final assessment, Colonel R. C. Stickney called him an "extremely well equipped and well qualified, capable, efficient, forceful, aggressive, experienced, alert and practical officer." Despite concerns about his health and the expense of moving him to Ohio, the army made a good bargain when it brought Hitt back for wartime duty.[28]

General Wallace first recommended Hitt for the Legion of Merit in July 1942. The Decorations Board of the Services of Supply approved the award, but it went no further. In August 1943 Wallace tried again, submitting a modified recommendation to the commanding general of the Army Service Forces. Chief of staff George C. Marshall's office rejected the award in October, noting that Hitt's service did not constitute "exceptionally meritorious conduct in the performance of outstanding service within the meaning of the law" governing the Legion of Merit.[29]

Hitt's war was nearly over. By mid-1943, the army had enough new, young officers to fill positions; it no longer needed to bend the retirement age rules to keep older, recalled officers in place. William Friedman, now in a position of intellectual but not command authority in Washington, bemoaned the fact that Hitt was forced to retire, commenting on the overlooked value of "a good many old-timers with active minds who could carry on more efficiently than younger men at desks," and he commiserated that he too was "a victim of arbitrary rulings but maybe it is all for the best." As 1943 wore on, Hitt told his father that he and Genevieve had "no plans for after the war, but like most people, want to get it over as soon as we can and then get a little much needed rest." They initially planned to return to Virginia. Hitt turned sixty-five on August 27, 1943—one year older than mandatory retirement age. He was officially released from duty as of January 20, 1944, but because he had accrued three months and twenty days of unused leave, he finished work on September 30. The family left Fort Hayes a week later, with Hitt nominally assigned to the Officer Replacement Pool at Fort Monmouth, New Jersey. The command held a formal retirement dinner to honor the end of his military career. Genevieve put some of her household goods on consignment with the Woman's Exchange in Columbus. The Hitts then packed up the remainder of their possessions and left active army service for good. But instead of heading east to Virginia, they went south to the warmer climes of San Antonio, Texas.[30]

11

The Old Soldier

I have to take things easy but, barring accidents, I am good for
a while yet and may outlive you all.

Parker Hitt, 1938

Though the army thought he was too old to serve, Hitt still had the energy and the desire to be useful. He considered retiring to Miami Beach, where his friend Harry Marks lived, but in the end, he decided San Antonio would be a better year-round location; it was Genevieve's hometown, the place where Parker and Genevieve had met, and Mary Lue's birthplace. Hitt was assuredly grateful not to be spending another winter in Front Royal. The wartime real estate market was tight, and though the Hitts found a house quickly, they were unable to take possession until later in the year and spent a few months in an apartment. Their new one-story home at 115 East Ashby Place had three bedrooms, two baths, a "very modern kitchen, a large glassed-in gallery, and a whole suite of closets grouped together beside lots of closet room in the bedrooms." The lot was not large, but it had a good lawn and nice shade trees; a shopping center was just a short walk away. Genevieve still had many friends in the city, some of them right in their new neighborhood, and Parker expected to find quite a few of his old friends in the area too.[1]

Hitt did not believe in sitting still. In October he went to Dallas to investigate the communications situation in the Eighth Service Command (corps areas had been renamed service commands); he had an idea he could serve as an intermediary between the telephone company and the army. The command had the situation under control, however, and Hitt was not needed. He then contemplated finding "some local business man who has to have his daily golf" and would give him "an afternoon job sitting in his office and amusing and holding off his callers." In the meantime, there was another battle to wage: the family's 9,000 pounds of household goods had been packed so that it weighed 14,500 pounds, well over Hitt's 11,000-pound shipping allowance. The army was demanding that he pay nearly $5 per 100 pounds of overage. The dispute lasted well into the new year, but Hitt won in the end.[2]

On New Year's Day 1944, with Big Boy sleeping "on the best rug," Parker wrote his customary letters while Genevieve made "enchiladas to start the New Year right." Genevieve's mother, "a very remarkable little woman and my favorite mother-in-law," spent the winter with the family. Mary Lue contemplated travel, having already explored Del Rio, Texas, and Villa Acuna, Mexico, with a friend. Genevieve and Mary Lue were "babying" Parker "as usual," but he humored them and tried to "growl as little as possible about it." Big Boy was "a lucky dog"; he had two meals a day "with real unrationed beef" and would soon have a fenced yard. Hitt told his sister of the "splendid markets" and "reasonable" prices in San Antonio; their house was only a block from a bus stop, making it easy to reach any part of the city. He was, however, concerned about whether the family could live on his retirement pay alone. The "critical old soldier" thought he might need to find a job as a plumber or night watchman to keep himself "from grouching over things," and he told his brother-in-law, "You fellows overseas are the ones who are going through hell these days and we old timers ought to keep our shirts on." Hitt was positively delighted to learn that his nephew, Edgar King Jr., was following in his footsteps as "a confirmed encyclopedia hound."[3]

William Friedman was glad to hear from Hitt, as he had not realized the family was now living in San Antonio. He passed on the news that Colonel George Bicher's wife, Mary, was in that city while her husband was stationed in London "in our line of work." Friedman, who was preparing a historical study of strip ciphers, was grateful for the information Hitt had shared about his inventions and bemoaned the fact that the work might never be published. Friedman hoped Hitt would find "something interesting to do" in retirement and thought the older man probably had "a good deal of energy which would be useful to some firm."[4]

George Cooper Hitt died on March 9, 1944, a few months shy of his ninety-fourth birthday. Parker, Genevieve, and Mary Lue traveled to Indianapolis for a private funeral service; George was interred in Crown Hill Cemetery next to his wife and parents (and near his friend James Whitcomb Riley) in a grave unmarked by a headstone. The Hitts returned to San Antonio after the funeral but did not stay long. Though they had been in the city for only six months and in their new house for just four, by April 6, the Hitts had decided to leave Texas, but they were not sure where they were going. They sold the house on April 18. By the end of the month, they were back in Front Royal and had repurchased Genlue Park.[5]

What went wrong in Texas? The decision was abrupt but not impulsive; there are no letters to explain what they were thinking. Perhaps

Genevieve and Mary Lue missed the farm, for the yard in San Antonio was small by comparison. Genevieve might have realized that, after so many years away, she did not like living so close to her family. Maybe Mary Lue missed her Virginia friends. They all might have been reminded of why they had been glad to leave Texas back in 1926. It could be that the Hitts decided they could live more cheaply and self-sufficiently at their old home in Virginia, although the cost of shipping their goods back east would have been a compelling disincentive for the frugal Hitt. But move they did. Parker had been so determined to leave Front Royal, but he would do anything to please Genevieve and Mary Lue, even if it meant enduring more winters at Genlue Park. Tot was surprised by the news but glad her sister would be "near enough to say hello once in a while."[6]

Lewis and Fannie Woodward, who had purchased Genlue Park and some land from the Hitts in 1940, were happy to sell the house and the main tract of land back to them but retained a small plot of land next to the house. Lewis had been called up by the army, so the Woodwards had moved to the West Coast and rented Genlue Park to a family named Kennedy. Genevieve was distraught when she returned to her beloved home and found not just disorder but extensive damage. Fannie was remorseful, writing, "I had no idea the average person could or would be so destructive to any property and I realize and regret that you found such a terrible condition." Lewis planned to negotiate with Genevieve for the cost of repairs but never got around to it. When, at the end of August, nothing had been resolved, Fannie, who did not want to handle the matter herself, suggested that the Hitts go ahead with the repairs and keep anything the Woodwards or the Kennedys had left behind.[7]

The Hitt family worked together to patch up the house and the gardens. When the growing season ended, Mary Lue expressed interest in finding another wartime job, as she had when they lived at Fort Hayes. On the evening of October 23, 1944, Parker phoned William Friedman about the possibility of finding a position for his daughter in the Signal Security Agency (SSA); Friedman sent the "necessary form" at once and promised that her application would get "prompt attention." He was not joking: even for a wartime hire, Mary Lue's paperwork was processed quickly. Despite the fact that Mary Lue was undoubtedly qualified for the job and would have been hired on merit, Friedman was delighted to use his influence to help the daughter of the man he revered. She was sworn in at Arlington Hall Station on November 9, well before the background investigation paperwork was complete. She earned $1,800 a year (the same salary she had made in her last job at Fort Hayes) as a cryptographic clerk in the Traffic Analysis and Control Office (B4B2). Mary Lue took up residence in Kansas Hall, part of the hastily constructed Arlington Farms housing development known as "Twenty-Eight Acres of Girls," where many young female government workers lived during the war. At thirty-two, though, Mary Lue was older than the recent college graduates.[8]

Mary Lue was a small player in the tremendous World War II cryptologic effort at Arlington Hall, a human machine composed largely of women. The army's code- and cipher-breaking organization had grown from the relatively small Signal Intelligence Service run by Friedman in the 1930s to a large, sprawling enterprise. By the time Mary Lue arrived, there were about 10,000 workers, and the SSA had demonstrated significant success against Japanese codes and ciphers; the agency was at the peak of its might. Though Friedman had been shunted aside for a military chief, he still held court as the chief of communications research and had considerable influence on the departments now run by his protégés Abraham Sinkov, Solomon Kullback, and Frank Rowlett.[9]

Just one letter survives from those Mary Lue wrote home while she worked at Arlington Hall, and it tells much about her experiences there. Her workload was heavy on Saturday, December 9, 1944, and she wrote from her desk at five in the evening because she could not wait to tell Parker and Gee Gee about her day. Mary Lue had been summoned to have tea at the headquarters building with the "Big Boss"—Friedman. Over tea and cookies, Friedman showed her one of his treasures—Parker's original sliding strip device—and they discussed his Voynich manuscript study group and gossiped about Herbert O. Yardley. Mary Lue was flabbergasted, but pleased, by Friedman's veneration of her father and proclaimed, "Anyone that has the *exalted* opinion of Pop that that guy has and who spreads it around the way that guy has, is for my money any day in the week." She told her parents, "I give you my word that the lowliest lieutenant stepping within the gates is taught about Pop first and then, much later, about his own particular duties and God." Friedman requested a signed photograph of Hitt for the collection of greats he displayed on his office walls. Mary Lue sent strict orders about which picture to send, how it should be inscribed, and how it should be framed to match the rest of Friedman's collection. Parker followed Mary Lue's instructions precisely. The photograph was inscribed: "To William F. Friedman, my friend of long standing in thought and work." Friedman sent his effusive praise back to Hitt, calling him the "father of cryptanalysis in the American Army."[10]

Mary Lue joined Friedman's study group that met to examine the (still) mysterious Voynich manuscript and attempt to decipher its secrets.

Parker sent her his thoughts on the matter, in the form of a memo he had written in 1926. Although the Voynich manuscript would interest her more in later years, the study group did not hold her attention for long; undoubtedly there were more interesting entertainments to occupy her time off. At some point during her short tenure with the SSA, Mary Lue smuggled some intercepted Japanese radio traffic out of the building and gave it to her father to examine. She may have done this with the tacit approval of Friedman, but even so, it was an alarming breach of security protocols. This may or may not have concerned Parker, who had been trusted with secret material for decades under a considerably less strict set of regulations than existed in 1944. Mary Lue's actions went undetected at the time, and she only admitted what she had done to David Kahn in 1972. Hitt's analysis of the material, if any, does not survive.[11]

Though she was quite capable at her job—her three evaluations were uniformly excellent, the highest possible score—Mary Lue evinced no desire to be a professional cryptologist. She had a natural ability and, of course, unusual early training from her parents, but she lacked a desire for full-time employment. Mary Lue was not destined to be one of the many women hired back by the army after the war to serve as the backbone of the cryptologic workforce up to and after the founding of the National Security Agency. Hired for the duration of the war, Mary Lue avoided the coming mass layoffs by resigning in August 1945, two days after the surrender of Japan, echoing her mother's departure from work after the 1918 armistice. Genevieve was ill again, and Mary Lue quit work to care for her. She had no regrets. She was paid for her unused leave, turned in her badge and her cigarette and gasoline ration cards, cleared out of housing, and headed home to Genlue Park. Parker later told Captain George E. McCracken, "It was a most interesting experience for her and she and I both hope that the office will keep her name on the list for the 'next time.' She is studying Russian in her spare moments, just for luck."[12]

With the war over and Mary Lue home, the elder Hitts settled into a comfortable retirement. They left their mountainside home only to visit friends and to shop in Washington and nearby Winchester. Parker and Genevieve's long-distance travel days were over. Instead, they spent their time reading and enjoying their land. Parker had bursts of invention, and Genevieve tended her farm. The family enjoyed a modest prosperity as the nation recovered from the Depression and the war.

Both Parker and Genevieve—aged sixty-seven and sixty, respectively, in 1945—had health issues. Genevieve had been periodically unwell in the years after her 1940 surgery. She was ill in March 1945 and again in August. When healthy, Genevieve concentrated on increasing her fruit production and keeping her chickens. Strawberries were too much work for too little profit, she decided, so she focused on raspberries, figs, peaches, apricots, plums, grapes, and apples. As late as 1957, she was planning a new apple orchard. The family's other food needs were met through frozen produce and meats from the new Safeway supermarket in Front Royal; they also bought a variety of products—dates, olive oil, tea, limes, avocados, canned tamales, salsa, and tortillas—in bulk by mail order from provisioners across the country. Genevieve had grown up eating Mexican food, and the whole family loved it; she also liked fried fish with cornbread and the local delicacy "creasy greens" (landcress), said to be "mighty good for you."[13]

In June 1946 Hitt became seriously ill. After weeks with a fever and suffering from hiccups for five days, he was admitted to the University of Virginia hospital in Charlottesville in early July with an irregular heartbeat and occasional edema. At first, the doctor saw no indication of congestive heart failure, but a few days later, Hitt seemed to have acute heart failure. His weight dropped from 185 to 171 pounds in five days. The doctor concluded that he was suffering from mild congestive heart failure secondary to auricular fibrillation and prescribed digitalis. The doctor in Charlottesville ordered Hitt's doctor in Front Royal to observe him carefully, "because I am not satisfied that we have found all of his ailments yet." Upon Hitt's release from the hospital, the doctor noted that he "was not as mentally alert as I would judge he was before his illness." Back home and confined to bed, Hitt fretted, "How the weeds do grow and how the little repair jobs do stack up." He kept his mind busy by examining photocopies of the Voynich manuscript, loaned to him by Friedman. It took months for Hitt to feel better, but in the meantime, he won a prize for his moss roses that summer. His mother-in-law remarked, "I am not surprised that you got a prize, I think you deserve a prize for everything you do, as everything you do is so well done."[14]

Parker had company while he recuperated. Genlue Park was "dog heaven." By the early 1950s, the family had at least four canines, including a Chesapeake Bay retriever named Bell. Parker suspected that Bell had "a touch of Golden retriever in her and is therefore part bloodhound. It makes a fine combination." The family enjoyed Sunday afternoon drives around the mountain, particularly when the fall foliage was at its colorful peak. Genevieve told her sister they got "a lot of fun out of the TV. Surprising what we can get out here in the mountains."[15]

As he kept up with changes to military pensions and benefits, Parker railed against the bureaucracy. When it became possible to take a pension for his Spanish-American War service, he did so; this lowered his retirement pay, but because the pension was not taxed, he saved money. Hitt did many of his own home repairs, and his quest for necessary parts or manuals resulted in some sharply worded correspondence with companies that were not providing timely service or not giving him his money's worth. A typical example was his aggravation when the manufacturer of his oil furnace kept referring him to its distributor in Richmond or to the local plumber, when all Hitt wanted was a set of instructions. He had the necessary tools and wanted to repair the furnace himself, noting that the plumber "has botched up so many other repair jobs that I would not think of letting him touch this machine even if he would come up in the mountain in an emergency." He also wrote to the Deepfreeze Company, the manufacturer of his freezer, with an idea to facilitate the removal of ice cube trays; the company passed his thoughts along to its engineering department.[16]

Hitt's desire to innovate was not confined to home appliances. His ingenuity could not be contained, and he was "always in such a hurry going from one thought to the next." When given the opportunity, he still tried to improve military operations. In October 1947 Hitt visited a friend at Vint Hill Farms Station, which, since World War II, had been an intercept site and training facility for the SSA and then the Army Security Agency (ASA). On his way home, he thought about the operators' "thankless task" of typing "number and letter code until they get dopy with it." He conceived a device to automate some of the intercept tasks and made a quick sketch when he got home; the device was based on a machine he had developed for IT&T that sent telegraph signals to a printer. The next morning, he mailed the sketch and a letter to General Spencer B. Akin, the army's new chief signal officer, and offered to visit Washington to talk to Signal Corps engineers. Akin mentioned to Hitt that a similar device had been developed during World War II, but he forwarded the idea to the ASA; there is no indication that the ASA followed up with him. A few years later, in 1953, Hitt sought the opinion of Bill Morrow of Crosby Enterprises regarding his concept for a device to detect incoming aircraft at altitudes below 5,000 feet; Hitt's device would send a radio message to a central tracking station and replace human plane spotters. He had approached Morrow because he was afraid the idea would be "pigeonholed and forgotten by the military." When he did not hear from Morrow after a month, he withdrew the offer.[17]

Genevieve's mother, Mary Lueise Carter Young, died on July 12, 1950, at age ninety-three. She left Genevieve a great deal of land in Texas, which Genevieve eventually sold to her sister, for "neither Parker or I can be bothered with this as it is all a bothersome subject. We are not young enough to cope and after all why should we." Genevieve was anxious to secure Mary Lue's future and believed the land sale, combined with her accumulated stocks and insurance policies, would provide about $40,000 for Mary Lue, which was not "much but it aint hay." If Mary Lue sold most of the land in Front Royal for $1,000 an acre, Genevieve thought she would be able to "manage a very good life for herself." Genevieve was less concerned about herself and Parker. They were content living on the pay he received, and she reckoned they "could spend a little more and add something worthwhile to our lives without having to save any of his pay. Our wants are few but what we have are expensive. Our next few years should be gay ones and I intend it shall be that way."[18]

One of the highlights of 1952 was the election of their friend Dwight D. Eisenhower to the presidency. The Hitts were half a generation older than Ike and Mamie, but the two couples remained friendly over the years. Genevieve mailed Mamie a letter and a copy of a speech given by a Virginia politician that Genevieve described as the "finest tribute to 'our Ike' that we have heard." In December 1952 Mamie sent the Hitts two tickets for the inauguration; Parker thanked her for "her thoughtfulness in remembering us," and he and Genevieve attended. The Hitts remained on the Eisenhowers' Christmas card list during his presidency and in the years that followed. In a New Year's Day letter, perhaps in 1955, Genevieve thanked Mamie for the Christmas card and told her, "Ike is proving you can wield a big stick with a gentle hand." She signed the letter, "Devotedly, Gee-Gee."[19]

Hitt was thrilled to receive an invitation to one of Eisenhower's "stag dinners" in 1955. On May 31 he joined Milton Eisenhower, W. Atlee Burpee, Oscar Hammerstein, Richard Rodgers, Samuel I. Newhouse, and others for a meal of French onion soup, roast pheasant sauterne with black cherries, grits, asparagus, salad, key lime pie, and all the trimmings. "I will always be grateful to Ike for having Parker in to such a wonderful party and for letting him have a sweet chat with Mamie," Genevieve wrote to Mamie's mother. Genevieve had not wanted to bother Mamie with a letter, as Ike had just suffered a heart attack. Mamie later thanked Genevieve for thinking of her, sent her love to Mary Lue and Parker, and told Genevieve, "The fact that you have gone through this same anxious time with your husband and that he has continued to be so well is most comforting to me."[20]

In *The Codebreakers,* David Kahn tells of Eisenhower visiting the Hitts in Front Royal during both World War II and his presidency. It is impossible to corroborate these stories, and they seem improbable. The Hitts were in Columbus, Ohio, for most of the war, and Ike was in Washington or Europe, so it is extremely unlikely that one morning the Hitts "stumbled across Ike, stretched out asleep in the living room of their home." And if President Eisenhower slipped out of the White House to play poker with Hitt in Front Royal (a story Mary Lue shared with friends), he managed to evade both the Secret Service and the secretarial recordkeeping that surrounds the presidency. Eisenhower did not play poker with subordinates, but Hitt was not his subordinate when they first met; both men did, however, play bridge. Though these stories are hard to prove, it is impossible to say with certainty that they are untrue; perhaps Mary Lue misremembered places and dates and some of these events occurred in the 1920s or 1930s.[21]

The close relationship between the Hitts and the Gruenerts faded as time went on; their lives diverged when Parker retired and George Gruenert was promoted to general. Florence and George, on what would be their last visit to Genlue Park in the 1950s, "did not realize . . . that this house is no longer full of servants." As a result, Mary Lue apparently took the brunt of the Gruenerts' demands and told her mother, "Never again." The family lost another good friend in the spring of 1954 when Harry New's widow, Catherine, died. She left a bequest of $1,000 to each of them. Hitt's comrades from World War I were slipping away too. In March 1950 he surveyed the remaining members of the Baltic Society, asking them whether the society should continue, and if so, should it continue with male descendants only or with "any qualified *person.*" The results of the survey are unknown, but it seems there was no clamor to continue. The Baltic Society had last met on May 28, 1949, the thirty-second anniversary of their voyage, with Fox Conner presiding. In 1940, of the original 191 members, 30 had died and 11 had dropped out of sight. By 1950, some of the most prominent members had died—George Patton in 1945, James Harbord in 1947, and John J. Pershing in 1948.[22]

Hitt threw his energy into a new organization. In 1950 he attended the second reunion of the Society of Germanna Colonies, a group comprising descendants of Germans who had settled in Virginia in 1714 and 1717. Parker's ancestor Peter Hitt had been in the first group. By 1953, Hitt was treasurer of the organization. He became close to the society's president, Brawdus Martin, who was "elated" to find Parker looking so well when he visited Genlue Park for a Sunday afternoon picnic in August

1953. Parker and Mary Lue (Genevieve may not have been up to the trip) joined Martin in a long excursion in September that included a clambake at "Warwick Banks," a house on the Northern Neck of Virginia, with stops to visit Ferry Farm (George Washington's childhood home), Wakefield, and Stratford Hall (the Lee family plantation). Hitt carefully plotted the mileage on the back of an envelope, calculating it would take three and a half to four hours to make the 143-mile trip from Front Royal. The next summer, the trio took a trip to Virginia's Middle Neck, "leaving the cool mountains during the heat of summer" to visit Tappahannock, "where it is said our illustrious ancestors landed in 1714." Martin dramatically recounted the scene: "Miss Mary Lue's dainty foot pressed the accelerator of her fiery chariot doing 50 miles per hour—that took our ancestors two days to cover doing one step in front of the other," while "the Colonel relaxed and flung his eyes over the Countryside and caught a whiff of 'Boots and Saddles' and the memory of yesterday colored his cheeks with enthusiasm."[23]

Mary Lue and her mother enjoyed life in the mountains and accepted the fact that they had to travel if they wanted to go shopping. Genevieve told her sister, "This is rather an easy family to clothe. We all like nice things but good ones so we are not always buying." Parker preferred standard-issue army shoes, and when Genevieve heard a rumor in 1956 that the shoes might be discontinued, she asked Tot (who had access to a military exchange) to buy two pairs for him. Mary Lue rejoiced when she learned that a shopping center—with a Woodward & Lothrop and a Garfinkle's—was under construction in Winchester, about twenty-five miles away. "It will keep us from ever having to take that 69-mile trip to Washington that we hate so much because the traffic is now beyond anything you can imagine. Civilization is creeping up on us and it has its advantages and disadvantages." Genevieve was slowly downsizing her garden by 1956, for it was becoming too much for her to manage; she relied instead on frozen vegetables from Safeway. Parker built Genevieve a tray-style bird feeder for her kitchen window, and she delighted in the cardinals, "my red birds," that fed there. They went to town once a day for mail, "if it isn't snowing."[24]

In late 1955 Hitt, looking back on his career, wrote about his two stints with the School of Musketry. He used information he had compiled for Major Truman Smith in 1929, when Smith was preparing a history of the Infantry School. Hitt's finished article, "A Brief History of the School of Musketry," appeared in the July 1961 issue of *Military Review,* a Command and General Staff College publication. The retired colonel was happy to receive $50 for his effort.[25]

Hitt wrote to the National Inventors Council in April 1960 with an idea for improving the short-range firepower of the M-14 rifle. He suggested a smoothbore design and a bullet made of two to four elements that would fly apart when fired; because the bullets would have no spin, they would not travel as far. Hitt thought the projectiles could be made of hard and heavy linotype metal. The council rejected his suggestion in May, as it did not meet the criterion of being sufficiently "new, unique, or useful," but it retained the idea for potential future use.[26]

Genevieve's digestive illness was diagnosed as cancer, and although the doctors told her it had been "cured," she had to be careful what she ate. She suffered several cases of what was treated as flu during the 1950s, and in March 1959 she had a heart attack. The night of the attack, the doctor told Mary Lue they were "sitting on a powder keg and he didn't know how it was coming out." Genevieve decided, "I had better do as they said from there on," and she gave up smoking. If her old friend from 1918, Captain Nicholas Szilagy, could see her now, she told her sister, "he would say there is one glamor girl who has fallen to pieces." Parker, too, was ailing; he had a chronic cough attributed to cigarettes, "so poor man he is trying not to smoke." Despite all this, Genevieve insisted, "One thing I refuse to do is worry about anything what so ever." A Mrs. Kidwell came in some days to do housework, and Mary Lue managed to do all the cooking with some assistance from Genevieve. Genevieve washed the dishes (and Parker dried them) when Mrs. Kidwell was not there because Mary Lue "hates housework . . . it is news when she picks up a broom and while she will wash dishes when she must, she fights it every step of the way." Aware of the passage of time, she told Tot, "I hope that time never comes, but one of us will leave the other, so what have you."[27]

Genevieve was the first to go. She died of congestive heart failure on February 6, 1963. On her death certificate, her occupation is listed as "retired code and cipher expert." Parker and Mary Lue scattered her ashes on the farm she loved so much.[28]

In his retirement, Parker continued to correspond with William Friedman. The two men had a long but sporadic relationship based on mutual admiration and their shared interest in the obscure field of cryptology. Friedman used the information he obtained from Hitt in both his historical work and his series of lectures to employees of the National Security Agency in the 1950s. He also cited Hitt's work in his multivolume books *Military Cryptanalysis* and *Military Cryptanalytics*. As the health of both men declined, they lost contact. Friedman died on November 12, 1969. There is no indication that Elizebeth Friedman and Genevieve Hitt, who met only once, maintained any sort of relationship.[29]

William Friedman did his bit to keep Hitt's name alive at the National Security Agency, but it was David Kahn who preserved Hitt's legacy as a cryptologist with his book *The Codebreakers.* Kahn, who expressed an interest in codes and ciphers at an early age, first wrote to Hitt in 1949, asking him to autograph his copy of Hitt's *Manual.* In November 1962 Kahn contacted Hitt with some questions, and Parker suggested that he read Friedman's *Elements of Cryptanalysis,* if he could find it. He also suggested that Kahn contact Friedman, "one of my protégés," while he gathered some material, as it would take "a little time to get together the information you ask for but I will get it for you." Hitt's longer letter written a few days later explained his history and warned Kahn not to trust the writings of Herbert O. Yardley.[30]

Kahn was rarely at a loss for words, but he professed it difficult "to express my appreciation and gratitude." He visited Front Royal in late December 1963, and after that visit Mary Lue began sorting through her father's papers and sent two large boxes of them to Kahn. She told Kahn, "It does not seem possible that so much ground could have been covered and so much accomplished in one lifetime."[31]

In mid-1963 Hitt responded to a memo asking for contributions to the new First Army Museum on Governors Island and offered material from his service in France. The deputy information officer, Lieutenant Colonel William K. Blanchard, told Hitt he would be in Washington in the fall and offered to visit Front Royal to see what Hitt had. On February 27, 1964, Hitt mailed two packages containing codebooks, a photograph, and his September 1918 memo directing a radio deception operation, as well as other papers. When the museum opened, some of Hitt's contributions were displayed in a case representing signals work.[32]

A huge party took place in Gettysburg, Pennsylvania, for Dwight Eisenhower's seventy-third birthday on October 12, 1963. More than 350 people attended, including Walter Annenberg, W. Atlee Burpee, Jimmy Doolittle, Allen Dulles, William Randolph Hearst, J. Willard Marriott, Laurance S. Rockefeller, and Parker Hitt. It was one of the few events Hitt attended after Genevieve's death; Mary Lue drove him to Pennsylvania, and they stayed overnight. The day began with informal get-togethers (and golf for those who were so inclined) and concluded with a cocktail party and dinner that included "only one speech," apart from Eisenhower's own brief remarks. "I found the food to be as good as the company," Eisenhower wrote afterward. Hitt was honored to attend and happy to pay his respects to his "oldest friend." In his acceptance letter, Hitt suggested that he would be the oldest Republican at the party, "as my political activities started at the age of ten," referring to his trip on Benjamin Harrison's inauguration train. It was undoubtedly the last time he saw Ike and Mamie.[33]

An illness in early 1964 was serious enough to worry his sister-in-law Tot, but Parker persevered. In December 1966 Mamie Eisenhower told Mary Lue, "Some day we are going to drive to Front Royal to see you," for "we love our old friends," but this probably did not happen. Parker Hitt's final years were lived quietly with his daughter and his dogs at Genlue Park. Mary Lue looked after him until the end.[34]

In February 1971 Hitt fell at home and broke his hip. He was taken to the hospital in Front Royal and never left. He died with Mary Lue by his side on March 2, 1971, less than six months before his ninety-third birthday. Mary Lue scattered his ashes on the farm, as she and Parker had done eight years earlier for Genevieve. There was no service, no ceremony. The final newspaper story about Hitt was his obituary, written by Kahn, who remembered him as a cryptologist. But he had been so much more.[35]

12

Legacy

Sailing away from me, with no farewell!
Ah, Parker Hitt and sister Muriel
And Rodney, too, and little Laurance—all
Sailing away—just as the leaves, this Fall!
James Whitcomb Riley, "The Witheraways"

Parker Hitt sailed away from life with no farewell. He was proud of his work but did not draw attention to himself. He did not commission a biography or write his memoirs; he wanted neither a tombstone nor an obituary. Although the bulk of Hitt's career was unrelated to intelligence, he left a significant legacy in that field and is honored in the Military Intelligence Hall of Fame and the Cryptologic Hall of Honor at the National Security Agency (NSA). Two buildings on the NSA's Texas campus are named for Parker and Genevieve Hitt.

Hitt led a useful and purposeful life, one of import and influence, perseverance and luck. He worked hard, jumping from project to project, but did not miss out on the pleasures of life. Genevieve was less driven by achievement, but she was always busy—often involved in unconventional pursuits for a woman of her time. She too sought satisfaction and enjoyment from life.

The Hitts' daughter, Mary Lue, was single-minded in her devotion to her parents: their choices directly influenced how she lived her life. Despite being raised to be self-sufficient and independent minded, Mary Lue apparently never envisioned a life separate from her family. Though she worked for some time as an insurance agent and was a notary public, "sitting in an office is not her idea of something to do." Her greatest pleasures were tennis, swimming, gardening, and world affairs and politics; she had suitors but never married. Mary Lue inherited Parker's nose and Genevieve's dark eyes and hair, and she learned from both parents to do whatever she wanted to do. Genevieve called her daughter the "only really contented person I have ever known." She abhorred dishonesty and considered her aunt Tot the most honorable person she knew (presumably after her parents). "Everybody likes Mary Lue, and she likes everybody, so I suppose that's why she has such a good time," Genevieve once told her own mother. And Mary Lue loved living at Genlue Park.[1]

A staunch Republican like her parents and grandparents, Mary Lue was active in local politics. She frequently served as an election judge, and at least once she was a delegate at Virginia's Seventh District Republican Party Convention. Friends remembered her lively personality; she was a good cook who introduced them to Mexican food and was famous for her homegrown red raspberries. Like her father, she loved dogs and called her black Labrador retriever Iris "a wonderful person." Mary Lue maintained a lively intellectual interest in unsolved ciphers; after Parker's death, she made it her mission to protect her parents' legacy in the cryptologic world. Although she sold some of Hitt's books, she sorted and preserved a vast quantity of papers and artifacts. She donated an assortment of papers and Parker's one surviving 1916 sliding strip device to the Military Intelligence Museum at Fort Huachuca when he was inducted in the Military Intelligence Hall of Fame in 1988. Hitt Hall, on the Huachuca campus, was named in his honor in 1995. Mary Lue also sent material to David Kahn and corresponded with Louis Kruh, a friend of Kahn's and a cofounder of the journal *Cryptologia*. Kruh, who amassed a collection of cryptologic papers, books, and curiosities, shared Mary Lue's interest in the Beale cipher. Mary Lue claimed she had solved it, and the two spent several years exchanging thoughts on the subject.[2]

In the 1970s Mary Lue sold some land to a young veterinarian and his wife, David and Evie Moreman. The couple became her friends, and their daughter, Jennifer, grew up swimming in her pool and playing in the Genlue Park garden. The Moremans became her family, and they watched out for her as she aged. When Mary Lue died on January 25, 1997, the Moremans and Jennifer's husband, Kevin Mustain, continued to preserve the contents of the house and the memory of Parker and Genevieve.

Hitt considered himself "an all-round engineer," and although he regretted not graduating from Purdue, he had "not done so badly for my country and myself." His choice of an army career may have been impulsive at first, inspired by his uncle's stories and the desire to do something patriotic, but the fact that he did not abandon the military after his experience in Cuba indicates that something about army life appealed to him. And once he chose that direction, he gave little thought to leaving the army until he had served thirty years. He even actively sought to return to service in 1939, when it would have been easy to stay at home. Hitt did not follow a traditional career path and occasionally made moves that hindered his advancement; at times, the army did not know what to do with him. What others may have perceived as perpetual reinvention was, from Hitt's perspective, a progression of technical achievement. Though he started as an Infantry officer, he was first promoted to colonel while working for the Signal Corps and returned to that rank as a member of the General Staff.[3]

Hitt's parents and grandparents prized usefulness above all other qualities, a philosophy that went hand in hand with their strong Methodist beliefs. Hitt was a useful and irrepressibly inventive officer. He had a confident, can-do demeanor; thought deeply and carefully about problems; and was clever with his hands, building prototypes of his inventions from readily available materials (for example, improvising a cooling system for machine guns from some bathroom hose and the tip of a hat cord). Senior officers wanted Hitt in their organizations because he possessed intelligence and common sense. He was skilled at conveying information to others and a good teacher. In every new assignment, Hitt inevitably found an unusual way to improve procedures, equipment, or techniques; he innovated whether it was part of his job or not. When he left the army, he preferred to wear short sleeves, which eliminated the bother of rolling up long sleeves whenever he tinkered with something.[4]

Most people who knew Hitt liked him, but he sometimes rubbed new acquaintances the wrong way; his intelligence and self-assurance could come across as arrogance. His intellectual confidence was overwhelming; if he did not know something, he would look it up and remember it. His mind was always working. On occasion, when he believed he was right, he held to a point of view without considering whether his criticism was politic or warranted. Hitt also had physical confidence and was accustomed to drawing attention because of his unusual height. His mother, a student of physical culture, emphasized exercise and physical well-being, which he continued to value, despite his serious injuries and illnesses. It is easy to imagine that less secure officers felt intimidated or threatened by Hitt's abilities.

Hitt lacked a well-placed sponsor or mentor and apparently did not aspire to the rank of general. His casual approach to his career progression allowed superiors to take advantage of his work ethic and technical abilities. Early in his service, Hitt had bad luck with superior officers: the seven colonels in charge of the 22nd Infantry during his years with that organization appreciated his achievements but never seemed to take to him as a person. His early captains, George Detchemendy and William Wassell, had their own career issues: one quit the army in disgust, and the other had a troubled marriage and an early death. Brigadier General John Henry "Machine Gun" Parker, who was still a captain when Hitt worked alongside him, was too wrapped up in promoting his own career to support the junior officer, but he was happy to use Hitt's technical advancements on the range. Colonel Samuel Reber of the Signal Corps was a mentor of sorts, encouraging Hitt to break ciphers, but Reber's mismanagement of aviation matters and subsequent disgrace meant that he could not advocate for Hitt in Washington after early 1917. Colonel Ralph Van Deman, in Military Intelligence, would have been happy to guide Hitt but never had the opportunity. The closest thing to a mentor in Hitt's life was General Edgar Russel of the Signal Corps, who encouraged Hitt's work at the Signal School, made sure he became an instructor there, and convinced Pershing that Hitt was needed in France. Major General Charles S. Farnsworth, the chief of Infantry in 1923, tried to look out for Hitt (and improve his chances for promotion) when he pushed him to join the Command and General Staff School's class of 1924, but Hitt rejected the offer because he was bored with school assignments.

He was not ignorant of army politics but did not engage in politicking; he knowingly made career choices based on personal interest rather than a desire to get ahead. He entered the army as an enlisted engineer in a volunteer unit after first seeking a commission. When he received his commission, it was in the Infantry, not the Engineers; whether this was the army's choice or Hitt's is uncertain, but he never attempted to switch to the Corps of Engineers, and there is no evidence that the Signal Corps interested him at the time. Perhaps he enjoyed the life of a soldier, and he had ample opportunity to use his engineering skills in the Philippines. Between 1906 and 1910, Hitt educated himself in communications technology, and he was well prepared when he found himself at the Signal School rather than the School of the Line. He enjoyed his detail as an instructor, but he either could not or would not switch from the Infantry to Signals when he left the school in 1915.

At the start of World War I, the Signal Corps had only fifty-five officers and was badly deficient in technical talent; Hitt once again leaped in to fill the breach, holding one of the most important Signal Corps positions in the American Expeditionary Forces (AEF). Although the Signal Corps needed Hitt, it did not treat him as one of its own; had he been a member of that corps, he surely would have been promoted to brigadier general. Edgar Russel recognized his abilities and tried but failed to get Hitt to transfer to Signals after the war. Hitt was hesitant because he had a low opinion of the technical skills of some of the senior officers. And

Russel's request in early 1919 came at the worst time for Hitt to make a life-changing decision; he was exhausted (and often ill), overworked, and worried about his family, and he wanted to go home. Hitt chose to stay with the Infantry and accepted an assignment to the Army War College, which led to years of teaching and staff work. Hitt's bias against Signal Corps officers was confirmed by George O. Squier's congressional testimony in 1919; Squier's comments made it impossible for Hitt to reconsider a move to Signals. By the time he returned to a real Infantry job in 1924, Hitt was behind the knowledge curve and lacked allies.

The decision not to transfer to the Signal Corps was the last major turning point of Hitt's military career. Had he listened to Russel, it is conceivable that he could have become chief signal officer (CSO) following George Gibbs's retirement in 1931. Gibbs was replaced by Irving Carr, who, like Hitt, had started out as an infantry officer. During the war, Hitt both supervised and outranked Carr; when Carr fell ill in 1919, Hitt took his place as CSO of Third Army. Had Hitt had a senior mentor in addition to Russel, he might have made the move to the Signal Corps. Hitt advanced through merit rather than politics, and he never expressed regret at what turned out to be a bad decision for his personal advancement in the army.

Elizabeth Barnett Hitt was an enormous influence on her son. Parker learned from an early age that women are capable of demanding work, organization, and intellectual achievement. When he finally married, it was to a spirited woman with a quick mind and a head for finances. Genevieve Young Hitt had no early career aspirations but took an interest in Parker's cipher studies and found she had an aptitude for the work. Unwittingly, she broke ground for women in the field by doing unpaid work for the government in 1915 and 1916, and her wartime work in the Southern Department's Intelligence Office was a matter of pride for both herself and her husband. Genevieve's niece, Jean Young Fish, remembered her as "truly a very remarkable person who in many respects lived before her time." Together, Parker and Genevieve raised a strong-willed young woman, Mary Lueise Hitt, who also had a brief stint as a cryptologist during World War II. Her parents gave her the freedom to be herself, did not pressure her to marry, and allowed her to live as she wished, with no expectations based on gender.[5]

As early as 1914, Hitt believed the army should consider using female telephone operators in wartime, and he helped bring the concept to fruition in 1917 and 1918. Hitt's support of and care for the women in

France demonstrated not just his innate courtesy and gallantry but also his understanding of women as part of a team making a significant contribution to the war effort. Raised by a mother who considered herself a feminist, Hitt was a feminist too.[6]

Despite his cipher devices, his cipher work, and his *Manual,* Hitt never considered himself a professional cryptologist. To him, the "cipher game" was a hobby and later an avocation, although, by the end of World War II, he was pleased to be counted "among those who have contributed to the curious business" of signals intelligence. The cryptologic world, however, considers him a pioneer in the field. Within the US Army, it is fair to say that Parker Hitt was to cryptology as Benjamin Foulois was to aviation and John Henry Parker was to machine guns. Hitt's greatest influence extends beyond his cipher devices, for his work with the Signal Corps during World War I marks him as a progenitor of twentieth-century signals intelligence and communications security systems. On page two of Hitt's *Manual,* in a discussion of "equipment for cipher work," he emphasizes the importance of each field army having an office "where all ciphers intercepted . . . should be sent at once for examination"; he places this work within the army's Intelligence Section. He suggests that "a special radio station, with receiving instruments only, should be an adjunct to this office and its function should be to copy all hostile radio messages whether in cipher or plain text," and he states that this facility should operate twenty-four hours a day. Hitt, writing in 1915, was describing a signals intelligence system that would not exist in the US Army until 1918. Radio intercept for the purpose of military intelligence was first practiced in the 1905 Russo-Japanese War; however, most of the belligerents in World War I did not have functioning intercept services or signals intelligence organizations when the war started. Hitt understood the need for such a service, and he seemingly had no specific knowledge of signals intelligence work in Europe to assist his thinking on the subject. During the Punitive Expedition in 1916, working both from home at Fort Sill and in the field on the Texas-Mexico border, Hitt was one of a handful of army personnel who served as unofficial cryptologists, receiving the code and cipher messages intercepted by radio stations and turning them into actionable intelligence. These men did not work in the tidy, well-equipped spaces envisioned by Hitt; they worked in the field or at home on their own time, doing the tasks that would later be performed by MI-8 in Washington.[7]

Hitt had a deeper understanding of communications technology than most serving signal officers in 1917. He understood how the technology worked, the advantages it provided to commanders, and the security risks involved, particularly with radio. Hitt was an early proponent of communications security, not only using codes and ciphers but also devising systems of call words and call signs to protect the identities of communicators even if their messages were read by the enemy. The United States was technologically unprepared for the signals intelligence war in 1917, both on the home front and in France. Hitt knew what was needed in France and helped make it happen. He was the critical link that enabled the three parts of the AEF's cryptologic organization, split between Military Intelligence and the Signal Corps, work well; he provided guidance, support, and sometimes supervision to the three men commanding the organizations: Frank Moorman (whom Hitt had trained in cipher work), Robert Loghry, and Howard R. Barnes. The AEF cryptologists had to get smart quickly, and they received advice from the British and French on organization, methodology, techniques for breaking German codes, traffic analysis, direction finding, and code compilation. Hitt advised and influenced this nascent cryptologic system. Because he understood the adversary's signals intelligence capabilities, Hitt advocated radio silence to deny the enemy knowledge of the order of battle, employed radio deception to trick the enemy with false signals, and stressed the importance of codes to slow the enemy's ability to exploit messages. AEF radio collection and direction-finding operations were, by the end of the war, more efficient than those of the French.[8]

Hitt's guidance and enthusiasm influenced both Moorman, who would continue to work for the Signal Corps after the war, and the great cryptologist William F. Friedman, who, among other things, constructed codes for the Signal Corps in the 1920s. It was Friedman who ensured that the United States retained cryptologic skills after the war. Friedman helped organize and pack up the work of the G2A6; in the 1930s he reissued many reports written by the AEF cryptologic organizations, and he used AEF organizational principles as a template for his Signal Intelligence Service (SIS). Many of these principles, cultivated by Friedman, were employed during World War II and retained when the NSA was established in 1952.

In 1916 Hitt envisioned that the work of radio intelligence would be split between Military Intelligence and the Signal Corps; in the AEF, the analytical work was conducted by the intelligence staff (breaking codes and ciphers and reporting intelligence), while the Signal Corps collected signals and compiled codes. In the 1920s the army struggled over the proper placement of cryptology, and when Friedman went to work for the

Signal Corps in 1921, he supported the idea of combining the three elements of cryptologic work into one organization. By design or default, the Signal Corps won the battle when the Military Intelligence Division's MI-8 (Yardley's "Black Chamber") closed in 1929 and was replaced in 1930 by Friedman's SIS, subordinate to the Signal Corps. Hitt contributed in a small way to the Signal Corps' victory, as his two acolytes Moorman and Friedman campaigned for the corps' control of cryptology. In the end, Hitt—Van Deman's first choice to be chief of MI-8—had greater influence on the direction of twentieth-century signals intelligence than did the man who took the MI-8 job, Herbert O. Yardley.[9]

One wonders what influence Hitt had on Dwight D. Eisenhower's view of intelligence. Eisenhower was an active consumer of signals intelligence as a commander in World War II and later as president. He first met Hitt in 1916 and was certainly aware of Hitt's reputation as "a shark on ciphers," as well as Genevieve's work for the Southern Department during World War I. It is possible that Ike discussed radio intelligence with Hitt during the 1920s when the couples regularly socialized. Neither man left any written record of conversations they had on the subject; it is impossible to know whether Eisenhower's views on the importance and validity of ULTRA intelligence during World War II were affected by anything he learned from Hitt.

Parker Hitt was a man of many talents. He could shoot, hunt (and clean his kill), ride a bicycle and a horse, climb a tower, conduct a survey, draw a map, play the banjo and baseball, dance, fish, drive a car and a dogsled, send Morse code, construct a code, build a telephone switchboard and a rifle target, modify a machine gun, fix a boiler, repair a lawn mower and a sewing machine, replace a marine engine, pilot a boat, write a book, play bridge, engineer a bridge, improve a signal lantern, drill troops, fight a battle, erect telephone poles, string telephone wire, fly a Wright plane, give a speech, teach a class, operate a radio, invent a cipher device, care for dogs, make architectural drawings, design a building, develop a war plan, kill an adversary, recover a body, plan a funeral, raise a gunboat, put up a tent, set up a machine gun, cook a meal, make ice cream, ice skate, solve a cipher, dig a garden, comfort a child, and complain to higher authorities. He survived disease, typhoons, two train wrecks, a fall from a horse, combat, and a serious health crisis in middle age. He was a good correspondent, a voracious reader, a talented artist, a caring son, a loving spouse, a tolerant parent, and an advocate for women in the workplace. Hitt was frugal and cranky, courteous and gallant; he was devoted to the army and patriotic, and he cut a fine figure in his dress blues. He knew two presidents, two senators, innumerable other elected officials, and a poet. He respected others for the work they did and earned the loyalty of those who served with him; people were glad to know him. He had a straightforward view of the world as something to be mastered. He was ingenious.[10]

Hitt led his own life, unencumbered by expectations, and he wanted others to do the same. He was not one for hero worship and desired no tribute or monument. From Indianapolis to Front Royal, he followed his instincts and lived a life of usefulness, great accomplishment, and modest comfort. Hitt enjoyed life, for as the card Genevieve gave him in 1933 jokingly reminded him, he would be a "long time dead."[11]

Acknowledgments

Research is not a solitary endeavor; many people assisted me in this journey, and this book has benefited from their contributions. David Moreman, Evie Moreman, Kevin Mustain, and Jennifer Mustain have my deepest thanks for preserving the Hitt legacy; Parker Hitt's story would not be complete without their gracious assistance. I am also grateful for the assistance of the Hitt and Young families: Peter Hitt, grandson of Parker's brother Rodney; Jean Young Fish; Vivienne Young Kinnear and her husband Bob Kinnear; and Laura Young Underwood. Both families shared stories, letters, and pictures and provided encouragement. My former colleagues at the National Security Agency's Center for Cryptologic History, particularly Dr. William J. Williams and Dr. David A. Hatch, supported my desire to tell Parker Hitt's story. Dr. Thomas A. Johnson made the link to Front Royal. Rene Stein and her successor at the National Cryptologic Museum Library, Rob Simpson, watched out for new Hitt references and located obscure sources. Special thanks to David Kahn for passing the torch and encouraging my work. The professional research done by Jonathan Webb Deiss of soldiersource.com saved me hundreds of hours and uncovered unexpected treasures.

Dozens of librarians, archivists, historians, and museum personnel were patient with my queries and generous with their time. Particular thanks are due to Eric Van Slander at the National Archives and Records Administration, College Park; Jacqueline B. Davis at the Fort Sam Houston Museum; Kelvin Crow, Kathleen Buker, and the staff of the Frontier Army Museum at Fort Leavenworth; Lori S. Stewart and Paul Pipik at the US Army Military Intelligence Center of Excellence at Fort Huachuca; Barbara Taylor at the Fort George G. Meade Museum; Floyd Hertweck, Susan Thompson, and Chrissie Reilly at the US Army Communications-Electronics Command (CECOM) History Office; Herb Pankratz, Timothy Rives, and Chalsea Milner at the Dwight D. Eisenhower Presidential Library; Patrick Farris, Judith Pfeffer, and James Hefline at the Warren County (Virginia) Heritage Society; Paul Barron, Jeffrey Kozak, and Melissa Davis at the George C. Marshall Foundation Research Library and Archives; Elaine Hinds and Mark Remington of St. Mary's School in

San Antonio; the staff of the Texana Room at the San Antonio Public Library; and the San Antonio Genealogical and Historical Society.

I am grateful for long-distance assistance from Towana Spivey at the Fort Sill National Historic Landmark Museum, Richard L. Baker at the Army Heritage and Education Center, Roger Hardig and Jennifer E. Capps at the Benjamin Harrison Presidential Site, Katie Davis at Kent State University, Mandy Wise at the University College London, Teressa Williams of the Anchorage Museum, Eugene Rutigliano at the Beeghly Library of Ohio Wesleyan University, Laurie A. Preston of the McGraw-Page Library at Randolph Macon College, and Ursula Romero at the Lilly Library in Bloomington, Indiana. At Purdue University I received assistance from David Hovde in the University Archives and Special Collections, Donna Pusey in the Office of the Registrar, and Bob Mindrum of the Purdue Memorial Union. David Hardin at the National Archives in St. Louis kept an eye on my pandemic-stalled request for photographs. To all the others who took the time to answer my questions, I thank you for your diligence.

Many individuals contributed information or documentation or lent a hand with research, including Becca Antonoplos, K. B. Barcomb, Steven M. Bellovin, James A. Bruce, Laurence M. Burke II, Elizabeth Cobbs, Tony Comer, Michael Doidge, Thomas Fife, John Fox, Jill Frahm, Louise Arnold Friend, Barbara J. Hardie, Lisa Long, Susan McClure, Jim Reeds, Ray Sadler, Ellouise Schoettler, Dwight Sullivan, Carolyn Timbie, Erwin Tiongson, Ryan Wadle, General Sam S. Walker, Tricia Washer, and Matthew Westfall. Still others provided critical advice, encouragement, and counsel: Craig Bauer, John Ferris, David Kohnen, Liza Mundy, Rebecca Robbins Raines, Rose Mary Sheldon, David J. Sherman, Kent Sieg, Paul Thomsen, and Mitchell Yockelson. Natalie O'Neal and Sarah Olson at the University Press of Kentucky guided me through the publication process with care and professionalism. I am indebted to Linda Lotz for her careful copyediting. All remaining errors are my own.

My husband, Andrew H. Smoot, whose genealogical connection to Parker Hitt inspired me to pursue Hitt's story, demonstrated extraordinary patience during my work on this book. He provided critical support in the roles of research assistant, chauffeur, cryptologic stevedore, editor, and wise counselor.

Notes

Abbreviations

ACA	American Cryptogram Association
ACOS	Assistant Chief of Staff
AEF	American Expeditionary Forces
AG	adjutant general
AGO	Adjutant General's Office
AHEC	Army History and Education Center, Carlisle, PA
ASC	Archives and Special Collections
AWC	Army War College
CO	commanding officer
COS	chief of staff
CSO	chief signal officer
DKC	David Kahn Collection
E	entry
EBH	Elizabeth Barnett Hitt
EPL	Eisenhower Presidential Library
ESFC	Elizebeth Smith Friedman Collection
FH	*Some Family History Covering the Hitt, Smith, John, Graves, and Barnett Ancestry,* by George Cooper Hitt
GCH	George Cooper Hitt
GO	General Order
GPO	Government Printing Office
GY	Genevieve Young
GYH	Genevieve Young Hitt
HQ	headquarters
IHS	Indiana Historical Society
ISR	Individual Service Record
IT&T/ITT	International Telephone and Telegraph
LH	Laurance Hitt
LYK	Louise Young King
MEP	Mamie Eisenhower Papers
MHB	Muriel Hitt Brandon
MID	Military Intelligence Division
ML	George C. Marshall Foundation Research Library and Archive
MLCY	Mary Lueise Carter Young
MLH	Mary Lueise Hitt

213

MMC   Moreman-Mustain Collection
NARA   National Archives and Records Administration, Washington, DC
NARA CP National Archives and Records Administration, College Park, MD
NCML   National Cryptologic Museum Library
NPRC   National Personnel Records Center, St. Louis, MO
OCSO   Office of the Chief Signal Officer
OMPF   Official Military Personnel File
OPF   Official Personnel File
PH   Parker Hitt
PHP   Parker Hitt Papers
PUL   Purdue University Libraries
RG   Record Group
RH   Rodney Hitt
SHSC   Shortridge High School Collection
SRH   Special Research History
SO   Special Orders
TFC   Timbie Family Collection
WD   War Department
WFP   William F. Friedman Papers
WFF   William F. Friedman
YFL   Young Family Letters

Preface

Epigraph: PH, *Manual for the Solution of Military Ciphers* (Fort Leavenworth, KS: Press of the Army Service Schools, 1916), 1.

Note on Terminology

1. WFF, "Six Lectures on Cryptology," in Center for Cryptologic History, *The Friedman Legacy: A Tribute to William and Elizebeth Friedman* (Fort George G. Meade, MD: National Security Agency, 2006), 6–8.

Introduction

Epigraph: WFF's inscription in Hitt's copy of William and Elizebeth Friedman's book *The Shakespearean Ciphers Examined* (Cambridge: Cambridge University Press, 1957), MMC.

1. Hitt's last words were, "I should have had more dogs." This is according to David Moreman, who heard the story from Mary Lue Hitt. David and Evie Moreman, oral history, March 23, 2009. Hitt wrote, "Success in dealing with unknown ciphers is measured by these four things in the order named: perseverance, careful

methods of analysis, intuition, luck." PH, *Manual for the Solution of Military Ciphers* (Fort Leavenworth, KS: Press of the Army Service Schools, 1916), 1.

2. This transition is well detailed in Edward M. Coffman, *The Regulars: The American Army 1898–1941* (Cambridge, MA: Belknap Press of Harvard University Press, 2004).

3. Betsy Rohaly Smoot, "An Accidental Cryptologist: The Brief Career of Genevieve Young Hitt," *Cryptologia* 35, no. 2 (2011): 166.

4. Samuel Reber to PH, January 4, 1915, NCML, DKC, PHP.

5. WFF, inscription.

1. The Making of the Man

Epigraph: GYH to MLCY, August 2, 1911, YFL.

1. The name Parker, popular in the nineteenth century, had a resurgence in the 1990s and into the early decades of the twenty-first century.

2. Muriel was born in 1880, Rodney in 1882, and Laurance in 1887. *FH,* DePauw University Archives and Special Collections, Hitt Family Papers (MC 34), 63.

3. Wilbur Hitt, Compiled Service Records, NARA, RG 94; Wilbur Hitt, Pension Files, NARA, RG 15, C2488352; *FH,* 63–64.

4. *FH,* 61; GCH, ed., *Western Collegian* (Delaware, OH), March 8, 1871, 4. Material related to George C. Hitt as paymaster is in NARA, RG 99, E 7, box 126, E 9, vol. 24. William A. Jones, *Report upon the Reconnaissance of Northwestern Wyoming, Including Yellowstone National Park, Made in the Summer of 1873* (Washington, DC: GPO, 1875); Paul K. Walker, introduction to *Exploring Nature's Sanctuary* (Washington, DC: GPO, 1985).

5. *FH,* 67, 65; Elizabeth Barnett, baptismal certificate, March 25, 1873, Trinity Cathedral Episcopal Church; "United States Births and Christenings, 1867–1931," FamilySearch database https://familysearch.org/ark:/61903/1:1:XLLL-J6X (accessed March 25, 2020).

6. *FH,* 67, 65.

7. *FH,* 69, 56; "Mrs. Hitt Passes Away," *Brookville (IN) Democrat,* August 3, 1905, 1; PH to EBH, September 22, 1905, MMC.

8. *FH,* 69–70; "Mrs. George C. Hitt Holds Enviable Record as Leader among 'Progressive' Club Women of Hoosier Capital," *Indianapolis Star,* April 15, 1912, 7; GYH to MLCY, August 11, 1911, YFL.

9. "Mrs. George C. Hitt Holds Enviable Record," 7; GYH to MLCY, August 11, 1911.

10. Berry Robinson Sulgrove, *History of Indianapolis and Marion County Indiana* (Indianapolis: L. H. Everts, 1884), 214F–G; "Booth Tarkington and the League of Nations: Advice for Senator Harry S. New," *Indiana Magazine of History* 84, no. 4 (1988): 343–53; Chandler Lighty, "A Brief History of the *Indianapolis*

Journal," Hoosier State Chronicles: Indiana's Digital Newspaper, August 16, 2013, https://blog.newspapers.library.in.gov/indjournalhistory/ (accessed September 14, 2019); Elizabeth J. Van Allen, *James Whitcomb Riley: A Life* (Bloomington: Indiana University Press, 1999), 220; Marcus Dickey, *The Maturity of James Whitcomb Riley* (Indianapolis: Bobbs-Merrill, 1922), 159.

11. Van Allen, *Riley,* 220; Charles W. Calhoun, *Benjamin Harrison* (New York: Henry Holt, 2005), 64; C. W. Fairbanks, ed., *Western Collegian,* April 17, 1872, 4; "Harrison en Route," *Wichita Eagle,* February 26, 1889, 2.

12. "Testimonials for George C. Hitt," *Indianapolis Journal,* October 11, 1890, 8; "Vice Consul Changes," *Pittsburgh Dispatch,* October 26, 1890, 9; *FH,* 68.

13. George C. Hitt family, Enumeration District 8, *Census Returns of England and Wales, 1891* (Kew, England: National Archives of the UK, Public Record Office, 1891), 6; H. J. K. Usher, C. D. Black-Hawkins, and G. J. Carrick, *An Angel without Wings: The History of University College School 1830–1980* (London: University College School, 1981), 38; PH, "Experiences in an English School," *Shortridge High School Annual* (1894), 31–32, IHS.

14. *FH,* 69; GCH to James Whitcomb Riley, January 21, 1891, Riley mss., courtesy Lilly Library, Indiana University, Bloomington, IN (the quote is actually from Riley's poem "Our Hired Girl"; the girl was courted by "the Raggedy Man"); "Deputy Consul Hitt Resigns," *New York Times,* January 5, 1892, 2; Passenger Lists of Vessels Arriving at New York, New York, 1820–1897, National Archives Microfilm Publication M237, roll 581, NARA, RG 36; Ancestry.com, *New York, Passenger and Crew Lists (including Castle Garden and Ellis Island), 1820–1957.*

15. Little did Hitt know that on June 11, 1910, he would be in the final month of his army service in Alaska. Laura Sheering Gaus, *Shortridge High School 1864–1981: In Retrospect* (Indianapolis: IHS, 1985), 15, 43–44; *Dawn,* May 6, 1893, box 18, folder 2, SHSC, IHS; Promotion List, Grade 11A, June 1894, Promotion List, Grade 12, June 14, 1895, SHSC, IHS; "Prophecy" section, *Shortridge High School Annual* (1895), 58–59, IHS.

16. Commencement Program, 1895, box 6, folder 7, SHSC, IHS; "Those Who Will Read," *Indianapolis Journal,* April 28, 1895, 7; "High School Commencement," *Indianapolis News,* June 12, 1895, 2; "High School Commencement," *Indianapolis Journal,* June 11, 1895, 3; "Class of 85 Members," *Indianapolis Journal,* June 12, 1895, 8; *Shortridge High School Annual* (1895).

17. "They Are on Tour," *Wheeling (WV) Daily Intelligencer,* July 1, 1895, 6. At a rate of about fifty miles a day, the pair should have made it to Connecticut in sixteen days. See http://www.bicyclehistory.net/bicycle-history/history-of-bicycle/ (accessed September 16, 2019); Fred C. Kelly, "The Great Bicycle Craze," *American Heritage* 8, no. 1 (December 1956): 69–73.

18. Class of 1899 of Purdue University, "Looking Backward," *Debris* (1899), ASC, PUL, http://earchives.lib.purdue.edu/cdm/search/searchterm/PUD00012 (accessed September 25, 2018); Class of 1898 of Purdue University, *Debris* (1898), 44, 46, 76, ASC, PUL, http://earchives.lib.purdue.edu/cdm/search/searchterm

/PUD00011 (accessed September 27, 2019); Class of 1896 of Purdue University, *Debris* (1896), 72, 93, 158, ASC, PUL, http://earchives.lib.purdue.edu/cdm /search/searchterm/PUD00009 (accessed September 27, 2019); Class of 1897 of Purdue University, *Debris* (1897), 92, ASC, PUL, http://earchives.lib.purdue.edu /cdm/search/searchterm/PUD00010 (accessed September 27, 2019); James H. Smart to Calvin Dewitt, June 27, 1899, PH, OMPF, NPRC.

19. "Record of Parker Hitt," Office of the Registrar, Purdue University; "According to Mr. Hitt," *Indianapolis Star,* August 29, 1896.

20. Department of Civil Engineering, *Debris* (1899); "Record of Parker Hitt"; "Looking Backward," *Debris* (1899).

21. *Debris* (1896), 102; *Debris* (1898), 100, 90; *Debris* (1897), 197.

22. "Record of Parker Hitt"; Smart to Dewitt, June 27, 1899; "Tau Beta Pi," *Debris* (1899).

23. Carmen Gonzalez Lopez-Briones, "The Indiana Press and the Coming of the Spanish-American War, 1895–1898," *Atlantis* 12, no. 1 (1990): 165–76; *Indianapolis Journal,* February 18, 1898, quoted in Clifton J. Phillips, *Indiana in Transition: The Emergence of an Industrial Commonwealth, 1880–1920* (Indianapolis: Indiana Historical Bureau and IHS, 1968), 59; "Indiana Responds to the War," https://www.in.gov/history/2418.htm (accessed September 28, 2019); Indiana Adjutant General's Office and 61st Indiana General Assembly, *Record of Indiana Volunteers in the Spanish-American War—1899* (Indianapolis: W. B. Burford, 1900), 12–13.

24. "Col. Hitt Will Speak at Winchester Rites," clipping from unknown newspaper, November 10, 1938, MMC; typed copy of speech delivered November 11, 1938, MMC.

25. Unlike some contemporaries (such as future Marine Corps Major General Smedley D. Butler), Hitt was in no position to lie about his age to gain a commission. Charles W. Fairbanks to Secretary of War, June 15, 1899, NARA, RG 94, E 25, box 893, file 135657; "Personal and Social," *Indianapolis Journal,* June 14, 1898, 3; "2nd Engineers Company Muster-in Roll and 2nd Engineers Company Description, Physical Records, and Enlistment, Volunteers," NARA, RG 94, E 522; "For the Engineer Corps," *Indianapolis Journal,* June 22, 1898, 3.

2. The Making of the Soldier

Epigraph: PH to GCH, May 30, 1942, MMC.

1. Indiana Adjutant General's Office and 61st Indiana General Assembly, *Record of Indiana Volunteers in the Spanish-American War—1899* (Indianapolis: W. B. Burford, 1900), 63; Patrick McSherry, "Camp Wikoff," Spanish-American War Centennial website, http://www.spanamwar.com/campwikoff.html (accessed March 8, 2015); Company D Muster Roll, August, September, and October 1898, and 2nd Engineers Muster-out Roll, NARA, RG 94, E 522, box 3191.

2. PH to GCH, November 27, 1924, MMC; "Second Volunteer Engineers Reach Havana," *San Francisco Call*, November 26, 1898, 2; PH to Dax Buell, April 8, 1938, MMC; Fitzhugh Lee, "Report of the Commanding General of the 7th Corps, Headquarters Department of the Province of Havana & Pinar Del Rio, August 15, 1899," in "Annual Report of Major General John R. Brooke, US Army, Commanding the Division of Cuba," 1899; PH, typed speech delivered November 11, 1938, in Winchester, VA, MMC.

3. "Personal and Social," *Indianapolis News*, February 9, 1899, 8; 2nd Engineers Company Return for February 1889, NARA, RG 94 E 522; PH to Buell, April 8, 1938.

4. Edward M. Coffman, *The Regulars: The American Army 1898–1941* (Cambridge, MA: Belknap Press of Harvard University Press, 2004), 15–16; Charles W. Fairbanks to Secretary of War, March 10, 1899, PH, ISR, NARA, RG 94, E 25, box 893, file 135657; "Second Lieutenants," *Indianapolis Journal*, March 14, 1899, 1; telegram from Fairbanks to Henry C. Corbin, March 27, 1899, PH, ISR; telegram from Assistant AG Schwan to Fairbanks, April 1, 1899, PH, ISR; Company D Muster Roll, March and April 1899, and 2nd Engineers Company Muster-out Roll, NARA, RG 94, E 522, box 3191; "Personal and Social," *Indianapolis Journal*, May 20, 1899, 3.

5. James H. Smart to Calvin Dewitt, June 27, 1899, and Christopher C. FitzGerald to Dewitt, July 14, 1899, PH, OMPF.

6. PH to AG, August 15, 1899, PH, OMPF; examination papers, PH, ISR. Although Hitt's weight fluctuated during his time in the service, it seems unlikely that it approached 175 pounds; this was apparently a polite fiction. His weight when he enlisted was 161 pounds. The US Army's "Table of Physical Proportions for Height, Weight, and Chest Measurement" (established in 1887) had a top height of seventy-three inches (two inches shorter than Hitt) and a required weight of 176 pounds. *Manual for the Medical Department, United States Army* (Washington, DC: GPO, 1896), 56; Proceeding of a Board of Officers, September 5, 1899, PH, ISR.

7. There is no indication that the Hitt family made this request; Fairbanks, who referenced the suggestion of "friends," proposed that Hitt go to the 5th, 6th, 8th, 10th, 12th, 22nd, or 23rd Regiment. Fairbanks to Corbin, October 10, 1899, PH, ISR; AG Office to Commanding General, Department of California, October 11, 1899, PH, ISR. The current motto of the 22nd, "Deeds Not Words," was in occasional use at the time but did not become official until 1923. See 1st Battalion, 22nd Infantry website, http://1-22infantry.org/ (accessed October 24, 2014). Timothy K. Nenninger, *The Leavenworth Schools and the Old Army: Education, Professionalism, and the Officer Corps of the United States Army, 1881–1918* (Westport, CT: Greenwood Press, 1978), 55–56.

8. "The Thirty-Eighth Here," *Hawaiian* (*Honolulu*) *Star,* December 2, 1899, 5; PH to Dr. Edward A. Rusk, September 22, 1947, MMC.

9. The complicated history of this conflict is cogently explained in David J. Silbey, *A War of Frontier and Empire: The Philippine-American War, 1899–1902* (New York: Hill and Wang, 2007).

10. "Recent Deaths," *Army and Navy Journal* 37, no. 45 (July 7, 1900): 1061; PH OMPF; "Report of Engagement on Mount Balubad," August 11, 1900, in *Annual Reports of the War Department for the Fiscal Year Ending June 30, 1900* (Washington, DC: GPO, 1900); PH, ISR; "In the Phillipines [*sic*]," *Belvidere (IL) Daily Republican*, August 15, 1900, 3.

11. PH, ISR; PH, OMPF; PH, Diary, January 1901, MMC. It is possible that Hitt kept diaries before this time, but none have been found in his papers.

12. George A. Detchemendy, "Experiences at Baler," *San Francisco Call*, March 23, 1902, 14; PH, "A Side Light on the Capture of Aguinaldo," NCML, DKC, PHP.

13. PH, Diary, August 30, 1901; Detchemendy, "Experiences at Baler."

14. PH, Diary, July 30, 1901; Detchemendy, "Experiences at Baler."

15. Hitt knew Rubio, who was one of his hunting guides. Some accounts say this happened on February 5, but Hitt says February 6. PH, "Side Light on the Capture of Aguinaldo."

16. For varying accounts of these incidents, see Silbey, *War of Frontier and Empire*, 174; David Haward Bain, *Sitting in Darkness: Americans in the Philippines* (Boston: Houghton Mifflin, 1984), 96; Brian McAllister Linn, *The Philippine War 1899–1902* (Lawrence: University Press of Kansas, 2000); Frederick Funston, *Memories of Two Wars: Cuban and Philippine Experiences* (New York: C. Scribner's Sons, 1911), 389. Newspaper accounts include "Soldier with a Record," *Indianapolis Journal*, March 1, 1902, 1. See also PH, "Side Light on the Capture of Aguinaldo." According to David Kahn, Hitt solved Philippine insurgents' ciphers during Aguinaldo's insurrection, a claim that contradicts contemporary evidence and one that I cannot support. See David Kahn, *The Reader of Gentleman's Mail* (New Haven, CT: Yale University Press, 2004), 11. I am grateful to Dr. Erwin Tiongson of the Walsh School of Foreign Service at Georgetown University, who found Hitt's personal copy of Funston's book in a used bookstore in August 2017 and donated it to the National Cryptologic Museum Library.

17. PH, Diary, March 14, 16, 1901; report of the Board of Officers meeting, March 16, 1899, in Baler, PH, ISR; correspondence between Hitt, Fairbanks, and AG Corbin, June and July 1901, PH, ISR.

18. For a full account of this event, see Matthew Westfall, *The Devil's Causeway: The True Story of America's First Prisoners of War in the Philippines, and the Heroic Expedition Sent to Their Rescue* (Guilford, CT: Lyons Press, 2012), 276–77, 282. A typical newspaper article was "Honor for Lieut. Hitt," *Indianapolis Journal*, December 29, 1901, 12. See PH, Diary, August 31–September 5, 1901; PH to "Jeb," November 30, 1937, MMC; PH, report, NARA, RG 391, E 1706, box 1.

19. PH, Diary, October 1901; PH, OMPF.

20. PH, Diary, January and February 1902; PH, OMPF; "Hancock's Tempestuous Voyage from the Philippine Islands," *San Francisco Call*, February 26, 1902, 5.

21. "Soldier with a Record"; GCH to PH, February 20, 1932, MMC; "Resigned from Army," *Boston Globe*, March 1, 1902, 7. Detchemendy, who

appears to have been an alcoholic and mentally unstable, was pushed over the edge by his time at Baler. Westfall, *Devil's Causeway,* 282–84, cites a March 18, 1903, report by a medical examining board.

22. PH, Diary, January 1901–October 1903; "Soldiers Injured in Wreck," *(Philadelphia) Times,* March 12, 1902, 3; PH to AG, April 28, 1920, NARA, RG 92, E 257, box 1; PH to AG, May 5, 1903, April 21 and 26, 1902, PH, ISR; "City Life," *Indianapolis Sun,* April 17, 1902, 1.

23. M. O. Smith, W. H. Wassell, and Daniel S. Appleton, *History of the Twenty Second Infantry 1866–1922* (Governors Island, NY, 1922), 85; PH, OMPF; PH to AG, July 31, 1902, PH, ISR; examination results, March 21, 1901, PH, ISR.

24. PH, Diary, January 1901–October 1903; "Trains Collide," *Arkansas (Little Rock) Democrat,* September 17, 1902, 2.

25. PH to AG, February 16, 1903, PH, ISR; Dr. William H. Corbusier indorsement, February 20, 1903, PH, ISR; PH, Diary, January 1901–October 1903; PH, OMPF.

26. PH, OMPF; PH, Diary, January 1901–October 1903; note relieving Hitt from treatment, July 1, 1903, PH, ISR; AGO, SO 154, July 2, 1903, PH, ISR.

27. PH, Diary, January 1901–October 1903; "The Drift of the Day," *Arkansas Democrat,* October 7, 1903, 5.

28. Marahui is now typically rendered Marawi. It is recently known for the five-month battle in 2017 between the Philippine government and jihadist militants. PH, Diary, January 1901–October 1903, October–December 1903; "Personal and Social," *Indianapolis News,* November 9, 1903, 8; PH, OMPF; Smith et al., *History of the Twenty Second Infantry,* 86.

29. For an excellent discussion of this period, see Ronald K. Edgerton, *American Datu: John J. Pershing and Counterinsurgency Warfare in the Muslim Philippines, 1899–1913* (Lexington: University Press of Kentucky, 2020), 97–98, 226–29. See also www.morolandhistory.com (accessed October 18, 2014); Coffman, *Regulars,* 76.

30. Some of Hitt's maps are in NARA, RG 395, E 4006, box 2; PH, Diary, 1904–1906. The relationship with Mary Wassell was apparently not sexual; it may have started as a favor to Wassell, whose marriage had been troubled for some time.

31. "The Ramaien Expedition," http://1-22infantry.ord/history3/ramaien.htm (accessed October 18, 2014); Edgerton, *American Datu,* 105; PH, Diary, January–February 1904; PH, "Amphibious Infantry," *United States Naval Institute Proceedings* 64, no. 420 (February 1938): 234–50.

32. William H. Wassell, "Report of Operations of 3rd Battalion, 22nd Infantry, Expedition against Taraca, April 2, 1904 to April 10, 1904," NARA, RG 94, E 25, file 529713; PH, OMPF; Edgerton, *American Datu,* 106–7; PH, Diary, April 2–10, 1904.

33. Wassell, "Report of Operations of 3rd Battalion"; PH, OMPF; Edgerton, *American Datu,* 106–7; PH, Diary, April 2–10, 1904. The Silver Star awarded in

1925 was called the Silver Citation Star; it had been devised in July 1918 as a silver star suspended from a campaign ribbon. Holders of the Citation Star were allowed to exchange it for the new Silver Star medal that replaced it in 1932. Hitt did not receive his medal until May 1927. The stop at Dalama may have been where the photograph of the officers of the 22nd Infantry was taken; it is now in the PH Photograph Collection, Philippine Photographs Digital Archive, Special Collections Library, University of Michigan.

34. PH, ISR; PH, draft, "The Story of the Lake Lanao Fleet," MMC (later published, slightly altered, as PH, "Amphibious Infantry"); Secretary of the Navy, *Annual Reports of the Navy Department for the Year 1905* (Washington, DC: GPO, 1906), 486–87, 1236. Army and navy doctrine and responsibilities for inland waterways are mentioned in Alfred T. Mahan, *The Gulf and Inland Waters* (New York: Charles Scribner's Sons, 1883), and were still under discussion in the early years of the twentieth century. See John B. Hattendorf et al., *Sailors and Scholars: The Centennial History of the U.S. Naval War College* (Newport, RI: Naval War College Press, 1984), 53–54.

35. PH, "Story of the Lake Lanao Fleet"; PH, Diary, April 14, 1904–December 18, 1905.

36. PH, Diary, October 1905; PH, "Story of the Lake Lanao Fleet."

37. Sketch of the "Admiral of Lake Lanao," PH Photograph Collection, Philippine Photographs Digital Archive, Special Collections Library, University of Michigan; A. B. Feuer, *Combat Diary: Episodes from the History of the Twenty-Second Regiment, 1866–1905* (New York: Praeger, 1991), 168–69; PH, Diary, July 31–August 1, 1904.

38. Feuer, *Combat Diary,* 168–69; PH, Diary, September 23 and 24, 1904.

39. Feuer, *Combat Diary,* 168–69; PH, Diary, October 24, 1904.

40. PH, "Story of the Lake Lanao Fleet"; PH, Diary, December 27 and 28, 1904.

41. Efficiency report, June 30, 1905, PH, ISR; PH to EBH, September 22, 1905, MMC. Jones later authored the landmark Philippine Autonomy Act of 1916, which promised Philippine independence.

42. PH to EBH, September 22, 1905.

43. PH, Diary, January 1906.

44. National Park Service, "Fort Barry History Tour: An Army Post Standing Guard over the Marin Headlands," 2011; PH, Diary, January–February 1906; "Regimental History of the 22nd US Infantry 1906," NARA, RG 391, E 1713, box 1, 10–11; PH, Diary, April 8, 1906.

45. PH, Diary, April 18, 1906; "List of Persons Occupying Quarters in the Infantry Cantonment, Presidio of San Francisco," n.d. (but lists earthquake refugees), NARA, RG 393, E 520, box 25; PH to AG, "Monthly Report for Camp 8 for June 1906," NARA, RG 393, E 521, box 2.

46. "Regimental History of the 22nd US Infantry 1906," 11–12; PH to AG, October 31, 1906; PH to Military Secretary, October 12, 1906, January 26,

1907; request for leave, September 29, 1906, all in NARA, RG 94, E 340B, box 65; "Last Ball of Season Given at Alcatraz," *San Francisco Call,* February 13, 1907, 5; Steven M. Bellovin, "Frank Miller: Inventor of the One-Time Pad," *Cryptologia* 35, no. 3 (2011): 203–22. Wassell became ill at Goldfield, Nevada, and died on March 7, 1908, at Fort Bayard, New Mexico.

47. David A. Armstrong, *Bullets and Bureaucrats: The Machine Gun and the United States Army* (Westport, CT: Greenwood Press, 1982), 141, 151; "Regimental History of the 22nd US Infantry 1906," 13, citing WD, GO 113, June 19, 1906, and Headquarters, 22nd Infantry, GO 14, July 1, 1906; PH to Adjutant, 22nd Infantry, February 24, 1907, NARA, RG 391, E 1706, box 1; "Regimental History of the 22nd US Infantry 1907," NARA, RG 391, E 1713, box 1; PH, OMPF.

48. PH, ISR; PH to EBH, July 26, September 12 and 20, 1907, MMC.

49. PH, "Analysis of Volleys Fired at 2400 Yards by the School of Musketry," September 20, 1907, NARA, RG 94, E 25, box 4674; PH, "A Brief History of the School of Musketry," *Military Review* (July 1961): 88; PH to GCH, October 18, 1907, MMC.

50. PH, "Brief History," 86; PH to EBH, November 10, 1907, MMC; Armstrong, *Bullets and Bureaucrats,* xiv.

51. PH to EBH, December 4, 1907, MMC; PH to AG, November 30, 1907, PH, ISR.

52. PH to EBH, December 9, 1907, MMC.

53. "Regimental History of the 22nd US Infantry 1907"; Clayton D. Laurie and Ronald H. Cole, *The Role of Federal Military Forces in Domestic Disorders 1877–1945* (Washington, DC: Center of Military History, 1997), 192–201.

54. PH to EBH, December 9, 1907, MMC; PH to GCH, December 12, 1907, MMC; Laurie and Cole, *Role of Federal Military Forces,* 192–201.

55. Laurie and Cole, *Role of Federal Military Forces,* 192–201; PH to EBH, December 16, 22, 1907, MMC; PH, ISR.

56. PH to GCH, January 24, 1908, MMC; PH, ISR; PH, "Brief History," 87; Armstrong, *Bullets and Bureaucrats,* 157; John H. Parker, "Progress in Machine Gun Development," *Journal of the United States Infantry Association* 5, no. 1 (July 1908): 1–13.

57. Hitt's report and related indorsements, March–October 1908, NARA, RG 156, E 28A, box 2139; Chief of Ordnance to AG, July 30, 1909, PH, ISR; PH, "Brief History," 90.

58. Multiple memos, May–July 1908, NARA, RG 156, E 28A, box 2129, file 1391885.

59. He gave at least ten formal lectures and many informal ones. PH, ISR; PH to Adjutant, 22nd Infantry, April 29, May 4, 1908, NARA, RG 391, E 1707, box 2.

60. Marion P. Maus to Alfred Reynolds, June 7, 1908; Reynolds to COS Department of California, June 8, 1908; Reynolds to Maus, June 8, 1908; Reynolds to AG, June 10, 1908, all in NARA, RG 391, E 1707, box 2; "Scandal at

Presidio," *Santa Cruz (CA) Evening News,* January 25, 1909, 5; PH to EBH, July 25, 1908, MMC; Frederick Funston to AG, June 11, 1908, PH, ISR.

61. PH, "Brief History." Hitt cites a 1909 inspector general's report that states the equipment was still packed in its original shipping boxes. PH to GCH, October 23, 1927, MMC.

62. PH to GCH, June 11, 1908, MMC; PH to EBH, July 8–12, 1908, MMC. Hitt had been told Nome was *"the* post of them all."

63. PH to EBH, July 25, August 14, 1908, MMC.

64. "Regimental History of the 22nd US Infantry 1909," NARA, RG 391, E 1713, box 1, 3; PH to EBH, July 25, August 14, December 28, September 21, 1908, MMC; efficiency report, year ending June 30, 1909, PH, ISR.

65. PH, addition to building no. 2, Fort Davis, Alaska (technical drawing), 1910, Anchorage Museum; PH to EBH, October 11, December 14, August 14, September 21, November 18–22, 1908, MMC; Ashley Bowman, *The Arctic Brotherhood: The Story of Alaska-Yukon's Most Influential Order* (Skagway, AK: Lynn Canal Publishing, 2014), 100, x, 141–44, 124. Hitt's roommate West later froze to death at Fort Davis in February 1911 while breaking a trail in a blizzard; West liked Nome so much that he had transferred to the 16th Infantry to stay there. http://www.ancestoryarchives.com/2019/02/remembering-solomon-bertram-west.html (accessed May 26, 2020).

66. PH to EBH, July 12, October 16 and 28, 1909, MMC; PH to GCH, September 11, 1909, MMC.

67. "Transport Buford Arrives in Port," *San Francisco Call,* August 1, 1910, 13; "Twenty-Second Goes to Texas Post Today," *San Francisco Chronicle,* August 2, 1910, 16; "Regimental History of the 22nd US Infantry 1910," NARA, RG 391, E 1713, box 1.

68. PH to EBH, May 17, 1911, MMC.

3. Genevieve Young

Epigraph: GY to her future mother-in-law, EBH, May 31, 1911, MMC.

1. Advertisement, *La Grange (TX) Journal,* August 27, 1885, 1; Jean Young Fish, conversation with the author, September 22, 2011; Vivian Young Kinnear, "Franklin Early Young (1854–1932)" (unpublished genealogy).

2. Vivian Young Kinnear, "From Ireland to Texas: Samuel Armstrong Young (1787–1867)" (unpublished genealogy); Jean Young Fish, "Tradition of the Young Family as Handed down from Generation to Generation" (unpublished manuscript held by the Young family); *General Alumni Catalogue of New York University 1833–1907* (New York: General Alumni Society 1907), 290. Genevieve's mother probably did not realize that she was a third cousin to General William Harding Carter; see William Harding Carter, *Giles Carter of Virginia* (Baltimore: Lord Baltimore Press, 1909). P. B. Carter registered to vote in La

Grange on January 30, 1868, after twelve months in the state. "Texas, Voter Registration Lists, 1867–1869," Ancestry.com; original data, 1867 Voter Registration Lists, microfilm, Texas State Library and Archives Commission, Austin (accessed December 30, 2019).

3. *Daniel's Texas Medical Journal* 6, no. 8 (February 1891): 361; "Pioneer Texas Physician Succumbs," *San Antonio Light,* December 20, 1932, 5A; *Texas State Journal of Medicine* 2, no. 7 (November 1906): 192; GYH to MLCY, August 2, 1911, YFL.

4. GY to Eleanor Onderdonk, August 21, 1897, MMC; Cecilia Steinfeldt, *The Onderdonks: A Family of Texas Painters* (San Antonio, TX: Trinity University Press, 1976), 173; Kemper Diehl, *Saint Mary's Hall: First Century* (San Antonio, TX: St. Mary's Hall, 1979), 3, 18–21, quoting the autobiography of Mrs. Nellie Bartlett; Wallace Carnahan, attestation to Genevieve Young's education, May 21, 1903, MMC; Betsy Rohaly Smoot, "An Accidental Cryptologist: The Brief Career of Genevieve Young Hitt," *Cryptologia* 35, no. 2 (2011): 166. The average surgeon earned $1,635 annually in 1900. Gilson Willets, *Workers of the Nation: An Encyclopedia of the Occupations of the American People and a Record of Business, Professional and Industrial Achievement at the Beginning of the Twentieth Century* (New York: P. F. Collier and Son, 1903).

5. "Ex-Governor Has Young Bride," *El Paso Herald,* August 22, 1903, 1; "Broke Collar Bone," *Houston Post,* March 21, 1905, 2; "Galveston, Harrisburg & San Antonio Railway Company v. Franklin E. Young," *Texas Civil Appeals Reports* 54 (March 1907): 430–34. The $15,000 Young received in 1903 would be equivalent to more than $457,000 in 2020 dollars; https://www.in2013dollars.com/us/inflation/ (accessed July 6, 2020).

6. "Social News and Gossip," *San Antonio Gazette,* July 25, 1907, 6; society page, *San Antonio Light,* March 6, 1909, 3; "History of the Travis Park United Methodist Church," http://travispark.org/760730 (accessed December 30, 2014); society page, *San Antonio Express,* October 15, 1908, 6; "Society," *San Antonio Light,* February 21, 1909, 14.

7. Susanne Wilcox, "The Unrest of Modern Women," *Independent* 67 (July 8, 1909): 63, as quoted in James R. McGovern, "The American Woman's Pre–World War I Freedom in Manners and Morals," *Journal of American History* 55, no. 2 (September 1968): 322; Dorothy Schneider and Carl J. Schneider, *American Women in the Progressive Era, 1900–1920: Change, Challenge & the Struggle for Women's Rights* (New York: Anchor Books, 1993), 16; Jean Young Fish, speech at the dedication of a building in honor of her aunt, Genevieve Young Hitt, April 13, 2012.

8. GY to EBH July 8, 1911, MMC.

9. George S. Simonds (later a major general) was with the 22nd Infantry in 1900 at the same time as Hitt; their paths would cross throughout their careers. "Regimental History of the 22nd US Infantry 1910," NARA, RG 391, E 1713, box 1; "Soldiers Interested in Sham Battle Thursday," *Galveston Daily News,*

August 16, 1910, 3; "Court Martial at Fort Assembles Thursday," *San Antonio Light & Gazette,* September 6, 1910, 5; "Announce Program for Quarterly Field Meet at Fort Sam Houston," *San Antonio Light & Gazette,* September 15, 1910, 2; Marlborough Churchill, memo, August 10, 1910, NARA, RG 393, E 4878, box 63; Reynolds to Adjutant, Fort Sam Houston, September 11 and 27, 1910, NARA, RG 393, E 4881, box 65; PH, "A Brief History of the School of Musketry," *Military Review* (July 1961).

10. PH to EBH, September 22, 1905, MMC.

11. Genevieve's height is given as five feet eight inches on her World War II ration card, MMC; she may have been an inch taller in her youth. Fish conversation, September 22, 2011; PH to EBH, May 17, 1911, MMC; advertisement, *San Antonio Express,* November 9, 1910, 7; "Society News," *San Antonio Light & Gazette,* November 10, 1910, 8.

12. PH, OMPF; PH to David Kahn, November 26, 1962, NCML, DKC; PH to GYH, December 10, 1917, MMC.

13. PH to EBH, May 17, 1911, MMC; PH, December 29, 1910, and subsequent indorsements, NARA, RG 393, E 101, file 7618.

14. "Kreuger-Westervelt Wedding," *San Antonio Express,* February 3, 1911, 8; society page, *San Antonio Light,* April 9, 1911, 14.

15. John M. Manguso, *Maneuver Camp, 1911: Transformation of the Army at Fort Sam Houston* (San Antonio, TX: Fort Sam Houston Museum, 2009), 21–27, 94–97.

16. "U.S. Troops over Line within Week, Is Belief," *Indianapolis Star,* March 9, 1911, 1. Hitt's pay of $200 a month is equivalent to about $5,400 in 2020 dollars, and $240 equals nearly $6,500; https://www.in2013dollars.com/us/inflation/ (accessed July 6, 2020).

17. PH to EBH, May 17, 1911, MMC.

18. W. S. Scott to CO, Fort Sam Houston, February 23, 1911, NARA, RG 393, E 4881, box 72; Benjamin Foulois, ISR, NARA, RG 94, E 25, box 2369; Juliette A. Hennessy, *The United States Army Air Arm April 1861 to April 1917* (Washington, DC: GPO, 1985), 39–45. The Collier plane probably left Texas in March, per Laurance M. Burke II, email to the author, March 1, 2021.

19. William C. Pool, "The Origin of Military Aviation in Texas, 1910–1913," *Southwestern Historical Quarterly* 58, no. 3 (January 1955): 342–71; "Gen. Carter Will Review All Troops," *San Antonio Light,* May 26, 1911, 6; "Camp Awakened by Reveille of Aero Motors," *San Antonio Express,* April 30, 1911, 19; US Air Force Fact Sheet, "Fort Sam Houston Pilot Training."

20. Foulois, ISR; PH, undated note, MMC.

21. Pool, "Origin of Military Aviation in Texas," 364; PH, undated note, MMC.

22. PH to EBH, May 17, 1911, MMC; PH to GYH, May 20, 1918, MMC.

23. GY to EBH, May 31, 1911, MMC; PH to EBH, May 17, 1911, MMC.

24. "At Ft. Benjamin Harrison," *Indianapolis News,* June 17, 1911, 19; PH, OMPF.

25. Marriage license, Bexar County, TX, 31788; MLCY to GYH, July 21, 1911, MMC; GYH to EBH, July 23, 1911, MMC; PH to GYH, December 10, 1917, MMC; "Weddings," *San Antonio Express,* July 18, 1911, 8. The newspaper announcement mistakenly said the groom was a member of the 10th Cavalry.

26. PH to EBH, July 23, 1911, MMC; GYH to EBH, July 23, 1911, MMC.

4. The Making of the Expert

Epigraph: PH, commentary on James G. Taylor's conference paper, November 22, 1911, NARA CP, RG 457, E 9032, box 793.

1. GYH to MLCY, August 2, 1911, YFL; MLCY to GYH, July 21, 1911, MMC.

2. The Hitts lived in rooms 3 and 4A. "Residence List of Officers on Duty at the Post of Fort Leavenworth, the Army Service Schools, and the United States Military Prison," February 10, 1913, 4, Special Collections, Combined Arms Services Library, Fort Leavenworth, KS; John W. Partin, ed., *A Brief History of Fort Leavenworth 1827–1983* (Fort Leavenworth, KS: Combat Studies Institute, 1983), 31; "Large Number of Officers at Fort Leavenworth," *Fort Leavenworth News,* March 8, 1912, 7; EBH to GYH, September 15, 1911, MMC.

3. GYH to EBH, September 25, 1911, MMC.

4. Kelvin Dale Crow, *Fort Leavenworth: Three Centuries of Service* (Fort Leavenworth, KS: Command History Office, 2010), 4; Rebecca Robbins Raines, *Getting the Message Through: A Branch History of the US Army Signal Corps.* (Washington, DC: GPO, 1996), 120–21.

5. Truesdell and Voris began their careers in the Infantry but were detailed to Signals before they attended the school. Gibbs became a lifelong friend. Truesdell, another good friend, served as a signal officer in World War I; he became a brigadier general and was commandant of the Command and General Staff School during World War II. Voris, named for his uncle, a Civil War general, served with Hitt in World War I. *Army Schools Annual Reports, 1912* (Fort Leavenworth, KS: Army Service Schools Press, 1912), 27, 55; A. Lincoln Lavine, *Circuits of Victory* (New York: Doubleday, 1921), 111. Hitt learned Spanish at the school and probably refreshed his college French during his free time, as much of the literature on codes and ciphers was in that language.

6. The cipher disk used by the army at this time employed monoalphabetic substitution—two standard alphabets, one in forward order (ABC . . .) and the other in reverse order (ZYX . . .), aligned on two celluloid disks that could be rotated. *Army Schools Annual Reports, 1912,* 56, 60–62; PH to David Kahn, November 26, 1962, NCML, DKC; GYH to EBH, September 25, 1911, MMC.

7. GYH to EBH, October 7, 1911, MMC.

8. A complete technical discussion of Hitt's cipher work can be found in Betsy Rohaly Smoot, *The Cipher Game: The Cryptologic Work of Colonel Parker Hitt,*

Genevieve Young Hitt, and Mary Lue Hitt (Fort George G. Meade, MD: Center for Cryptologic History, forthcoming). According to David Kahn, conference 4 took place on December 20, 1911, which agrees with copies of conference papers collected by George Fabyan; however, according to Truesdell, it occurred in October. The December date is probably correct, as Muirhead's article was published in October. David Kahn, *The Codebreakers* (New York: Scribner, 1996), 321; "Military Cryptography" (a collection of conference papers), George Fabyan Collection, Library of Congress; Truesdell file, NARA, RG 94, E 324, box 1393; *Army Schools Annual Reports, 1912,* 62; Captain Murray Muirhead, "Military Cryptography," *Journal of the Royal United Service Institute* 55, no. 404 (October 1911): 1321–32; comments on Muirhead's "Military Cryptography," ML, WFP, item 524; Steven M. Bellovin, "Vernam, Mauborgne, and Friedman: The One-Time Pad and the Index of Coincidence," in *The New Codebreakers: Essays Dedicated to David Kahn on the Occasion of His 85th Birthday,* ed. Peter Y. A. Ryan, David Naccache, and Jean-Jacques Quisquater (New York: Springer, 2016), 40–66; PH, commentary on Taylor's paper, November 22, 1911, NARA CP, RG 457, box 793; Betsy Rohaly Smoot, "Parker Hitt's First Cylinder Device and the Genesis of U.S. Army Cylinder and Strip Devices," *Cryptologia* 39, no. 4 (2015): 316.

9. "Society," *Indianapolis News,* November 1, 1911, 7; "Secretary of War and Chief of Staff Visit Post," *Fort Leavenworth News,* November 18, 1911, 1.

10. GYH to EBH, November 6, 1911, MMC. The bridge was the Whiskey River Bridge, which was torn down in 1914.

11. Leave of absence, NARA, RG 393, E 101, file 7618; "General Mention," *San Antonio Express,* January 3, 1912, 16; "Informal Dance," *Leavenworth Times,* January 11, 1912, 5; "Signal Corps Ball," *Fort Leavenworth News,* February 10, 1912, 1; "Heard at the Signal Corps Ball," *Fort Leavenworth News,* February 23, 1912, 2; PH to GCH, March 14, 1912, MMC. Drum's wife, Mary Reaume, came from Indianapolis and may have known Hitt.

12. Smoot, "Hitt's First Cylinder Device," 318. The chronology of these events is quite confused. Hitt, thirty-five years after the fact, conflated dates and events in his letter to Friedman. PH to WFF, August 9, 1947, NCML, DKC, PHP.

13. Craig Bauer believes that Friedman took the name "star cipher" from a row of stars in Hitt's original alphabets, designed to separate letter from numbers. Craig Bauer, *Unsolved: The History and Mystery of the World's Greatest Ciphers from Ancient Egypt to Online Secret Societies* (Princeton, NJ: Princeton University Press, 2017), 361; WFF, *Several Machine Ciphers and Methods for Their Solution,* Riverbank Laboratories Publication 20 (1918), in *The Riverbank Publications,* vol. 2 (Laguna Hills, CA: Aegean Park Press, 1976); PH to WFF, August 9, 1947; *Army Schools Annual Reports, 1912,* 59.

14. Voris's thesis was "War Department Telegraph Field Code," and Taylor's was "Codes and Ciphers," NARA CP, RG 111, E 44, box 400. See Craig Bauer *Secret History: The Story of Cryptology* (Boca Raton, FL: Chapman Hall, 2013), 245. Hitt used Truesdell's frequency counts in his *Manual.*

15. "Snow Storm," *Fort Leavenworth News,* March 1, 1912, 1; GYH to EBH, March 7, 1912, MMC; PH to GCH, March 14, 1912, MMC; Academic Board to PH, May 24, 1912, NARA CP, RG 111, E 44, box 394; PH to GCH, March 14, 1912.

16. PH to Director, Signal School, May 2, 1912, NARA CP, RG 111, E 44, box 387; George Whitehall, Acting Director of the Signal School, to CSO, May 3, 1912, NARA CP, RG 111, E 44, box 387; Edgar Russel to PH, August 5, 1913, MMC; PH to Russel, August 8, 1913, MMC; George I. Back, "The Telephone: Commercial v. Military History and Development," *Signal Corps Bulletin* 42 (March 1928): 14; PH, "Testing of Dry Cells," NARA CP, RG 111, E 44, box 400.

17. *Army Schools Annual Reports, 1912,* 62; Bruce W. Bidwell, *History of the Military Intelligence Division, Department of the Army General Staff: 1775– 1941* (Frederick, MD: University Publications of America, 1986), 90–91; Ralph Weber, ed., *The Final Memoranda* (Wilmington, DE: SR Books, 1988), xiv–xv; Raines, *Getting the Message Through,* 165–66.

18. Efficiency report, June 1912, PH, OMPF; "Service Schools to Close June 21st," *Fort Leavenworth News,* June 8, 1912, 1; PH, request for leave, June 26, 1912, NARA, RG 393, E 101, file 7618; Leonard Wood to CSO, May 29, 1912, NARA CP, RG 111, E 44, box 395; CSO to Wood, July 18, 1912, NARA CP, RG 111, E 44, box 395.

19. Telegrams from PH to Signal School, August 12, 1912, 10:40 a.m., and August 13, 1912, 1:31 p.m., NARA, RG 393, E 101, file 7618.

20. PH to GYH, August 28, 1912, MMC. Cora's role in the household is unknown. The address was 240-A Auger Avenue, according to the Fort Leaven- worth Exchange Directory, June 1913, 74. See Fort Leavenworth and Kansas City Army Corps of Engineers, *Historic Home Guide: Fort Leavenworth, Kansas* (n.p., n.d.); building floor plans were provided by Kelvin Crow.

21. Raines, *Getting the Message Through,* 120; James Hagood, "The Man- chu Law and Detached Service," *National Service with the International Digest* 6, no. 4 (October 1919): 210–12. The origin of the slang term "Manchu law" is unknown, but it is probably derogatory.

22. *Army Schools Annual Reports, 1913* (Fort Leavenworth, KS: Army Ser- vice Schools Press, 1913), 52; PH to GYH, September 2 and 5, 1912, MMC.

23. *Army Schools Annual Reports, 1913,* 60; PH to Russel, August 8, 1913, MMC.

24. The house was at 271-A Meade Avenue. R. L. Polk, *Ft. Leavenworth Directory* (Leavenworth City, 1913–1914), 427; "Residence List," February 10, 1913, 4; Fort Leavenworth, *Historic Home Guide* and building floor plans; GYH to MLCY, n.d. [spring 1913], YFL. Twenty dollars was more than enough to buy a Victrola, the cheapest of which cost $15. In 2020 dollars, the $20 gift was equivalent to about $518 (or more than $1,000 for the two of them); https:// www.usinflationcalculator.com/ (accessed June 12, 2020).

25. GYH to MLCY, n.d. [spring 1913].

26. The house was at 328C Meade Avenue. "Student Officers Report for Duty," *Leavenworth Times,* August 6, 1913, 5; Fort Leavenworth, *Historic Home Guide* and building floor plans.

27. *Army Schools Annual Reports, 1914* (Fort Leavenworth, KS: Army Service Schools Press, 1914), 46, 49–50; PH, "A Simple Transposition System," Signal School lecture, n.d., ML, WFP, item 523. International Morse code, referred to as "Continental" code, differed from Samuel Morse's original creation, known as American Morse code. PH to Russel, August 8, 1913.

28. PH to Russel, August 8, 1913; PH to OCSO, through Signal School, November 17, 1915, MMC; OCSO to Hitt, January 13, 1914, MMC; "The Doggett Formula," *Electrical World* 68, no. 5 (January 31, 1914): 259–60; Leonard Wildman to Russel, April 22, 1914, NARA CP, RG 111, E 44, box 458.

29. PH to WFF, August 9, 1947; PH to Wildman, Director, Army Signal School, December 19, 1914, NARA CP, RG 111, E 44, box 477.

30. William Friedman was intimately involved with construction of the M-138 and CSP-488 devices, and he was familiar with Hitt's early work. PH to Wildman, December 19, 1914; Wildman to CSO, December 22, 1914, NARA CP, RG 111, E 44, box 477; PH to WFF, March 12, 1949, August 7, 1930, NCML, DKC, PHP; PH to Colonel Hamlin, September 10, 1943, NCML, DKC, PHP. Hitt's device was destroyed in the October 30, 1918, fire at Souilly, France; Genevieve's device is in the US Army Military Intelligence Museum collection at Fort Huachuca, Arizona.

31. *Army Schools Annual Reports, 1914,* 54; PH to Wildman, February 19, 1914, and Wildman indorsement, NARA CP, RG 111, E 44, box 449; Russel on behalf of CSO to Wildman, February 28, 1914, NARA CP, RG 111, E 44, box 449.

32. GYH to EBH, October 29, 1914, MMC; "Telephone Society Meets," *Leavenworth Times,* March 3, 1914, 10; "Explain Working of Wireless: Capt. Parker Hitt Gives Interesting Address at Men's Club," *Leavenworth Times,* March 22, 1914, 7; PH to Russel, October 7, September 15, 1914, NARA CP, RG 111, E 44, box 468. The material came from Russel on October 10. GYH to EBH, October 29, 1914, MMC.

33. GYH to EBH, October 29, 1914; "Telephone Society Meets," *Leavenworth Times,* November 10, 1914, 6; PH, talk, November 9, 1914, MMC. Hitt received permission to have the talk published in *Southwestern Telephone News* on November 17, 1914, NARA, RG 393, E 101, file 7618.

34. "Work of the Signal Corps," *Army and Navy Register* 57, no. 1801 (January 23, 1915): 97–98.

35. "Signal Corps Men Well on Way to Southern Border," *Leavenworth Times,* April 28, 1914, 3; PH, OMPF; *Army Schools Annual Reports, 1914,* 46; *Army and Navy Register,* May 2, 1914, 564; *Army and Navy Register,* May 20, 1914, 700.

36. The Larrabee cipher is a Vigenère cipher (a 26 × 26 square with 26 mixed alphabets within the square and an alphabetic key on both axes) written in chart form. The Playfair cipher, invented by Charles Wheatstone, places an alphabet

into a 5 × 5 square; only the keyword is required to encipher and decipher messages. For an excellent description of how the Playfair cipher works, see Bauer, *Secret History,* 168–72. PH to 2nd Division COS, May 19, 1914; memorandum from COS to J. F. Bell, May 28, 1914, NCML, DKC, PHP.

37. C. R. Krauthoff to J. F. Bell, June 12, 1914, MMC; Major D. J. Carr indorsement, June 16, 1914, MMC; Timothy K. Nenninger, *The Leavenworth Schools and the Old Army: Education, Professionalism, and the Officer Corps of the United States Army, 1881–1918* (Westport, CT: Greenwood Press, 1978), 68–69; PH to Bell, fifth indorsement, June 18, 1914, MMC.

38. Bell to PH, August 20, 1914, MMC.

39. Bell to PH, August 20, 1914; PH, OMPF.

40. *Army Schools Annual Reports, 1914,* 37; *Army Schools Annual Reports, 1915* (Fort Leavenworth, KS: Army Service Schools Press, 1915), 41–56.

41. PH to CSO, November 2, 1914, NARA CP, RG 111, E 44, box 472; Russel to PH, November 3, 1914, NARA CP, RG 111, E 44, box 465; Russel to PH, June 18, 1914, January 18, 1915, NARA CP, RG 111, E 44, box 458.

42. PH to WFF, August 9, 1947; H. M. O'Bleness to PH, January 19, 1917, and PH to O'Bleness, January 25, 1917, NCML, DKC, PHP. In 1807 Dr. William Blair, an Englishman, published a book used by the Signal Corps during the Civil War. See David W. Gaddy, "The First U.S. Government Manual on Cryptography," *Cryptologic Quarterly* 11, no. 4 (1992). Kahn, *Codebreakers,* 324, notes that there were only two American works on cryptography prior to Hitt's: Joseph O. Mauborgne's *An Advanced Problem in Cryptography and Its Solution* (Fort Leavenworth, KS: Press of the Army Service Schools, 1914) and a small 1874 work by Harvey Gray called *Cryptography.* PH to Kahn, November 26, 1962, NCML, DKC; Herbert O. Yardley, *The American Black Chamber* (New York: Ballantine Books, 1931), 3; David Kahn, *The Reader of Gentleman's Mail* (New Haven, CT: Yale University Press, 2004), 11; Helen Fouché Gaines, *Elementary Cryptanalysis: A Study of Ciphers and Their Solution* (Boston: American Photographic Publishing, 1939). Hitt's *Manual* was reprinted by Aegean Park Press in 1976.

43. PH to Kahn, November 26, 1962. Hitt told Kahn that this work was his "last contact with official cryptography." Samuel Reber to PH, January 4, 1915, and PH to Reber, January 8 and 9 1915, NCML, DKC, PHP.

44. PH to Henry E. Eames, February 17, March 6, 1915, MMC; Eames to PH, March 3 and 15, 1915, MMC; Reber to Army Signal School, February 20, 1915, NCML, DKC, PHP; McAndrew to George Fabyan, April 2, 1917, NARA CP, RG 165, E 65, box 1876, file 4131-27; PH, *Manual for the Solution of Military Ciphers* (Fort Leavenworth, KS: Press of the Army Service Schools, 1916), vi.

45. Mauborgne's *An Advanced Problem in Cryptography and Its Solution* discussed the Playfair cipher in 1914; Hitt wrote the preliminary note for the book. GYH to EBH, May 13, 1915, MMC; PH to GCH, May 27, 1914, MMC; PH to Service School Press, December 16, 1915, NARA, RG 393, E 101, file 7618;

Pertinent Pointers for Patrons of the Book Department, undated pamphlet, NCML, DKC, PHP; PH to AB STRUSE, February 25, 1940, NCML, DKC, PHP.

46. GCH to PH, February 24, 1916, MMC; Kahn, *Codebreakers,* 322–23.

47. PH to AG, November 7, 1914, NARA CP, RG 393, E 101, file 7618.

48. It was particularly surprising that the normally frugal Hitt wanted to use his own money for the trip; he probably believed the experience was worth the price. The request went to Pershing and Funston because, by the time it had worked its way through channels, Hitt had been assigned to a command subordinate to those two generals. PH to AG, January 29, 1915, with sixteen subsequent indorsements, including Wildman (February 1, 1915) and Peyton March (n.d. [February 1915]), MMC and NARA CP, RG 393, E 101, file 7618.

49. GYH to EBH, March 8, 1915, MMC; WD, SO 19, para. 31, February 1, 1915; WD, SO 25, para. 23, January 30, 1915; WD, SO 26, para. 18, February 3, 1915; Southern Department, SO 56, para. 3, March 11, 1915, all in MMC; PH to Russel, February 2, 1915, NCML, DKC, PHP.

50. GYH to EBH, February 19, March 8, 1915, MMC; PH, "Memorandum for Board on Electric Signal Lanterns" March 2, 1915, MMC.

51. GYH to EBH, March 8 and 19, 1915, MMC; WD, SO 122, para. 45, July 1, 1915, MMC.

52. GYH to EBH, May 13, 1915, MMC; various correspondence regarding the field code and preamble cipher, NARA CP, RG 111, E 44, box 508; John N. Greely to PH, August 15, 1915, NCML, DKC, PHP; "Militia Signal Corps Men Have No 'Soft Snap,'" *Leavenworth Times,* June 11, 1915, 3; Leonard Wildman to PH, June 18, 1915, PH, OMPF. It was Reber who called Hitt "a shark on ciphers." Reber to PH, January 4, 1915, NCML, DKC, PHP.

53. W. S. Nye, "The Field Artillery School," *Military Engineer* 29, no. 164 (March–April 1937): 109–10; "Aero Squadron at Fort Sill," *Muskogee County (OK) Democrat,* July 8, 1915, 3; draft general orders, May 1915, NARA, RG 94, E 25, box 7086.

54. GYH to EBH, October 26, 1915, MMC; PH to War Department COS, September 27, 1916, NARA CP, RG 165, E 65, box 2139.

55. It is one of those strange coincidences that Childs—J. Rives Childs— would later work in the G2A6 Code and Cipher Section in France and gain renown breaking ciphers. His famous encounter with Parker Hitt is discussed in chapter 5. PH to GCH, July 7, 1915, MMC; GCH to PH, July 4, 1915, MMC; LH to PH, November 5, 1915, MMC; PH to LH, November 10, 1915, MMC.

56. PH to EBH, September 27, 1915, MMC; GYH to EBH, October 26, 1915, MMC; PH to AG, October 11, 1915, NARA CP, RG 111, E 44, box 519; Martin B. Madden to AG, November 15, 1915, PH, ISR; PH to Commandant, School of Musketry, "New Design for a Battle Sight," November 4, 1915, MMC; Chief of Ordnance to AG, December 29, 1915; PH to Commandant, December 29, 1915; School of Musketry to Ordnance Department, March 27, February 3,

1917, all in NARA, RG 94, E 26, box 3265; Tasker Bliss to COS, January 26, 1917, NARA, RG 94, E 25, AGO file 2342067.

57. Ordnance Department to AG, December 24, 1915, referencing PH to Ordnance Department, December 14, 1915, MMC; PH to Commandant, School of Musketry, December 6, 1916, MMC; PH to AG, first indorsement, December 11, 1916, MMC.

58. AG to PH, October 7, 1915; Reber to PH, October 11, 1915; William A. Mann to Presiding General Court-Martial, October 12, 1915; PH to Reber, October 20, 1915, all in NCML, DKC, PHP; GYH to EBH, October 26, 1915, MMC. For a good description of von Papen's failures as an intelligence officer, see John F. Dooley, *Codes, Ciphers and Spies: Tales of Military Intelligence in World War I* (New York: Springer, 2016), 163–75.

59. GCH to PH, January 14, 1916, MMC.

60. CSO to AG, "Radio Stations on Mexican Border," March 23, 1916, NARA CP, RG 111, E 45, box 1759; David A. Hatch, "The Punitive Expedition: Military Reform and Communications Intelligence," *Cryptologia* 31, no. 1 (2007): 38–45.

61. "Oklahoma Troops Ready to Entrain," *Morning Tulsa (OK) Daily World,* March 11, 1916, 3; WD, GO 32, May 7, 1916, MMC; "Troops from Fort Sill Are Ordered to Border," *Cleburne (TX) Morning Review,* May 9, 1916, 6; Charles H. Harris III and Louis R. Sadler, *The Archaeologist Was a Spy: Sylvanus G. Morely and the Office of Naval Intelligence* (Albuquerque: University of New Mexico Press, 2003), 17; Stephen Fuqua to PH, May 22 and 27, 1916, NCML, DKC, PHP; messages between Southern Department intelligence officer and PH, November 25–December 1, 1916, NARA CP, RG 457, E 9032, box 793; memos between Southern Department and Fort Sill, July 27, August 1 and 4, 1916, NARA, RG 94, E 25, box 8365; returns of the 19th Infantry, NARA, RG 391, E 1665, box 2.

62. Army COS to PH, June 28, 1916; PH to Army COS, September 26, 1916; PH to Reber, March 10 and 25, 1917, all in NCML, DKC, PHP; Basil M. Manly, "Sherlock Holmes of the World, That's Uncle Sam!" clipping from unidentified Chicago newspaper, September 17, 1917, NARA CP, RG 165, E 65, box 2241.

63. PH to Commandant, School of Musketry, April 25, 1916, MMC; PH and Thomas W. Brown, *Description and Instructions for the Use of the Fire Control Rule* (Washington, DC: US Infantry Association, 1917); WD Bulletin 49, November 20, 1916, AGO file 2414426-A, MMC; PH to GYH, April 21, 1918, MMC.

64. Terrence J. Gough, "Isolation and Professionalization of the Army Officer Corps: A Post-Revisionist View of the Soldier and the State," *Social Science Quarterly* 73, no. 2 (June 1992): 423. Gough cites Robert C. Kemble, *The Image of the Army Officer in America: Background for Current Views* (Westport, CT: Greenwood Press, 1973), 111–16, and Edward M. Coffman, *The Old Army: A Portrait of the American Army in Peacetime, 1784–1898* (New York: Oxford

University Press, 1986), as well as Gibbs memo, January 10, 1910, George Gibbs Papers, Library of Congress, 401–2, 439. PH, OMPF.

65. WD, SO 114, para. 30, MMC, ordered Hitt to report to the chief of staff for duty in Washington. Telegraphic orders issued the same day (MMC) ordered him to report to Major General John J. Pershing.

66. The kimono may have been one Hitt bought impulsively on a shopping trip in Nagasaki in January 1906. PH to GYH, May 6, 12, 1918, MMC.

5. To France

Epigraph: Ralph Van Deman to GYH, July 18, 1917, MMC and NARA CP, RG 165, E 65, box 2241.

1. PH to Samuel Reber, January 4, 1917, MMC; Reber to PH, January 8, 1917, MMC.

2. The division began as a section and then a branch; this work refers to all phases of the organization as the Military Intelligence Division (MID). For its early history, see Bruce W. Bidwell, *History of the Military Intelligence Division, Department of the Army General Staff: 1775–1941* (Frederick, MD: University Publications of America, 1986). The Bureau of Investigation (BOI), predecessor of the Federal Bureau of Investigation (FBI), needed the messages from the *Dresden* and *Sacramento* to support a Department of Justice neutrality trial. Messages between Ralph Van Deman, Bruce Bielaski, Hitt, Joseph O. Mauborgne, John M. Manly, and George Fabyan, April–June 1917, NARA CP, RG 165, E 65, box 2241.

3. Van Deman's note is referenced in PH to GCH, May 16, 1917, MMC. Russel was Pershing's CSO in the Southern Department; Pershing arrived in Washington on May 10 and chose Russel to accompany him to France. By the time Russel arrived in Washington, he knew he wanted Hitt as his assistant.

4. WD, SO 114, para. 30, May 17, 1917, MMC, ordered Hitt to report to the COS for duty in Washington. Telegraphic orders issued the same day (MMC) ordered him to report to Major General John J. Pershing. Memos between Van Deman, Fabyan, and PH, April 21, 26, and 30, May 7, 15, and 19, 1917, NARA CP, RG 165, E 65, box 2241; telegram from PH to GCH, May 19, 1917, MMC; PH to GYH, May 22, 1917, MMC.

5. PH to GYH, May 22, 1917; temperature data obtained from https://www .weather.gov/media/lwx/climate/dcatemps.pdf (accessed October 5, 2020); Van Deman to Fabyan, May 23, 1917, NARA CP, RG 165, E 65, box 2241.

6. PH to GYH, May 22, 1917. The change of station put Hitt in the 57th Infantry, but he never served in the unit. HQ 57th Infantry, GO 1, para. 1, item 9, June 1, 1917, MMC; WD, SO 125, para. 10, May 31, 1917, MMC.

7. Van Deman to Fabyan, May 23, 1917; Van Deman to Manly, September 15, 1917, NARA CP, RG 165, E 65, box 2241; Van Deman to GYH, July 18, 1917, MMC; Herbert O. Yardley, *The American Black Chamber* (New York:

Ballantine Books, 1931), 11; David Kahn, *The Reader of Gentleman's Mail* (New Haven, CT: Yale University Press, 2004), 19–21; Bidwell, *History of the Military Intelligence Division,* 164–65.

8. PH to GYH, May 24, 1917, MMC; PH to EBH, May 24, 1917, MMC. The Bell men were William F. Repp and Rexford M. Glaspey, both commissioned as first lieutenants. A. Lincoln Lavine, *Circuits of Victory* (New York: Doubleday, 1921), 124–25.

9. Order from AG to proceed to France, May 26, 1917, MMC; John J. Pershing, *My Experiences in the World War* (New York: De Capo Press, 1995), 41–44.

10. PH to GYH, May 25, 1917, MMC; Van Deman to Fabyan, May 19, 1917, NARA CP, RG 165, E 65, box 2241; Betsy Rohaly Smoot, "An Accidental Cryptologist: The Brief Career of Genevieve Young Hitt," *Cryptologia* 35, no. 2 (2011): 168–70; Center for Cryptologic History, *The Friedman Legacy: A Tribute to William and Elizebeth Friedman* (Fort George G. Meade, MD: National Security Agency, 2006), 146; Ronald Clark, *The Man Who Broke Purple: The Life of Colonel William F. Friedman, Who Deciphered the Japanese Code in World War II* (Boston: Little, Brown, 1977), 59; Fabyan to Van Deman, June 11, 1917; GYH to Van Deman, July 3, 1917; Van Deman to GYH, July 18, 1917, all in NARA CP, RG 165, E 65, box 2241.

11. PH, "Personal Narrative," January 4, 1919, NARA CP, RG 120, E 2040, box 132.

12. David F. Trask, *The AEF & Coalition Warmaking, 1917–1918* (Lawrence: University Press of Kansas, 1993), 24; PH to GCH, November 24, 1918, MMC. For a discussion of troop movements, see David R. Woodward, *The American Army and the First World War* (Cambridge: Cambridge University Press, 2014), 156–71.

13. *Chronology of the Signal Corps,* NARA CP, RG 120, E 2040, box 131, 1–2; PH, "Personal Narrative"; PH to GYH, June 15 and 21, July 20, August 8, 1917, MMC.

14. Lavine, *Circuits of Victory,* 111; PH to GYH, August 8, 1917, MMC; *Chronology of the Signal Corps,* 2–4.

15. PH to GYH, June 21, July 8 and 20, August 8, 1917, MMC; *Chronology of the Signal Corps,* 2–4; *War Department Annual Reports, 1919* (Washington, DC: GPO, 1920), 1241; telegram from Chief of the French Army Telegraphic Service to GQG [Grand Quartier Général, or GHQ] of the Armies of the North and Northeast, July 7, 1917, MMC; AEF, SO 30, July 8, 1917, MMC; PH, "Report on Inspection Trip to the 20th Army Corps," July 12, 1917, NARA CP, RG 120, E 2040, box 178 (unfortunately, most of the locations have been censored); AEF, SO 34, July 12, 1917, MMC; luncheon menu, July 11, 1917, MMC (Mary Lue Hitt believed the cowboy resembled her father, according to Kevin Mustain, emails to the author, February and March 2020); Woodward, *American Army,* 105; PH, Statement of Preferences, July 24, 1919, PH, OMPF; Hugh Drum, PH Efficiency Report, 1919, PH, OMPF.

16. PH to GYH, August 16, 19, and 30, September 13, 1917, MMC; PH, OMPF.

17. Trask, *AEF & Coalition Warmaking*, 20–24; PH to GYH, August 30, September 2, 1917, MMC; PH, billet assignment, n.d., MMC.

18. *Chronology of the Signal Corps*, 6–10; PH to GYH, September 30, October 27 and 28, 1917, MMC; Edgar Russel to AEF COS, September 27, 1917; Kirby Walker to Russel, October 24, 1917; Russel to Walker, October 25, 1917, all in NARA CP, RG 120, E 267, box 3236.

19. PH to GYH, November 11, December 10, 1917, MMC.

20. PH to GYH, December 30, 1917, January 13 and 18, 1918, MMC. Genevieve's letters to Parker did not survive the war and may have burned in the Souilly fire in October 1918.

21. Fox Conner, memorandum on Operations Section organization at Chaumont, December 8, 1917, MMC; LeRoy Eltinge, memo on Third Section organization, February 25, 1918, MMC.

22. James G. Harbord, AEF COS, SO 15, January 15, 1918, NCML, DKC, PHP; PH, handwritten notes of board meetings, January 18 and 25, 1918, MMC; "World War I," in *Historical Background of the Signal Security Agency (SRH-001)*, vol. 2, NARA CP, RG 457, E 9002, 27, 36–37. Military Intelligence Code Number 5, released in July 1918, was almost immediately compromised; a new War Department telegraphic code was not issued until 1921.

23. PH to GYH, January 20, 27, and 29, February 9, March 17, 1918, MMC.

24. AEF, SO 92, April 2, 1918, MMC; PH to GYH, February 23, April 2, 1918, MMC; Eltinge to Harbord, February 15, 1918, NARA CP, RG 120, E 267, box 3212; Russel to Harbord, February 22, 1918, NARA CP, RG 120, E 267, box 3236.

25. PH to GYH, February 9, March 24, 1918, MMC. Hitt had sold 100 rules by mid-March 1918.

26. PH to GYH, March 17 and 24, 1918, MMC; AEF CSO, Monthly Report, July 1918, NARA CP, RG 120, E 2042, box 33; George S. Simonds to PH, March 30, 1918, NCML, DKC, PHP. The listening stations were installed in February 1918. For the locations of the various listening and intercept stations, see Betsy Rohaly Smoot, *From the Ground Up: American Cryptology during World War I* (Fort George G. Meade, MD: Center for Cryptologic History, forthcoming).

27. PH to George Gibbs, February 28, 1931, NARA CP, RG 111, E 45, box 398. Hitt was answering an inquiry from Gibbs, then CSO, about the "genesis of the action which brought about the formation of the group of women telephone operators." In 1931 Hitt recalled that the discussion happened at Rue de la Boetie and surmised it had taken place in July or August 1917; however, it must have been between mid-June and mid-July 1917. Lavine, *Circuits of Victory*, 491; Elizabeth Cobbs, *The Hello Girls: America's First Women Soldiers* (Cambridge, MA: Harvard University Press, 2017), 69–71.

28. PH to GYH, April 21 and 30, 1918, MMC; invitation from Julia Russell to PH, n.d., MMC; PH to GYH, May 20, 1918, MMC.

29. PH to GYH, April 14 and 21, 1918, MMC; PH to EBH, April 21, May 12, 1918, MMC; Russel to George Gibbs, NARA CP, RG 120, E 267, box 3236; PH to GYH, May 20, 1918, MMC.

30. Mark Ethan Grotelueschen, *The AEF Way of War: The American Army and Combat in World War I* (Cambridge: Cambridge University Press, 2007), 74; AEF, SO 15, May 31, 1918, MMC; PH to GYH, June 9, 1918, MMC; medical records, PH, OMPF.

31. PH to GYH, June 19 and 24, 1918, MMC.

32. PH to G3, July 2, 1918, NCML, DKC, PHP.

33. PH to G3, July 17 and 18, 1918, NCML, DKC, PHP. After the offensive, the 38th became known as "The Rock of the Marne," a nickname later used by the entire 3rd Division. The French and Americans had a difficult relationship at 3rd Division HQ; see Edward G. Lengel, *Thunder and Flames: Americans in the Crucible of Combat, 1917–1918* (Lawrence: University Press of Kansas, 2015), 334–35.

34. Betsy Rohaly Smoot, "Impermanent Alliances: Cryptologic Cooperation between the United States, Britain, and France on the Western Front, 1917–1918," *Intelligence and National Security* 32, no. 3 (2017): 365–77.

35. Smoot, *From the Ground Up*.

36. Frank Moorman to PH, October 16, 1917, NARA CP, RG 120, E 105, box 5761; Moorman to Arthur Conger, March 19, 1918, NARA CP, RG 120, E 105; Dennis Nolan to AEF COS, March 20, 1918, NARA CP, RG 120, E 105; Moorman to Nolan, June 17, 1918, NARA CP, RG 120, E 105, box 5768; PH to Nolan, July 12, 1918, NARA CP, RG 120, E 105; Smoot, *From the Ground Up*.

37. PH to Sosthenes Behn, April 2, 1918, MMC; memo dated April 23, 1918, and initialed by PH, MMC; telegrams between PH and Behn, May 23, 1918, MMC.

38. PH to Nolan, March 17, 1918, NARA CP, RG 120, E 105. Using the female code, Parker Hitt, CSO of First Army, would be referred to as Bertha Hart. WFF, *American Army Field Codes in the American Expeditionary Forces during the First World War* (Washington, DC: GPO, 1942), 245; published as SRH 315, NARA CP, RG 457, E 9002, box 86.

39. Moorman to Nolan, "Use of Plett's [*sic*] Cipher," June 19, 1918, NARA CP, RG 120, E 105; Marlborough Churchill to S. L. H. Slocum, June 11, 1918, NARA CP, RG 165, E 65, box 3862; memo from John Powell to Malcolm Hay, June 12, 1918, NARA CP, RG 165, E 65, box 3862. Hay and Pletts worked in MI1(b) in London; Hitchings worked in MI1(e) at British Army HQ in France.

40. Childs later had a distinguished career as a US diplomat. J. Rives Childs, *Let the Credit Go* (New York: K. S. Giniger, 1983), 30–31; David Kahn, *The Codebreakers* (New York: Scribner, 1996), 327; WFF, *American Army Field Codes*, appendix 10, 9–17.

41. Childs, *Let the Credit Go*, 30–31; Kahn, *Codebreakers*, 327; Yardley, *American Black Chamber*, 17–18. There are slight variations between Childs's official 1918 account and the memoir he wrote later in life. Friedman examined this story in 1942 and supported Childs's 1918 account. See WFF, *American Army Field Codes*, appendix 10, 9–17.

42. Hay to Moorman, June 24, 1918, NARA CP, RG 120, E 105, box 5763; Russel to Howard R. Barnes, July 16, 1918, NCML, Barnes Papers.

43. Barnes to Russel, "Transmission of Code Messages by Radio," September 2, 1918; "Construction of a New Code for Transatlantic Communications," November 16, 1918; Russel to Gibbs, November 22, 1918; Henry G. Gale to Executive Officer, February 24, 1919; Russel to George O. Squier, "Code Compilation Section of the American E.F.," April 11, 1919, all in NARA CP, RG 457, E P11, box 214. This code, short title SIGRIM, was used by the War Department until 1943–1944, when it was replaced by the War Department Telegraphic Code of 1942 (SIGARM). See http://chris-intel-corner.blogspot.com/2014/03/united-states-cryptologic-security.html (accessed October 5, 2018); *Report of the Code Compilation Section, General Headquarters, AEF December 1917–November 1918*, 42, later SRH 321, NARA CP, RG 457, E 9002, box 88.

44. WFF to Elizebeth S. Friedman, July 13, 1918, ML, ESFC, box 2, folder 4; WFF to E. S. Friedman, n.d. [probably August 1, 1918], ML, ESFC, box 2, folder 5.

45. See Grotelueschen, *AEF Way of War*, particularly 25–58, for a discussion of doctrinal differences between the AEF and the Allies.

46. PH to AG, May 23, 1917, PH, ISR; WD, SO 125, para. 10, May 31, 1917, MMC; PH to GYH, February 16, 1919, April 14 and 21, May 12 and 28, June 9, 1918, MMC; Memorandum 50 from Fort Sam Houston, March 16, 1918, MMC.

47. Memorandum 50 from Fort Sam Houston, March 16, 1918.

48. George Fabyan to Van Deman, March 22, 1918, NARA CP, RG 165, E 65, box 2243; WFF to E. S. Friedman, August 7, 1918, ML, ESFC, box 2, file 15. The visiting officer was probably Colonel R. G. Van Horn, a Signal Corps officer who knew the Hitts.

49. Memos to GYH and her worksheets, 1917, NCML, DKC, PHP; GYH to EBH, October 27, 1917, MMC; Smoot, "Accidental Cryptologist," 168–69.

50. PH to GYH, March 10, 1918, MMC; "In Society," *San Antonio Light*, October 25, 1917, 6. Genevieve later referred to herself during this period as a "glamor girl." GYH to LYK, March 18, 1961, YFL.

51. Leonard T. "Gee" Gerow was a friend of the Hitts as well. Walton H. Walker (writing from Luxembourg) to GYH, January 20, 1919 (misdated 1918), MMC; Walker to GYH, February 3, 1946, MMC. In 1946 Walker addressed her as "Genevieve Darling" and asked, "How could you have thought that I might have forgotten? I've thought of you constantly through the years, and never has a promotion or honor come to me that I haven't wanted to tell you about it." He

professed that he had "the same feeling for you that I had at the start of my career. *You* more than anyone else are responsible for any success I have attained." Walker and Genevieve resumed communications in October 1945, likely prompted by a meeting between Tot and Walker at Fort Bliss earlier in 1945, when Walker said of Genevieve, "I love her as much as I ever did." LYK to GYH, September 5, 1945, MMC. Most of Walker's papers and memorabilia, apart from collections at the Marshall Library and the Virginia Military Institute Archives, were destroyed. General Samuel Sims Walker (Walton Walker's son), telephone conversation with the author, February 16, 2011.

52. GYH to EBH, July 27, October 19, 1918, MMC.

53. GYH, OPF, Civilian Personnel Records, NPRC; Smoot, "Accidental Cryptologist," 168–69; John M. Manguso, *The Quadrangle: Hub of Military Activity in Texas; an Outline History* (San Antonio, TX: Fort Sam Houston Museum, 2009), 68; PH to GYH, May 28, 1918, MMC. The Southern Department intelligence officers worked in rooms 5 and 6.

54. GYH to EBH, May 28, 1918, MMC; PH to WFF, August 9, 1947, NCML, DKC, PHP; Smoot, "Accidental Cryptologist," 168–71; MLH to Louis Kruh, n.d., NCML, Louis Kruh Collection; MLH to Kahn, n.d., NCML, DKC, PHP. Yardley was probably referring to Military Intelligence Code Number 5. See John F. Dooley, *Codes, Ciphers and Spies: Tales of Military Intelligence in World War I* (New York: Springer, 2016), 193–206, for the full story.

55. GYH to EBH, May 28, 1918, MMC.

56. PH to GYH, June 9, July 3 and 14, 1918, MMC; Fabyan to WFF, August 8, 1918, ML, ESFC, box 1, folder 42.

57. Influenza Encyclopedia, www.influenzaarchive.org/cities/san-antonio.html# (accessed October 12, 2020); GYH to EBH, July 27, October 19, November 4, 8, and 12, 1918, MMC.

58. Robert L. Barnes to MID, September 12, 1918, NARA CP, RG 165, microfilm M1194, roll 97, MID 9685-316, 1–7; GYH, OPF; Smoot, "Accidental Cryptologist," 171.

59. PH to GYH, multiple letters, July–September 1918, MMC; PH to MLH, July 30, 1918, MMC.

6. Chief Signal Officer

Epigraph: PH to GYH, October 8, 1918, MMC.

1. Bruce Wedgwood, "Personal Narrative," NARA CP, RG 120, E 2040, box 131; First Army CSO, Report, July 1918, NARA CP, RG 120, E 2042, box 33; First Army CSO, Report, August 1918, NARA CP, RG 120, E 2042, box 34; PH to GYH, August 26, 1918, MMC; Dulany Terrett, *The Signal Corps: The Emergency; the United States Army in World War II* (Washington, DC: Office of the Chief of Military History, 1956), 134. Terrett quotes Pershing's direction to Russel

that the Signal Corps had responsibility for "communications from St. Nazaire to the barbed wire." Memorandum, Move of First Army HQ, August 11, 1918, NARA CP, RG 120, E 765, box 18.

2. *US Army Field Service Regulations 1914* (Washington, DC: GPO, 1914), 22; Rebecca Robbins Raines, *Getting the Message Through: A Branch History of the US Army Signal Corps* (Washington, DC: GPO, 1996), 185. See Hugh G. J. Aitken, *The Continuous Wave: Technology and American Radio, 1900–1932* (Princeton, NJ: Princeton University Press, 1985), for an in-depth discussion of the capabilities of early radio technologies.

3. PH to all officers of First Army, August 5, 1918, NARA CP, RG 120, E 765, box 18; PH to COS and ACOS First Army, September 3, 1918, NARA CP, RG 120, E 786, box 214; PH to all officers with operations telephones, September 11, 1918, NARA CP, RG 120, E 765, box 72.

4. PH to Edgar Russel, August 17, 1918, MMC.

5. Memorandum, HQ 32nd Division, July 30, 1918, NARA CP, RG 120, E 1241, box 22; PH to First Army units, August 19, 1918, NARA CP, RG 120, E 1018, box 160; PH to Colonel R. McCleave, August 20, 1918, NARA CP, RG 120, E 765, box 47.

6. A. Lincoln Lavine, *Circuits of Victory* (New York: Doubleday, 1921), 491; PH to Russel, August 18, 1918, mentioned in PH, "Personal Narrative," January 4, 1919, NARA CP, RG 120, E 2040, box 132; PH, "A Study of the Service of Women Telephone Operators of the AEF," November 13, 1918, NARA CP, RG 111, E 45, box 400; PH to GYH, April 21, March 10, 1918, MMC; Suzanne Prevot to PH, December 8, 23, 1919, MMC. Berthe Hunt thought Prevot was Hitt's special friend, according to Elizabeth Cobbs (telephone conversation with the author, December 18, 2015). Berthe Hunt Diary, August 29, 1918, 36, Collection of the National World War I Museum and Memorial, Kansas City, MO.

7. PH to telephone operators, "Secret Orders," August 19, 1918, TFC; Elizabeth Cobbs, *The Hello Girls: America's First Women Soldiers* (Cambridge, MA: Harvard University Press, 2017), 193, 229, citing Grace Banker Diary, 52, TFC; Lavine, *Circuits of Victory,* 492; PH, memorandum, August 26, 1918, TFC; PH, "Personal Narrative." Julia R. Russell (1881–1967) was not, as some thought, the daughter of General Edgar Russel.

8. Wedgwood, "Personal Narrative"; George C. Pratt, "Personal Narrative," NARA CP, RG 120, E 2040, box 130; George C. Pratt, "Our Radio Work in France," *Western Electric News* 8, no. 3 (May 1919): 3.

9. PH, "Explanation and Execution of Plans for St. Mihiel Operation and Argonne-Meuse Operation to November 11, 1918," January 13, 1919, NARA CP, RG 120, E 765, box 76; PH, "Personal Narrative."

10. PH, "Explanation and Execution of Plans"; PH, "Personal Narrative." Tongas received the American Distinguished Service Medal for his efforts during the war. WD, GO 87, 1919.

11. PH, "Report of the Chief Signal Officer, First Army," January 5, 1919, NARA CP, RG 120, E 24, box 3396.

12. "History of the Activities of the Radio Division," NARA CP, RG 120, E 2040, box 131, 9; George Gibbs to PH, August 3, 1918, and Willey Howell to PH, August 3, 1918, both in NARA CP, RG 120, E 765, box 189; G2A6, Weekly Code Section Report, September 10, 1918, NARA CP, RG 120, E 105, box 6696; First Army, Summary of Intelligence No. 8, September 6, 1918, NARA CP, RG 120, E 765, box 11; "Listening Station Report Week Ending September 12, 1918," September 14, 1918, NARA CP, RG 120, E 24, box 3367; Charles Matz to Frank Moorman, September 16, 1918, NARA CP, RG 120, E 105, box 5767. The Saint-Mihiel attack was the first time the US Army used the terms "D-day" and "H-hour."

13. Betsy Rohaly Smoot, *From the Ground Up: American Cryptology during World War I* (Fort George G. Meade, MD: Center for Cryptologic History, forthcoming). A few postwar accounts imply that Matz was at the meeting, but Matz's own account does not. L. W. Comstock, "Lecture to Post-Graduate Students," June 22, 1926, NARA CP, RG 38, E 1029, box 32; Mark Ethan Grotelueschen, *The AEF Way of War: The American Army and Combat in World War I* (Cambridge: Cambridge University Press, 2007), 112–13; Matz to Moorman, September 16, 1918. Others agree with Matz's conclusions about the importance of radio intelligence to Pershing's decision, including Comstock, "Lecture to Post-Graduate Students"; George E. Krumm and Willis H. Taylor Jr., "Wireless in the AEF," *Wireless Age* 7, no. 4 (January 1920): 12; William E. Moore, "The Crisis of St. Mihiel," *American Legion Weekly* 4, no. 23 (June 9, 1922): 7–8, 26; and Thomas M. Johnson, *Our Secret War: True American Spy Stories 1917–1919* (Indianapolis: Bobbs-Merrill, 1929), 15–16.

14. PH, "Personal Narrative."

15. "Clarkes Summit Notes," *Scranton (PA) Republican,* November 15, 1918, 11; Cobbs, conversation with author; Hunt Diary, 40–41; PH to GYH, September 15, 1918, MMC; Banker Diary, 50; Cobbs, *Hello Girls,* 203–5. Cobbs also cites Hunt's "Real Thrills in This Operator's War," *Telephone Bulletin* (New England Telephone Company), March 1919, 1.

16. PH, "Report of Chief Signal Officer"; Cobbs, *Hello Girls,* 229–33; George D. Beaumont, "Personal Narrative," NARA CP, RG 120, E 2040, box 132; "Praises Officers," *Fort Wayne (IN) News and Sentinel,* January 28, 1919, 2.

17. PH, "Report of Chief Signal Officer"; PH, memo, September 18, 1918, referenced in First US Army Museum to PH, March 13, 1964, MMC; James H. Hallas, *Squandered Victory: The American First Army at St. Mihiel* (Westport, CT: Praeger, 1995), 230–32; *The United States Army in the World War 1917–1919,* vol. 8 (Washington, DC: Center of Military History, 1948), 75.

18. First Army CSO, Report, September 1918, NARA CP, RG 120, E 2042, box 34; PH, "Signal Communication for Higher Command," September 21, 1923, MMC; PH, "Report of Chief Signal Officer," 6.

19. PH, "Signal Communication"; PH, "Report of Chief Signal Officer," 8; Raines, *Getting the Message Through,* 190; "Report of the Radio Officer, First Army," September 29, 1918, NARA CP, RG 120, E 2042, box 34.

20. PH, "Explanation and Execution of Plans"; First Army CSO Report, October 1918, 2, NARA CP, RG 120, E 2042, box 35.

21. Cobbs, *Hello Girls,* 239–40; Banker Diary, October 20, 1918, 87; Hunt Diary, October 19, 20, 1918, 49–50.

22. *Annual Report of the Chief Signal Officer to the Secretary of War 1919* (Washington, DC: GPO, 1919), 336–37; Charles Matz, "Final Report of First Army," November 25, 1918, in *Final Report of the Radio Intelligence Section, General Staff, AEF GHQ,* Enclosure C, 36, NARA CP, RG 457, E 9002, box 10. There were many newspaper articles about this operation, including "Yanks Tricked Huns: Officers Created Mythical Army on the Etain Front," *Washington Post,* October 26, 1919, 25. The story also appeared in "That Phantom Yankee Army on the Verdun Front," *Literary Digest* 63, no. 10 (December 6, 1919), and Lavine, *Circuits of Victory,* 542–43.

23. Cobbs, *Hello Girls,* 244–46; Adele L. Hoppock Mills, "Signal Corps Reminiscences," Matt Herron Papers; Lavine, *Circuits of Victory,* 576–77; Hunt Diary, 51; PH, "Study of Service of Women Telephone Operators," November 13, 1918. There is no entry for First Army CSO files in NARA, RG 120; records of First Army's signal effort can be partially reconstructed from material filed with the AEF CSO and other organizations. Hitt told William Friedman that his device was destroyed in the fire; PH to WFF, March 12, 1949, NCML, DKC, PHP.

24. PH, "Signal Communication"; George C. Marshall, *Memoirs of My Services in the World War 1917–1918* (Boston: Houghton Mifflin, 1976), 193–94.

25. PH to GCH, November 24, 1918, MMC.

26. PH, "Signal Communication."

27. First Army CSO Report, October 1918; Russel to PH, November 7, 1918, and PH to Russel, November 15, 1918, NARA CP, RG 120, E 2040, box 157.

28. PH to GYH, November 24, 1918.

29. PH to GYH, November 24, 1918, January 5, 1919, MMC; menu/place card, MMC; PH, "Signal Communication."

30. PH to GYH, January 18, February 2, 1919, MMC.

31. PH to GYH, January 18, 1919.

32. Genevieve knew that some army wives, including Lily Marshall and Florence Simonds, were staying with "quite a large Army colony" at a boardinghouse called Carter Hall in Warrenton, Virginia. It was "an inexpensive pleasant place to be" and was nearer to New York, should their husbands get home. She probably chose Winchester for similar reasons. GYH to EBH, November 4, 1918, MMC; PH to GYH, February 11, March 6 and 11, April 5, May 5, 1919, MMC; "Winchester," *Richmond Times-Dispatch,* April 20, 1919, pt. 3, 5.

33. PH to GYH, February 11, 1919; Henry G. Gale to Executive Officer, February 24, 1919, NARA CP, RG 457, E P11, box 214.

34. PH to GYH, February 11 and 16, 1919, MMC. Voris was "furious."

35. File of papers relating to the car accident, MMC.

36. PH to EBH, March 9, 1919, MMC; PH to CO Nice Leave Area, "Request for Investigation of Overcharge," March 15, 1919, MMC; CO Riviera Leave Area to PH, April 17, 1919, MMC; PH to GYH, March 6, 1919.

37. PH to GYH, March 24, 1919, MMC; Wedgwood to PH, March 22, 1919, MMC; Donald B. Sanger for Gibbs to PH, "Letter of Instructions," March 20, 1919, NCML, DKC, PHP.

38. PH to GYH, April 5 and 15, May 5 and 18, 1919, MMC; Bender to PH, March 25, 1919, MMC; AEF, SO 92, para. 2, April 2, 1919, PH, OMPF; Services of Supply No. 1676-8, para. 11, June 21, 1919, NCML, DKC, PHP.

39. AEF, SO 98, para. 173, April 8, 1919, MMC; PH to GYH, April 15, May 5 and 29–31, 1919, MMC; Grotelueschen, *AEF Way of War,* 353; John B. Wilson, "Mobility versus Firepower: The Post–World War I Infantry Division," *Parameters* 13, no. 3 (September 1983): 48; PH to Third Army Adjutant, June 20, 1919, NARA CP, RG 120, E 973, box 135. The other members of the board were Major Generals John L. Hines and William Lassiter and Brigadier Generals Hugh Drum and William Burtt.

40. "Report of the Superior Board on Organization and Tactics," 95, http://cgsc.cdmhost.com/cdm/ref/collection/p4013c0117/id/808 (accessed May 30, 2020); Raines, *Getting the Message Through,* 219; John B. Wilson, *Maneuver and Firepower: The Evolution of Divisions and Separate Brigades* (Washington, DC: Center of Military History, 1988), 82–86; Wilson, "Mobility versus Firepower," 48.

41. PH to GYH, February 2, 1919, November 24, 1918, MMC; GYH to EBH, October 19, 1918, MMC. Hitt counted the "fighting Signal Corps" as himself, Edgar Russel, George Gibbs, Hanson B. Black, Alvin Voris, Karl Truesdell, Owen Albright, John E. Hemphill, George E. Kumpe, R. G. Van Horn, and James G. Taylor.

42. PH to Russel, May 13, 1919, NARA CP, RG 120, E 973, box 135.

43. PH to Russel, May 13, 1919.

44. AEF, SO 110, para. 16, April 20, 1919, NARA CP, RG 120, E 267, box 135; PH to GYH, April 15, 1919, MMC; PH to G3, Third Army, April 28, 1919; J. Watson to Hitt, May 1, 1919, both in NARA CP, RG 120, E 973, box 134. Carr did not actually leave France until the end of May 1919; he had arrived in mid-November 1917. Carr would serve as CSO of the US Army from 1931 to 1934.

45. PH, "Signal Communication."

46. PH, multiple memos, April 12–June 20, 1919, NARA CP, RG 120, E 267, box 134; PH, memorandum, May 31, 1919, NARA CP, RG 120, E 973, box 135.

47. PH to GYH, June 8, 1919, MMC; PH to Third Army Adjutant, June 20, 1919.

48. PH to GYH, May 29–31, 1919, MMC; PH to EBH, June 8, 1919, MMC; Russel to PH, June 18, 1919, and PH to Russel, June 20, 1919, NARA CP, RG 120, E 973, box 135.

49. PH to GYH, June 19–20 and 29, 1919, MMC.

50. PH to GYH, June 29, 1919.

51. Russel, PH Efficiency Report, March 15, 1918; Fox Conner, PH Efficiency Report, July 24, 1918; Hugh Drum, PH Efficiency Reports, April 20, 1919, and December 15, 1918; Malin Craig, PH Efficiency Report, June 20, 1917; Joseph Dickman, PH Efficiency Report, July 19, 1919; Russel letters, July 10, January 14, 1919, all in PH, OMPF.

52. John J. Pershing, PH Efficiency Report, September 30, 1918, PH, OMPF.

7. Jack-of-All-Trades

Epigraph: Memo from LeRoy Eltinge, Acting Chief of AEF G3, to AEF Chief of Staff James Harbord, February 15, 1918, NARA CP, RG 120, E 267, box 3212.

1. PH, "Explanation and Execution of Plans," January 13, 1919; Dennis Nolan to James McAndrew, May 10, 1919; McAndrew to George C. Marshall, May 22, 1919, all in NARA CP, RG 120, E 16, 17, 18, box 101. The AWC was briefly called the General Staff College before reverting to its original name in 1921.

2. Photographs, NARA CP, RG 111, SC Photos 162060 and 162055; PH, OMPF.

3. "Guns to Welcome Gen. Pershing Today," *Washington Post,* September 12, 1919, 1; PH to Grace Banker, October 24, 1919, TFC. The Signal Corps' photographic lab moved to Washington Barracks in 1919.

4. Phyllis L. McClellan, *Silent Sentinel on the Potomac: Fort McNair, 1791–1991* (Bowie, MD: Heritage Books, 1993), 1, 67; PH, OMPF.

5. McClellan, *Silent Sentinel,* 133; Harry A. Smith, "General Staff College Course," *Infantry Journal* 18 (January 1921): 51–57.

6. George S. Pappas, *Prudens Futuri: The US Army War College 1901–1967* (Carlisle Barracks, PA: Alumni Association of the US Army War College, 1967), 97; efficiency rating, December 31, 1919, PH, OMPF.

7. PH to George Fabyan, January 3, 1920, MMC. Vernam's telecipher device used key tape with random characters; Vernam and Mauborgne are credited with inventing the one-time pad, although some believe the credit should be shared with Friedman and Hitt. Steven M. Bellovin, "Vernam, Mauborgne, and Friedman: The One-Time Pad and the Index of Coincidence," in *The New Codebreakers: Essays Dedicated to David Kahn on the Occasion of His 85th Birthday,* ed. Peter Y. A. Ryan, David Naccache, and Jean-Jacques Quisquater (New York: Springer, 2016), 40. Vernam's work is discussed in depth in David Kahn, *The Codebreakers* (New York: Scribner, 1996), 394–403. For a discussion of one-time pads, see Craig Bauer, *Secret History: The Story of Cryptology* (Boca Raton, FL: Chapman Hall, 2013), 103–15.

8. Fabyan to PH, November 29, 1919, NCML, DKC, PHP. The musical cipher, dated December 1, 1919 (NCML, DKC, PHP), reads when broken: "Mary is a good name. Mary Lue is pretty. My name is plain old fashioned Elizabeth."

9. Suzanne Prevot to PH, December 8, 1919, MMC; John L. Carney to PH, September 2, 1920, MMC; PH to Carney, September 3, 1920, MMC; Mark J. Ryan to PH, October 11, 1920, MMC; PH to "to whom it may concern," October 12, 1920, MMC. Hitt had a soft spot in his heart for the Signal Corps' pigeons. One of his cherished possessions was a photograph of the legendary World War I pigeon Cher Ami.

10. Entry card, December 23, 1919, MMC; Florida, Passenger Lists, 1898–1963, Ancestry.com, original data from Selected Passenger Lists and Manifests, NARA; PH to Fabyan, January 1, 1920, MMC.

11. PH to Joseph O. Mauborgne, February 3, 1920 (missing first page), MMC; "Carrier Telegraph from Coast to Coast, Long Lines," March 1922, 7–10, https://earlyradiohistory.us/1922cc.htm (accessed November 16, 2018); Mauborgne to PH, February 7, 1920, NCML, DKC, PHP; James A. Reeds, email to the author, March 29, 2018. The Signal Corps' electrical engineering laboratory was in Washington, but the radio laboratory was at Camp Alfred Vail, New Jersey.

12. PH, OMPF; F. R. Curtis to CO, Camp Alfred Vail, May 17, 1920, MMC; draft memo from Commandant, General Staff College, to AG of the Army, May 21, 1920, MMC; Pappas, *Prudens Futuri*, 104.

13. EBH to PH, September 24, 1920, MMC; GYH, OPF; Kenneth D. Ackermann, *Young J. Edgar: Hoover, the Red Scare and the Assault on Civil Liberties* (New York: Carroll & Graf, 2007), 340–41; Betsy Rohaly Smoot, "An Accidental Cryptologist: The Brief Career of Genevieve Young Hitt," *Cryptologia* 35, no. 2 (2011): 172; assignment order, 1920, PH, OMPF. In 2020 dollars, a full colonel's pay was about $6,400 a month and a major's $4,300. Genevieve's annual salary was nearly $15,500 in 2020 dollars, or $1,550 a month; her bonus was worth about $3,100. https://www.usinflationcalculator.com/ (accessed July 25, 2020).

14. Hitt is not listed as an occupant of quarters 7; the most likely explanation is that the Gowens, the listed residents, moved out that summer and the Hitts moved in. In 1987 General Colin L. Powell occupied these quarters while serving as national security adviser to President Ronald Reagan. *The United States Army and Navy Journal and Gazette of the Regular and Volunteer Army* 57, pt. 2 (June 26, 1920): 1345; McClellan, *Silent Sentinel*, 89–92, 233; Mamie Doud Eisenhower to her parents, n.d., EPL, Barbara Eisenhower Papers, box 1, folder "Family Letters 1920"; bridge "orders," n.d., MMC; Jean Young Fish, conversation with the author, September 22, 2011.

15. PH, statement of preference, n.d. (probably autumn 1920), MMC; PH's typed copy of George O. Squier's testimony, MMC; Terrence J. Gough, "Isolation and Professionalization of the Army Officer Corps: A Post-Revisionist View of the Soldier and the State," *Social Science Quarterly* 73, no. 2 (June 1992): 430;

"Experts Will Confer," *Indianapolis News,* September 18, 1920, 14; PH to New, March 12, 1921, MMC. Squier, who had impressive academic and scientific credentials, wanted to build a larger group of professionally competent signal officers who were not tied to other branches of the army; he probably did not intend to insult Hitt.

16. GCH to PH, October 4, 1920, MMC.

17. Hitt also taught the G1 course in the autumn of 1921. "Course at the Army War College, 1921–1922, Volume I, G-1 Part 1, Lectures," NARA CP, RG 165, E UD7, box 14; index cards relating to AWC held at AHEC; Chief of Infantry to PH, December 27, 1920, MMC; efficiency report, December 31, 1920, PH OMPF; PH to Banker, February 8, 1921, TFC.

18. WD, GO 75, December 23, 1920, PH, OMPF; WD, SO 302-0, December 24, 1920, para. 37, PH, OMPF; Stephen Fuqua to PH, December 28, 1920, and PH to Fuqua, undated handwritten response, MMC; PH to William Weigel, December 28, 1920, MMC; PH to Banker, February 8, 1921.

19. "Terrific Explosion Outside Morgan's Office," *Wall Street Journal,* September 17, 1920, 3; Bruce W. Bidwell, *History of the Military Intelligence Division, Department of the Army General Staff: 1775–1941* (Frederick, MD: University Publications of America, 1986), 275.

20. PH to Colonel Brown, February 21, 1921, MMC; PH to G. A. Lynch, February 17, 1921, MMC; James L. Collins to PH, March 21, 1921, NARA CP, RG 165, E 65, box 368; PH to Collins, February 9, June 9, 1921, MMC; Collins to PH, February 19, 1921, MMC. Collins, who became a major general, was the brother of General Joseph Lawton "Lightning Joe" Collins and the father of both Brigadier General (and army historian) James Lawton Collins Jr. and astronaut Major General Michael Collins.

21. Marlborough Churchill, "The Military Intelligence Division General Staff," *Journal of the United States Artillery* 52, no. 4 (April 1920): 295, 311–12.

22. Collins to PH, February 1, 1921, and PH to Collins, February 11, 1921, NARA CP, RG 165, E 65, box 2292; PH to MID, March 26, 1921, NARA CP, RG 165, E 65, box 2285; PH to MID, February 11, April 13, July 18, 1921, NARA CP, RG 165, E 65, box 368.

23. PH to Dennis Nolan, April 13, 1921, MMC; Claude T. Rice to PH, April 27 and 29, June 28, 1921, MMC; M. J. McKenna to PH, June 10, 1921, MMC.

24. PH to MID, "State Department Code," August 11, 1921; Mathew C. Smith to W. L. Hurley, August 16, 1921, both in NARA CP, RG 165, E 65, box 1877; Charles J. Scully to J. Edgar Hoover, August 11, 1921, www.footnote.com /image/5272115 (accessed March 28, 2009), original data from NARA CP, Investigative Case Files of the Bureau of Intelligence, 1908–1922, RG 65, microfilm M1085, roll 908, 2.

25. Invitation to Baltic Society dinner, n.d., MMC; "Lt. Col. Behn Weds Miss Dunlap," *Philadelphia Inquirer,* June 1, 1921, 2; efficiency ratings, January 31–August 24, 1921, PH, OMPF.

26. Joseph W. Bendersky, *The "Jewish Threat": Anti-Semitic Politics of the U.S. Army* (New York: Basic Books, 2000), 171; Joseph W. Bendersky, "The Absent Presence: Enduring Images of Jews in United States Military History," *American Jewish History* 89, no. 4 (December 2001): 418–19; Roy Talbert Jr., *Negative Intelligence: The Army and the American Left, 1917–1941* (Jackson: University Press of Mississippi, 1991), 211.

27. PH to GCH, July 29, 1921, MMC; PH, OMPF.

28. PH to George S. Gibbs, February 26, 1916, NCML, DKC, PHP; "'Just a Plain Nut' on Code Study Says Friedman, Famed in Oil Case," *Washington Evening Star*, March 8, 1924, 4. Some of the notable cases are detailed in Betsy Rohaly Smoot, *The Cipher Game: The Cryptologic Work of Colonel Parker Hitt, Genevieve Young Hitt, and Mary Lue Hitt* (Fort George G. Meade, MD: Center for Cryptologic History, forthcoming).

29. WFF to PH, April 13, 1922, NCML, DKC, PHP; PH, review, *Signal Corps Bulletin* 25 (May 1924); WFF to PH, April 19, 1923, NCML, DKC, PHP.

30. Correspondence between Albert Osborn and PH, 1920–1924, NCML, DKC, PHP; B. E. Brigman to PH, December 7, 1924, NCML, DKC, PHP; Edwin L. Miller to PH, February 7, 11, 1922, MMC; PH to Miller, February 9, 1922, MMC. Brigman was the author of "Midnight Oil," a story published in *Real Detective Tales*, February and May 1924.

31. Kahn, *Codebreakers*, 767–68; PH to John F. Byrne, March 7, August 14, 1922; Byrne to PH, March 19, 1922, all in NCML, DKC, PHP. Byrne's article, "Here Is an Absolutely Secret Cipher; Can't Be Deciphered without the Key," supposedly appeared in the *New York Herald* on June 8, 1921 or 1922; the clipping does not include the year. J. F. Byrne, *Silent Years: An Autobiography with Memoirs of James Joyce and Our Ireland* (New York: Farrar, Straus & Young, 1953).

32. PH to GCH, October 19, 1921, MMC; report card for MLH, Georgetown Visitation Convent, December 19, 1921, MMC; commissary receipts, n.d., MMC; MLH to GYH, n.d. (1923, based on context), MMC. When confronted, Genevieve Hitt acknowledged that she had given her daughter the cigarettes. Oral history with David E. Moreman and Evie Moreman, March 23, 2009. McClellan, *Silent Sentinel*, 92, 236, lists later occupants of quarters 11 as Generals Mark Clark and A. W. Vanaman in the 1940s and 1950s and several US surgeon generals in the 1980s.

33. "Course at the Army War College, 1921–1922, Volume I, G-1 Part 1, Lectures"; index cards relating to AWC; PH, "The Attack and Defense of Halifax, Nova Scotia: A Preliminary Study," paper prepared for AWC, July 26, 1922, MMC; efficiency report, June 30, 1922, PH, OMPF.

34. PH, "Graphic Presentation," AWC lecture, NARA CP, RG 165, E UD7, box 19; list of courses, AWC, 1923–1924, NARA CP, RG 165, E UD7, box 2.

35. PH, remarks following the presentation of the report of the committee on the British Empire, G-2 Course 17, 1922–1923, NARA CP, RG 165, E UD7, box 17.

36. "Mrs. George C. Hitt Dies Suddenly at Her Home in Worcester, Mass.," *Indianapolis Star,* March 4, 1923, 1; untitled item, *Indianapolis Star,* March 5, 1923, 6; GCH to PH, June 23, 1923, MMC.

37. Medical records; efficiency report, June 30, 1923; assignment preferences, all in PH, OMPF.

38. PH, "Signal Communication for Higher Command," AWC lecture, September 1923, MMC.

39. Chief of Infantry to PH, October 5, 1923, MMC; PH indoresment, October 9, 1923, MMC.

40. GYH to GCH, December 7, 1923, MMC.

41. PH, "Period of Informative Studies Orientation, G-1 Course," NARA CP, RG 165, E UD7, box 19; Henry Dickinson, "Why the Army War College," *Cavalry Journal* 33, no. 135 (July 1924): 302–7.

42. PH to GCH, March 20, 1924, MMC.

43. PH to GCH, April 15, May 23, 1924, MMC. George Gruenert, like Hitt, had enlisted during the Spanish-American War and served in Cuba and the Philippines before being commissioned in 1901. Gruenert became a lieutenant general and directed the army's investigation of the Japanese attack on Pearl Harbor.

44. Memorandum, May 29, 1924, NARA CP, RG 165, E UD7, box 18; WD, SO 34, June 10, 1924, PH, OMPF; PH, "Memorandum for My Successor," July 1, 1924, MMC.

45. PH to GCH, April 15, 1924, MMC; PH, OMPF.

46. PH to GCH, July 15, October 8, 1924, MMC; Certificate of Personal Property, July 5, 1924, MMC; GYH to GCH, August 24, 1924, MMC.

47. PH to GCH, July 15, 1924, MMC; GYH to GCH, August 23, 1924, MMC.

48. Hitt's class included Colonels Edgar T. Collins, Stanley H. Ford, David L. Stone, John L. De Witt, Duncan Major, H. P. McAdams, and Dana T. Merrill and Lieutenant Colonels H. Clay M. Supplee, George Herbst, Wait C. Johnson, and Stephen O. Fuqua. Efficiency report, September 30, 1924, PH, OMPF; *Infantry School News* 3, no. 5 (September 26, 1924): 5; no. 7 (October 10, 1924): 1–2; no. 8 (October 17, 1924): 6; no. 14 (November 28, 1924): 3; no. 15 (December 5, 1924): 3; *A History of the Infantry School* (Fort Benning, GA, 1945); *The Doughboy* (US Infantry School, Fort Benning, GA, 1924), all in digital collection, Maneuver Center of Excellence, Donovan Research Library; PH to GCH, October 8, November 27, 1924, MMC; W. A. Dumas to PH, February 5, 1925, MMC.

49. H. E. Knight for Chief of Infantry to AG, January 22, 1925, PH, OMPF; Dumas to PH, February 5, 1925, MMC.

50. Robert C. Davis to ACOS, G1, March 6, 1925; John B. Bennett to COS, March 12, 1925; AG to Chief of Infantry, March 17, 1925, all in PH, OMPF; Briant H. Wells to PH, March 23, 1925, MMC; PH to GCH, April 20, 1925, MMC.

51. PH to GCH, November 27, December 21, 1924, MMC.

52. GYH to GCH, June 7, 1925, MMC.

53. Efficiency report, June 30, 1925, PH, OMPF; C. D. Eddleman to PH, March 19, 1962, MMC; PH to Eddleman, n.d., MMC.

54. PH, "Code for Feb 25, 1925," MMC; PH, "Plan for Reorganization of the Infantry Regiment," September 1, 1925, MMC; two handwritten notes, n.d. and September 3, 1927, MMC.

55. Efficiency report, June 30, 1925; PH to GCH, February 24, 1926, MMC.

56. PH to GCH, August 15, November 2, December 14 and 27, 1925, MMC.

57. PH to GCH, December 14, 1925, February 24, 1926, MMC; "1926—The U.S. Army Air Corps Act," https://www.afhistory.af.mil/FAQs/Fact-Sheets/Article/459017/1926-the-us-army-air-corps-act/ (accessed May 17, 2020).

58. WD, SO 49, para. 16, March 1, 1926, PH, OMPF; efficiency reports, March 4, June 30, 1926, PH, OMPF; Paul B. Malone to PH and AG, July 14, 1924, NCML DKC PHP.

59. PH to GCH, July 5, 1936, MMC; PH, OMPF.

60. PH to GCH, July 29, 1926, n.d. (autumn 1926), MMC; GCH to PH, February 8, 1927, MMC. The Cordova is now the President Madison Apartments.

61. PH to GCH, May 5, 1927, MMC.

62. PH to GCH, December 28, 1926, MMC; Joni Guhne, "Sherwood Forest Still a Merry Place," *Baltimore Sun,* March 30, 2003, Real Estate sec., 1; PH to GCH, May 5, 1927, MMC. Gunston Hall was a leading school for girls in Washington. The building now houses the National Museum of American Jewish Military History.

63. PH to GCH, June 7, August 11, 1927, MMC; PH, OMPF.

64. PH, OMPF; PH to GCH, August 11, 1927.

65. PH to GCH, August 11, September 2, 1927, MMC; GYH to PH, August 22, 1927, MMC; Warren County Deed Book 30/395, deed made September 12, 1927, and executed October 6, 1927, Philip Stickley et al. to Genevieve Hitt. Genevieve paid $6,875 cash; this would be about $101,000 in 2020 dollars. https://www.usinflationcalculator.com/ (accessed July 25, 2020).

66. PH to GCH, September 2, 1927.

67. PH to GCH, October 23, 1927, MMC; Edith Jackson, Front Royal, Virginia, "Genlue Park," Works Progress Administration of Virginia Historical Inventory, Warren County, August 21, 1936, http://image.lva.virginia.gov/VHI/html/28/0264.html (accessed May 23, 2020); Judy Reynolds and Pat Windrow, Front Royal Walking Tour Guide, https://frontroyalva.com/DocumentCenter/View/166/Front-Royal-Walking-Tour-PDF (accessed May 23, 2020); David Edwards, "An Evaluation of Architectural Historic and Archaeological Resources in Warren County," Valley Region Historic Preservation Plan (Richmond: Virginia Division of Historic Landmarks, 1985); GCH to PH, May 31, 1928, MMC.

68. PH to GCH, August 11, October 23, 1927, MMC; PH to Miss Merrill at Briarcliff, carbon copy to MLH, November 1, 1927, MMC.

69. Benjamin Franklin Cooling, "Dwight D. Eisenhower at the Army War College, 1927–1928," *Parameters* 5, no. 1 (1975); PH to GCH, October 23, December 23, 1927, MMC.

70. PH to GCH, April 11, 1928, MMC; receipt from Beaux-Arts Tours, May 16, 1928, MMC. The full cost of the trip was $785, or about $11,770 in 2020 dollars. https://www.usinflationcalculator.com/ (accessed May 17, 2020).

71. Associated Press, "$300,000,000 Wire Merger Underway," *News Journal* (Wilmington, DE), March 20, 1928, 20; PH to Sosthenes Behn, March 21, 1928, and Behn to PH, March 23, 1928, both in NCML, DKC, PHP; PH to GCH, June 6, 1928, MMC. Dollar figures calculated at https://www.usinflationcalculator.com/ (accessed May 17, 2020)

72. PH to GCH, June 6, July 4, 1928, MMC. Hitt had been promoted to full colonel in September 1927. By January 1928, he was number 512 on the promotion list; he crept up to number 485 in July 1928. He thought he would reach brigadier general in 1935 (with no increase in retirement pay). If he had stayed in the army, he would have attained retirement age (sixty-four) in 1942, although he might have been kept on a bit longer because of the war. IT&T (now ITT) did not respond to multiple requests for details about Hitt's employment.

8. Commerce

Epigraph: GCH to PH, June 6, 1928, MMC.

1. Behn "gloried in the title, all of the military trappings, and even the supposed glamour of combat. This could be seen later on when he surrounded himself with former military and naval officers, many of whom he had met during the war." Robert Sobel, *ITT: The Management of Opportunity* (1982; reprint, Washington, DC: Beard Books, 2000), 32; Sosthenes Behn, "Personal Narrative," January 22, 1919, NARA CP, RG 120, E 2040, box 133.

2. Sobel, *ITT,* 31.

3. PH to Sosthenes Behn, June 16, 1928, NCML, DKC, PHP.

4. MLH to PH, August 3 and 27, 1928, MMC; MLH to GYH, August 5 and 13, 1928, MMC; PH to GCH, October 23, 1928, MMC.

5. Directory, International Telephone Building, May 1, 1931, NCML, DKC, PHP; PH to GCH, September 18, 1928, MMC.

6. PH, first draft of proposal, September 7, 1929, NCML, DKC, PHP; PH to GCH, September 18, October 23, December 11, 1928, MMC; PH to GCH, May 8, 1929, MMC; Friedman grille, MMC, copy available at https://www.marshallfoundation.org/blog/friedmans-christmas-cards/ (accessed May 27, 2020); Dr. Harlow Brooks to PH, February 5, 1929, MMC.

7. Some companies that asked IT&T to assess their devices also submitted them to the US government for evaluation, which was usually performed by William Friedman. AB Cryptograph was run by Boris Hagelin and later became

Crypto AG. William Friedman, Frank Rowlett, and Abraham Sinkov comprehensively broke the Kryha in 1933 while testing it for the government, more than three years after Hitt's work. See Ronald Clark, *The Man Who Broke Purple: The Life of Colonel William F. Friedman, Who Deciphered the Japanese Code in World War II* (Boston: Little, Brown, 1977), 130–33. A discussion of other systems Hitt evaluated can be found in Betsy Rohaly Smoot, *The Cipher Game: The Cryptologic Work of Colonel Parker Hitt, Genevieve Young Hitt, and Mary Lue Hitt* (Fort George G. Meade, MD: Center for Cryptologic History, forthcoming); F. Hutchinson to A. A. Clokey, June 20, 1929, NCML, DKC, PHP; PH, "Notes on Decipherment of Kryha Ciphers," December 2, 1929, transcript of document by Philip Marks, 2009, http://cryptocellar.org/Kryha (accessed May 19, 2020), original documents in TICOM Collection T2510, box 129, Politisches Archiv des Auswaertigen Amts, Berline, Bestand Rueckgabe TICOM; PH to GCH, January 30, 1930, MMC; PH to Clokey, July 18, 1929, NCML, DKC, PHP; W. C. Peterman to PH, August 12, 1929, NCML, DKC, PHP; PH to GCH, May 8, June 20, 1929, MMC.

8. See David Kahn, *The Codebreakers* (New York: Scribner, 1996), 415–25, for discussion of these developments.

9. PH, Ciphering and Deciphering Apparatus, US Patent 1,848,291, filed August 13, 1930, and issued March 8, 1932; PH, Printing Telegraph System, US Patent 1,872,951, filed May 6, 1930, and issued August 23, 1932; PH, Device for Insuring Privacy of Reception of Printing Telegraph Messages, US Patent 1,834,278, filed June 16, 1930, and issued December 1, 1931.

10. PH to Peterman, October 16, 1929, NCML, DKC, PHP; PH, Ciphering Apparatus, US Patent 2,028,508, filed August 7, 1931, and issued January 21, 1936. The slits to view the keyword hark back to Hitt's 1912 manual cylindrical device. The paper strips are in NCML, DKS, PHP.

11. PH to GCH, December 11, 1929, January 30, May 27, 1930, MMC; GYH, Illuminating Device for Dial Telephones, US Patent 1,747,976, filed March 22, 1929, and issued February 18, 1930; handwritten note, PH to Behn, n.d., with Behn's penciled remark, MMC. In 1945 Genevieve listed her patent in the Register of Patents for License or Sale, having not yet sold the rights. GYH to the Commissioner of Patents, November 11, 1945, MMC.

12. GYH to PH, November 13, 1929, MMC. Squier's life and inventions are discussed in Paul W. Clark and Laurence A. Lyons, *George Owen Squier: U.S. Army Major General, Inventor, Aviation Pioneer, Founder of Muzak* (Jefferson, NC: McFarland, 2014).

13. "Prize Rooster Is Leader of Show Flock of South," *Boston Traveler,* January 21, 1930, 13; PH to GCH, January 30, 1930, MMC.

14. PH to GCH, May 27, 1930, MMC.

15. Sobel, *ITT,* 72–73; PH to GCH, July 28, 1930, MMC.

16. PH to GCH, July 28, 1930, MMC; GYH to GCH, August 7, 1930, MMC; PH to GCH, September 8, 1930, MMC; Diane M. Dale, "The Boundary

Dilemma at Shenandoah National Park," *Virginia Environmental Law Journal* 15, no. 4 (Summer 1997): 611. "Young" Stephen Reynolds may have been the son of Major Stephan Reynolds, who in 1927 was stationed at the Quartermaster's Depot in Front Royal.

17. PH to GCH, September 8, 1930, MMC; Hernand Behn to PH, September 10 and 25, 1930; PH, "Memorandum for File—Scrambler Operation," October 8, 1930; memorandum to Hitt, October 23, 1930, all in NCML, DKC, PHP.

18. Organizational chart of ICL, November 1, 1930, NCML, DKC, PHP; Harry New to GYH, October 28, 1930, MMC; PH to GCH, November 18, 1930, MMC.

19. PH to GCH, December 24, 1930, MMC.

20. PH to GCH, February 27, July 27, 1931, MMC; Joseph Wenger to PH, February 2, 1931, NCML, DKC, PHP. Although Wenger investigated many machines in the early 1930s, the navy did not begin to use electromechanical cipher machines for its own communications until the 1940s. John Ferris, email to the author, September 2020, regarding Wenger's reports from the early 1930s. Wenger, later a rear admiral, was the first vice director of the National Security Agency in 1952, after a long cryptologic career with the navy.

21. PH to GCH, February 27, April 2 and 7, 1931, MMC.

22. GYH to MLCY, May 22, 1931, YFL; PH to GCH, May 6, June 1, July 27, 1931, MMC.

23. Memos between PH and Signal Corps, September 29–October 10, 1931, https://www.nsa.gov/Portals/70/documents/news-features/declassified-documents /friedman-documents/reports-research/FOLDER_532/41771569081065.pdf (accessed November 17, 2018); PH to George S. Gibbs, December 30, 1931, NCML, DKC, PHP; Frank B. Rowlett, *The Story of Magic* (Laguna Hills, CA: Aegean Park Press, 1998), 71; PH to David A. Salmon, October 31, 1931, NCML, DKC, PHP. It is not clear why Friedman and Crawford traveled to New York to see the machine when it was being set up in Washington at around the same time.

24. State Department to War Department, October 29, 1931, https:// www.nsa.gov/Portals/70/documents/news-features/declassified-documents /friedman-documents/reports-research/FOLDER_532/41771549081063.pdf (accessed November 17, 2018); Rowlett, *Story of Magic,* 70–74.

25. Rowlett, *Story of Magic,* 72–74; Salmon to CSO, November 11, 1931, https://www.nsa.gov/Portals/70/documents/news-features/declassified-documents /friedman-documents/reports-research/FOLDER_532/41771519081060.pdf (accessed November 17, 2018); William Friedman, "Report on Investigation for the Department of State of the Cipher Machine Submitted for Their Consideration by the International Telephone and Telegraph Company," November 16, 1931, https://www.nsa.gov/Portals/70/documents/news-features/declassified-documents /friedman-documents/reports-research/FOLDER_532/41771479081056.pdf (accessed November 17, 2018). The "temporary" Munitions Building and its twin, the Navy Building, were torn down in 1970; the Vietnam Memorial now occupies part of the land where the Munitions Building once stood.

26. Friedman, "Report on Investigation."

27. *Principles of Solution of Cryptograms Produced by the I.T.&T. Cipher Machine* (Washington, DC: GPO, 1934), later released as SRH 330, NARA CP, RG 457, E 9002, box 89; Friedman, "Report on Investigation."

28. Rowlett, *Story of Magic,* 72–74. Although Rowlett's account is credible, he seems to describe only the first test, and the timeline might be compressed.

29. Solomon Kullback, oral history interview, August 26, 1982, NSA-OH-1982-17, 23–25, https://www.nsa.gov/Portals/70/documents/news-features/declassified-documents/oral-history-interviews/nsa-oh-17-82-kullback.pdf (accessed November 18, 2018); *Principles of Solution of Cryptograms;* Gibbs to Clokey, "Cipher Typewriter Development," March 29, 1932, NCML, DKC, PHP. Dollar figures calculated at https://www.usinflationcalculator.com/ (accessed December 12, 2020).

30. PH to Gibbs, "The Electric Scrambler and the Cipher Typewriter," December 30, 1931; Gibbs to Clokey, "Cipher Typewriter Development," March 29, 1932, both in NCML, DKC, PHP. The device Hitt describes in the letter does not match any of the patents he received, and the details cannot be found in any known collection of Hitt's papers; they may be in ITT's files.

31. Army Security Agency, *History of Converter M-134-C,* vol. 1 (Washington, DC: Army Security Agency, n.d.), 18, 27–32; Timothy Mucklow, *The SIGABA/ECM II Cipher Machine: "A Beautiful Idea"* (Fort George G. Meade, MD: Center for Cryptologic History, 2015), 19.

32. James A. Reeds, Whitfield Diffie, and J. V. Field, eds., *Breaking Teleprinter Ciphers at Bletchley Park: An Edition of I. J. Good, D. Michie and G. Timms; General Report on TUNNY with Emphasis on Statistical Methods (1945)* (Piscataway, NJ: Wiley–IEEE Press, 2015), xxxii; Clokey to P. R. Arendt, Gesellschaft fur Telephon und Telegraphenbeteiligungen, Berlin, December 10, 1930, NCML, DKC, PHP; PH to GCH, May 6, 1931, MMC; Army Security Agency, *European Axis Signal Intelligence in World War II as Revealed by "TICOM" Investigations and by Other Prisoner of War Interrogations and Captured Material, Principally German,* vol. 2, *Notes on German High-Level Cryptography and Cryptanalysis* (Washington, DC: Army Security Agency, 1946), 21; Reeds et al., *Breaking Teleprinter Ciphers,* 567–68; James A. Reeds, email to the author, March 23, 2018.

33. Kullback oral history, 23–25. Hitt's account is in an undated draft of a letter, possibly intended for the CSO in the late 1940s; Hitt believed he had not received proper credit for the cryptographic devices he invented for the army. It is not clear whether this letter was ever sent. PH, undated account, MMC; James A. Reeds, emails to the author, November 16–17, 2016.

34. Comptroller, IT&T, to PH, September 19, 1931, MMC; IT&T to PH, September 9, November 27, 1931, MMC; PH to Gibbs, January 29, 1932, MMC.

35. D. T. Finney to PH, February 1, 1932, MMC; Gibbs to PH, January 30, 1932, MMC; GCH to PH, February 3, 1932, MMC; September 1940 medical

exam, PH, OPF. Gastroesophageal reflux disease (GERD) is the most common cause of noncardiac chest pain, and Hitt had a history of acid troubles. See https://my.clevelandclinic.org/health/diseases/15851-gerd-non-cardiac-chest-pain (accessed January 11, 2021).

36. GCH to PH, February 6 and 20, 1932, MMC.

37. PH to A. H. Griswold, January 28, 1932; PH to Behn, January 29, 1932, MMC. Griswold, a civilian engineer from the Pacific Telephone and Telegraph Company, was the first commander of the AEF's 411th Telegraph Battalion; in March 1918 General Edgar Russel made him director of the AEF's Telephone and Telegraph Department. Charles H. Moore, ed., *Memories of the 411th Telegraph Battalion in the World War Here and "Over There"* (Reno, NV: A. Carlisle, 1919), 16. Dollar figures calculated at https://www.usinflationcalculator.com/ (accessed May 19, 2020).

38. Behn to PH, January 30, 1932, MMC; H. B. Orde to PH, June 22, 1932, MMC; GCH to PH, March 17, 1932, MMC.

39. Sobel, *ITT,* 76; Clokey to PH, April 30, 1932, NCML, DKC, PHP; Orde to PH, June 22, 1932, MMC; PH to Orde, June 26, 1932, MMC; Gibbs to PH, April 7, 1933, MMC. A concise explanation of Behn's calamitous deal can be found in Christian Stadler, *Enduring Success: What We Can Learn from the History of Outstanding Corporations* (Stanford, CA: Stanford University Press, 2011), 80–81.

9. Retreat

Epigraph: GYH to Sosthenes Behn, n.d. [1932], MMC.

1. "Dr. Hugh H. Young to Address Baltic Society Next Saturday," *Baltimore Sun,* May 25, 1932, 24; Harry S. New to PH, July 22, 1932, MMC.

2. PH to AG, "Request for Assignment to Active Duty," June 1, 1933, MMC; Harold L. Ickes, *Back to Work: The Story of PWA* (New York: Macmillan, 1935), 16–18; PH to James W. Adams, June 27, 1933, MMC; GCH to PH, August 4, 1933, MMC; Philip B. Fleming to PH, May 13, 1937, MMC; PH to Fleming May 18, 1937, MMC.

3. PH to J. P. Borden, July 31, November 8, 1932, MMC; PH to IT&T, December 28, 1932, MMC.

4. Protective Association for Married Men card, 1933; GCH to PH, June 3, 1933; LH to PH, August 5, 1933; *Encyclopedia Britannica* receipt, August 31, 1936, and payment card showing that the set was paid off in January 1938; PH to GYH, August 28, 1912, all in MMC.

5. MLCY to GYH, January 26, 1942; "Old Virginia Fig" recipe and distilling instructions, n.d.; GCH to PH, January 25, 1935; PH to George Gruenert, June 1, 1937, all in MMC; GYH to MLCY, June 13, 1932, YFP.

6. PH to Dax Buell, April 8, 1939, MMC; property records, Warren County, VA; Darwin Lambert, *The Undying Past of Shenandoah National Park.* (Lanham, MD: Roberts Rinehart, 1989), 287. The Shenandoah National Park Act of 1926 authorized the National Park Service to accept donations of land and permitted the transfer of land from the commonwealth of Virginia. Virginia established the State Commission on Conservation and Development that year, and in 1928 the legislature passed the Virginia National Park Act and Public Park Condemnation Act, allowing the state to take land through eminent domain. Unlike Genevieve, most landowners did not challenge the findings of appraisers. State Commission on Conservation and Development v. G. Y. Hitt, etc., Chancery Court, Warren County, VA, Case 1937-035, Library of Virginia Archives.

7. GYH to MLCY, June 13, 1932, YFL; Journal of the Convention, 1934, MMC; GCH to GYH, August 27, 1934, MMC; Pauline Sabin to GYH, November 7, 1933, MMC.

8. PH to Gruenert, undated draft in pencil, likely January 1937, MMC; multiple articles, *Key West Citizen,* March 13–26, 1935; oral history with David and Evie Moreman, March 23, 2009.

9. LH to PH, December 21, 1932, MMC; "H. S. New, Former Cabinet Member, Dies in Maryland," *Modesto (CA) Bee and News-Herald,* May 11, 1937, 5; "New Rites Conducted at Capital," *Pharos-Tribune* (Logansport, IN), May 11, 1937, 1; "Scenes and Events in the Career of Harry S. New," *Indianapolis News,* May 10, 1937, 1; PH to George Gruenert, June 22, 1937, MMC.

10. Social column, *Richmond Times-Dispatch,* November 19, 1937, 12; PH to "Jeb," November 30, 1937, MMC; PH to Byrne, December 18, 1937, NCML, Byrne Chaocipher Collection; "Colonel Hitt Arrives Here Accompanied by His Wife and Daughter Miss Mary Lou [sic]," *Key West Citizen,* December 23, 1937, 1; "Various Army Officers and Their Families Visit Here," *Key West Citizen,* December 29, 1937, 6; C. C. FitzGerald to PH, January 10, February 3, 1938, MMC.

11. Thomas M. Johnson to PH, August 17, 1931, and PH to Johnson, August 21, 1931, NCML, DKC, PHP. Johnson would contact Hitt again in 1936 about his nongovernmental cipher stories; Hitt referred him to Paulus.

12. GCH to PH, March 17, 1932, MMC; PH to Fabyan, March 7, 1932; Roy Paulus to PH, March 15, April 20, 1934; PH to Paulus, March 17, 1934, all in NCML, DKC, PHP.

13. PH to Paulus, April 27 and 30, July 3, November 17, December 11, 1934; Paulus to PH, May 3, 1934, all in NCML, DKC, PHP; GCH to PH, January 25, 1934, MMC.

14. Paulus to PH, May 8, June 30, 1934; PH to Paulus, May 9, June 1, July 3, 1934, all in NCML, DKC, PHP. The name Cryptogame is probably unrelated to the nineteenth-century graphic narrative by Rodolphe Töpffer, *Histoire de Monsieur Cryptogame.*

15. Paulus to PH, August 11, 1934; PH to Paulus, August 13, December 11, 1934; set of Cryptogame cards, all in NCML, DKC, PHP. Although the Boy

Scouts had fun with the Cryptogame cards, Hitt was unable to get them interested in a merit badge for cipher work.

16. PH, "Ciphers and Their Solutions," unpublished manuscript (six chapters), [1935], NCML, DKC, PHP; PH to Jerome S. Meyer, January 7, 12, and 27, 1935; Meyer to PH, January 22, 1935, all in NCML, DKC, PHP. The date of Hitt's unpublished manuscript (1935) was determined from a reference to the International Telecommunications Conference of 1934 as having taken place "last year."

17. Paulus to PH, June 1, October 16, November 27, 1935, October 12, 1937; PH to Paulus, July 30, October 6, December 18, 1935, all in NCML, DKC, PHP; PH, *The ABC of Secret Writing* (New York: Puck Products, 1935); PH, "A Tale of the Rio Grande," *New York National Guardsman* 13, no. 7 (October 1936): 19, 22.

18. Dwight D. Eisenhower to PH, November 7, 1936, March 16, 1937, MMC; PH to Eisenhower, January 7, 1937, MMC. Hitt's penciled notations on the January 1937 letter indicate that he had already obtained most of this information from other sources, but it seems he did not tell Eisenhower that his work was duplicative.

19. PH to Gruenert, undated pencil draft of letter from January 1937, April 5, June 1 and 23, 1937, MMC; Gruenert to PH, April 29, May 27, 1937, MMC; Tomas Ceoma to Gruenert, May 22, 1937, MMC; PH, "Amphibious Infantry;" *United States Naval Institute Proceedings* 64, no. 420 (February 1938): 234–50.

20. Donald Millikin to PH, September 11, 1933, MMC. Millikin wanted to know whether Hitt was going to republish his *Manual.* Many ACA members teased Hitt about his nom, thinking it might be of Greek origin or perhaps a "naughty word." But PHERTIKRAT was simply an anagram of PARKER HITT. Hitt assigned the numbers 0–9 to his name and then mixed them so that the even-numbered letters were arranged to form PHERT and the odd-numbered letters spelled IKRAT (0=P, 1=A, 2=R, 3=K, 4=E, 5=R, 6=H, 7=I, 8=T, 9=T). History of the American Cryptogram Association, http://www.cryptogram.org/about-the-aca/history/ (accessed June 28, 2017).

21. George C. Lamb to PH, April 8, 1938, MMC; Herbert O. Yardley, *The American Black Chamber* (New York: Ballantine Books, 1931); Herbert O. Yardley, "Secret Inks," *Saturday Evening Post,* April 3, 1931, 3–5, 140–45; Herbert O. Yardley, "Codes," *Saturday Evening Post,* April 18, 1931, 16–17, 141–42; Herbert O. Yardley, "Ciphers," *Saturday Evening Post,* May 9, 1931, 35, 144–49; WFF to PH, May 16, November 17, 1931, MMC; PH to WFF, May 20, 1931, MMC; PH to CSO, September 10, 1931, MMC; PH to BNATURAL, December 13, 1940, NCML, DKC, PHP; PH to David Kahn, August 3, 1963, NCML, DKC; MLH to Louis Kruh, April 1988, NCML, Kruh Collection. Friedman also sent his memo to Frank Moorman, Hitt's former student and head of the AEF's G2A6, and to two of Friedman's closest colleagues from G2A6.

22. Lamb to PH, March 30, 1939, MMC; O. D. Williamson to PH, April 15, 1938, MMC; Helen Fouché Gaines to PH, April 26, 1938, MMC. Helen Fouché

Gaines, a native of Arkansas, was a regular contributor to the *Cryptogram*. Gaines often referred to Hitt as "Ferdy," an affectionate diminutive of his nom.

23. PH to Gaines, October 8, 1939, NCML, DKC, PHP. About Gaines's use of his name in the book, Hitt wrote, "I don't like the 'great Parker Hitt' either, you just leave me out of your dambook [*sic*] and let me criticize it later." PH to Gaines, December 23, 1938, NCML, DKC, PHP.

24. PH to Gaines, December 23, 1938; WFF quoted in a letter from PH to Lamb, December 11, 1938, NCML, DKC, PHP; WFF to PH, December 7, 1938, MMC; PH to WFF, November 21, 1938, MMC.

25. PH to DAMON, February 24, 1939, NCML, DKC, PHP; Townsend Morgan to PH, April 12, 1938; Solar-Sturges Mfg. Co. to PH, April 19, 1938; inventory of property moved from Front Royal to Columbus, OH, December 11, 1940, all in MMC.

26. "Col. Hitt Will Speak at Winchester Rites," clipping from unknown newspaper, November 10, 1938; typed speech delivered November 11, 1938, MMC; "City and State to Participate in Honors to Martial Heroes in Fitting Exercises," *Richmond Times-Dispatch*, November 11, 1937, 3.

10. Return to Service

Epigraph: Samuel Reber to PH, January 8, 1917, MMC.

1. WFF to PH, April 4, 1939, NCML, DKC, PHP.

2. PH to Helen Fouché Gaines, July 1, 1939, MMC; GENEAL to PH, September 25, 1939; POPPY to PH, June 5, 1939; "The Unsolved Benjamin Franklin Cipher," *Cryptogram,* December 1935; PH to POPPY, June 7, August 11, 1939; POPPY to PH, August 9, 1939, all in NCML, DKC, PHP.

3. PH to POPPY, August 27, 1939; WFF to PH, September 29, 1939, both in NCML, DKC, PHP. No information about the ACA's wartime work has been found, but a June 1951 memo from WFF to William G. Bryan of the ACA indicates that recruiting efforts among the ACA were not worth the amount of work required to establish contacts—of eighty-eight contacted, only three were accepted (twenty-five failed to respond, fifty-eight declined, and two were rejected). https://www.nsa.gov/Portals/70/documents/news-features/declassified-documents/friedman-documents/correspondence/FOLDER_010/41698059073739.pdf (accessed November 17, 2018).

4. Franklin Delano Roosevelt, Proclamation 2453(1), September 5, 1939, and Proclamation 2487(1), May 27, 1941; copy of memorandum for the record dated September 1939, MMC; PH to AG, September 9, 1939; Third Corps Area indorsement, September 11, 1939; AG to PH, September 16, 1939, all in PH, OMPF.

5. WFF to PH, January 10, 1940; PH to WFF, January 12, 1940; correspondence between WFF and PH, January–March 1940, all in NCML, DKC, PHP. The intercepted German messages likely came from Hitt's ACA colleague BIMBO, a Canadian who had a shortwave radio.

6. PH to RH, March 6, 1940, MMC; MHB to PH, n.d., MMC; multiple letters between the Hitt siblings, MMC.

7. Fred Hallford, July 3, 1940, GYH, OMPF; BIMBO to PH, November 3, 1940, MMC.

8. "Pershing Gives Talk on War at Dinner of Baltic Society," *Washington Sunday Star,* June 2, 1940, A-8; personnel file index sheet AG 210.851, February 3, 1940, PH, OMPF; Eastman to PH, September 17, 1940, PH, OMPF.

9. RH to PH, September 11, 1940, MMC; LH to PH, September 16, 1940, MMC; PH to Clyde Eastman, September 21, 1940, PH, OMPF.

10. PH to Eastman, September 20, 1940, PH, OMPF. This letter refers to the examination being complete; however, the examination paperwork is dated September 21.

11. Notation, September 27, 1940, on paperwork dated September 21, 1940; OCSO to AG, October 8, 1940; PH to AG, October 11, 1940, all in PH, OMPF.

12. Informal action sheet, October 18, 1940, with reply from J. R. Darnall, October 21, 1940; WD, SO 249, para. 30, 1940, both in PH, OMPF; PH to William S. Warford (BOBHITE), November 26, 1941, MMC.

13. MHB to PH, October 26, 1940, MMC; Warren County, VA, Deed Book 49, 96–99. The property, originally in Genevieve and Parker's names, had been put in Genevieve and Mary Lue's names in 1933.

14. PH to Colonel Pleas B. Rogers, Front Royal Remount Deport, November 4, 1940, MMC; PH to Greyvan Lines, November 15, 1940, MMC; PH to Greyhound Lines, November 18, 1940, MMC.

15. PH to BNATURAL, December 12, 1940, MMC.

16. PH to GYH, November 2, 1940, MMC. The move to quarters 21 had taken place by May 1942; they were in quarters 13 by January 1943. Addresses reconstructed from letters in MMC. The Columbus Army Depot, which opened in 1918, is now the site of the Defense Supply Center, Columbus.

17. PH, OMPF; F. E. Stoner to PH, October 24, 1940, MMC; PH to Eastman, November 6, 1940, MMC.

18. PH to Eastman, November 6, 1940; Eastman to PH, November 9, 1940, MMC; Spencer B. Akin to PH, December 4, 1940, NCML, DKC, PHP. For details on SIGABA, see Timothy Mucklow, *The SIGABA/ECM II Cipher Machine: "A Beautiful Idea"* (Fort George G. Meade, MD: Center for Cryptologic History, 2015), 19. For details on Hitt's recommendations, see Betsy Rohaly Smoot, *The Cipher Game: The Cryptologic Work of Colonel Parker Hitt, Genevieve Young Hitt, and Mary Lue Hitt* (Fort George G. Meade, MD: Center for Cryptologic History, forthcoming).

19. Multiple SOs, 1941–1943, in PH, OMPF; PH to Adamson, May 18, 1943, MMC. About seeing Pershing at the 1941 dinner, James Harbord said: "I have never felt more like weeping, without actually doing it, than I did at that moment." Donald Smythe, "The Baltic Society," *Army* 28, no. 2 (February 1978): 42.

20. PH to John F. Landis, December 9, 1940, MMC; Landis to PH, December 3, 1940, MMC; news item in *Military Engineer* 33, no. 180 (1940): 260; George

Luberoff and PH, exchange of letters, September 5 and 8, 1941, NCML, DKC, PHP. The three correspondence courses mentioned by Landis were Elementary Cryptography, Advanced Cryptography, and Elementary Cryptanalysis.

21. Correspondence between Sixth US Civil Service District and Fifth Corps Area Commander, October 27–31, 1941, MLH, OPF, Civilian Personnel Records, National Personnel Records Center, St. Louis, MO; PH to GCH, May 30, 1943, MMC.

22. Dan Van Voorhis to MLH, May 17, 1942; Ken E. "Buck" Hunter to MLH, June 7, 1942, January 16, 1943; Harry Simms to MLH, December 30, 1942, January 22, July 11, 1943; Frederick Eckley Craig to MLH, November 12, 1942, April 1 and 27, 1943; Robert H. Oppenheimer to MLH, September 5, 1943, all in MMC; GYH to MLCY, December 15, 1942, YFL; MLCY to GYH, May 22, 1941, January 26, 1942, December 4, 1941, MMC.

23. Message with annotation by PH, December 7, 1941, MMC; "Citizen Defense Program Takes Definite Shape," *Repository* (Canton, OH), January 1, 1942, 11; "Army Chief Praises Radio Corps Here," *Zanesville (OH) Times Recorder,* March 8, 1942, 10; "Footnotes about Fighters," *East Liverpool (OH) Evening Review,* January 21, 1942, 9; PH to GCH, May 30, 1942, MMC.

24. PH to Army Historical Section, March 9, 1942; Army Historical Section to PH, March 12, 1942; CSO H. C. Ingles to PH, September 13, 1943, all in MMC.

25. GYH to MLH, November 8, 12, and 18, 1942, MMC; GYH to MLCY, December 15, 1942, YFL. Muriel's husband, John Judah Brandon, died in 1931.

26. GYH to MLH, November 8, 12, and 18, 1942; MLCY to GYH, July 4, 1942, MMC; GYH to MLCY, December 15, 1942, YFL.

27. Merrill G. Beck to PH, September 1, 1944, July 16, 1945, MMC; Gruenert to PH, March 15, 1943, YFL.

28. Efficiency reports, June 30, 1941, June 30, December 31, 1942, June 30, 1943, PH, OMPF.

29. Fred C. Wallace to Director, Military Personnel, Services of Supply, July 8, 1942; Wallace to Commander, Army Service Forces, August 29, 1943; J. A. Ulio, AG, to Wallace, October 11, 1943, all in PH, OMPF.

30. WFF to PH, January 5, 1944, MMC; PH to GCH, May 30, 1943, MMC; PH to WFF, July 26, 1943, NCML, DKC, PHP; SO 236/1, August 24, 1943, and SO 237, October 1, 1943, PH, OMPF; Fort Hayes Woman's Exchange to GYH, April 22, 1944, MMC.

11. The Old Soldier

Epigraph: PH to Dax Buell, secretary for the Purdue class of 1899, April 8, 1939, MMC.

1. Harry Marks to PH, September 24, 1943, MMC; PH to Wilson, September 9, 1943, January 4, 1944, MMC; PH to MHB, January 1, 1944, MMC. The

identity of Parker's correspondent Wilson is unknown, but they corresponded as early as 1943 on genealogical matters; he was likely a descendant of Martin Hitt's brother Peter.

2. PH to Wilson, January 4, 1944; PH, certification of goods shipped, December 2, 1943, MMC; refund from War Department, February 11, 1944, MMC.

3. PH to MHB, January 1, 1944; PH to Wilson, January 4, 1944; PH to Edgar King, January 16, 1944, MMC.

4. WFF to PH, January 5, 1944, MMC; William Friedman, *The History of Army Strip Cipher Devices July 1934–October 1947* (Washington, DC: Army Security Agency, 1948).

5. "George Hitt, Ex-Newspaper and Business Leader, Dies," *Indianapolis News,* March 9, 1944, 12; MHB to PH, April 6, 1944, MMC; Bexar County land records, April 18, 1944.

6. Beck to PH, September 1, 1944, MMC; LYK to GYH, n.d., MMC. Vivian Young Kinnear, Genevieve's great-niece, believes she did not enjoy living near her family. Kinnear, email to the author, May 25, 2020.

7. Warren County, VA, Deed Book 57, 11; Fannie Mae Woodward to GYH, May 6, August 30, 1944, MMC.

8. WFF to PH, October 24, 1944, MMC; MLH, OPF. Friedman's letter indicates that Hitt had called him the previous evening. Friedman checked with SSA chief Colonel Preston Corderman to make sure it was okay to handle the situation as a personal letter rather than an official memo. Undated routing slip, https://www.nsa.gov/Portals/70/documents/news-features/declassified-documents/friedman-documents/correspondence/FOLDER_365/41734109077334.pdf (accessed November 18, 2018). For details on the young women employed at Arlington Hall Station during World War II, see Liza Mundy, *Code Girls* (New York: Hachette, 2017), 35–55.

9. The work of the SSA during World War II is documented in *History of the Signal Security Agency,* vol. 1, *Organization 1939–1945* (Washington, DC: Army Security Agency, 1948), https://www.nsa.gov/Portals/70/documents/news-features/declassified-documents/cryptologic-histories/history_of_the_signal_security_agency_vol_ISRH364.pdf, and *History of the Signal Security Agency,* vol. 2, *The General Cryptanalytic Problem* (Washington, DC: Army Security Agency, 1946), https://www.nsa.gov/Portals/70/documents/news-features/declassified-documents/cryptologic-histories/History_Vol_2.pdf (accessed July 5, 2021).

10. MLH to her parents, December 9, 1944, MMC; WFF to PH December 21, 1944, MMC. The sliding strip was probably the device submitted to the CSO in December 1914.

11. PH to MLH, December 17, 1944, MMC. A small amount of traffic and a handwritten note from Kahn document Mary Lue's April 1972 admission that she had smuggled the messages out of the building. NCML, DKC, PHP, "WWII Cryptanalysis" folder.

12. MLH, OPF; PH to George E. McCracken, February 6, 1946, MMC.

13. MLCY to GYH, March 27, 1945, MMC; GYH to LYK, July 21, 1956, YFL; MLH and GYH to LYK, December 31, 1956, YFL; correspondence with various food providers, 1947–1958, MMC; GYH to LYK, December 25, [1955], YFL.

14. George Evans to PH, September 11, 1946, MMC; Dr. S. D. Blackford to Dr. Dixon Whitworth, July 16, 1946, MMC; PH to WFF, August 14, 1946, and WFF to PH, August 16, 1946, NCML, DKC, PHP; MLCY to PH, n.d., MMC (this letter is in an envelope dated February 4, 1947, but it may be misdated, as it mentions weather in May).

15. GYH to LYK, March 17, 1961, YFL; PH to Mrs. Whaley, n.d. [probably 1950s], MMC; GYH to LYK, n.d. [1950s], July 21, 1956, YFL.

16. PH to Timkin Silent Automatic Division, December 9, 1948; PH to L. B. Dutrow, October 3, 1947; Dutrow to PH, October 15, 1947; H. J. Gastman, Deepfreeze Appliance Division, to PH, October 2, 1953; PH to Director, Veterans' Bureau, May 7, 1946; PH to Veterans Administration, September 2, 1947; Veterans Administration to PH, September 23, 1947; PH to Harry F. Byrd, February 5, 1960, all in MMC.

17. MLH to Louis Kruh, January 1, 1979, NCML, Kruh Collection; PH to Spencer B. Akin, October 2, 1947, MMC; Akin to PH, October 17, 1947, MMC; PH to Bill Morrow, January 29, February 20, March 10, 1953, MMC. The World War II intercept station was housed in a barn and designated Monitoring Station #1. The facility is now a winery.

18. GYH to LYK, March 11, 1961, YFL.

19. GYH to Mamie Doud Eisenhower, October 18, 1952; M. D. Eisenhower to GYH, November 10, 1952; PH to M. D. Eisenhower, December 14, 1952, all in EPL, MEP, box 18, Correspondence; Christmas card list 1953, EPL, Dwight D. Eisenhower Papers as President (Ann Whitman File) 1953–1961, Name Series, box 4; GYH to M. D. Eisenhower, January 1, [1955], EPL, MEP, box 18.

20. Dwight D. Eisenhower to PH, May 5, 1955, and PH to D. D. Eisenhower, May 8, 1955, MMC; stag dinner guest list and menu, EPL, White House Social Office: Records, box 50, folder "5-31-55 Stag dinner" and President's Appointment Books, May 31, 1955, 7; GYH to Mrs. Doud, October 9, 1955; M. D. Eisenhower to GYH, October 14, 1955, both in EPL, MEP, box 18.

21. David Kahn, The Codebreakers (New York: Scribner, 1996), 325; oral history with David and Evie Moreman, March 23, 2009. The Eisenhower Library has no record of Eisenhower making an evening trip to Front Royal while president. Herb Pankratz, email to the author, January 24, 2011.

22. GYH to LYK, March 16, 1961, YFL; L. A. Gravelle to PH, June 11, March 1, 1954, October 9, 1953, MMC; PH to D. B. Guynn, March 12, 1950, MMC; Donald Smythe, "The Baltic Society," Army 28, no. 2 (February 1978): 41–42.

23. Peter Hitt to PH, May 31, 1950, MMC; Brawdus Martin to PH, September 28, 1956, August 18, 1953, undated note, July 1, 1954, MMC. "Boots and Saddles" is an army bugle call.

24. GYH to LYK, March 17, 1961; MLH and GYH to LYK, December 31, 1956; GYH to LYK, July 21, 1956; GYH to LYK, March 17, 1961, all in YFL.

25. PH to War College, November 19, 1955; Kenneth E. Lay to PH, July 5, 1961; Truman Smith to PH, June 14, 1929; PH to *Military Review,* April 26, 1961, payment June 29, 1961, all in MMC. Smith's history was never published, but a draft is in the digital collection of the Maneuver Center of Excellence, Donovan Research Library, Fort Benning, GA.

26. PH to National Inventors Council, April 20, 1960, MMC; National Inventors Council to PH, May 19, 1960, MMC.

27. GYH to LYK, March 11 and 16, 1961, YFL; MLH and GYH to LYK, December 31, 1956, YFL.

28. Commonwealth of Virginia Death Certificate, Genevieve Young Hitt, file number 6795, February 6, 1963.

29. WFF lectures in Center for Cryptologic History, *The Friedman Legacy: A Tribute to William and Elizebeth Friedman* (Fort George G. Meade, MD: National Security Agency, 2006); WFF, *Military Cryptanalysis,* 4 vols. (Washington, DC: GPO, 1936–1941); WFF, *Military Cryptananalytics,* 2 vols. (Washington, DC: GPO, 1956, 1959).

30. Kahn to PH, November 19, 1962, and PH to Kahn, November 22, 1962, NCML, DKC, PHP; PH to Kahn, November 26, 1962, NCML, DKC. According to Kahn, Hitt autographed his copy of the *Manual* on August 27, 1949 (Hitt's seventy-first birthday).

31. Kahn to PH, November 27, 1962, December 20, 1963, MMC; Kahn to MLH, January 28, February 29, 1964; MLH to Kahn, [February 1964]; Kahn to PH, May 4 and 22, 1966; PH to Kahn, May 9, 1966, all in NCML, DKC, PHP. The papers Mary Lue sent to Kahn form the heart of his collection of Hitt's papers.

32. Press release, "War Mementos Needed for First Army Museum," June 28, 1963, MMC; William K. Blanchard to PH, July 23, 1963, MMC; Joseph H. Ewing to PH, March 13, 1964, MMC. The museum was transferred to Fort George G. Meade in 1966, but by 2018, Hitt's material was no longer in the archive. All that remained of the signal communications exhibit was a photograph, taken at an angle and from a distance.

33. Organizing Committee to PH, September 10, 1963, and PH, undated copy of reply, MMC; List of Attendees, EPL, Post-Presidential Papers, 1963, Principal File, box 10; Eisenhower to Toddie Lee Wynne, October 14, 1963, EPL, Post-Presidential Papers, 1963, Principal File, box 69.

34. LYK to MLH, May 26, 1964, MMC; Mamie Eisenhower to MLH, December 5, 1966, MMC. Mamie's letter is interesting; she is responding to a letter from Mary Lue and professes ignorance of Genevieve's death more than three years earlier. Hitt had seen the Eisenhowers in the fall of October 1963, but they likely had little time to converse, given the crush of partygoers.

35. David and Evie Moreman, oral history, March 23, 2009; "Col. Parker Hitt, 93, Cryptology Expert," *New York Times*, May 28, 1971, 36. Note that Hitt was ninety-two when he died; he would have turned ninety-three on August 27, 1971.

12. Legacy

Epigraph: James Whitcomb Riley, "The Witheraways (Set Sail, October 15, 1890)," in *The Complete Poetical Works of James Whitcomb Riley* (Blooming-ton: Indiana University Press, 1992), 461. Riley was dismayed when the Hitt children did not say good-bye before moving to London.

1. Certificate of qualification, Virginia Bureau of Insurance, May 7, 1946, MMC; Warren County Order of Law Index 1946–1974, qualification as notary public; GYH to MLCY, June 23, 1932; GYH to LYK, March 16, 1961; GYH to LYK, July 21, 1956, all in YFL.

2. Kevin Mustain, conversation with the author, March 23, 2009; Barbara Tuttle to MLH, May 1, 1995; James A. Chambers to MLH, August 7, 1995; Paul Hockman to MLH, letter of appointment, June 29, 1962, all in MMC; Lisa Long, email to the author, January 4, 2014 (Long's mother was a friend of Mary Lue Hitt); David Kahn and Louis Kruh correspondence in MMC; NCML, DKC, PHP; and NCML, Louis Kruh Collection.

3. PH to Dax Buell, April 8, 1939, MMC.

4. GYH to LYK, March 17, 1961, YFL.

5. Jean Young Fish, speech at the dedication of a building in honor of Gene-vieve Young Hitt, April 13, 2012.

6. GCH to PH, June 23, 1923, MMC.

7. PH to George McCracken, February 6, 1946, MMC; PH, *Manual for the Solution of Military Ciphers* (Fort Leavenworth, KS: Press of the Army Service Schools, 1916), 2.

8. In later years, Hitt told David Kahn he was "never mixed up" in the work of the G2A6, although he unofficially helped with the codebooks; he said nothing about the Radio Section. In the same letter he admitted, "I am getting to be an old man and memory for little things is sometimes hazy." PH to Kahn, August 4, 1963, NCML, DKC.

9. There is increasing evidence that the formation of the Signal Intelligence Service contributed to the demise of MI-8. Yardley had success with codes and ciphers but was less knowledgeable than Hitt about other aspects of cryptologic organization; he was also much more ambitious and lazier than Hitt.

10. GYH to EBH, October 29, 1914, MMC.

11. Protective Association for Married Men card, 1933, MMC.

Selected Bibliography

Archives and Libraries

Anchorage (Alaska) Museum Library and Archives
Archives of DePauw University and Indiana United Methodism, Greencastle, IN
Dwight D. Eisenhower Presidential Library, Abilene, KS
Fayette County Heritage Museum and Archives, La Grange, TX
George C. Marshall Research Library and Archives, Lexington, VA
    Elizebeth S. Friedman Collection
    William F. Friedman Papers
    George C. Marshall Collection
    Walton H. Walker Collection
Ike Skelton Combined Arms Research Library, Fort Leavenworth, KS
Indiana State Historical Society, William Henry Smith Memorial Library, Indianapolis, IN
Indiana State Library, Indianapolis, IN
    George C. Hitt Papers
    Harry S. New Collection
Indiana University, Lilly Library, Bloomington, IN
    George C. Hitt manuscripts
    L. Payne manuscripts
    James Whitcomb Riley manuscripts
Kent State University Special Collections and Archives, Kent, OH
Library of Congress, Washington, DC
    George Fabyan Collection
Library of Virginia, Richmond, VA
Maneuver Center of Excellence, Donovan Research Library, Fort Benning, GA
National Archives and Records Administration, Washington, DC, and College Park, MD
    RG 15 Records of the Department of the Veterans Administration
    RG 36 Records of the US Customs Service
    RG 38 Records of the Office of the Chief of Naval Operations
    RG 65 Federal Bureau of Investigation Records
    RG 92 Records of the Office of the Quartermaster General
    RG 94 Records of the Adjutant General's Office 1780s–1917
    RG 99 Records of the Office of the Paymaster General
    RG 111 Records of the Chief Signal Officer
    RG 120 Records of the American Expeditionary Force

263

PARKER HITT

RG 156 Records of the Office of the Chief of Ordnance
RG 159 Records of the Office of the Inspector General (Army)
RG 160 Records of the 5th Service Command
RG 165 Records of the War Department General and Special Staff
RG 391 Records of US Regular Army Mobile Units 1821–1942
RG 393 Records of US Army Continental Commands 1821–1920
RG 394 Records of US Army Continental Commands 1920–1942
RG 395 Records of US Army Overseas Operations and Commands 1898–1942
RG 407 Records of the Adjutant General's Office 1917–
RG 457 Records of the National Security Agency
National Cryptologic Museum Library, Fort George G. Meade, MD
  Barnes Papers
  Byrne Chaocipher Collection
  David Kahn Collection
  Louis Kruh Collection
National Personnel Records Center, St. Louis, MO
Nevada State Museum, Las Vegas
New York Public Library, Rare Book and Manuscript Division, New York, NY
Ohio Wesleyan University Archives, Delaware, OH
Purdue University Libraries e-Archives, West Lafayette, IN
Randolph-Macon College, Flavia Reed Owen Special Collections and Archives,
  Ashland VA
  J. Rives Childs Collection
University of Alaska–Fairbanks, Elmer E. Rasmuson Library
  Alaska and Polar Regions Collections and Archives
University of Michigan Library Special Collections, Ann Arbor, MI
US Army History and Education Center, Carlisle, PA
Virginia Military Institute Archives, Lexington, VA
  Walton H. Walker Collection

Privately Held Papers

Matt Herron Papers
Moreman-Mustain Collection of Parker Hitt material
Timbie Family Collection
Young Family Letters

Published Sources

Ackermann, Kenneth D. *Young J. Edgar: Hoover, the Red Scare and the Assault on Civil Liberties*. New York: Carroll & Graf, 2007.
Aitken, Hugh G. J. *The Continuous Wave: Technology and American Radio, 1900–1932*. Princeton, NJ: Princeton University Press, 1985.

American Battle Monuments Commission. *American Armies and Battlefields in Europe*. 1938. Reprint, Washington, DC: Government Printing Office, 1995.

Armstrong, David A. *Bullets and Bureaucrats: The Machine Gun and the United States Army*. Westport, CT: Greenwood Press, 1982.

Bain, David Haward. *Sitting in Darkness: Americans in the Philippines*. Boston: Houghton Mifflin, 1984.

Bauer, Craig. *Secret History: The Story of Cryptology*. Boca Raton, FL: Chapman Hall, 2013.

————. *Unsolved: The History and Mystery of the World's Greatest Ciphers from Ancient Egypt to Online Secret Societies*. Princeton, NJ: Princeton University Press, 2017.

Bellovin, Steven M. "Frank Miller: Inventor of the One-Time Pad." *Cryptologia* 35, no. 3 (2011): 203–22.

————. "Vernam, Mauborgne, and Friedman: The One-Time Pad and the Index of Coincidence." In *The New Codebreakers: Essays Dedicated to David Kahn on the Occasion of His 85th Birthday*, edited by Peter Y. A. Ryan, David Naccache, and Jean-Jacques Quisquater. New York: Springer, 2016.

Bendersky, Joseph W. *The "Jewish Threat": Anti-Semitic Politics of the U.S. Army*. New York: Basic Books, 2000.

Bidwell, Bruce W. *History of the Military Intelligence Division, Department of the Army General Staff: 1775–1941*. Frederick, MD: University Publications of America, 1986.

Calhoun, Charles W. *Benjamin Harrison*. New York: Henry Holt, 2005.

Cashman, Sean Dennis. *America in the Gilded Age: From the Death of Lincoln to the Rise of Theodore Roosevelt*. New York: New York University Press, 1984.

Center for Cryptologic History. *The Friedman Legacy: A Tribute to William and Elizebeth Friedman*. Fort George G. Meade, MD: National Security Agency, 2006.

Center of Military History. *Order of Battle of the United States Land Forces in the World War*. Washington, DC: Government Printing Office, 1931.

Childs, J. R. "My Recollections of G.2 A.6." *Cryptologia* 2, no. 3 (1978): 201–14.

[Childs, J. Rives]. *Before the Curtain Falls*. Indianapolis: Bobbs-Merrill, 1932.

Childs, J. Rives. *Let the Credit Go*. New York: K. S. Giniger, 1983.

Churchill, Marlborough. "The Military Intelligence Division General Staff." *Journal of the United States Artillery* 52, no. 4 (April 1920): 293–315.

Clark, Paul W., and Laurence A. Lyons. *George Owen Squier: US Army Major General, Inventor, Aviation Pioneer, Founder of Muzak*. Jefferson, NC: McFarland, 2014.

Clark, Ronald. *The Man Who Broke Purple: The Life of Colonel William F. Friedman, Who Deciphered the Japanese Code in World War II*. Boston: Little, Brown, 1977.

Clendenen, Clarence C. *Blood on the Border: The United States Army and the Mexican Irregulars*. London: Macmillan, 1969.

Cobbs, Elizabeth. *The Hello Girls: America's First Women Soldiers*. Cambridge, MA: Harvard University Press, 2017.

Coffman, Edward M. *The Regulars: The American Army 1898–1941*. Cambridge, MA: Belknap Press of Harvard University Press, 2004.

———. *The War to End All Wars: The American Military Experience in World War I*. Lexington: University Press of Kentucky, 1998.

Cosmas, Graham A. *An Army for Empire: The United States Army in the Spanish-American War*. College Station: Texas A&M University Press, 1994.

Crow, Kelvin Dale. *Fort Leavenworth: Three Centuries of Service*. Fort Leavenworth, KS: Command History Office, 2010.

Diehl, Kemper. *Saint Mary's Hall: First Century*. San Antonio, TX: St. Mary's Hall, 1979.

Dooley, John F. *Codes, Ciphers and Spies: Tales of Military Intelligence in World War I*. New York: Springer, 2016.

Edgerton, Ronald K. *American Datu: John J. Pershing and Counterinsurgency Warfare in the Muslim Philippines, 1899–1913*. Lexington: University Press of Kentucky, 2020.

Eisenhower, John D. *Intervention! The United States and the Mexican Revolution, 1913–1917*. New York: W. W. Norton, 1993.

Eisenhower, Susan. *Mrs. Ike: Portrait of a Marriage*. Sterling, VA: Capital Books, 1996.

Fagone, Jason. *The Woman Who Smashed Codes*. New York: HarperCollins, 2017.

Feuer, A. B. *America at War: The Philippines, 1898–1913*. Westport, CT: Praeger, 2002.

———. *Combat Diary: Episodes from the History of the Twenty-Second Regiment, 1866–1905*. New York: Praeger, 1991.

Finnegan, John Patrick. *Military Intelligence*. Washington, DC: Center of Military History, 1998.

Foulois, Benjamin D., with C. V. Glines. *From the Wright Brothers to the Astronauts: The Memoirs of Major General Benjamin D. Foulois*. New York: McGraw-Hill, 1968.

Frahm, Jill. "The Hello Girls: Women Telephone Operators with the American Expeditionary Forces during World War I." *Journal of the Gilded Age and Progressive Era* 3, no. 3 (July 2004): 271–93.

Friedman, William F. *American Army Field Codes in the American Expeditionary Forces during the First World War*. Washington, DC: Government Printing Office, 1942.

———. "A Brief History of US Cryptologic Operations 1917–1929." *Cryptologic Spectrum* 6, no. 2 (Spring 1976): 9–14.

———. *The History of Army Strip Cipher Devices July 1934–October 1947*. Washington, DC: Army Security Agency, 1948.

———. *Military Cryptanalysis*. 4 vols. Washington, DC: Government Printing Office, 1936–1941.

———. *Several Machine Ciphers and Methods for Their Solution*. Riverbank Laboratories Publication 20. 1918. In *The Riverbank Publications*. Vol. 2. Laguna Hills, CA: Aegean Park Press, 1976.

———. "The Use of Codes and Ciphers in the World War and Lessons to Be Learned Therefrom." *Signal Corps Bulletin* 101 (July–September 1938).

Funston, Frederick. *Memories of Two Wars: Cuban and Philippine Experiences*. New York: C. Scribner's Sons, 1911.

Gaddy, David. "The Cylinder-Cipher." *Cryptologia* 19, no. 4 (1995): 385–91.

Gaines, Helen Fouché. *Elementary Cryptanalysis: A Study of Ciphers and Their Solution*. Boston: American Photographic Publishing, 1939.

Gaus, Laura Sheerin. *Shortridge High School 1864–1981: In Retrospect*. Indianapolis: Indiana Historical Society, 1985.

Gilbert, James L. *World War I and the Origins of the U.S. Military Intelligence*. Lanham, MD: Scarecrow Press, 2012.

Gough, Terrence J. "Isolation and Professionalization of the Army Officer Corps: A Post-Revisionist View of the Soldier and the State." *Social Science Quarterly* 73, no. 2 (June 1992): 420–36.

Grotelueschen, Mark Ethan. *The AEF Way of War: The American Army and Combat in World War I*. Cambridge: Cambridge University Press, 2007.

Hallas, James H. *Squandered Victory: The American First Army at St. Mihiel*. Westport, CT: Praeger, 1995.

Harris, Charles H., III, and Louis R. Sadler. *The Archaeologist Was a Spy: Sylvanus G. Morely and the Office of Naval Intelligence*. Albuquerque: University of New Mexico Press, 2003.

———. *The Border and the Revolution: Clandestine Activities of the Mexican Revolution: 1910–1920*. Silver City, NM: High-Lonesome Books, 1988.

———. *The Secret War in El Paso: Mexican Revolutionary Intrigue, 1906–1920*. Albuquerque: University of New Mexico Press, 2009.

Hatch, David A. *The Dawn of American Communications Intelligence*. Fort George G. Meade, MD: Center for Cryptologic History, 2019.

Headrick, Daniel R. *The Invisible Weapon: Telecommunications and International Politics 1851–1945*. Oxford: Oxford University Press, 1991.

Hennessy, Juliette A. *The United States Army Air Arm April 1861 to April 1917*. Washington, DC: Government Printing Office, 1985.

Hitt, Parker. *The ABC of Secret Writing*. New York: Puck Products, 1935.

———. "Amphibious Infantry." *United States Naval Institute Proceedings* 64, no. 420 (February 1938): 234–50.

———. "A Brief History of the School of Musketry." *Military Review* (July 1961): 86–90.

———. *Manual for the Solution of Military Ciphers*. Fort Leavenworth, KS: Press of the Army Service Schools, 1916.

———. "A Tale of the Rio Grande." *New York National Guardsman* 13, no. 7 (October 1936): 19, 22.

Hitt, Parker, and Thomas W. Brown. *Description and Instructions for the Use of the Fire Control Rule.* Washington, DC: US Infantry Association, 1917.

James, Winston. *Holding Aloft the Banner of Ethiopia: Caribbean Radicalism in Early Twentieth-Century America.* London: Verso, 1998.

Johnson, Thomas M. *Our Secret War: True American Spy Stories 1917–1919.* Indianapolis: Bobbs-Merrill, 1929.

———. "Secrets of the Master Spies: Code and Cipher Stories of Statecraft and Battle." *Popular Mechanics* 57, no. 4 (April 1932): 636–40.

Kahn, David. *The Codebreakers.* New York: Scribner, 1996.

———. *The Reader of Gentleman's Mail.* New Haven, CT: Yale University Press, 2004.

Kruh, Louis. "The Evolution of Communications Security Devices." *Army Communicator,* Winter 1980.

———. "The Genesis of the Jefferson Bazeries Cipher Device." *Cryptologia* 5, no. 4 (October 1981): 193–208.

Krumm, George E., and Willis H. Taylor Jr. "Wireless in the AEF." *Wireless Age* 6, no. 12 (September 1919): 12–18; 7, no. 1 (October 1919): 9–21; 7, no. 4 (January 1920): 12–19; 7, no. 7 (April 1920): 10–14.

Lambert, Darwin. *The Undying Past of Shenandoah National Park.* Lanham, MD: Roberts Rinehart, 1989.

Laurie, Clayton D., and Ronald H. Cole. *The Role of Federal Military Forces in Domestic Disorders 1877–1945.* Washington, DC: Center of Military History, 1997.

Lavine, A. Lincoln. *Circuits of Victory.* New York: Doubleday, 1921.

Lengel, Edward G. *Thunder and Flames: Americans in the Crucible of Combat, 1917–1918.* Lawrence: University Press of Kansas, 2015.

———. *To Conquer Hell: The Meuse-Argonne, 1918.* New York: Henry Holt, 2008.

Linn, Brian McAllister. "Peacetime Transformation in the U.S. Army, 1865–1965." In *Transforming Defense,* edited by Conrad C. Crane. Carlisle Barracks, PA: Strategic Studies Institute, US Army War College, 2001.

———. *The Philippine War 1899–1902.* Lawrence: University Press of Kansas, 2000.

Manguso, John M. *Maneuver Camp, 1911: Transformation of the Army at Fort Sam Houston.* San Antonio, TX: Fort Sam Houston Museum, 2009.

———. *A Pocket Guide to the Cavalry and Light Artillery Post, Fort Sam Houston, Texas.* San Antonio, TX: Fort Sam Houston Museum, 2007.

———. *The Quadrangle: Hub of Military Activity in Texas; an Outline History.* San Antonio, TX: Fort Sam Houston Museum, 2009.

Marshall, George C. *Memoirs of My Services in the World War 1917–1918.* Boston: Houghton Mifflin, 1976.

Mauborgne, Joseph Oswald. *An Advanced Problem in Cryptography and Its Solution*. Fort Leavenworth, KS: Press of the Army Service Schools, 1914.

McClellan, Phyllis. *Silent Sentinel on the Potomac: Fort McNair, 1791–1991*. Bowie, MD: Heritage Books, 1993.

Moore, William E. "The Crisis of St. Mihiel." *American Legion Weekly* 4, no. 23 (June 9, 1922): 7–8, 26.

Moorman, Frank. "Code and Cipher in France." *Infantry Journal* 16, no. 12 (June 1920): 1039–44.

Muirhead, Murray. "Military Cryptography." *Journal of the Royal United Service Institute* 55, no. 404 (October 1911): 1321–32.

———. "Military Cryptography: A Study of Transposition Cipher Systems and Substitution Frequency Tables." *Journal of the Royal United Service Institute* 56, no. 418 (1912): 1665–78.

Mundy, Liza. *Code Girls*. New York: Hachette, 2017.

Nenninger, Timothy K. *The Leavenworth Schools and the Old Army: Education, Professionalism, and the Officer Corps of the United States Army, 1881–1918*. Westport, CT: Greenwood Press, 1978.

Odom, William O. *After the Trenches: The Transformation of US Army Doctrine, 1918–1939*. College Station: Texas A&M University Press, 1999.

Pappas, George S. *Prudens Futuri: The US Army War College 1901–1967*. Carlisle Barracks, PA: Alumni Association of the US Army War College, 1967.

Partin, John W., ed. *A Brief History of Fort Leavenworth 1827–1983*. Fort Leavenworth, KS: Combat Studies Institute, 1983.

Perry, Jeffrey B. *Hubert Harrison: The Voice of Harlem Radicalism, 1883–1918*. New York: Columbia University Press, 2009.

Pershing, John. J. *My Experiences in the World War*. New York: De Capo Press, 1995.

———. *My Life before the World War, 1860–1917: A Memoir*. Edited by John T. Greenword. Lexington: University Press of Kentucky, 2013.

Phelps, William Lyon, ed. *Letters of James Whitcomb Riley*. Indianapolis: Bobbs-Merrill, 1930.

Phillips, Clifton J. *Indiana in Transition: The Emergence of an Industrial Commonwealth, 1880–1920*. Indianapolis: Indiana Historical Bureau and Indiana Historical Society, 1968.

Pool, William C. "The Origin of Military Aviation in Texas, 1910–1913." *Southwestern Historical Quarterly* 58, no. 3 (January 1955): 342–71.

Powell, Edward Alexander. *The Army behind the Army*. New York: Charles Scribner's Sons, 1919.

Raines, Rebecca Robbins. *Getting the Message Through: A Branch History of the US Army Signal Corps*. Washington, DC: Government Printing Office, 1996.

Ray, Max A. *The History of the First United States Army from 1918 to 1980*. Fort George G. Meade, MD: First United States Army, 1980.

Reeds, James A., Whitfield Diffie, and J. V. Field, eds. *Breaking Teleprinter Ciphers at Bletchley Park: An Edition of I. J. Good, D. Michie and G. Timms; General Report on TUNNY with Emphasis on Statistical Methods (1945)*. Piscataway, NJ: Wiley–IEEE Press, 2015.

Rowlett, Frank B. *The Story of Magic*. Laguna Hills, CA: Aegean Park Press, 1998.

Sampson, Anthony. *Sovereign State: The Secret History of ITT*. London: Hodder and Stoughton, 1973.

Schauble, Peter Lambert. *The First Battalion: The Story of the 406th Telegraph Battalion, Signal Crops, US Army*. Bell Telephone Company of Pennsylvania, 1921.

Schneider, Dorothy, and Carl J. Schneider. *American Women in the Progressive Era, 1900–1920: Change, Challenge & the Struggle for Women's Rights*. New York: Anchor Books, 1993.

———. *Into the Breach: American Women Overseas in World War I*. New York: Viking, 1991.

Segovia, L. *The Full Story of Aguinaldo's Capture*. Translated by Frank de Thoma. Reprint, Manila, Philippines: MCS Enterprises, 1969.

Sievers, Harry J. *Benjamin Harrison: Hoosier Statesman*. Newtown, CT: American Political Biography Press, 1996.

Silbey, David J. *A War of Frontier and Empire: The Philippine-American War, 1899–1902*. New York: Hill and Wang, 2007.

Smith, G. Stuart. *A Life in Code: Pioneer Cryptanalyst Elizebeth Smith Friedman*. Jefferson, NC: McFarland, 2017.

Smoot, Betsy Rohaly. "An Accidental Cryptologist: The Brief Career of Genevieve Young Hitt." *Cryptologia* 35, no. 2 (2011): 164–75.

———. *The Cipher Game: The Cryptologic Work of Colonel Parker Hitt, Genevieve Young Hitt, and Mary Lue Hitt*. Fort George G. Meade, MD: Center for Cryptologic History, forthcoming.

———. *From the Ground Up: American Cryptology during World War I*. Fort George G. Meade, MD: Center for Cryptologic History, forthcoming.

———. "Impermanent Alliances: Cryptologic Cooperation between the United States, Britain, and France on the Western Front, 1917–1918." *Intelligence and National Security* 32, no. 3 (2017): 365–77.

———. "Parker Hitt's First Cylinder Device and the Genesis of U.S. Army Cylinder and Strip Devices." *Cryptologia* 39, no. 4 (2015): 315–21.

———. "Pioneers of U.S. Military Cryptology: Colonel Parker Hitt and His Wife, Genevieve Hitt." *Federal History Journal* 4 (2012): 87–100.

Sobel, Robert. *ITT: The Management of Opportunity*. 1982. Reprint, Washington, DC: Beard Books, 2000.

Steinfeldt, Cecilia. *The Onderdonks: A Family of Texas Painters*. San Antonio, TX: Trinity University Press, 1976.

Talbert, Roy, Jr. *Negative Intelligence: The Army and the American Left, 1917–1941*. Jackson: University Press of Mississippi, 1991.

Terrett, Dulany. *The Signal Corps: The Emergency; the United States Army in World War II*. Washington, DC: Office of the Chief of Military History, 1956.

Thomas, Evan. *The War Lovers: Roosevelt, Lodge, Hearst, and the Rush to Empire, 1898*. New York: Back Bay Books, 2010.

Trachtenberg, Alan. *The Incorporation of America: Culture and Society in the Gilded Age*. New York: Hill and Wang, 1982.

Trask, David F. *The AEF & Coalition Warmaking, 1917–1918*. Lawrence: University Press of Kansas, 1993.

Usher, H. J. K., C. D. Black-Hawkins, and G. J. Carrick. *An Angel without Wings: The History of University College School 1830–1980*. London: University College School, 1981.

Van Allen, Elizabeth J. *James Whitcomb Riley: A Life*. Bloomington: Indiana University Press, 1999.

Westfall, Matthew. *The Devil's Causeway: The True Story of America's First Prisoners of War in the Philippines, and the Heroic Expedition Sent to Their Rescue*. Guilford, CT: Lyons Press, 2012.

Wilson, John B. *Maneuver and Firepower: The Evolution of Divisions and Separate Brigades*. Washington, DC: Center of Military History, 1998.

———. "Mobility versus Firepower: The Post–World War I Infantry Division." *Parameters* 13, no. 3 (September 1983): 47–52.

Winkler, Jonathan Reed. *Nexus: Strategic Communications and American Security in World War I*. Cambridge, MA: Harvard University Press, 2008.

Woodward, David R. *The American Army and the First World War*. Cambridge: Cambridge University Press, 2014.

Wooster, Robert, ed. *Soldier, Surgeon, Scholar: The Memoirs of William Henry Corbusier 1844–1930*. Norman: University of Oklahoma Press, 2003.

Yardley, Herbert O. *The American Black Chamber*. New York: Ballantine Books, 1931.

Yockelson, Mitchell. *Forty-Seven Days: How Pershing's Warriors Came of Age to Defeat the German Army in World War I*. New York: New American Library, 2016.

———. "The United States Armed Forces and the Mexican Punitive Expedition: Part 1." *Prologue* 29, no. 3 (Fall 1997): 256–62.

Index